MISSION *at* NUREMBERG

MISSION *at* NUREMBERG

An American Army Chaplain and the Trial of the Nazis

TIM TOWNSEND

Wm
WILLIAM MORROW
An Imprint of HarperCollins *Publishers*

HarperCollins books may be purchased for educational, business, or sales promotional use. For information please e-mail the Special Markets Department at SPsales@harpercollins.com.

A hardcover edition of this book was published in 2014 by William Morrow, an imprint of HarperCollins Publishers.

FIRST WILLIAM MORROW PAPERBACK EDITION PUBLISHED 2015.

Designed by Jamie Lynn Kerner

Library of Congress Cataloging-in-Publication Data has been applied for.

ISBN 978-0-06-199720-4

HB 03.20.2024

Do not be overcome by evil, but overcome evil with good.

—ROMANS 12:21

CONTENTS

MISSION *at* NUREMBERG

CHAPTER 1

Death by Hanging

There had been men who had thought they could make a pet of cruelty,
and the grown beast had flayed them.

—REBECCA WEST

WILHELM KEITEL HAD BEEN general field marshal, second only to
Adolf Hitler in Germany's military hierarchy. Now, on a cold, rainy
October morning, at 1:00 A.M. in 1946, he stood shackled to a guard
outside cell 8 of Nuremberg's Palace of Justice. In half an hour,
Keitel would be hanging by his neck from a rope, his hands tied
behind his back with a leather bootlace, a black hood over his head.
Outside the prison, no moon marked the sky above the destroyed
city of Nuremberg.

The prison's commandant, U.S. Army colonel Burton Andrus,
spoke loudly, with both custom and history in mind. His voice was
high pitched but authoritative, and it echoed off the prison's dull
stone walls and traveled up the metal staircases, past the mesh wiring
that had been strung across the three tiers of cells to prevent suicides.

It traveled past a small chapel that had been created by knocking down the wall between two cells.

Andrus felt the weight of the moment, but he didn't relish it. He walked along the cell block on the first level, stopping at each prisoner's cell and repeating his sentence. The men had heard the same words two weeks earlier when the justices of the International Military Tribunal read the verdicts and sentences aloud in court.

The colonel was simply going through with a formality—required by the army's standard operating procedure and the Geneva Convention. The men in these cells were the former elite of the Third Reich, but they had long since been stripped of any military rank or privilege. In Nuremberg's prison, they were treated by most as persons without status.

The other major war criminals—those who had avoided the tribunal's supreme penalty and had been moved to the prison's second tier—could hear the details of each sentence as Andrus stopped at the cells. So could those on the third tier, the lesser Nazi criminals, used as witnesses by prosecution attorneys for testimony that had convicted the men below.

Andrus's strict adherence to by-the-book army rules and regulations had become something of a joke among the courtroom lawyers, and a headache to the twenty-one Nazis in his care during the yearlong trial. Before being assigned to Nuremberg, Andrus had served under General George Patton. He idolized Patton and tried to emulate him. He once wrote to a friend, "I will go anywhere with Georgie, anytime, for any purpose."

This morning Andrus was dressed, as he always was, in his green, four-pocket uniform tunic with brass buttons imprinted with the United States coat of arms—an eagle carrying thirteen arrows in one talon and an olive branch in the other. The colonel wore a burnished steel olive-drab helmet and carried a riding crop tucked under his arm.

Andrus was anxious and annoyed as he eyed Keitel. This was

the date the tribunal had set for the executions, and while the prisoners didn't know it officially, most of them had guessed these were their final hours. Earlier in the night, Hermann Goering, Germany's former reichsmarshal, Hitler's designated successor and the former head of Germany's air force, had killed himself by swallowing cyanide, cheating justice and outfoxing Andrus, who had vowed that his prison would be suicide-free. The commotion that followed Goering's death had woken the other prisoners. At 12:45 A.M., they were told to dress and were given their last meal: sausage, potato salad, cold cuts, black bread, and tea.

Most didn't touch the food. Keitel had made his bed and asked for a brush and duster to clean his cell.

Like Andrus's, Keitel's life had been ruled by army regulations. Since his capture by the Allies eighteen months earlier he had played the part of a disciplined soldier. His bearing was erect, his silver hair and mustache always perfectly trimmed. A year earlier, when Keitel arrived at the Nuremberg prison, Andrus had torn the shoulder boards from the general's uniform. He'd told Keitel he was no longer a soldier; he was now a war criminal. Nevertheless, each day in court, Keitel had proudly worn the plain tunic, blooming breeches, and black boots of a Wehrmacht officer. Keitel's defense attorney had played on the notion of following orders. He had only been doing a job he'd trained for his entire life. Keitel's commanding officer was the führer, and questioning orders was never even a consideration.

The tribunal had seen it differently. "Superior orders, even to a soldier, cannot be considered in mitigation where crimes so shocking and extensive have been committed," the justices had said about Keitel's defense. They found him guilty on all four counts of the Nuremberg indictment. When the justices told Keitel he'd been sentenced to death, the general nodded curtly and left the courtroom.

Now Keitel was hearing his sentence for the second and final time. "Defendant Wilhelm Keitel," Andrus announced, "on the counts of the indictment on which you have been convicted, the Tribunal has sentenced you to death by hanging."

Once Andrus had moved to the next prisoner and Keitel had returned into his cell, a stocky man with glasses, receding gray hair, and a doughy face followed the field marshal to his cot. Chaplain Henry Gerecke, a captain in the U.S. Army, was carrying a Bible. He asked Keitel if he'd like to pray.

Gerecke (rhymes with "Cherokee") had also been rattled by Goering's suicide. An ocean away, Gerecke's St. Louis Cardinals had been battling the Boston Red Sox in the World Series. The prison's other chaplain, Father Sixtus O'Connor, was rooting for the Sox. Though from upstate New York and really a Dodgers fan, he'd chosen Boston in a bet with Gerecke. They had been in the guards' booth on the prison floor awaiting a telephone call when Goering bit down on the cyanide. With the Palace of Justice locked down for the executions, the only way the chaplains and guards had of receiving updates after each half inning was through phone calls from an American officer outside the prison walls. Just after a call came in that Boston's Dom DiMaggio had doubled in the top of the eighth, driving in two runs to tie St. Louis, Goering's guard began yelling that something was wrong; Gerecke was the first to get to the reichsmarshal as he died.

Two hours later, Gerecke was with Keitel. They sank to their knees in Keitel's cell, and Gerecke began to pray in German. Andrus's words must have triggered in Keitel the realization that his life was over, because his soldierly demeanor was suddenly shattered. His voice faltered. His prayer trailed off. He began to weep, then sobbed uncontrollably, his body jerking as he gasped for air. Gerecke raised his hand above Keitel's head and gave the general a final benediction. Most likely it was Martin Luther's favorite, from the book of Numbers: "The Lord bless you, and keep you; The Lord make his face shine on you, and be gracious to you; The Lord lift up his countenance on you, and give you peace." Then the chaplain was called to the next cell, and he rose to his feet.

A LITTLE MORE THAN three years earlier, on June 3, 1943, Henry Gerecke was late for dinner. He burst through the front door and bounded up the wide wooden steps, two and three at a time, leading to the three-bedroom apartment at 3204 Halliday Avenue in south St. Louis that he shared with his wife, three sons, and sister-in-law. Gerecke's wife, Alma, was the only one home. Her younger sister, Ginny, was out. The couple's youngest son, fifteen-year-old Roy, was at a church youth group meeting. Gerecke's two older sons had already joined the army. The eldest, twenty-two-year-old Hank, was in the Aleutian Islands, fighting off the Japanese threat to the North American mainland. Twenty-one-year-old Carlton—everyone called him Corky—was training at Fort Bliss, Texas, for the Normandy invasion that would take place the next year.

As Henry reached the top of the steps, panting, he knew he was about to tell a woman with two sons in the war that her husband was headed there, too. That, *and* he was late for dinner. He walked through the long hallway, over the creaking hardwood floorboards toward the back of the apartment, where the kitchen was, and sat down at the table. Alma's back was to him. His dinner was already on the table. It was lukewarm, but Henry began shoveling the food down, praising Alma for her cooking. Alma was silent.

"Do you know something?" he asked brightly. "I got the idea today I'd like to join the Chaplains Corps." More silence. Henry kept eating. Still nothing from his wife. "I asked you something," he said.

"I heard you," Alma said, finally. "I've heard you right along." She took her time. She dried another dish. "But I want to tell you something. If the army has come to such straits that men of your age have to go into the Chaplains' Corps, I feel sorry for the army."

Alma had a point. By the summer of 1943, the army was desperate for chaplains. It needed thousands more. The ratio of one army chaplain for every thousand soldiers was better than in the First World War, when the ratio was one chaplain for every twenty-four hundred men. But it wasn't quite good enough. "As the tempo of the war increases, the soldiers' interest in spiritual matters also increases," General William R. Arnold, the army's chief of chaplains, told a newspaper that summer. "Reports from our chaplains in the battle areas tell of the increased opportunities afforded them and because such conditions prevail, I believe you will agree that we dare not fail these men by not supplying them with enough chaplains."

He urged church organizations to "rob their parishes of priests and ministers, if necessary, to supply spiritual advisors for our troops." Arnold stressed that the army wanted chaplains under the age of forty-five for service with combat troops. "At present there are no vacancies for those over 50."

Gerecke's fiftieth birthday was two months away. Alma's joke about the Chaplain Corps was her way of letting her husband know she'd accepted the situation. She knew he had already made up his mind.

Their marriage was of the opposites-attract variety. Henry was short and portly; Alma was tall and beautiful. He came from farm country; she from the city. (When they met, in the 1920s, his relatives from downstate referred to her as "the flapper.") Henry was an idealist; Alma was a materialist. He was dedicated to the poor; she wanted fur coats and big cars. He played the supplicant and she was the roost ruler, though they both knew the opposite was true. He had nicknames for her: Boss, Speaker of the House, Brown Eyes. She called him Henry.

Gerecke had decided to become an army chaplain, and he hadn't consulted his wife about it. Three-quarters of the men in Alma's family would be at war, but after twenty-five years of marriage, she also knew there wasn't much she could do about her husband's decision.

Gerecke volunteered just before his birthday, and two months later he reported for duty at the Chaplains School at Harvard University. Five weeks after that, the army assigned him to the Ninety-

Eighth General Hospital, a newly formed unit at Fort Jackson, South Carolina. For the next several months, he wasn't even sure the Ninety-Eighth would be called overseas. But in February 1944, the army directed the hospital unit to Camp Myles Standish in Massachusetts, and then on to England. Eighteen months later Gerecke was in Germany and was handed an assignment he was allowed to refuse. He could go home to St. Louis, to Halliday Avenue, to Alma. Instead, he took the assignment, and later he considered his time in Nuremberg the most important year of his life. Gerecke's ministry at Nuremberg has been called "one of the most singular . . . ever undertaken by U.S. Army chaplains." It was a historic experiment in how good confronts radical evil. And at its center was a farm kid from Missouri.

Gerecke, the Lutheran preacher from St. Louis who ministered to the agents of the Third Reich, was one player in a judicial improvisation we now call simply the Nuremberg trials. They were "trials"—plural—because the most famous proceeding, officially called the Trial of the Major War Criminals before the International Military Tribunal, was only the first in a series that took place in the German city of Nuremberg lasting until 1949. But that first trial overshadows the rest. When most people refer to "Nuremberg," they mean the Trial of the Major War Criminals. For the first time in history, the international community held a state's major leaders accused and convicted them of conspiring to commit crimes against humanity. Nuremberg was, in the words of one of its American prosecutors, "a bench mark in international law and the lodestar of thought and debate on the great moral and legal questions of war and peace."

One actor in that historic examination of evil was an unassuming man whose importance to the trials revealed itself only in time. Hans Fritzsche, on trial as Hitler's radio propaganda chief and a member of Gerecke's Nuremberg flock, wrote later that when Gerecke first arrived at the prison in November 1945, just days before the trials began, the chaplain "made scarcely any impression on us. Some of us may even have smiled at his simple, unequivocal faith and unpretentious sermons." It was the victorious Allies who were judging the crimes of the Nazi leaders at Nuremberg, but it would be a pastor of the Lutheran Church–Missouri Synod who would try and convince those criminals that it was really God's judgment that they should fear.

For Gerecke, the decision to accept the assignment wasn't easy. He wondered how a preacher from St. Louis could make any impression on the disciples of Adolf Hitler. Would his considerable faith in the core principles of Christianity sustain him as he ministered to monsters? During his months stationed in Munich after the war, Gerecke had taken several trips to Dachau. He'd seen the raw aftermath of the Holocaust. He'd touched the inside of the camp's walls, and his hands had come away smeared with blood.

The U.S. Army was asking one of its chaplains to kneel down with the architects of the Holocaust and calm their spirits as they answered for their crimes in front of the world. With those images of Dachau fresh in his memory, Gerecke had to decide if he could share his faith, the thing he held most dear in life, with the men who had given the orders to construct such a place.

Fritzsche wrote later:

> Pastor Gerecke's view was that in his domain God alone was Judge, and the question of earthly guilt therefore had no significance so far as he was concerned. His only duty was the care of souls. In a personal prayer which he once made aloud in our queer little congregation he asked God to preserve him from all pride, and from any prejudice against those whose spiritual care had been committed to his charge. It was in this spirit of humility that he approached his task; a battle for the souls of men standing beneath the shadow of the gallows.

WHEN GERECKE RETURNED TO Keitel's cell about thirty minutes after his initial visit in those early morning hours, he was visibly shaken from just having escorted Joachim von Ribbentrop, Hitler's foreign minister, to the gallows. It was the first time Gerecke had seen someone put to death. Now he was at Keitel's cell, and the two again prayed through Keitel's tears.

But then it was time to go, and they started down the corridor. Andrus was in front, his cavalry boots clacking on the prison's cement floor. He was followed by Gerecke, then Keitel, who was handcuffed to a guard. They walked out the door and into the cold, wet darkness of the courtyard that separated the cell block from the prison gymnasium where the gallows had been erected hours earlier.

Outside the walls of the Palace of Justice, Nuremberg tried to get along as best it could. Ninety percent of the beautiful medieval city had been destroyed by Allied bombs. Now its residents slept wherever they found warmth—between large pieces of broken masonry, behind the crumbled wall of a former church, in the dark cellars of demolished homes. Near the city's ancient imperial castle, a group of children had hung Hermann Goering in effigy, then built a bonfire, marching around it and watching its shadows play on the rubble.

When Andrus reached the gymnasium door, he knocked to let those inside know the next prisoner was ready. A military police officer opened the door, and Andrus led the other men in. They blinked their eyes in the bright lights. Looming ahead of them, just to the left, were two black gallows, which, in the words of the lieutenant in charge, were "huge, foreboding and hopelessly out of place next to the basketball hoop at the end of the chamber." A third gallows, held in reserve in case one of the other two failed, stood to the right. A curtain next to it hid eleven wooden coffins. The gym was a grimy building with nothing much in it other than two iron stoves in one corner. One of the walls had a single poster of a U.S. Army—

sponsored slogan seen everywhere in occupied Nuremberg over the last year: "VD walks the Streets."

Left of the main gallows, the four tribunal judges sat at folding tables, and near them, at four other tables, were eight members of the press. After taking three steps into the gym, Keitel was stopped by another MP who removed his shackles. Keitel's eyes went instinctively to the first gallows, where he saw a rope, taut and twisting. He knew Ribbentrop was dying on the other end. Two MPs took Keitel by the arms, and Gerecke followed as they stood Keitel before the tribunal. The judges asked him to state his name.

"Wilhelm Keitel!" the general said, loudly and clearly.

He then turned on the heels of his gleaming black boots and walked briskly up the thirteen steps of the second gallows. Gerecke followed him up, and the two men looked at each other. Gerecke began a German prayer he had learned from his mother. The chaplain knew Keitel's mother had taught him the same verse as a child, and the general joined Gerecke in prayer.

The prayer was just one thing the two men had in common. Brunswick was another. Keitel had been raised on a farm outside Brunswick in central Germany, and Gerecke's great-grandfather had left that city when he sailed to America. Keitel had hoped to follow his family's farming tradition, but his father pushed him into the army instead, and he became a professional soldier. In 1940, Hitler appointed him general field marshal. He was the führer's closest military adviser and most dependable sycophant—an obsequious figure, the archetypal Nazi bootlicker.

Keitel was ten years older than Gerecke, but both men had been brought up on farms, and both had married the daughters of brewers. During the year of the trial, Gerecke and Keitel had become close. Gerecke found that Keitel was always "devotional in his bearing" when the chaplain visited his cell. He found the field marshal penitent and "deeply Christian." Keitel was interested especially in hymns and verses from scripture that dealt with the evidence of

God's love for man, and man's redemption from sin through Christ's death on the cross.

Gerecke was very slow to give Holy Communion to a new, or returning, Christian. He needed to be convinced that a candidate not only understood the significance of the sacrament, but that, "in penitence and faith," he was ready for it. This was the real reason Gerecke took the Nuremberg assignment. These were men who had spit on the notion of traditional Christianity while promoting an idea that a cleansed Germany would mean a better world and a more pure future. They had broken a contract with God, set down in the Ten Commandments, and Gerecke believed his duty as a Christian minister was to bring redemption to these souls, to save as many Nazis as he could before their executions. After studying the sacrament during the first months of the trial, Keitel asked Gerecke if he could celebrate Communion under the chaplain's direction. The general chose the Bible readings, hymns, and prayers for the ritual and read them aloud. He knelt by the cot in his cell and confessed his sins.

"On his knees and under deep emotional stress, [Keitel] received the Body and Blood of our Savior," Gerecke wrote later. "With tears in his voice he said, 'You have helped me more than you know. May Christ, my Savior, stand by me all the way. I shall need him so much.'"

Henriette von Schirach, the wife of Hitler Youth leader Baldur von Schirach, who was also on trial at Nuremberg and was a member of Gerecke's prison flock, spoke to Gerecke shortly after the verdicts were announced by the court. Gerecke had given a sermon about the trial from the pulpit of a small, five-hundred-year-old church he pastored in Mögeldorf, a village in the eastern part of Nuremberg, where his congregation was mostly other American officers and enlisted men, with a few Germans included.

"The church was half destroyed and one could see the sky through the burnt-out roof," Schirach wrote. "Gerecke preached in

English. His subject—the executions. He did not want our men"—the Nazi prisoners—"to be killed."

Gerecke told Schirach the executions would take place in the gymnasium of the prison, not—as rumored—in public, in the square outside Nuremberg's great St. Lawrence Church where Hitler had spent hours reviewing the troops as they marched past during the Nuremberg rallies.

"Gerecke had made friends with Field Marshal Keitel, Hitler's military adviser," she wrote. "They were about the same age, but Keitel's sons had been killed or captured while Gerecke's sons were alive. Physically there was a certain resemblance between them—both had short grey hair and jovial expressions. The pastor was bound to take the farewell from the prisoner very hard."

After reaching the top of the thirteen steps of the gallows, Keitel was asked if he had any last words.

"I call on the Almighty to be considerate of the German people, provide tenderness and mercy," he said. "Over two million German soldiers went to their death for their Fatherland. I now follow my sons."

A United Press account reported that the field marshal then "thanked the priest who stood beside him." Then the executioner pulled a lever, and just twenty minutes after Gerecke and Keitel had first kneeled in prayer on the general's cell floor, Keitel dropped through the platform's trapdoor.

In the seconds that followed, the only sound in the gym was the creaking of the rope against its huge steel eyebolt at the top of the gallows. Gerecke walked out into the rain to retrieve the next prisoner.

CHAPTER 2

Zion

God our Father has made all things depend on faith so that whoever has faith will have everything and whoever does not have faith will have nothing.

—MARTIN LUTHER

IN 1918, WHEN HENRY met Alma Bender, at the Lutheran Church of Our Redeemer in south St. Louis, the Benders were living about four blocks from the church and a fifteen-minute walk to Otto Stifel's Union Brewery, where Alma's father, Jacob, worked as a brewer.

Jacob Bender's own father had come to St. Louis from Baden-Württemberg, Germany, in the middle of the nineteenth century. Jacob married an American girl, Alma Isselhardt, from Staunton, Illinois, and they had three children. Roy and his little sisters, Alma and Virginia, grew up in St. Louis, in an apartment next to their grandparents and close enough to Jacob's workplace—and several other breweries—that, for Alma, the earthy, sweet fragrance of hops in the wind became the smell of growing up.

After Alma and Henry were married, on July 23, 1919, Henry

moved in with his in-laws. The wedding was a happy moment in a difficult year for the family. That fall, as Henry began his second year at Concordia, the U.S. Congress adopted the Volstead Act, which enabled it to pass the Eighteenth Amendment in favor of Prohibition, putting many people in St. Louis, including Jacob Bender and his boss, Otto Stifel, out of work. The next year, Stifel—in what became a pattern for beer barons of the time—shot himself.

The second crisis that fall emerged from the seminary itself. Studying at Concordia was something Henry had been dreaming about since high school. But the seminary, Henry was told, did not allow its students to be engaged or married (or to sing "frivolous and uncouth songs," "read romances," or play cards). Concordia tossed him out for marrying Alma, and he had to go to work answering correspondence in the office of New World Commercial Co., an insurance agency in downtown St. Louis. Henry feared he would never become a preacher.

The entire family was now living above Wehrenberg's Tavern on Cherokee Street, which Fred Wehrenberg, a former blacksmith, had opened at the turn of the century with the help of Otto Stifel and William Lemp. There was an ornately carved hardwood bar with brass tap handles, posters of beautiful women promoting various beer brands lining the walls, and sawdust covering the floor. All Fred had to do was serve the beer and the various German-style salted foods—pretzels, spiced ham, potato salad, roast mutton, sauerkraut, pickled pig's feet—that kept customers thirsty.

Groups gathered at tables for games of poker, bridge, or gin rummy and listened to piano and accordion music. Chess and checkers players hovered over the boards balanced on oak beer barrels. Customers huddled in "hot stove leagues" engaged in debates about boxing or baseball. In the garden, beer drinkers tossed horseshoes.

As other bars opened nearby, Fred and his wife, Gertrude, decided on a gimmick to make themselves stand out. At the 1904 World's Fair in St. Louis's Forest Park, Fred had seen an exhibit that featured a replica of a train car that people clambered into. Once they were seated, images of the Alps flickered by outside the car's windows, giving those seated inside the impression of motion.

Wehrenberg "saw how the crowds were flocking to the exhibit" and realized what a boon this new technology could be for beer sales. Within two years, he'd set up an annex to the saloon for motion pictures with the original bar serving as a kind of early concession stand. So when the Benders and Gereckes moved into the Wehrenbergs' old apartment above the saloon, the bar was still lively, despite Prohibition.

Henry was the sole provider for his now-pregnant wife, her parents, and her six-year-old sister, all living in the Cherokee Street apartment. His relationship with his own parents, already strained because Henry had married a city girl, nearly ruptured completely at the beginning of 1921 after Henry's little sister, Nora, died of meningitis at age seventeen. Henry's mother had begged her husband to let Nora see a doctor, but he refused. Herman Gerecke denied that his daughter was very sick, and besides, he said, doctors cost too much.

Herman relented eventually, but it was too late. Henry was furious with his parents but also with himself for not protecting Nora from their father's ignorance and miserliness.

There had been almost no time for grieving Nora's death. A month later, Alma and Henry's first child was born. They named him for his father and grandfathers, Henry Herman Jacob Gerecke, but Alma and Henry called him Hank.

When he'd first arrived in St. Louis in 1918, Henry had become friendly with a prominent Lutheran pastor, Rev. Richard Kretzschmar, and his family, who allowed him to live in their basement before he started seminary. After Concordia forced Henry to withdraw because of his marriage, Pastor Kretzschmar directed Henry's private studies, with the approval of a Concordia faculty committee and the help of individual professors. In the summer of 1920, Henry took classes at Harris Teachers College and St. Louis University so he could get out of the insurance business and into teaching as he pursued his private studies in theology. In the fall of 1921, he started teaching at Emmaus Lutheran, where Kretzschmar was pastor. Henry taught there for five years, later calling it "the beginning of my comeback."

Life was lively, if crowded, above a tavern in Prohibition St. Louis. And it became even more so in January 1922, when Corky was born exactly eleven months after Hank's arrival. But Corky and his grandpa Bender lived together for only a short time. Just ten days after Corky arrived, Jacob, who had been suffering from ulcers, died of a stomach hemorrhage at age forty-nine.

When Hank and Corky were a little older—four or five—Alma's mother often sent them downstairs with a bucket and a dime to Wehrenberg's with explicit instructions not to spill any "near-beer," a malted beverage with trace amounts of alcohol popular during Prohibition, on the way back up to the apartment. Their reward was a sip from the bucket. At the end of each day, the boys ran down to the front of the building to watch for Henry as he arrived home from work on his bike, a black briefcase swinging from the handlebars. Henry, a dedicated musician, practiced violin, piano, and trumpet in the little apartment. His trombone playing made his young sons cry, so Alma made him practice in the bathroom.

In the fall of 1925, after years of extracurricular help from Kretzschmar and other Concordia professors working with him in their free time, Gerecke passed his exams at Concordia and graduated, making him eligible to be "called" to lead a congregation as its pastor. The Lutheran Church–Missouri Synod divides the country up into geographical districts, each with an elected president and a certain number of congregations. District presidents traditionally have some influence in matching up ministers and congregations in his district.

When Gerecke became eligible for call, Kretzschmar was a

district president of the synod, and he engineered Gerecke's call to the ministry. Kretzschmar had also cofounded the church's KFUO radio station in St. Louis in 1924 and would be influential in developing Gerecke's side career in broadcasting. After teaching for five years at Emmaus, on January 24, 1926, Gerecke, at age thirty-two, was ordained at Christ Lutheran Church and installed as its pastor by Rev. A. P. Feddersen. Christ Lutheran was about three miles from Wehrenberg's, at an address that shared a name with Gerecke's mother and grandmother—3506 Caroline Street. Two years later, in 1928, as Henry was settling in to life leading a congregation, Alma gave birth to the couple's third son, Roy David.

In the small vicarage house, Alma and Henry had one room, with the three boys in another, two of them—Hank and Corky—sharing a bed and constantly fighting. Grandma Bender and Aunt Ginny—a not-very-auntly eleven-year-old when they moved in—had a room as well.

As is traditional in churches, cliques within the congregation tested Gerecke at first and tried to keep him in line with their goals and agendas. One of the first summers there, the congregation was meeting in the church hall, and all the windows were open to the St. Louis humidity. The family was sitting on the back porch and could hear raised voices as Gerecke led the meeting inside.

Finally, they heard Gerecke boom, "If you want to step out into the alley, I'll show you who's running this church!"

Afterward, Grandma Bender counseled her son-in-law. "Henry," she said, "you can't talk to the congregation like that."

He sure could, Gerecke told her. "They've got to realize who is in charge."

After the trial period, the cliques settled into their own debates and left Gerecke to run the church. As for the vicarage, each year a committee of church members came in and fixed anything that was broken and gave the place a fresh coat of paint. Alma supplied the food—her braunschweiger sandwiches were a favorite. On Gerecke's fifth anniversary as pastor, the congregation threw him a surprise party.

St. Louis has always been a Catholic town, and Christ Lutheran existed within the borders of Immaculate Conception parish. That church was about nine blocks away from Christ Lutheran, and the neighborhood between the churches was populated by Catholics. Most of Hank's and Corky's friends were Catholic. Henry got along well with the priests at Immaculate Conception and with his Catholic neighbors, often attending the wakes of those who died. Even though they were only a few miles from their old apartment, Hank and Corky were still the new kids, and their Lutheranism was an invitation for childhood cruelty.

One afternoon, when Hank was about eight, a group of teenagers approached him on the street outside Christ Lutheran and "beat the hell" out of him. He ran inside the house and told his father, who ran after the teens, eventually capturing all four of them. He dragged them back, two in each hand, to the house and called out to Hank, "Which one?"

The Gereckes socialized with other Lutheran pastors and their wives. Their best friends were Pastor Henry "Woods" Holls and his wife, whom the kids called "Aunt Agnes." The couples and their friends gathered at each other's homes to play bridge and talk or attended functions at each other's churches. Occasionally, on a Sunday after services, they'd all pile their kids in cars and drive out to the banks of the Meramec, a tributary of the Mississippi that flows through the Ozarks.

Gerecke thought dancing was "sinful" in those days, but he loosened up later. He hated smoking and forced those who were going to light up to retreat elsewhere. His dress style was the same on Sunday as on any other day of the week—a dark suit and tie. He wore a black gown over his suit when he was preaching, and a homburg hat when he was outside. He never donned a clerical collar for worship services, but he always wore a watch on his left wrist, rimless glasses, and a cross on a chain tucked into his suit pocket. His sermons were casual but authoritative, and he wrote them in outline form in order to better speak off the cuff when he felt the need. When Gerecke delivered a sermon, every person in every pew felt like he was speaking just to them—an effect similar to a meaningful conversation with a learned friend. Preaching was perhaps Gerecke's greatest talent as a minister.

Grandma Bender could be a dire presence in the little apartment. One time, when Hank stole some money out of his grandmother's purse, she taught him a lesson by turning on the stove and forcing his hand over the fire—not close enough to burn him, just enough to get his attention. And on the rare occasions when Henry's parents visited, the country versus city feud continued. The Gereckes blamed Alma for Henry's awkward withdrawal from Concordia. Herman Gerecke hadn't wanted his son to be a preacher, but once Henry was traveling down that road, Herman didn't want any bumps in the way. For the Gereckes, Alma represented an obstacle, and they saw her parents as a potential corrupting influence on their grandchildren.

There wasn't a lot of love going the other way either. Whenever the Gereckes came up to St. Louis to visit, Grandma Bender called her grandchildren over to her and instructed them: "When your Grandma Gerecke comes over, she's going to kiss you. Don't kiss her back."

Like a lot of people who are hard on their children, Herman Gerecke was a pushover with his grandchildren. On visits to St. Louis or when the family traveled down to Cape Girardeau, Herman loved taking the boys for long walks, showing them off to his friends and buying them the ever-present near beer and pails of ice cream.

Grandma Bender had a soft spot for Henry, and he for her. She often took his side in family debates. She lent him money to buy a car from someone's estate—a Marmon Roosevelt. On Saturday nights, he would drive down near the Mississippi where the German bakeries were and buy his mother-in-law her favorite brain sandwiches.

In 1932, Hank, now eleven, came home from school and his mother called him into the kitchen. "Your father has something to tell you," she said. Grandma Bender had died of a ruptured gangrenous appendix, at age fifty-one. Years before her death, she had lost a child—her oldest, Roy, who had died in the First World War. On her deathbed, she didn't ask after Alma—her oldest daughter, who had taken her widowed mother into her home, or Ginny—her seventeen-year-old youngest child. She spoke only about her dead son.

Soon after his mother-in-law's death, Gerecke realized he was bored with congregational life. For a couple of years, he'd been doing mission work in his free time among the "unchurched" in St. Louis's poor black neighborhoods, and he'd come to love this work more than what he was doing with his own flock. He wanted to be among people he felt were more desperately in need of hearing the Gospel message. The members of his congregation, sitting in the pews at Christ Lutheran, were good, faithful Christians. They had their problems, like anyone else, Gerecke believed, but they were already on a path toward a salvation they could grasp. Gerecke had become more interested in the city's wounded, those who were at risk of dying without hearing God's message of love for them.

In 1935, five years into the Great Depression, Gerecke told the family they were moving from the Christ Lutheran vicarage, and he would no longer be the pastor there. He told Alma they were going to have to find an apartment to rent and he would be a missionary. Alma was shocked, but her husband had made up his mind. That May, Gerecke "followed a call," leaving a job with a decent salary and housing, to work for a fraction of the pay ministering to the city's poor, its old, insane, sick, and criminal.

ON A LITTLE HILL off County Road 226, about ten miles west of the Mississippi River, the white-shingled spire of Zion Lutheran Church is just one of many shooting up from the corn and sorghum fields around Gordonville, Missouri. This is middle America, straight out of the picture-book imaginations of Americans who have never been to their country's vast center. Farmers still wear denim overalls while pitching hay high into the storage spaces under the gambrel roofs of their red prairie barns. The inscription above the doors of the church, a little brick building that's home to one of the oldest faith communities in Missouri, gives visitors a clue as to its founders' heritage. "Deutsch Zions Kirche" it reads—Zion German Church. And on the cornerstone below:

Ev. Luth. Zions Kirche
U.A.C.
1865—1915

When the Civil War ended in 1865, the farmers of southeastern Missouri, near Cape Girardeau, wanted desperately to leave four years of brutality behind. So they banded together to share their faith. The "U.A.C." on the cornerstone of Zion Lutheran Church was a confession of what it was. The initials, which stand for Unaltered Augsburg Confession, signaled that these men and their families were true German Lutherans, followers of the original splinter group to break away from the Roman Catholic Church.

More than three centuries earlier, their ancestors—including Martin Luther and his friend, the theologian Philipp Melanchthon—were called before Charles V, the Holy Roman Emperor, who wanted to halt the growing divide between Luther and Pope Clement VII. At the Diet of Augsburg in 1530, Melanchthon presented Charles with twenty-eight articles of faith that both disputed charges of heresy made by Catholic loyalists and made clear the theological differences at the root of the Reformation.

The Augsburg Confession was signed by German secular rulers and magistrates—dukes and princes (and also by the mayor and council of Nuremberg). The document was read aloud to Charles V, an event that took two hours, and while it failed to bring unity to Christian Europe, it became the foundational document for the Lutheran denomination.

Ten years later, Melanchthon revised the Confession—a version that was later adopted by John Calvin—and in the generations that followed, some Lutheran churches distinguished themselves from others by the initials U.A.C. to signal that their congregation abided by the original, unaltered Augsburg Confession.

In and around Gordonville, a group of Lutheran farmers—William Hager, Ludwig Siemers, Friedrich Schwab, William Schneider, George Keller, George Siemers, Samuel Nussbaum, and William Gerecke—were intent on abiding by Augsburg. Three months after the end of the war, on August 13, 1865, they signed the original constitution for Zion Lutheran Church. In doing so, William Gerecke—Henry Gerecke's grandfather—became one of Zion's charter members.

When Wilhelm Gerecke arrived in America from Brunswick in 1855, he was nineteen years old. He'd made his way to Missouri and bought 150 acres of land near Gordonville. By the time he was twenty-four years old, Wilhelm had become an American citizen and anglicized his name to William. He was a small-time farmer by 1860, using about a third of his land to keep his horse, two "milch cows," and three hogs and to grow 150 bushels of wheat and 300 bushels of corn.

In southeastern Missouri in the middle of the nineteenth century, corn was king, rising eight feet from the often inexpertly plowed land. Oats and wheat were afterthoughts, planted between corn rows and cultivated in the winter after the corn had been husked. Only workhorses were rewarded with ear corn, and then only when they were working. In the winter, they were let out into the fields and woods to fend for themselves, just like the farmers' sheep, cows, and hogs.

Many farmers were working just to feed their families. Before there were barns, farmers used horses to separate wheat grain from stalk on giant threshing floors cleared in the fields, and they used hand-cranked mills to divide the wheat from the chaff. Families grew potatoes, turnips, pumpkins, watermelons, muskmelons, onions, and lettuce on small pieces of cleared land near the farmhouse. They raised pole beans by letting them climb the many cornstalks. William Gerecke's life on the farm was severe and simple, qualities that would influence his offsprings' frugality—and eventually come to haunt his descendants.

Lessons in agriculture had followed William across the Atlantic, but so had civil war. When war came, Missouri—a border state—was hit hard. William enlisted in the Union Army in 1863. By then he had married a fellow German immigrant, Caroline Luecke, two years his junior and from Hanover, Germany, just forty miles from Brunswick. When William went off to war, at age twenty-seven, the couple's first child, Louis, was less than a year old, and Caroline was pregnant with their second son, Herman. He was born on December 27, 1863.

William Gerecke and his fellow farmers were exhausted by war and its violence, and they banded together in an act of faith to found Zion. But on November 6, 1865, three months after forming the church, William died at age twenty-nine, leaving Caroline to look after the farm and raise Louis and Herman. Henry Wessel, who owned an adjoining farm to the Gereckes', became the boys' guardian, and on Valentine's Day 1867, he married Caroline. Nine months and two days later, Caroline gave birth to her third son, whom she named William.

When their father died, Louis Gerecke was three years old and Herman was not yet two. Henry Wessel raised the boys as his own, and he preserved William Gerecke's farm for them. Each year, Wessel calculated the amount of interest his wife's sons received from their $693.14 inheritance. In 1873, after taxes and probate court fees, their total balance was $773.90. By 1882, when the boys were eighteen and nineteen, the balance was $1,335.82, the equivalent of nearly $30,000 today—and there was the farm.

On November 3, 1892, Herman married a woman with the same first name—and from the same town as—his mother: Caroline Kelpe from Hanover, Germany. She went by "Lena." He was twenty-nine, she was twenty and the couple moved into the farmhouse that William Gerecke had left to his sons nearly thirty years earlier. Exactly nine months later, on August 4, 1893, their first child was born. On August 27, Henry (Heinrich) Friedrich Gerecke was introduced to the Christian world at Zion Lutheran, the church his grandfather had formed in the wake of war.

A key article in the Augsburg Confession says that man cannot be forgiven for his sins through his own "merits, works or satisfactions." Luther's friend Melanchthon wrote that "we receive forgiveness of sin and become righteous before God by grace, for Christ's sake, through faith." That theology became central to the work of William Gerecke's grandson.

HERMAN, LENA, AND HENRY lived on the Gerecke farm, off County Road 203, for ten years before Lena had another child—a girl this time. Leonora Gerecke was born April 13, 1903. The family called her Nora, and she was soon joined by a playmate—Fritz—when the Gereckes adopted a second cousin, Fred Conrad Gerecke, who was six years younger than Henry.

Herman, like most farmers, thought of his work as a family project, and Fred's addition to the family was as much an economic decision as a personal one. Henry and Fred worked as farm laborers alongside men Herman hired to help bring in the harvest, fix ailing machinery, and plow the fields.

By 1908, Henry was fourteen and felt a call to the ministry. He'd seen a man named Billy Sunday preach, and he was hooked.

Sunday, a former center fielder for the Chicago White Stockings, had quit the major leagues in the late nineteenth century to devote himself full time to ministry. After the turn of the century, he was leading outdoor tent revivals in small towns around the Midwest.

By 1910, "the baseball evangelist," as he came to be known, was drawing thousands to his revivals. His populist preaching style enraged the clerical establishment, but charmed the rural masses. He was a tiger onstage, constantly prowling, never stopping for more than an instant, often jumping around or standing on chairs. One writer called him a "gymnast for Jesus." The pace of his sermons—accelerating one moment, decelerating the next, all in the service of creating tension—kept audiences rapt, until the payoff line, when they would burst with laughter, rise to their feet in applause, or grab for the hand of a loved one nearby in heartbreak—whatever Sunday had intended.

Sunday's message wasn't new among evangelical Christians: the secular world is dangerous; alcohol is the devil; the Bible is the inerrant word of God; accept Jesus as your personal savior. But his vocabulary was filled with slang, his antics from the pulpit were hugely entertaining, and his conversion record was unmatched.

Thousands heeded Sunday's altar calls over the weeks at any given revival. Between 1896 and 1907, Sunday mostly visited towns in Iowa, Illinois, Missouri, Indiana, Minnesota, Nebraska, and Colorado. The towns where he set up his wooden tabernacles were mostly small: Leon and Exira, Iowa; Rantoul and Prophetstown, Illinois; Lima and East Liverpool, Ohio. "What he lacked in originality of ideas," wrote one Sunday biographer, "he made up for with a fertility of expressive imagination and a talent for buffoonery which transcended the banality of his message."

By 1917, Sunday was considered by many the "greatest revivalist in American history, perhaps the greatest since the days of the apostles." Some said he was "the greatest preacher since John the Baptist."

Billy Sunday may have inspired young Henry Gerecke to preach, but Henry's father wasn't about to make his path to the pulpit an easy one. Herman was dead against his oldest son having a career in the church, and Lena didn't have much of a say in the matter. Herman told Henry he could be a farmer or a teacher. If Henry chose the latter, Herman said, he'd pay part of his tuition to the teacher's college at nearby Southeast Missouri State.

Henry didn't want to be a teacher, and he certainly didn't want to farm. But his sense of loyalty and responsibility were strong, and he remained on the farm until he was nineteen years old. Finally, in 1912, he left Cape Girardeau and traveled west to the plains and the campus of St. John's Academy and College in Winfield, Kansas.

His biggest problem there was money. Henry had no help from his father, so he landed a succession of jobs as he entered prep school—cleaning toilets and spittoons at a department store in nearby Wichita, and harvesting wheat as a farm laborer. Winfield, a college town of eight thousand residents, was populated mostly by retired farmers. The 1917–1918 St. John's *Bulletin,* a promotional pamphlet selling the school to Lutheran parents, points out the town's "many paved and well-shaded streets, neat cottages and lawns, splendid residences and electrical 'white ways.'"

While plenty of trains came through Winfield—the Santa Fe, Southern Kansas, Florence–El Dorado, Frisco, Missouri Pacific—the town had no "railroad shops—which often bring an uncultured class of citizens." The college was in east Winfield and connected to downtown by streetcar. The dormitory was a three-story stone building that slept 140 students and was "lighted with electricity, heated by steam" and "equipped with a modern vacuum-cleaning apparatus."

Breakfast was from 6:30 A.M. to 6:50 A.M. ("Grace will be said at table, and general good order preserved.") Morning study followed, from 7:00 A.M. to 7:45 A.M. After an inspection, classes commenced in the main hall. Aside from gatherings of the literary and musical organizations, vacant periods were to be devoted to study. "Lounging in the halls or expectorating in the building cannot be tolerated." Attendance at morning and evening devotions was "considered self-evident" to aid in the development of "a truly Christian character."

Devotions were at 10:15 A.M. and after dinner, which was at 5:30 or 6:00, depending on the season. A student could smoke in the studies, but not cigarettes, and only if he was seventeen years old and had the permission of his parents. He could not visit the picture shows or theaters, and "flirtations" were prohibited. "This includes all attentions to the other sex not called for by ordinary courtesy."

St. John's was a six-year prep school and college ministerial program for what would become the Lutheran Church–Missouri Synod, a place where young men who thought they might want to join the ministry came to earn their college degree before entering a graduate-level Lutheran seminary.

In 1847, a group of northern German immigrants to the United States had come together in Chicago to form the German Evangelical Lutheran Synod of Missouri, Ohio, and Other States. Its goal was a network of churches that would preach and teach "confessional Lutheranism," a traditionalist branch of the denomination that stressed a strict adherence to the Book of Concord, the sixteenth-century collection of authoritative documents, called *confessions*, that define the central doctrines of Lutheranism.

Pastors and congregations who wanted to join the new denomination were required to accept a document called the "Scriptures of the Old and New Testaments as the written Word of God and the only rule and norm of faith and practice." It described the backbone of Protestantism: the notion of *sola scriptura*—that the biblical texts, not the dictates of the men who built the Catholic Church, contain the only infallible tenets of the Christian faith. Members also were required to accept all the symbolic books of the Lutheran Church "as a true and correct statement and exposition of the Word of God . . . the three Ecumenical Creeds, the Unaltered Augsburg Confession, the Apology of the Augsburg Confession, the Smalcald Articles, the Large Catechism of Luther, the Small Catechism of Luther, and the Formula of Concord."

The core group that formed this new Lutheran branch had fled Germany in 1839 after the German government forced it to merge with Calvinists. The synod's new constitution required new members to renounce "unionism"—worshipping with Christian clergy of other denominations—and "syncretism"—the fusion of different religions. Finally, new synod members had to agree to use "doctrinally pure agendas, hymnbooks, and catechisms." On the denomination's centennial, in 1947, the church changed its named to the Lutheran Church–Missouri Synod.

During Gerecke's years at St. John's, the school held tight to its Saxon roots, largely because of instructions from Synod headquarters. The college imported textbooks from Germany so that Latin, Greek, and Hebrew could be taught in German rather than in English. Evening chapel services were conducted in German. Dormitory rules and report cards were issued in German. The local Lutheran church in Winfield offered services in German once a week. The students were given Reformation Day off.

The ministerial program was the main course at St. John's, though it also offered a classical course that emphasized the languages, literature, and "the antiquities of Greece and Rome," and a scientific course for students interested in mathematics and science. Young women could enroll at St. John's and take business classes "and by close application soon become proficient in Shorthand, Typewriting and Bookkeeping." Tuition was $1.00 per week and board was $90 per year. Books were $10 per year and expenses for "electric light" averaged twenty-five cents per month. Laundry was "best sent home by parcel post."

In the fall of Gerecke's sophomore year of college at St. John's, Wichita Natural Gas Co. struck oil in El Dorado, fifty miles north of the school. The well, Stapleton #1, led to the discovery of a massive oil field that covered thirty-four square miles and became the largest single-field producer of oil in the country. The El Dorado field created its own bustling business district with the population of Butler County nearly doubling between 1910 and 1920, which created plenty of jobs for starving college students—including Gerecke.

The one-dollar-per-week tuition expense didn't apply to students in the ministerial course. Their tuition was paid by the synod with the understanding that "students who abandon the course are liable for full amount of back tuition." Ministerial students concentrated on religion and languages, and graduates were admitted to the synod's seminaries on the basis of their diplomas from St. John's. "Such graduates," the *Bulletin* promised, "if they have completed our full German course, will be able to use also the German fluently in the pulpit and in conversation."

Gerecke started at St. John's in 1913, at age twenty. In the high school, Gerecke took sacred literature, beginning Latin, ancient and medieval history, geometry, biology, and three units each of English and German. He got mostly Bs in English, rhetoric, and literature. He also got Bs in Hebrew, though he hated it. In German and Greek, he earned a mix of Bs and Cs. In Latin he fared better with Cicero (B/B-) than Virgil (B/C).

When he wasn't working or studying, Gerecke had plenty of other distractions. He played basketball his freshman year, took part in the Student's Mission Society, and was a member of the student council, rising to president of the student body and of the St. John's Class of 1918. The St. John's yearbook, *The Saint*, called him "the best man for the job." But music was Gerecke's true love—he played piano and violin at St. John's, and his senior year quote, from George Eliot, underscored his devotion to it: "There is no feeling, except the extremes of fear and grief, that does not find relief in music." He played violin for the school's Arion Quintet and sang in the Senior Octet, which performed often "spicy selections" during literary meetings and other public occasions. Gerecke was a founding member of the college orchestra and was its president all four years of college. The orchestra bought five pianos that it rented out to fund its concerts and *The Saint* proclaimed "the excellent success of this organization must largely be given to [Gerecke's] credit."

Gerecke, whom his classmates nicknamed Grex ("herd" in Latin, a play on both his name and childhood on the farm), also took part in the school's literary societies, whose purpose was "to extend classroom learning." In 1915, school officials added a second society—Demosthenian—to longtime society Chrysostomos and began an annual intersociety contest, pitting students against one another in oration, reading, and debate. Two students from each society competed in each of the three disciplines and were then ranked by faculty. The team with the best overall ranking won the Faculty Loving Cup. According to *The Saint,* the ultimate purpose of Chrysostomos was not to create "stars" for the literary battles against Demosthenian, but "to produce and develop every grain of literary ability present. . . . We have persistently tried to develop hidden mental treasures in every individual member."

In the 1918 intersociety contest, Gerecke—who grew a beard and began smoking a pipe while in college—was one of two students on the Chrysostomos oration team. He placed fourth of four, and Chrysostomos lost the Faculty Loving Cup to Demosthenian. "Let us nourish the hope that Chrysostomos may ever uphold that beacon of thoroughness for which she has always stood," the society's members wrote in *The Saint.* "May she hold firm to the spirit of diligent application, which in due time spells progress. *Vivat, crescat, floreat* (Live long, grow, flourish) Chrysostomos!"

When the United States declared war on Germany in 1917, the need for oil grew dramatically, and by 1918, the El Dorado field was producing 13 percent of the country's oil production and 9 percent of the world's. By the end of the war, the Kansas oil fields were among the most productive in the nation. While Gerecke's job in those fields may have been contributing to the war effort, he was young and patriotic and wanted to do more. During one visit home to Missouri in 1917, he decided to enlist in the army and lined up outside the recruiting station in Cape Girardeau.

By then Herman had leased the farm to a relative and moved Lena, Fritz, and Nora into a house on Pacific Street in town. Herman found Henry at the recruiting station and yanked his son out of line. Herman's views on war were even more unfavorable than his views on religion, and no son of his was going to volunteer for battle.

"You can't go to war," Herman told him. "You're in divinity school."

In 1942, when Herman was on his deathbed, he asked after his grandson Hank. Henry couldn't bring himself to tell his father the truth: that Hank had joined the army and was fighting the Japanese in the Aleutian Islands. Instead, he told Herman that Hank was "on a trip."

By the time Henry left Kansas in 1918, he'd picked up a nick-name, improved his German, gained some weight, and obtained the first college degree in his family's history. (*The Saint* said Grex hadn't "been 'Hooverizing' very much," a reference to a request by Herbert Hoover—then the head of the U.S. Food Administration under President Woodrow Wilson—that Americans cut back on their eating to help the war effort.) He was twenty-four years old and ready for seminary at Concordia in St. Louis. Gerecke moved to the heart of Missouri Synod scholarship just as the church was celebrating the four hundredth anniversary of the beginning of the Reformation, an exciting time to be studying to become a pastor.

Soon after arriving in the big city, Henry met a seventeen-year-old Famous-Barr department store candy counter girl named Alma. She was lively and beautiful, with big brown eyes. Their children later called the meeting "Dad's Waterloo."

REV. F. W. HERZBERGER, the Baltimore-born son of a Civil War chap-lain, founded the St. Louis Lutheran City Mission in 1899 after conducting a church service for the homeless in a tavern on South Second Street in St. Louis. Herzberger was educated in the Missouri Synod system in schools and seminaries across the country.

"He had a genuine sympathy for all classes of unfortunates, and was instrumental in his institutional work to bring many a wanderer back to the Fold, and bring Christian solace to the sinner in the dying hour," wrote Gerecke's friend "Woods" Holls, who began working with Herzberger at City Mission in 1919 and was instrumental in recruiting Gerecke.

Another pastor wrote that Herzberger had "an understanding love, and compassion for souls even among the lowliest and the poorest." Herzberger's motto came from a famous verse in the Gospel of Matthew: "I was naked and you gave me clothing, I was sick and you took care of me, I was in prison and you visited me."

Herzberger died in August 1930, at age seventy-one, less than five years before Gerecke took his place leading City Mission. When Gerecke joined the organization, the Reverend Walter Ellwanger, who had joined City Mission in 1930 after Herzberger died, was running its school and first mission chapel on the Mississippi, a few blocks south of the site where Eero Saarinen would build the Gateway Arch thirty years later. When he joined the mission, Ellwanger had discovered that children were not bringing their lunches to school because there wasn't anything to eat in their own kitchens. He found many of them behind a nearby pickle factory next to the river, scrounging for scraps in the factory dump. By 1938, he was running a school lunch program that fed St. Louis kids fourteen thousand meals a year.

Holls was doing most of the institutional work, visiting hospitals and sanitariums around the city. The men ran City Mission from an office on Fourth Street, next to its mission chapel and underneath the Municipal Bridge that brought trains across the river. When Gerecke took over as executive missioner, the organization bought a second chapel, for $5,000, in north St. Louis. They called it Good Shepherd Lutheran Church, and Gerecke became its pastor, holding services at 10:45 A.M. and 8:00 P.M. each Sunday.

He installed a cross on top of the building and opened the doors for business, recruiting the destitute from the local neighborhood as his congregation. "The large neon cross lights the way on 10th St.," he wrote in the City Mission newsletter. The City Mission office moved with Gerecke to Good Shepherd, enabling him to organize the nonprofit more efficiently. He hired a secretary, Dorothy Williams, who worked every day but Saturday and who kept all the mission's records organized and answered the office phones.

Gerecke designed a new City Mission letterhead and listed the organization's departments as "Gospel Preaching in City Institutions," "Missions and Mission Schools," "Prison Welfare," "Court Work," "Social Service and Christian Charity," "Child Saving Work," "Follow-Up Work," "Care for the Aged and Incurables," and "Rescue Endeavors." The letterhead gave each missionary's home address and phone number (Gerecke's was GRand 8858). A City Mission stamp that decorated its newsletter showed Christ, arms outstretched, floating above the Mississippi with St. Louis in the background. "Rebuild Lives with Christ," the stamp said in bold letters at the top. And below: "The Gospel is unchanged and unchanging, but it changes men."

The Lutheran Deaconess Association provided the missioners with one full-time nurse to help with its visits to Robert Koch Hospital, one of several sanitariums the missioners frequented. Gerecke managed about eighty-five student volunteers working for City Mission throughout the city and another sixty-five from Lutheran congregations.

"Ours is the busiest little one-man office in St. Louis," Gerecke wrote. "Your City Mission business is God's big business in St. Louis."

Just a few months after taking the job, Gerecke realized that if he was going to help the city's poor during the Depression, he had to do something to create jobs to lift their spirits. In the fall of 1935, he registered Lutheran Mission Industries with the state and began asking congregations, and anyone else, for old newspapers and magazines, rags, old clothing, and broken furniture.

He borrowed a broken-down Chevrolet paneled truck and hired two men from Good Shepherd to drive it and collect the donations. He opened a warehouse to store the donations, then sorted and stacked the paper, cloth, and glass into lots, which were then sold at two storefronts Gerecke opened near both mission chapels. The goal was employment, and Gerecke hired men from Good Shepherd and Ellwanger's congregation as drivers, sorters, and sellers. Eventually, Lutheran Mission Industries had three trucks, with two men each driving through the city and suburbs—north and northwest on Mondays, Wednesdays, and Fridays; south and southwest on Tuesdays, Thursdays, and Saturdays, making an average of twenty-five stops a day.

More men worked in the warehouse unloading the trucks, sorting, breaking glass into lots, and reloading trucks for delivery to the stores. Two men worked in each store, which were open every day. Men were paid a dollar a day for their work. Foremen were paid two dollars a day. "Whatever the business brings in is divided among the help after operating expenses have been paid," Gerecke wrote. "This is Christian Charity in the real sense of the word because the men want work and not sympathy."

Gerecke advertised that Lutheran Mission Industries sold "the lowest priced second-hand goods in the city." Poor families at the two mission congregations qualified for help to buy clothes or other goods through Mission Industries by obtaining a "charity tag" from Gerecke or Ellwanger. Men who needed clothes could come to the organization and "work the value of their needs in our warehouse," Gerecke wrote. "They always get a bargain."

Clothing was important, and several St. Louis stores donated clothes to the Lutheran Mission Industries cause. In order to keep this side business going, Gerecke constantly badgered Lutherans to either contribute or buy. He hit people up for everything from trucks to their address books.

"Since the first of November, prices on paper hit the bottom and at this very moment because of the RECESSION we are struggling desperately to keep Mission Industries going," he wrote in 1938. "We ask a favor of you. May we have your family mailing list in order to contact all our people with a card or letter asking for cast-off materials such as old clothing, broken furniture, cardboard, newspapers and magazines? . . . We keep fifteen men at work whose families would have been in desperate circumstances without your help."

Nearly everything—the trucks, the warehouse, and the store space—was donated by Lutherans, but there were expenses. Trucks broke down, warehouses burned, pipes froze.

"We can't keep up with the calls and are badly in need of another truck," Gerecke wrote in another plea, suggesting pastors put a free ad for Lutheran Mission Industries in their parish paper. Expenditures exceeded $700 a month. "There's no allowance for up-keep of our cars or rent. The situation is desperate. What shall we do? We need the encouragement of your prayers more than you realize. Our work is with the unfortunates, discouraged, the poor, the sick and the dying. May He bless you richly."

Less than a year after joining City Mission, Gerecke began working with prisoners in the downtown city jail. He held services at the jail at 9:00 A.M. on the first and third Sundays of each month. At first, about fifteen to twenty prisoners showed up. Gerecke began to bring in music—"the Gospel Songbird, Loretta Rolfingsmeyer," the Girls Gospel Harmony Trio from Overland, Missouri, and cornet and piano players. By the third year of this program, more than a hundred prisoners turned out for the services.

"Without boasting, the Lutheran services are the only protestant [sic] services well attended in that institution," Gerecke wrote in a newsletter. "The prisoners know without special announcement that the Lutheran services are holding forth. . . . Sometimes the guards join in the service."

By 1940, Gerecke was "much excited about the attendance at Jail. Remember, the prisoner is not compelled to attend church. The average for Nov. was nearly 160. Even the guards pick up a hymnal to join in singing those fine old Gospel hymns. Does that crowd sing! Sorry we can't invite your people to these services. With Wilma at the piano, Ralph on the cornet, and the pilgrim singers adding their harmonies, believe me, brother, that crowd sings. Even killers will listen to a blood-bought Gospel."

Gerecke also made his way to the Missouri State Penitentiary in 1940—a visit he called "a high spot"—where he spoke to eleven hundred fifty men. "They seemed visibly touched," he wrote. "When Chaplain Lindsay asked the men about a return visit, they answered with a tremendous applause. We shall see them again. This may be the opening of a large field. God has been good to us."

Unsurprisingly, money was a constant issue for a charity operation during the Great Depression. Two of the synod's districts contributed to the agency's budget, which was $11,000 in 1938, about $175,000 in today's dollars. But at the end of that year, City Mission was $500 ($7,500 today) in the red.

Gerecke wrote to the delegates at each Lutheran congregation in the district: "We must have better financial support of work if we are to carry on with the present arrangement. Where shall we get it? Under what circumstances and when? If no financial help comes our way, we will be compelled to retrench our activities in the very near future. Some of you say 'NO' to this, but what can we do about it? . . . You say, 'Have faith.' Thank you we do, but how long shall we go on deeper and deeper into debt with no reasonable assurance to be able to pay back?"

The lack of funding was not only a business issue; it influenced the morale of the three missionaries. "When we see only money matters in our work we become terribly depressed because of low funds," Gerecke wrote at one point, "but when we think of spiritual matters we know the command of Jesus that we are to go out and find the lost and wandering for heaven."

When eight hundred people attended City Mission's fortieth anniversary service, the collection plate brought in $208.64. Gerecke called the haul "a grand success."

Ellwanger ran the mission day school and original chapel on the south side. Holls was responsible for about 230 Lutheran patients out of 3,700 who suffered from "mental and nervous disorders" at the City Sanitarium on Arsenal Street in south St. Louis, and 120 Lutherans at the City Infirmary, which housed "the aged, infirm and poor," next door. Holls also traveled to the U.S. Veterans Hospital in Jefferson Barracks, about fifteen miles south of the city, and conducted services at St. Louis's Lutheran Convalescents Home, Barnes Hospital, and the Home for the Friendless. Gerecke, who also ran the business end of City Mission, was in charge of the Lutheran Mission Industries, pastored his congregation of one hundred at Good Shepherd, and did as much missionary work as Holls.

On Wednesdays, Gerecke went to the City Workhouse, a medium-security prison, at noon, and gave a sermon to the men as they ate in the mess hall. Wednesday evenings, he visited tuberculosis patients at the City Hospital and attended the spiritual needs of those in isolation wards. Three times a week, he made the rounds at Koch Hospital, visiting the two hundred patients under City Mission's spiritual care. On Friday mornings, he visited the isolation patients at Mount St. Rose, a Catholic sanatorium on the far south side of the city. Sundays were Gerecke's busiest days. In 1941, he wrote in a City Mission newsletter about a typical one:

First service, fifteen miles from home, at 6 a.m. Another at 7:45 a.m. A hurry up trip to Jail for a 9 a.m. service. Then Sunday School and Church service at 10:45 a.m. at the chapel. Several hos-

pital calls in the afternoon. Evening devotion at 6 p.m. at another
institution and evening service at 8 p.m. at the chapel. Your prayers
keep us going. God shall supply strength on the way.

A seminary student who worked at City Mission wrote in a 1941 newsletter about the long hours the missioners put in:

The work of a city missionary taxes a man's energy to the utmost.
Pastor Gerecke and the other men sometimes preach as many as seven
or eight sermons per Sunday (5 is normal) and they often are called
to the death beds of two or more patients in one night at some city hos-
pital or institution. They never seem to complain, however, because of
the personal joy which one receives in administering to sick brethren
and sisters who need comfort from God's Word.

Gerecke also made weekly visits to the government's Marine Hospital, west of the city in Kirkwood, and once a month he conducted a service and Bible class for unmarried mothers at the Bethesda Hospital and Home for Incurables, just a block from his former pulpit at Christ Church.

The missioners kept track of everything and anything they could—lists of sermon attendance figures, visitation requests, baptisms, confirmations, marriages—for their annual report. For Gerecke, it would turn out to be good training for the army. In 1937, for instance, Gerecke counted 17, 614 "hearers"—those who'd heard him speak in some capacity about the faith. The three men together baptized 28 adults and 59 children, confirmed 28 adults and 17 children, communed 1,480, married 13 couples, and buried 52 dead that year. "The Gospel has been taught and preached," Gerecke wrote. "We leave the fruits of our work to the Holy Spirit."

Like the number-keeping, Gerecke would use much that he learned during his City Mission years as an army chaplain. In a pamphlet handed out at a service and dinner at the fortieth anniversary of City Mission, worshippers were given an overview of some of the work the missioners did each week.

At the Municipal Workhouse, the pamphlet read, Gerecke "preaches a brief Gospel sermon to a large audience in the 'mess hall' each Wednesday noon where men of both races listen with deep and grateful appreciation and God alone knows how many of these law violators have changed their manner of living as a direct result of these sermons and returned to Christ."

By 1941, Gerecke had gained large audiences at his lunchtime Workhouse sermons, "all working on 'spare-ribs' and not eating too loud," he wrote. "The authorities have been most kind. The prisoners have never disturbed the speaker."

Gerecke's heart was with these men, many of whom were on their way back out into society with little chance of getting a job. "What can be done for the ex-prisoner?" he wrote in 1941. "When out he needs work to support the family. Nobody seems to care."

Gerecke believed the work of City Mission was not just about comforting the sick and forgotten. It was about evangelization. He was an evangelical Christian a half century before that term gained political currency. Evangelicals take a verse in Matthew as the bedrock of their faith. In the Gospel's final scene, a resurrected Christ appears to his followers on a Galilee mountain and instructs them to make new disciples by baptizing them in the name of a new faith and by "teaching them to obey everything that I have commanded you." Remember, Christ says, in case his instructions are a little daunting, "I am with you always, to the end of the age."

Evangelicals take this directive, often called the Great Commission, very seriously, seeing it as responsibility to save souls that have been damned to an eternity separated from God. They see the world as a "mission field," filled with non-Christians who must be rescued. The Gospel is the life raft that can buoy these souls; the "good news" is that Jesus loves them, and to avoid hell all they need to do is to accept his message of love.

For Gerecke, those who had not taken Christ's message to heart urgently needed to. He looked among the wretched of St. Louis and saw what he often called "fields white for the harvest"—a phrase borrowed from the Gospel of John. He wrote in a newsletter about Koch Hospital, where one hundred and eighty of these souls "receive some form of personal instruction in God's word. We enjoy a splendid spirit of cooperation on the part of the doctors and nurses. Dr. Kettlekamp, head of the Hospital, is our friend. The field is white unto harvest. Pray for your laborers."

City Mission, he often said, was "a soul-winning agency." "Remember," he wrote, "we are after souls, lost, strayed souls. Some will miss Hell because you have sent us with the Gospel."

City Mission's "big job" was "to find souls for Christ," he wrote in another newsletter.

> *Quite often we find former members of the Lutheran Church in the neighborhoods of our settlement missions and in our city institutions. These we try to re-establish with the Church. The pastor is generally notified and every effort is made to encourage the individual to renew his confirmation vow. Then there are those who have never given a thought to God until affliction struck them down flat upon their backs in the hospital. Sometimes we never quite succeed in winning such discouraged people for Christ, but we keep on trying and consistently bring them the meaning of the cross.*

Gerecke was a serious evangelical, but his little chapel was called *Good* Shepherd. He was not a sheep stealer. His respect for faith in general gave him a healthy respect for all faiths, and his years living in a Catholic neighborhood gave him real-world experience with other Christians. In 1941, he wrote in the City Mission newsletter that the missioners were passing out new devotional booklets at Koch and City hospitals.

"Every new patient, if not Catholic, receives a booklet by the missioner upon his arrival," Gerecke wrote. "That's the opening wedge for spiritual healing. If he is a bona fide member of a protestant church, he is urged to call his pastor. Our missioner backs out of the picture."

During his nine years preaching at Christ Lutheran, Gerecke had honed his preaching skills and learned the power of a good story. His sermons, both at Christ Lutheran and Good Shepherd, kept people coming back each Sunday. Regulars knew Gerecke was wrapping up when he began a short story—usually about an average person—to illustrate the point of his sermon. Gerecke also realized he could use his monthly newsletters to harness the same storytelling power in writing as he did in his sermons. He believed pastors and delegates who read these newsletters could use the City Mission stories as fund-raising mechanisms as they asked for money from the pews on Sundays, or in their own church bulletins. Often he would end his stories with the phrase, "Tell it and print it."

He used only first names. Cathleen, he wrote one month, "was found in the TB Division of City Hospital #1. She had spent a number of years in institutions for TB patients and she became an arrested case . . . During the many moments of prayer and meditation spent at her bedside, we found her staunch and true to her Savior . . . Cathleen begged to be with her Lord. Last Tuesday morning we laid her to rest in Our Redeemer Cemetery."

He often used all capital letters for emphasis, in an effort to goad others to action: Lutherans owed it to themselves to see the City Mission work in person, he wrote: "Come and see for yourself. Then tell it to the congregation with a lot of enthusiasm. DO SOMETHING . . . Brother, if you feel we are wasting our time, tell us so and show us a way out. Become interested in a program for City Mission soul-winning. WELL?"

Sometimes, Gerecke just liked to turn a good phrase in the service of his never-ending, desperate search for financial support. "The summer is on, but there must be no letdown in City Mission work.

The old devil is terribly busy during the hot weather," he wrote in 1941. "Men and women are dying every day and the hospitals are crowded to the doors. Again, we say, the harvest is white. We need your help."

Another way Gerecke reached the city was through radio station KFUO-AM, founded by his mentor, Pastor Richard Kretzschmar, in 1924, just after the advent of commercial radio. Gerecke's *Moments of Comfort* was originally popular mostly in hospitals, but it soon caught on across KFUO's listening area, bringing him fan mail and even calls to his house. The show was a combination of scripture recitation and soothing sermonizing by Gerecke, whose voice had the depth and clarity of film stars of the decades that followed— Burt Lancaster and Robert Mitchum. Gerecke brought his favorite musicians and singers with him each week to provide background music and sing hymns.

The program also promoted the work of City Mission, allowing Gerecke to use the huge reach of radio to scare up more funding or to ask for old clothing and furniture for Lutheran Mission Industries. In turn, he promoted the show through the City Mission newsletter.

At the end of each *Moment,* Gerecke recited what he called a "mission prayer." But the words were really the lyrics of a nineteenth-century hymn: "Lord, lay some soul upon my heart and love that soul through me. And may I nobly do my part to win that soul for thee." The program and its host became so successful that a rival station, KMOX, approached Gerecke about a full-time broadcasting job. But he realized it would mean leaving the ministry and turned it down.

At City Mission, Gerecke had clearly found his life's calling. He enjoyed the frenetic pace, and he thrived on the energy it took to keep up with his schedule. Mostly, though, he loved the challenge of harvesting a mission field he believed so hungry for God's grace. All of that personal, professional, and sacred satisfaction, however, came at the expense of an easy home life. When Gerecke left Christ

Lutheran, he had to give up the vicarage, and the family moved to an apartment with creaky hardwood floors, three bedrooms, and one bathroom. It was about the same size the Gereckes were used to, but it was more cramped because Gerecke didn't have an attached office and the kids were now older.

Alma had a rule against children in the dining room except during meals, or in the family room—it was reserved for company—leaving the boys to make do in their small bedroom, the kitchen, or in the neighborhood outside. Life as a pastor's kid is never easy, but the boys' clothes and shoes frequently came off the Lutheran Mission Industries trucks, and this became well known at their school, leading to taunts of: "Hey, Gerecke got dressed on the charity trucks again." Naturally that led to fights.

Hank and Corky earned fifty cents a day sorting donated materials at the City Mission warehouse. They were so close in age they fought from the time they woke up until they went to sleep at night. Alma often had to use a "Wait until your father gets home" threat to settle them down. When Henry did get home, Alma would tell him what happened and demand that he discipline the boys.

He did as instructed, calling each of his sons into the bedroom, where he took off his belt and then issued his own instructions: "Make it sound like this hurts." And then he'd slap the bed hard with his belt, while his sons would smile gratefully and howl in fake pain.

"Okay, Henry. Stop it. You're hurting them," Alma would call from the kitchen.

As the wife of a pastor, Alma attended church and was part of the Ladies' Aid Society, but once her husband was no longer leading a regular congregation, some of those social responsibilities disappeared. The trade-off was financial. This was the Depression, and the Gerecke family's existence was hand to mouth. Henry was satisfied that they, as he liked to say, had a roof over their heads and food on the table. God would take care of the rest. But Alma liked cars and clothes. She liked money, and the absence of it became a major point of contention in their marriage.

Henry believed Thanksgiving was an important American holiday, writing in the City Mission newsletter: "This is Thanksgiving month. We are thankful. We have some very poor families who will be thankful, too. Understand?" One year when a destitute member of his Good Shepherd congregation invited the Gereckes to his hovel for Thanksgiving dinner, Henry accepted. Alma was furious, and at first she refused to go. But by Thanksgiving day she relented, and they all hopped in the car and made their way to a desperately poor section of the city to give thanks.

Gerecke's schedule made family outings like that rare. His children didn't see much of him during the week, so the boys looked forward to Saturday afternoons, which were often spent around the kitchen table, where they listened to a broadcast of the Metropolitan Opera on the radio. Gerecke told his sons stories about his childhood on the farm, or about working the Kansas oil fields. Gerecke hated to drive, so when Hank and Corky were old enough, they became his Sunday chauffeurs. Hank drove his father around for his marathon preaching circuit of hospitals, jails, convalescent homes, and churches. After a while, Gerecke let his son stay in the car.

"You've heard the sermon four times already," he'd say. "You can sit here and wait." But Hank always chose to go with his dad to the 9:00 A.M. services in the City Jail. Going inside a jail was too exciting for a teenager to miss.

Just before Christmas in 1940, Hank enlisted in the army. He was nineteen years old and five feet, six inches—short, like his father. When the Japanese bombed Pearl Harbor a year later, he was sent to the Aleutian Islands to defend them from Japanese forces. In the spring of 1942, five months after the United States declared war on Japan and Germany, the message of Lutheran Mission Industries became patriotic: "Mission Industries Trucks are busy collecting old clothing, furniture, rags, newspapers, magazines and iron," Gerecke wrote. "Save your old papers for Defense. We want to do our bit toward victory for our Country and every pound of paper you save will help to that end. At this moment we need your old overcoats for homeless men in the settlement missions." But gas rationing finally felled Gerecke's efforts, and he was forced to shutter the Industries arm of City Mission.

Corky followed Hank into the army in September 1942, when he was twenty years old (and five foot five). Suddenly, a house once crammed with people felt spacious—even Roy had his own room.

With two of his sons in the fight, Gerecke thought more and more about the war and less about City Mission. Readers of his April 1943 newsletter could tell that his heart was elsewhere: "Oliver Grosse assists at the piano," he wrote, listlessly. "Noonday talks on Wednesdays in dining hall. . . . Warden and guards cooperate to the last detail. . . . Every one is questioned about spiritual matters. Some are so young. All need Jesus."

By the time Gerecke wrote that newsletter, he had already asked for the synod's endorsement for him to volunteer for the army's Chaplain Corps. The Army and Navy Commission of the Evangelical Lutheran Synod of Missouri, Ohio, and Other States had received his application for ecclesiastical endorsement on February 8, 1943, and then the recommendation letters began to pour in.

Pastor O. Rothe of St. Paul's Lutheran Church in St. Louis said he believed Gerecke's "experience in hospitals, jails and other institutions qualify [*sic*] him, in my estimation, in a remarkable way, for the position of chaplain."

P. E. Kretzmann, director of Concordia's library, wrote the commission that if Gerecke "was not beyond the age limit, I feel that you will have a real acquisition."

The Reverend George Wittmer, who was the chairman of the City Mission board, said Gerecke had "proven himself to be a psychologist in his dealings with all types and classes of people from every stratum of society."

And Rev. Louis Wickham, whom Gerecke had replaced as head of City Mission in 1935 and was now a first lieutenant at Fort Hayes in Ohio, said his ten months in the chaplaincy had given him a perspective on the type of person it required.

"When I review in my mind the type of work required in the many situations that arise, I am confident that Brother Gerecke could efficiently and with distinction serve as a Chaplain," Wickham wrote. "He is very personal in his presentation and can inspire men. He can be emotional as well as stern. . . . I know of no reason why he will not make a GOOD chaplain, and the army knows there are too many of the other kind."

Wickham's letter to the synod's Army and Navy Commission was dated June 2, 1943, the day before Gerecke told Alma he planned to volunteer. At least a dozen men, and probably many more, knew Gerecke was joining the army before he told the mother of his children.

A week after the tense moment in the kitchen with Alma, Gerecke received word that the synod's Army and Navy Commission had approved his application and forwarded it to the army's Chief of Chaplain branch.

On July 15, the U.S. Army named Gerecke a chaplain (1st Lt.) and ordered him to report to Chaplain School at Harvard University a month later. In his last City Mission newsletter, written in August 1943, Gerecke told the delegates that he'd be replaced by an able pastor to lead the agency, but that *Moments of Comfort* would be "suspended for a time." He thanked people for listening.

"My dear Friends, I ask your blessings upon my new assignment," he wrote. "You and many others have sent good wishes for great spiritual blessings as a chaplain in the Army. . . . Keep your eyes fixed upon Jesus. If I have blundered, forgive me, please. If I have done normally well, thank God for it."

Then he quoted two verses from the Old Testament. From Genesis: "The Lord watch between me and you when we are absent one from another." And from Deuteronomy: "The eternal God is your refuge and underneath are the everlasting arms."

As Gerecke left the safety of St. Louis for the heart of the most violent, destructive war man had ever fought, he might have added a proverb he penned himself in the November 1941 City Mission newsletter. "God give us strength, to carry on through the shadows."

CHAPTER 3

God of War

Before you join battle, the priest shall come forward and address the troops. He shall say to them, "Hear, O Israel! you are about to join battle with your enemy. Let not your courage falter. Do not be in fear, or in panic, or in dread of them. For it is the Lord your God who marches with you to do battle for you against your enemy, to bring you victory."

—DEUTERONOMY 20:2–4

HENRY GERECKE RECEIVED A letter on June 23, 1943, from the army's Chief of Chaplains office informing him that he'd been provisionally recommended for the Chaplain Corps. Three days later, he sent a letter back to Washington. "Kind Sir!" Gerecke wrote. "The day I receive the official assignment shall be the happiest day of my life. My family, including two fine boys in the Army, are agreeable and praying blessings on me. There is no intention of backing down." On August 17, 1943, he said good-bye to Alma and fifteen-year-old Roy and reported for duty at Harvard the next day.

When he arrived on campus, Gerecke was given a welcome

letter written by the army chief of chaplains, General William R. Arnold, the first Catholic priest to become chief of chaplains and the first chaplain to rise to the rank of major general, a tradition the army has maintained ever since. Arnold called himself "a priest in khaki," but before entering the priesthood, he had held a number of jobs. He'd worked at his father's cigar-making operation in Worcester, Ohio; at a steel mill in Muncie, Indiana, where he was a bar straightener; and at the Hagenbeck-Wallace Circus in Peru, Indiana, where he worked—and sometimes bunked—with the performers. Arnold was ordained in 1908 and sent to the Philippines as a chaplain in the First World War.

In December 1937, Roosevelt appointed Arnold to head the Chaplain Corps, and at the end of the war—just before Gerecke was tapped for the job in Nuremberg—Pope Pius XII made him a bishop. Arnold later served nearly two decades as an aide to New York Cardinal Francis Spellman and as the Catholic Church's delegate to the military.

In his last days leading the Chaplain Corps, in 1945, Arnold wrote about his love for his fellow military priests, ministers, and rabbis in his book, *Soldiers of God*. For many soldiers, he wrote,

> *Chaplains of all faiths have been their sole link between the battlefield and home. These Chaplains volunteered to be with your men, to share the dangers of battle so they might help to keep alive the spiritual values for which we went to war—spiritual values without which lasting peace cannot be attained. In the performance of their duties, some of them have been wounded; others have died. The War Department has given to many of these clergymen the highest honors. These are your Chaplains. These are clergymen from your community. You have good cause to be proud of them.*

Arnold's letter to Gerecke at Harvard began: "With hearty congratulations and best wishes we welcome you to active duty with the Regular Army." This might have been a form letter, but it also served as a pep talk from the top chaplain in the country, and it gave Gerecke a good sense of what the chaplaincy expected of him and what he could expect from the army in return.

"Inconveniences, difficulties and hardships will be your portion," Arnold continued. "Military life is a life of discipline, and the essential military virtues of courage, loyalty, obedience, devotion, and self-sacrifice are also religious virtues."

Arnold spoke of "the alarming increase" in the number of young soldiers unfamiliar with God or religious worship. "How shall they know if they are not taught, and by whom shall they be taught if not by an able and zealous chaplain?" he asked.

Each chaplain's responsibility was tremendous, he wrote, and each chaplain's own salvation would be determined "by the efforts and sacrifices you make to teach and train men."

"Your earnest words, pregnant with Divine wisdom and power, will establish convictions and train consciences in these young men that will strengthen and comfort them every hour of every day," Arnold wrote, "in daylight or in darkness . . ."

EARLY IN THE FOURTH century, probably in 316, a boy named for Mars, the god of war, was born to a soldier and his wife in the village of Sabaria in modern-day Hungary. Only a few years before the birth of the boy, who would later be known as Martin of Tours, Constantine freed the Christians from two centuries of secret meetings, persecution, and murder. By declaring the Edict of Milan, Constantine—the leader of the Roman Empire—had allowed Christians to practice their faith openly.

While his parents worshipped and offered sacrifices to the Roman gods and the emperor himself, Martin, even as a child, was drawn to Christianity, specifically to its followers who had so recently been killed by Constantine's slaughterous predecessor Diocletian, and the ascetics—hermits who adopted a form of martyrdom by living a life of prayer, alone in the woods or the desert.

When Martin was fifteen years old, a decree was sent down from the emperor that required all sons of veterans to join the army, changing Martin's plans of a solitary life for Christ. Instead, Martin found himself a member of the extravagantly uniformed imperial guard, one of five hundred cavalrymen protecting the emperor himself during military campaigns.

The imperial guard was stationed in Amiens, a city in Gaul near the Roman frontier. During a particularly cold Amiens winter, in 335, many of the city's poor were freezing to death. One day, as Martin came through the city gates, he saw a beggar sitting on the ground, shivering. Martin had no money to give the man, so instead, he cut his cape in two with his sword and gave one half to the beggar. The white cape, lined with lambskin and fastened at the right shoulder with a broach, was distinct to the elite corps that protected the emperor.

The cape, or *chlamys,* gave the men their name—the *candidate*—or men clothed in white. Those watching the scene between the soldier and the beggar laughed as Martin put the other half of the white cape back around his own shoulders. That night Martin, who was still not baptized, dreamed that he saw Christ wearing the half of his cape he'd given to the beggar.

It was a scene straight out of the Gospels, when Matthew predicted that at the Second Coming, Christ will say, "Truly I tell you, just as you did it to one of the least of these who are members of my family, you did it to me."

Martin became a Christian, then a bishop, and he founded a monastery. After his death, he became France's patron saint, and his cape became an object of veneration, preserved in the city of Tours. For centuries, French kings carried the cape into battle in a portable shrine called the *capella.* The priest who cared for the shrine was called the *capellani,* or *chapelains* in French. In English it became "chaplain."

The relationship between war and the divine is ancient, and chaplains—though called something else—have been around a lot longer than the cape of St. Martin of Tours. It is said that soldier-priests once carried maces into battle to avoid spilling blood. The priests of Amun-Ra worked among the ancient Egyptian armies, and the priests of Joshua's forces carried the Ark of the Covenant, blowing rams' horns before the assault on Jericho.

In the United States, chaplains have been ministering for more than 230 years to the fifty-five million Americans who have served in the military. In the colonial period, civilian pastors simply volunteered their services to commanders in times of war. During the Pequot Wars, beginning in 1637, Samuel Stone of Hartford was the first military chaplain to begin his service in the New World. During King Philip's War in 1675, seven chaplains served in military units fighting Native Americans.

At the Battles of Lexington and Concord, which set off the Revolutionary War, four ministers were among the minutemen facing British general Thomas Gage's British troops on Lexington Green. Other pastors went to the battlefield to support their flocks fighting the British. Two hundred and twenty army and navy chaplains served during the Revolutionary War, but they received no military training and had no uniforms. At regimental inspections, when other soldiers raised their muskets at "present arms," chaplains often raised their Bibles.

In northern colonies, where Congregationalists were accustomed to choosing their own ministers, militias held boisterous elections to choose a chaplain from among many choices in the community. Chaplains counseled soldiers, led daily prayer services and Sunday worship services, and visited the sick and wounded, helping doctors where they could.

On July 29, 1775, the Continental Congress recognized chaplains as a distinct branch of the army and authorized one chaplain for every two regiments, setting pay at $20 per month, the same amount received by captains. On November 28, 1775, the Continental Navy adopted regulations allowing divine services on ships, and Congress appointed chaplains to serve in hospitals.

In the field, chaplains often had their own quarters or bunked with the commanding officer. Unlike the way the Chaplain Corps sees itself today—as a force that stands for free expression of religion—Revolutionary War chaplains were enforcers of religious responsibility among their troops. On August 23, 1776, Rev. Henry Melchior Muhlenberg, a Lutheran minister, endorsed Rev. Christian Streit for the Eighth Regiment of Regulars of Virginia, certifying that Streit was "an ordained Minister of the Gospel, sound in Protestant Principles and sober in life, desirous and virtuous to promote the Glory of God and Welfare of the State and therefore recommended to all Friends and Well-wishers of Religion and State."

Benjamin Franklin told the story of a "zealous Presbyterian" chaplain who was part of a militia guarding Pennsylvania's northwest frontier and who complained that too few of the militiamen attended worship services. Franklin suggested a creative solution. "It is, perhaps, below the dignity of your profession to act as steward of the rum," Franklin advised the chaplain. "But if you were to deal it out and only just after prayers, you would have them all about you." The chaplain liked the idea. "[N]ever were prayers more generally and punctually attended," Franklin reported.

When George Washington was desperate for a chaplain to minister to his drunken Virginia backcountry troops, he asked the governor to provide one, writing that the absence of a chaplain reflected "dishonor on the regiment." Some of Washington's soldiers told him they'd pay a chaplain's salary from their own pockets, but Washington said he'd rather have a chaplain appointed as an officer because that would have "a more graceful appearance." A chaplain, Washington wrote, "ought to be provided, that we may at least have the show if we are said to want the substance of Godliness." When Washington became commander of the Continental Army on July 2, 1775, he found fifteen chaplains among the army's twenty-three regiments. He encouraged the chaplains to lead weekly worship services, and he eventually admitted ministers of eight denominations into the chaplaincy and urged his commanders to facilitate the free exercise of religion among their troops.

In 1780, Washington and his British counterpart began working toward an agreement that chaplains captured during hostilities would be released instead of made prisoners of war, and two years later, Washington wrote that chaplains were "exempted from being considered as prisoners of War on either Side; and those then in Captivity were and have been Since mutually released." When the war was over, Washington's vision for a peacetime military included a chaplain in a staff officer's position for each regiment—recognition that a chaplain's duties extended beyond providing pastoral services to soldiers. Washington saw chaplains as integral to the military strategy, providing commanders with advice on matters dealing with morals, morale, and religion.

No Catholic chaplains served in the Revolutionary War or the War of 1812, but in 1846, President James Polk called together several bishops to discuss the Catholic chaplaincy and suggested they name two priests as chaplains. The bishops did so, and Polk appointed them. In 1850, the government put together a "Board of Clergymen" made up of chaplains and civilian clergy, whose job it was to screen army and navy chaplain candidates.

But looming war killed that church-state debate and by the beginning of the Civil War, in 1861, the military employed nearly four thousand chaplains of twelve denominations and multiple ethnic backgrounds. In 1862, Congress changed legislative language from "Christian denomination" to "religious denomination," allowing the first Jewish chaplain—Rabbi Jacob Frankel—to enter the army. Henry M. Turner, the first black army chaplain, served only black soldiers in the United States Colored Troops. Ella E. Gibson, an ordained minister of the Religion-Philosophical Society of St. Charles,

Illinois, received President Abraham Lincoln's somewhat reluctant approval as the first female chaplain, serving with the First Wisconsin Heavy Artillery. Among the thirteen hundred chaplains in the Confederate army was the first Native American chaplain, Unaguskee, who served with a Cherokee battalion in North Carolina.

In May 1861, the army ordered its commanders to appoint chaplains approved by their state governors. But soon complaints of uneducated, unprepared, or unethical chaplains surfaced, prompting Congress to create legislation requiring chaplains to be ordained. It also barred anyone "who does not present testimonials of his present good standing with recommendations . . . from some authorized ecclesiastical body." It was the first step toward ecclesiastical endorsement so central to today's Chaplain Corps.

When the War Department issued General Order 126 on September 6, 1862, requiring chaplains to be mustered into service by an officer of the Regular Army, it did not address age limits. Chaplain Charles McCabe of the 122nd Ohio Volunteers referred to a colleague, then sharing his prison cell, as "Father" Brown, not because the chaplain was a Catholic priest, but because he was eighty years old.

Americans fought the Civil War in the midst of the Second Great Awakening, the Christian revival movement that began in the late eighteenth century and set the stage for the evangelicalism that dominated war chaplaincy. "Evangelism [was] more than ever before the chaplain's first responsibility," according to one historian.

The misery of the war was surely a factor, too. After the Battle of Chancellorsville, which lasted one week in the spring of 1863 and resulted in thirty thousand dead, the chaplain of the Twenty-Sixth Alabama Regiment reported "100 converts a week for several weeks." That kind of carnage, perhaps, contributed to a softer evangelical sell by chaplains in tune with men traumatized by constant violence. Their sermons were less animated than those of the revivalists of the past. Less "emotional," according to historian Herman Norton.

"Holy barks, shouts, jerks and other such accomplishments which had typed American revivals since Jonathan Edwards were virtually absent." Chaplains were preaching to men fighting a harrowing war "who could not be scared into religion."

The fervor of religious services among Confederate forces in the winter of 1863–64 earned the season a nickname: "The Great Revival." The revival reached its height in the Army of Greater Virginia where soldiers were "converted by the thousands every week," according to Norton. Revivals in Dalton, Georgia, were "glorious" and "had no parallel." "In the coldest and darkest nights of the winter, the crude chapels were crowded and at the call for penitents, hundreds would come down in sorrow and tears." Forty-five thousand were converted in the Confederate army over four years of war.

When the Civil War was over, the Chaplain Corps shrank. Some chaplains did missionary work within the army for their churches during this quiet period, and officials moved to make some changes to the evolving military chaplaincy. The Act of April 21, 1904, created a grade structure and promotion policy among army chaplains and determined that all chaplains, regardless of rank, would be referred to only as "Chaplain." In 1909, the War Department created the position of chaplain assistant—an enlisted man who could help the chaplain with his duties.

A year before the United States entered the First World War, the National Defense Act authorized one army chaplain for each regiment of cavalry, infantry, field artillery, and engineers, a total of 85 chaplains. But by the time the country declared war on Germany in April 1917, there were still only 74 Regular Army chaplains on active duty. By the end of the war a year and a half later, the army had 2,217 chaplains. The army's quota for Catholic chaplains was 24 percent before the war, but rose to 38 percent during the war. Twenty-five Catholic priests ministered to the Catholic soldiers among the three hundred thousand troops.

The structure of the Catholic Church—which is organized

largely by geographical dioceses governed by a bishop, and diocesan priests who answer to that bishop—didn't meld well with military structure. Priests serving in various parts of the country, or the world, were unsure if they were to report to their home bishop or the bishop of the geographical area they were serving as chaplain. The Vatican recognized the problem and just two weeks after the United States entered the war, Pope Benedict XV named a bishop who would solely oversee military chaplains, an arrangement that still exists today.

During the course of the war, which for the United States lasted nineteen months, regulations for chaplains were altered several times to allow for additional priests. The age limits, since set at forty for the army and thirty-one for the navy, were raised to forty-five and forty before the end of the war.

Even with a more professional Chaplain Corps, the army was not prepared to outfit its chaplains as they mobilized for war. Individual churches, not the government, provided army chaplains with most of the supplies they needed to conduct services during the First World War: religious books and literature, ecclesiastical garments, altar equipment, portable Communion sets, typewriters.

Typewriters in particular came in handy for chaplains who handled miscellaneous duties that had little to do with their ordination. Chaplains often collected the dead after battle, for instance, before performing burial services and registering each grave. Graves had to be marked with a full name and the soldier's unit and date of death, and that information had to correspond with unit records. The grave location was then recorded with map coordinates. Chaplains also served as postal officers and censors during the war and were recruited as unit historians, librarians, mess officers, band directors, athletic officers, morale officers, venereal disease control officers, couriers, and rifle-range scorers.

The Second World War saw the largest military mobilization in American history. On December 7, 1941, when the Japanese bombed Pearl Harbor, there were only 140 Regular Army chaplains on active duty. Eventually, over the course of the war, 12,000 chaplains ministered to more than 16 million men and women in uniform in the United States and overseas.

The army required that each applicant for the chaplaincy be male, between the ages of twenty-three and thirty-four, ordained and in good standing with his denomination, a graduate of both a four-year college and a three-year theological seminary, and actively engaged in the ministry as his main job. The central organizing agency for the Chaplain Corps, the General Commission on Army and Navy Chaplains, received 4,000 applications in the first nine months of the war. In June 1942, the Chief of Chaplains office asked the General Commission to recruit up to 5,000 chaplains between July 1 and the end of the year—or about 175 per week—for the army alone.

In 1920, the army had assigned chaplains by denominational quota, determined by the Religious Census of 1916, and decided that the corps should be 25 percent Roman Catholic, 70 percent Protestant, and 5 percent held "for final adjustment." By 1940, the army was using the Yearbook of American Churches as its quota guide, attempting to better replicate the broader American religious population. Methodists had the largest quota of any Protestant church during the war. The army asked Methodist officials to contribute one thousand chaplains, and the Methodist Church considered four thousand applications.

The Lutheran Church–Missouri Synod functioned separately from the General Commission. It had formed its own Army and Navy Commission in 1936 and sponsored its first conference on chaplaincy in January 1941 to teach newly commissioned chaplains military procedure and pastoral duties—a sort of prep course before shipping its pastors off to Chaplain School.

The War Department continued to ask the churches for more chaplains throughout the war. At its peak in 1943, it authorized a quota of nine thousand chaplains. At its height in August 1945, at the end of the war, the corps had more than eight thousand chaplains on active duty.

Wartime chaplains continued to wear many hats. They were busy men who often heard the refrain, "tell it to the chaplain" bandied around camp. In 1942, each chaplain had an average of fifty-three personal conferences a day. The most popular topics of conversation were homesickness, suicidal feelings, marriage, and alcohol.

The nature of war tested the creativity and flexibility of chaplains looking for appropriate places to hold prayer and worship services. Often they resorted to barns, stables, wine cellars, attics, railroad stations, palaces, caves, and vaults below castles. Besides the usual sacred duties, on ships transporting troops overseas chaplains also organized boxing matches, orchestras, and movies.

To get from one place to the next in the field, they traveled by jeep, by truck, and on foot. As one historian put it, chaplains "climbed mountains, crossed rivers, lay for hours in foxholes, parachuted to safety when their planes were shot down and faced enemy fire in rescuing the wounded. All these were endured, that 'the bond between man and his God and his home might be maintained and strengthened.'"

With 478 casualties in the Second World War, the chaplain branch suffered the third-most combat deaths by percentage behind the air corps and the infantry. Some historians attribute those losses to the chaplains' "be there" philosophy. Many Catholic chaplains felt compelled to give last rites to dying troops and were killed as they did so. Others wanted to be on the front lines with their men to counsel them as much as they could and provide some sense of prayer and relief during battle.

Chaplains did, however, have help. A chaplain assistant was classified as a clerk-typist, but he often served as a chaplain's driver, jeep mechanic, organist, choir leader, and—because he could carry a weapon and the chaplain could not—protector.

The army relaxed education requirements and age limits as the need for chaplains grew. By August 1942, a bachelor of divinity degree was no longer required, and the age limit rose from thirty-four in the Regular Army and forty-two in the Reserves to fifty. At the height of the war, the War Department also scratched denominational quotas. Quotas had been determined based on proportional U.S. membership in the various denominations, but with the August 1942 chaplain shortage the Chief of Chaplains office notified the General Commission that chaplains were being accepted "regardless of quota." If a particular denomination couldn't fill its space, the army filled it with a chaplain from a different denomination that could.

The military chaplaincy in the United States has always been caught between two worlds. As a branch of the armed forces, it is a government agency guided absolutely by the Constitution and its amendments, particularly the first one. As an extension of the Christian church for much of its history, it is necessarily an evangelical institution, governed by those instructions of Christ to his apostles at the end of the Gospel of Matthew—to "make disciples of all nations."

Much of what chaplains have learned over the last century about how to incorporate their responsibilities as pastors into the duties as military officers has been taught at a version of the Chaplain School. In September 1940, the secretary of war asked the Chief of Chaplains office for "a brief study outlining the plans of the Chief of Chaplains for meeting the situation as regards the spiritual welfare of the Army." The office responded that it was "now apparent that provision should be made for the reactivation of the Chaplain's School."

A school for army chaplains had been founded in 1919—a five-week course that included classes on military custom and discipline, military law, army regulations, drill, and first aid—but it had gone dark during peacetime ten years later. By the time the Chaplain School was reactivated in 1941, all that was left was its name, a fund of $101.92, fifteen library books, and ten framed pictures of past classes.

The implementation of a new Chaplain School was accelerated by the Japanese attack on Pearl Harbor. It was reopened on December 9, 1941—two days after the attack.

The army's goal was a student body of between fifty and seventy-five Reserve and National Guard chaplains who would take twenty-five days (two hundred academic hours) of instruction during a one-month session. Classes would include: Organization of the Army, Army Morale, Military Law, Military Discipline, Grave Registration, Rules of Land Warfare, Map Reading, Military Sanitation and First Aid, and Defense Against Chemicals.

The purpose of the newly reopened school was, according to Army Regulation 350-1500:

> *to give chaplains specific training in ministering to the moral and religious needs of the military personnel, to acquaint them with the methods of work which experience has shown to be the most effective and with the customs of the service, to instruct them regarding the organization and administration of the Army and to promote cooperation and a fraternal spirit among chaplains.*

The school was set up at Fort Benjamin Harrison, Indiana, and the first class of 71 chaplains graduated on April 25, 1942. By the third class of students, school officials ignored the class size limit of 75 and brought in 148 chaplain candidates. Soon, classes of 300 made continuing at Fort Benjamin Harrison impossible, and the school moved to Harvard University. Duke University lost out because its classrooms were too small, and because the move there would have required the segregation of white and black students. By the end of the summer of 1942, classes at Harvard had grown to 450.

One year later, on August 18, 1943, Henry Gerecke walked onto the campus in Cambridge, Massachusetts, two weeks after his fiftieth birthday.

CHAPTER 4

This Too Shall Pass

When man thinks that his eyes are opened, and therefore that he knows what is good and evil, when man sets himself on the seat of judgment, or even imagines that he can do so, war cannot be prevented, but comes irresistibly.

—KARL BARTH

ABRAHAM LINCOLN FIRST BECAME a rising star in the Republican Party when he famously debated Stephen Douglas during the 1858 Illinois U.S. Senate race. A year later—the year before he was elected president—he spoke before the Wisconsin State Agricultural Society in Milwaukee.

"It is said an Eastern monarch once charged his wise men to invent him a sentence, to be ever in view, and which should be true and appropriate in all times and situations," Lincoln said. "They presented him the words: 'And this, too, shall pass away.' How much it expresses! How chastening in the hour of pride! How consoling in the depths of affliction! 'And this, too, shall pass away.'"

This phrase would come in handy for Chaplain Henry Gerecke

as he ministered to hundreds of wounded troops with the Ninety-Eighth General Hospital in 1944. "This too shall pass." It became his mantra as wave after wave of battered GIs were flown into the huge temporary hospital the Allies had set up in Hermitage, a village sixty miles west of London in Berkshire.

Gerecke's job encompassed more than simply ministering to the troops. His colleagues at the hospital also needed comfort and his motto helped them, too. He decided the Jewish doctors and nurses of the Ninety-Eighth would benefit from the services of a rabbi. Gerecke enjoyed his religious conversations with all his colleagues, but he also felt strongly that everyone in the unit should take part in the religious service particular to his or her own faith.

In May 1944, a month after the Ninety-Eighth arrived in Hermitage, Gerecke made sure that one layman among the 8 percent of the hospital's Jewish members led a weekly service. He searched for a local rabbi to visit the hospital, and that August a Rabbi Miller led two of the month's four Friday evening services.

When the High Holidays approached in September, Gerecke made arrangements for his Jewish colleagues to visit a nearby synagogue for what he called "atonement services" on Yom Kippur. Eventually, Gerecke recruited another local rabbi to make the regular rounds for the Ninety-Eighth's Jewish patients.

During the war, a company in the United States sold "GZY" rings for Americans at home to send to their loved ones fighting abroad. In Hebrew the letters were an abbreviation for *"Gamzu ya'avor,"* or "This too shall pass." The rings referred to a story attributed to King Solomon.

In one version, the king, in search of a cure for sadness, assembled his wise men together. They discussed the issue for a long time, then advised him to engrave a ring with the letters GZY. King Solomon did so and wore the ring constantly. "Every time he felt sad and depressed, he looked at the ring, whereon his mood would change and he would feel cheerful."

One of the Ninety-Eighth's Jewish nurses, whose father was a jeweler in New York City, had a ring made for Gerecke. It was inscribed with his motto in Hebrew, and she gave it to him as a Christmas present. Gerecke was surprised and moved. He wore it for the rest of his life.

Rarely did a chaplain remain with his original unit throughout the war, but Gerecke did. In fact, that's what most members of the Ninety-Eighth did. The unit was unusually close. It had coalesced into a team during the war and bonded as a family. In 1945, when the unit commander, Colonel James P. Sullivan, learned that the army would be breaking up the Ninety-Eighth as the war in Europe came to a close, his reaction mirrored his staff's.

"To a unit closely knit by thirteen months of operation with relatively few changes in officer and key enlisted personnel, readjustment came as a shock," Sullivan wrote. "Barring those physically disqualified, the vast majority of this organization would have desired to be committed as a unit, even for direct redeployment to the Pacific."

The Ninety-Eighth General Hospital had been activated at Fort Jackson in June 1943, nine months before the unit landed in England. Sullivan was named commander and received one officer and twenty-eight enlisted men from the Twenty-Eighth General Hospital in Swannanoa, North Carolina. For the next five months, Sullivan built his administrative officer staff and requisitioned enlisted personnel from the army's Medical Department Training Centers. Before shipping out in March 1944, Sullivan added professional and nursing staffs.

Throughout the war, the unit's numbers remained unusually steady, with about 500 enlisted men and 150 officers. Sullivan, from Chevy Chase, Maryland, was thirty-five when he was handed the responsibility of building an army hospital from scratch in the summer of 1943. An officer with the Army Medical Corps and a graduate of the Army Medical School and the Army Field Service School, during his six-year army career to that point he'd been stationed at various hospitals around the country, including two years in Puerto Rico, where he gained an interest in his eventual specialty—tropical medicine.

Gerecke was assigned to the Ninety-Eighth on August 24, 1943. The assignment had come within a week of Gerecke's arrival at Harvard and was an indication of how desperately the army needed to fill chaplain vacancies in units that were preparing to deploy overseas.

In his monthly reports for the army, Gerecke's love of numbers—so evident from his City Mission newsletters—flourished. The report worksheets didn't leave much space for commentary, but he told his story through meticulous counts of confessions heard, sex education classes given, or worship services led. The chaplain would file his second monthly report—after ninety-seven more classes and forty-nine more drill periods—less than a week after arriving at Fort Jackson on September 25, 1943.

Gerecke did not have a chapel where he could work when he arrived at Fort Jackson, so he held services in a classroom. His office, which lacked a typewriter, was in the barracks dayroom where soldiers in training gathered to relax and play Ping-Pong. The lack of appropriate space for services at Fort Jackson bothered Gerecke. He felt that worshipping God was a sacred activity, and that sacredness should be reflected in the worship venue. And as the months at Fort Jackson went by, he used his monthly reports to let his superiors in the Chaplain Corps know how he felt. For the next five months, until the unit was deployed, Gerecke was the only chaplain for its growing staff, about half of which was Protestant.

Gerecke participated in the unit's overnight training bivouacs in the field, often addressing large groups of soldiers with a spiritual message. He took part in all the training exercises: obstacle course, infiltration crawl, and road marches. He used these early days to get to know the members of the unit as he would any congregation. Though he disapproved of dancing, he attended the dances on post and while there, he distributed Protestant New Testaments and "publicity cards" announcing the time and place of his Sunday worship services.

Gerecke was drawn to volunteering for wartime service, but his attitude toward the military before he joined had not been positive. His secretary at the St. Louis Lutheran City Mission, Dorothy Williams, had been married to a GI, and the soldier had not treated her well. One day when "Dot," as Gerecke called her, came home from work, every item of furniture had disappeared. Her husband had sold it all and left town with a buddy. Gerecke had once visited Jefferson Barracks outside of St. Louis to perform services there and disapproved of the behavior he saw from some soldiers. He'd also inherited some aversion to the military from his father, who had yanked Gerecke from the First World War enlistment line. But that seemed to change once he came to know his colleagues at Fort Jackson and settled into army life. Its sense of order and discipline fit perfectly into the way Gerecke structured his own life and work.

Sullivan assigned eighteen-year-old Private First Class Tommy Geist from Jamaica, Queens, to be Gerecke's clerk. Geist had been drafted straight out of high school in April 1943, and after basic training at Camp Pickett, Virginia, that summer, he arrived at Fort Jackson in August, on the same day Gerecke started at Harvard. Someone had noticed in Geist's paperwork that he played the organ, and Sullivan pointed Geist toward the musically minded Gerecke. Like so many of the staff of the Ninety-Eighth, Geist was young and he looked up to the relatively ancient Gerecke, whom he called "Chappie." Geist said later that Gerecke "was like a father to me, all the way, straight through." In his monthly reports, Gerecke called Geist "an excellent pianist and organist for all my services."

In November, Gerecke presided over a devotion for thirteen German prisoners, using his language skills in the army for the first time. He preached outside the base, at Lutheran, Presbyterian, and Methodist civilian churches in Columbia, South Carolina, a practice he would continue at nearly every stop during his army career.

Gerecke gave two Thanksgiving services that fall, and he came to believe there was a growing interest in his work among the hospital staff.

In December, he organized Christmas services for soldiers already missing home, and he performed his first baptism, of the daughter of one of the Ninety-Eighth's sergeants. "I am happy and delightfully busy," he wrote. "There is a growing spirit of cooperation among the men." Appropriately enough for February, the chaplain performed his first wedding, marrying Captain Raymond T. Lathrem and his bride, Virginia Byrnside. Five months after leaving St. Louis, in the early days of 1944, Gerecke went home on a fifteen-day leave. He wouldn't see Alma again until December 1946.

Five months into his assignment, Gerecke found that his promotional efforts had worked. Attendance at Sunday services had doubled, and he continued to take part in as much of the daily life of the unit as he could. He gave two more sex lectures for 500 soldiers and screened the War Department movie *For God and Country* for 180 more.

The short film, set in a Second World War foxhole, starred Ronald Reagan as a Catholic chaplain coming to terms with the dangers of war. "Oh, heavenly Father," the chaplain prays at one point, "Grant us in this our time of peril the fullness of thy mercy. Forgive us who have sinned against thy holy name. Protect us from the dangers around us. And if it be thy will that we should die, bring us, oh Lord, to the shelter of thy heavenly gates."

After one of his men is shot leaving the foxhole, the chaplain attempts to save him and they're both killed by enemy fire. At the chaplain's funeral, the film's narrator says, "A soldier, unarmed, yet not unarmed. For what better weapons may a man carry with him into battle than those of courage, an unswerving devotion to his faith and to his fellow man?"

In March 1944, Sullivan received orders to move the hospital to England. Later that month, the Ninety-Eighth left Boston and sailed stormy seas to Bristol, where it arrived April 4. Gerecke proved sea-worthy, holding noon deck services each of the unit's twelve days afloat, and leading nine services on the two Sundays they sailed on the Atlantic.

The Ninety-Eighth's assignment was to take over a crumbling station hospital in Hermitage. After arriving in Bristol in southeast England, the unit traveled sixty miles east to Tidworth in Wiltshire for two weeks of orientation, arriving at the hospital grounds on April 18.

The 834-bed hospital was a series of cantonment-type brick buildings with corrugated steel half-pipe Nissen huts for personnel quarters, and soon the Ninety-Eighth was operational and taking patients. While the medical personnel saw patients, the rest of the unit was renovating the hospital's buildings and grounds, which were in poor physical condition, and increasing the hospital's phys-ical capacity to hold patients by 40 percent. Within a couple weeks, the unit had its first major activity when it received 281 "acute ortho-pedic cases" after a 101st Airborne Infantry Division practice jump went wrong.

To his surprise and delight, Gerecke found a dedicated hospi-tal chapel, a small wooden structure set in the woods, somewhat removed from the main camp. It was better than worshipping in a classroom, but crucial chaplaincy tools were still missing. In theory, the army provided each chaplain with an "outfit" that included a chest for hymnals, the hymnals themselves, a field desk, a chaplain's flag, a folding organ, and a portable typewriter. A Christian chap-lain's own denomination provided him with a folding altar and a brass Holy Communion kit.

In his first monthly report, Gerecke decided the "squeaky-wheel" approach might work with his superiors in the Chief of Chaplains office. "A fine chapel with office in rear," he wrote. However, "chap-lains outfit not complete. Our little organ is lent to us by the neigh-borhood vicar. We do not have our own organ or piano for the chapel. At the moment we have no hymnals. Hope to have at least a field organ and hymnals very soon."

On May 16, he received a letter from a senior chaplain. "In Par. 6b, it is noted that your Chaplain's Outfit is not complete. Will you advise this office what is being done to obtain these deficiencies?" When the appropriate gear arrived, Geist finally had an army-issue, GI field organ.

Inside, the chapel was surprisingly roomy and could seat two hundred. Gerecke and Geist set up a white altar with a black cross cut out of the center panel. Gerecke laid a white cloth on top of the altar and set a large wooden cross in the middle in front of the Bible. On either side of the cross, they kept either two candles or fresh flowers. Gerecke hung black drapes behind the altar and a large American flag above.

Geist was an accomplished musician, and when he wasn't playing Gospel hymns for Gerecke, typing up the chaplain's reports, driving him around in his jeep, organizing the chapel, or riding his bicycle, "Old Faithful," in service of whatever Gerecke needed him to do, he also played piano in the Ninety-Eighth General Hospital Orchestra.

Gerecke and Geist became close to Rev. O. E. Owens, the local vicar in Hermitage, and his wife, Win. The couple had twin daughters, Menna and Eryl, and Gerecke visited their home for dinner at least once each week. Pastor Owens helped the hospital chaplains when the patient load grew unmanageable. The Owens home was one of about three hundred British homes near Hermitage that welcomed members of the Ninety-Eighth during the hospital unit's yearlong stay.

Sullivan encouraged exchange visits for his staff with other Allied bases and British civilians. He invited both groups to dances on post and loaned out the Ninety-Eighth General Hospital Orchestra to other nearby units for their dances. He believed that recreation was an important component for patient recovery and staff morale, so he encouraged a lot of it. Immediately after the unit's arrival, he asked that three movies be shown each week. Over time there were nightly screenings in two locations on the hospital campus, and Sullivan requisitioned a local projectionist on a full-time basis.

There was a heavy emphasis on physical conditioning and re-conditioning at the Ninety-Eighth, and the unit offered daily calisthenics, road marches, and bike rides. A large Nissen hut was built to house a gymnasium. The unit organized frequent dances, including a monthly dance at the Corn Exchange—a nineteenth-century building once used as a corn and wool market in nearby Newbury that had been transformed into a public entertainment space—for the medical detachment. The nurses organized weekly dances at the Officers and Nurses Club, and enlisted men invited local girls to their dances.

Besides a dedicated chapel, another bonus, Gerecke noted, was that the army had finally supplied the Ninety-Eighth with a Catholic chaplain. The unit was made up of 56 percent Protestants by the time it reached England. But more than a third of the Ninety-Eighth was Catholic, and Gerecke was desperate for a priest to help minister to them.

That promising situation didn't last. Geist reported to Gerecke that the new Catholic chaplain treated his own clerk badly. "Stay out of it," Gerecke advised Geist. But not long afterward, as Gerecke approached the chapel office, he heard yelling, followed by a distinct slapping sound. Gerecke walked into the office and saw the private holding his jaw. He asked what had happened, but the clerk rushed past, and the priest ignored him. Gerecke reported the incident to Sullivan, who was Catholic. Within days Sullivan had the priest removed and put in a request with the Chief of Chaplains office for a replacement.

As Gerecke settled into a routine, he was pleased with how his colleagues were participating in worship and making it easy for patients, too. "Our Medical Staff is cooperating in every way that ambulatory patients may attend divine services," Gerecke wrote. "Many nurses attend with their charges."

In May, he led seventeen services for more than 500 people and had visited 750 patients in the hospital's wards. Gerecke met with every patient, either on the day he arrived or the next day. The chaplain received a daily sheet with the religious affiliation, ward number, and operation schedule for each new patient. Those scheduled for immediate surgery took priority on his visitation list. When the chaplain visited with patients, he typically started with a friendly greeting to everyone, then a walk up and down the rows of beds, stopping at the side of the most seriously wounded for a brief prayer with any patients who were conscious and able. Each time he met with a patient, he left a folder "containing a spiritual lift"— usually Christian tracts supplied by religious organizations in the United States and the name of the appropriate chaplain, based on the soldier's designated religious preference.

During one of his rounds, Gerecke discovered a soldier with a serious head injury. He'd lived through his operation but had permanently lost his sight. The soldier was a Missouri-Synod Lutheran from Nebraska who had performed his confirmation in German. After Gerecke said a prayer in German, the soldier wouldn't let go of his hand. Finally, he said, softly, "God, help me see again." The man wanted to know how his family would treat him now. Would his girlfriend still want to marry him? Gerecke had plenty of hospital ministry experience in peacetime, but sitting with young men whose lives had just changed so dramatically was new, and it took him some time to get used to it.

The body of a pilot named Henry Smith had been ripped apart by shrapnel. He was close to death for nearly a week after he arrived at the hospital. His nurse, one of Gerecke's Christian flock, asked the patient to allow the chaplain to pray with him. Breathing heavily, the pilot's words came in short bursts as he labored to say the Lord's Prayer with the chaplain. As they prayed, both Gerecke and the nurse dropped to their knees next to the pilot's bed. It was the first devotional prayer Smith had ever been part of, he told the chaplain later, and in the coming weeks he would not go to sleep until Gerecke visited his bed at 10:00 P.M. each night to pray with him.

Gerecke also talked to hundreds of men in the hospital's rehabilitation ward. The army had designated the Ninety-Eighth a Neurological Center in addition to its status as a general hospital. The influx of patients suffering from what the army then called battle fatigue meant another round of expansion to accommodate a program for soldiers suffering from the psychological horrors of war. The neuropsychiatric recovery section had its own corner of the hospital campus with 120 beds. Here patients were screened, sorted, and organized into platoons.

The symptoms may have been less severe than those Gerecke had been accustomed to in his visits to the asylums of St. Louis during the Depression, but these psychological wounds were fresher. The men were given lectures about combat fatigue and what the army was doing to try and help them deal with it. Most were given duties around the hospital, and after observation, some returned to duty. In the first two months of the hospital's British operation, 829 officers and enlisted men came through the doors of its neuropsychiatric division. More than 450 of those men were sent back to the United States.

AS GERECKE SETTLED INTO his new job in the military, back in St. Louis Alma's loneliness was mitigated slightly by an easier lifestyle. With three fewer bodies in the house, and money coming in from Henry's army paychecks—the first real money she'd seen in years— Alma could enjoy life a bit more. Hank, Henry and Alma's eldest and a first lieutenant, was sending his mother $100 a month from his army paycheck. Alma added some of that to what Henry was sending her, but she saved much of it for Hank (he later used it for his wedding to Millie Curtis, a pretty army nurse he met in France). Corky, the couple's second child, drew only a corporal's paycheck, so there wasn't much left over to send home to Mom. But the financial contributions from Henry, Hank, and Corky went only so far.

Like most of Henry's cars, the family's 1939 Chrysler Imperial came from an estate sale, and St. Louis Lutheran City Mission donors had helped the pastor pay for it. When Henry left for Harvard, he wasn't sure if the army would send him overseas. He wanted to keep the car—probably worth about $1,200—so that he wouldn't have to go through the trouble of finding another one if he was asked to return to St. Louis and serve the war effort from there. Alma didn't drive, and she had wanted Henry to sell the Imperial before he left for Harvard.

Instead, Henry made a deal with a friend—a woman named Rosella—to use the car while he was away. In May 1944, Henry sent a letter to his former secretary, Dot Williams, to help smooth things over with Alma. "Dot, if you can do something about the car business, I shall thank you for the rest of my life," he wrote. "Mrs. G. insists I sell it. For the sake of peace, I must sell it. The Hitch: Rosella does not want to deal with Mrs. G. . . . Maybe you can be the mediator as a special favor to me? Mrs. [Gerecke] claims she's persecuted because another woman is driving our car. Of course, Dot, you must be very subtle about this. If Rosella gives you an opening, just offer to lend a hand. Thanks, Dearie. I'm really anxious to get out of the dog-house."

Henry and Alma were both flirts, but Alma was beautiful, so her flirtations got her things. Apparently Dot wasn't able to broker a deal between Alma and Rosella, so when one of Alma's admirers offered to buy the car, telling her he'd take it off her hands for $600, she smiled and took the deal. She sent her husband $300 in England and bought a fur coat with her half.

FOR THE FIRST SIX weeks or so, the Ninety-Eighth functioned, as advertised, as a general hospital for American and Allied troops based in the United Kingdom. It also served as an outpatient clinic for thousands of GIs, treating eye, ear, nose, and throat; dental; venereal; dermatological; orthopedic; and neuropsychiatric conditions. The hospital was only fifteen miles east of the Ramsbury and Membury airfields, and in June, as the D-day landings began, the Allies used the Ninety-Eighth as a transit hospital for air evacuations from the Continent. The Ninety-Eighth was a big, busy place, and the busier it got, the bigger it had to become. As more patients arrived, the hospital expanded. Tents rose to accommodate 345 more beds and extra supplies.

The hospital had become its own small town. The unit built two messes—one for officers, one for enlisted men—and installed electric warming tables. The 786th Airborne Engineers helped the hospital's own men build gravel roads between wards. Twenty British civilians worked at the hospital as stenographers, carpenters, plumbers, electricians, seamstresses, laborers, stokers, and sewage attendants. The original sewage system was inadequate for the new hospital's numbers and had to be expanded. The unit built a combination post office and barbershop in one Nissen hut.

Six ambulances—really just retrofitted buses—supplied by the Newbury Chapter of the British Civilian Defense Organization picked up patients from one of the two airfields and brought them back to the hospital, where a receiving officer and assistants sorted and assigned the patients to the appropriate wards. There a ward officer checked casts and bandages and separated the patients into "evacuables" and "non-evacuables." When the officer recorded enough evacuables to fill a train (usually 292 patients), the patients were put back on a bus or ambulance and taken to Newbury Race Course to load onto the train, which delivered them to static hospitals in and around London for long-term treatment.

From June to November 1944, the unit received 16,380 patients from the front lines, about 95 percent of which were evacuated by train and treated elsewhere. The Ninety-Eighth's job was, actually, to stop the bleeding. They were treating men almost directly off the battlefield, trying to stabilize as many as they could and then get them out the door before more came in on the next flights.

As the Allies invaded Normandy that June, the army promoted Gerecke to captain, and he became the ranking chaplain officer at the hospital. (Another priest, Father Walsh, had by now replaced the problematic Catholic chaplain.)

Leaning on his old *Moments of Comfort* radio program, both in title and in feel, Gerecke instituted "Moments of Prayer," a short daily devotion at 3:15 P.M. in the chapel. "This spot offers daily opportunity to ambulatory patients and members of our personnel to meet in the Chapel for prayer," he wrote. "I read a portion of the Scripture and conduct the prayers during which time my clerk does a soft background of Gospel melodies. The attendance is small. The Chapel is too far removed from the patients."

The chapel's distance from the hospital's living and working areas led to another annoyance for the chaplain. He began noticing used condoms discarded in the vicinity of the chapel. First a few condoms, then many more as weeks went by. Gerecke complained to an embarrassed Sullivan that the wooded area around the chapel had apparently become a desirable location for clandestine sex among staff members.

But the chapel's distance from the wards never kept the Ninety-Eighth staff from summoning Gerecke when he was needed. One evening, a nurse called and asked him to report quickly to one of the wards housing the most seriously wounded. When Gerecke arrived, he made his way through the flurry of doctors and nurses to the correct patient. "God bless you, son," Gerecke said into the man's ear as he sat down next to the bed. The soldier's eyes opened, and he saw the cross on Gerecke's uniform. He gave the chaplain a sad smile and said he'd been brought up in a Christian home. Gerecke said the

Lord's Prayer, and the soldier followed by praying the Twenty-Third Psalm: "The Lord is my shepherd; I shall not want . . ." Gerecke sat with him, and later, when a nurse came by with another needleful of morphine, the soldier told her she was wasting her time. As he lay dying, the soldier looked at Gerecke, "The Lord is my shepherd," he said again.

Gerecke encountered only three atheists when he was with the Ninety-Eighth. One saw him from several beds away, as the chaplain was working his way from patient to patient. "Don't bother about me, I'm an atheist," he called out. Another smiled when Gerecke tried to hand him a devotional booklet and suggested the chaplain spend his time elsewhere. The third said he hadn't had time for religion before the war and refused to take it up until he could consider it more seriously when he returned home. Gerecke prayed at the beds of these men and blamed himself that he couldn't bring them around to the faith. "I failed to win any of these atheists," he said.

To mitigate the frenetic pace, long hours, and grim work, Sullivan tried to keep morale up with his team. Weekly bus trips took members of the command to Bournemouth, Oxford, or Stratford-Upon-Avon. As long as it was possible, everyone got one day off duty each week, and an occasional forty-eight-hour pass. Enlisted men who wanted to visit family, or visit cities in England, Scotland, or Wales, got five-day furloughs. Nurses could visit family, and those who were married were encouraged to visit their husbands if they were stationed in England. Each night, buses took off-duty staff members on Liberty Runs to Newbury. On the hospital campus, the unit put two Nissen huts together to form a patient dayroom—102 feet long by 16 feet wide—with a brick fireplace at each end, a bar, dartboards, a Ping-Pong table, pool and snooker tables, a radio, a library, a phonograph with records (classical and popular), a piano with sheet music, books, newspapers, British and American magazines, and writing tables. A hospital library stocked eighteen hundred books. The Ninety-Eighth basketball team—complete with uniforms supplied by the Special Services Division—practiced on a backboard near the rehab center and entered the Airborne League.

By August, Gerecke was visiting 2,000 patients each month and counseling more than 150 staff members. He made it a practice to seek out each member of the 650-member-strong Ninety-Eighth General Hospital staff to deliver a personal greeting when it was his or her birthday. Or, as the chaplain called it, "birthday anniversary." "You only have one birthday," he always said. "The rest of them are anniversaries of your birthday."

The hospital was chaotic, with medics moving hundreds of patients in and out of the various wards every hour of the day. The staff was overworked, and it showed at chapel, but Gerecke knew the reasons and tried to bring faith to the tired doctors and nurses, rather than wait for them to come to him. "There is splendid cooperation among the doctors, the nurses and the Chaplains," Gerecke wrote. But "members of our unit find it difficult to attend services due to the present status of our hospital."

He began saying short devotions at 12:45 each day, making it as easy as possible for the staff to take advantage of a short spiritual breather during the lunch hour. As candles on the altar flickered and Geist softly played a hymn in the background, Gerecke read a verse or two from the Bible, then simply prayed. Between prayers there was what the chaplain called a "be still and know that I am God" silence.

"It makes your heart skip a beat to see enlisted men, nurses, doctors and a few patients on their knees speaking to God," he wrote. "It's the sweetest ten-minute period in the whole day." Doctors and nurses handed Gerecke the names of the seriously sick. "Prayers for the sick ones here are my very own, and are ex corde"—from the heart—"to the nth degree," he wrote. "Others speak to me concerning their loved ones scattered all over the world."

Gerecke's loved ones were certainly scattered. That made an unexpected visit from his oldest son the highlight of an otherwise hellish September. Hank arrived in England and traveled straight from London to Hermitage. Gerecke picked him up from the train station at the Newbury racetrack in an ambulance. They hugged tight, overjoyed at the sight of each other, then retreated to Gerecke's quarters to catch up.

Hank, an officer with the army's military police, left in the morning but came back later that month, when the two went into town and had tea at the community hall. A four-piece orchestra playing the hall noticed the Yanks and began playing the "Star-Spangled Banner." But father and son were engrossed in conversation and didn't catch on at first. Finally, Gerecke noticed and both men scrambled to their feet, hands over hearts, just as the band finished the tune.

Gerecke took Hank to visit Rev. Owens and his family, and Hank attended his father's chapel services. On Saturday night, they went to the officers' club and Gerecke introduced Hank to his colleagues. Everywhere they went, Hank noticed that his father was greeted with beaming smiles, backslaps, and booming greetings of "Hey, Chappie!" or "Padre!" At the officers' club Hank was amazed and amused that a lot of the prettiest nurses were flirting with his father. "Dad, those girls are hitting on you," Hank said to the chaplain. "Happens all the time," Gerecke said smiling. "They think I'm safe."

Safe or not, the chaplain clearly enjoyed and encouraged the attention. After Hank had downed a few beers, they walked over to an officers' and nurses' dance where Hank had a couple more drinks. Gerecke sat and watched as his Ninety-Eighth friends danced. Knowing his father disapproved of dancing, Hank just sat next to him and drank another beer.

"Son, there are a lot of pretty nurses in this room," the chaplain said. "Why don't you go ask one of them to dance?" Hank was stunned, but he decided to take his father's advice. "By then I couldn't stand up to get out of my damn chair," Hank said later. "And Dad knew it. He just sat there laughing."

Hank's visits alleviated some of Gerecke's anxiety, but the grim work of the Ninety-Eighth was all-consuming. He was sitting with nearly a hundred patients a day, and he continued to try and convince his colleagues that their spiritual health was as important as their physical nourishment, especially in the turbulent atmosphere and individual stresses of life in a transit hospital.

He also knew that matters of life and death took priority, and that's where he spent most of his time. The medical staff often asked for his help. A soldier was brought in, unconscious and severely wounded, and the doctors asked Gerecke to pray for the man. For three hours he stood silently behind the surgeons as they operated, and prayed. When Gerecke visited the soldier as he was recuperating, he told Gerecke that he "wasn't ready" to die.

Another time, Gerecke was called to the side of a dying man. He joined a raft of doctors at the soldier's bed. As Gerecke bent over him, the man opened his eyes and asked, "Chaplain, am I going to die?" For a moment, Gerecke froze. The doctors and nurses looked at him expectantly, as Gerecke prayed for an answer. A nurse was about to fill the void, but a doctor stopped her. "God's children never die," Gerecke finally said. As the medical staff drifted away from the man's bed, Gerecke told the twenty-year-old that "Heaven's gate is opened by trusting Jesus, who died for you." He asked the soldier to repeat after him, and the soldier did: "Jesus, I trust Thee. Keep me safe for heaven." Gerecke never saw him again.

In the fall, the hospital expanded again as more patients continued to flow through its doors. The unit built an intricate drainage system to eliminate problems with standing water around the hospital grounds, another mess for patients, and a laundry facility with twelve fifteen-gallon tubs to accommodate 350 men per hour. The Red Cross expanded its craft room with tools and materials so patients with battle fatigue could do wood- and metalworking. Sullivan built a theater with a permanent stage, dressing rooms, and seating for 350.

Gerecke used all this activity to his advantage. "I am fortunate in having the friendship of the entire personnel," he wrote. "Many are reached in Mess Halls, Day Room, and Officer's Meetings."

Just as Gerecke had come around to appreciate the strictures and discipline of army life, the institution was changing him in different ways. He had witnessed the bonding that occurs under intense physical and psychological stress of a wartime hospital, and that in turn led to an acknowledgment that God couldn't possibly hold it against these doctors and nurses for blowing off steam through dancing and drinking a bit. He also knew, of course, that these were occasions for him to connect with his colleagues—opportunities for Gerecke's true goal: evangelization. And so, to the dances, USO shows, and basketball games he went.

The unit put on two patient dances in the fall in the new patient mess hall, with music provided by the Ninety-Eighth General Hospital Orchestra, and invited young ladies from local British welfare organizations to attend. The orchestra also played three music variety shows in the new theater, two enlisted dances, and two officers/nurses dances. The theater hosted three USO shows, a special service show, and a British show. The unit basketball team was playing a weekly schedule of four games in two leagues formed among nearby units.

Gerecke continued to encourage the Jewish members of the unit to hold services together, and in the absence of a Jewish chaplain or available local rabbi, a Jewish officer led the Friday evening services for about twenty-five staff members. In November, Gerecke arranged for thirty-three of his Jewish colleagues to attend Yom Kippur services at a local synagogue.

Gerecke held Thanksgiving services in November, and knowing how Christmas cheer would affect morale, he began planning for December. He formed caroling, flower, and decoration committees. "Our nurses are especially interested in this work," he wrote. "Friendly neighbors will provide Christmas trees."

The Allies had moved one thousand German POWs to a stockade near Hermitage, and Sullivan began using detachments of them for labor around the hospital. The staff laid out a baseball diamond with the help of the POWs. Dozens of prisoners helped with construction, sanitary projects, painting buildings, general maintenance, and kitchen patrol duties. They helped build three thousand feet of sidewalks among the buildings and a garbage incinerator. Because of Gerecke's knowledge of German, Sullivan asked him to help supervise the prisoners. "They have a chaplain, but I must watch him," Gerecke wrote. "Especially his sermon material concerning anything he might say against our government."

But he was also doing his best to convert the German POWs he encountered at the stockade. In October 1944, Gerecke sent a Western Union telegram to Paul Kretzmann, Concordia Seminary's librarian in St. Louis, who had written a recommendation for Gerecke to get into the Chaplain Corps.

"PLEASE RUSH GERMAN LITERATURE DEVOTIONALS CHRISTMAS CARD HYMN BOOKLETS FOR LARGE PRISON CAMP IN NEIGHBORHOOD," Gerecke wrote.

His country actually asked him to do much more. Two members of the Office of Strategic Services, the U.S. intelligence agency during World War II that preceded the CIA, came from London to visit the Ninety-Eighth. Gerecke later said they asked him to use his German to extract information from the POWs during confession. Gerecke had, indeed, begun to help the German chaplain with his pastoral duties among the prisoners, but he told the OSS men that he couldn't violate the privacy of the confessional, even in the service of national security.

At an army general hospital, patients were given "definitive treatment" then returned to duty if their units were in Britain or sent to replacement depots for reassignment. If patients needed prolonged treatment—defined as more than 120 days—the army sent them back to the United States. Patients who needed specialized treatment but could return to duty within three months were sent to other hospitals in England designated for whatever special treatment they needed.

At the end of November, the army returned the Ninety-Eighth from the status of a transit hospital to that of a general hospital and the patient flow from the two airfields slowed considerably. In October and November, when the Ninety-Eighth was taking wounded directly from the battlefields, it admitted 7,290 patients. In December, after the army had returned the Ninety-Eighth to the status of "general," it saw only 350 patients from the Continent. But it treated 533 patients based in the United Kingdom and gave another 6,280 outpatient care.

The pace change mattered for Gerecke only in the kind of work he was doing. Less time in the emergency and operating rooms meant doctors and nurses had more time for church. December is the busy season for anyone in the Christianity business anyway, and Gerecke saw the biggest chapel attendance spike in his army career with nearly one thousand coming to one or more of his thirteen Sunday services over the month. "We feel highly gratified at the response to our invitations to Christmas Services," Gerecke wrote. "The days are too short for two Chaplains to meet all spiritual opportunities in our large hospital. We pray for Guidance."

Sullivan noticed the chaplain's efforts during December, and in January, he wrote a note of commendation. Chaplain Gerecke, Sullivan wrote:

> . . . is to be commended upon the superior manner in which he has performed his duties during the year 1944. In the early months of the year, before the unit arrived in the United Kingdom, he was the only chaplain assigned, and by his devotion to duty, his broad tolerance, his concern for the spiritual needs of the entire unit regardless of creed, he established himself firmly as the counselor and guide of officer and enlisted personnel. The same paternal characteristics were shown

to patients. In the most difficult times, as a transit hospital, when large numbers of patients arrived on short notice and were evacuated within 12 to 24 hours, no man departed without the ministration and prayers of the chaplain. This officer exemplifies the best traditions of the Corps of Chaplains in the Ministry.

The relatively ponderous pace of patient loads didn't last long. During the winter, especially in January and February 1945, the hospital received thousands of soldiers from the front lines suffering the effects of the severe cold and arduous battles on the Continent. Trench foot, frostbite, and battle fatigue were the most common conditions.

The hospital received an average of about eleven hundred patients a week, but that number swelled to treat as many as fourteen hundred during heavy battle activity. As if there wasn't enough to keep the unit busy, on January 26 a fire destroyed the bar in the enlisted men's dayroom, forcing hundreds of thirsty off-duty soldiers into a cramped Special Services Building for beer.

Gerecke's ward visits increased again after the New Year, and he began taking cigarettes with him on his rounds to offer to the wounded, along with New Testaments and devotional booklets. One month he distributed "1,000 Scripture Calendar cards; 200 New Testaments; 1,000 Easter Crosses; 300 Plastic Crosses; 500 Devotional Tracts and 250 Devotional Booklets." Gerecke worked alongside twelve members of the British Women's Volunteer Services who visited patients four afternoons a week to sew and mend their clothing. The ladies also handed out matches—helpful for those who'd acquired a few cigarettes from Gerecke.

The cold was a killer for chapel attendance, and Gerecke again complained about its distance from the hospital's main action. "Suggest the English place Chapels in Hospital Areas thereby serving the spiritual needs of all ambulatory patients," he wrote. "The distance between Chapel and Hospital Area is too great, especially in bad weather."

Gerecke still had no doubt—despite all the commotion and life-and-death situations and new friendships and adventure of the past year—about the most important part of his job. On February 21, he baptized twenty-three-year-old Samuel K. Cressman from Lansing, Michigan, in the chapel. Second Lieutenant Nurse Nathalie La-Crouts was the witness. "Opportunities for individual soul-winning are tremendous," he wrote. "There's not enough time."

By now Geist was directing a chapel choir and a glee club. A member of the Ninety-Eighth, Captain Friedland, led Jewish services on Friday nights at six, and Gerecke convinced Sullivan to allow an army transport to shuttle a local rabbi, Rabbi Ginsberg, to the hospital twice a week to minister to Jewish patients. "Our Commanding Officer never hesitates to give every available help to his Chaplains," Gerecke wrote. "Our wounded men are deeply grateful."

In an efficiency report for Gerecke, written on March 1, Sullivan gave the chaplain the highest marks possible on categories like "attention to duty," "cooperation," and "judgment and common sense." His lowest marks, perhaps predictably for a somewhat plump fifty-one-year-old, were for "force" and "physical activity and endurance."

"A cheerful, loyal, devout officer," Sullivan wrote in the report, "intensely concerned in the spiritual welfare and morale of all members of the unit, tolerant and kindly to all, not sparing himself in the performance of duty. He has the affection as well as respect of all."

Sullivan's push for morale-boosting distraction expanded during the spring. The intrahospital softball league competition was fierce. The unit's clinicians, officers, patient detachment, administration, and mess each fielded a team. A Ninety-Eighth baseball team (with uniforms) formed to compete against nearby hospitals and other installations, playing six home games in March and April.

Sullivan chartered a boat for enlisted personnel to float from Oxford, down the Thames twenty miles and back. Staff and patients could play golf, tennis, and basketball, and the hospital loaned out fifteen bicycles for patients to explore the surrounding countryside. Anyone who had a camera could take his film to the hospital photo lab, where pictures could be developed and printed at cost.

Three days after the death of President Franklin D. Roosevelt in April 1945, Gerecke organized memorial services. "It was the desire of our Commanding Officer that ambulatory patients and members of the unit attend the Service of their choice," Gerecke wrote. That month, he also visited an American cemetery in Cambridge to take part in a mass burial. "An unforgettable experience," he wrote. "I feel more qualified to write better condolence letters."

As Allied forces began breaking through German defenses in May, the Ninety-Eighth had a new patient class: American soldiers flown in from newly liberated German POW camps. The unit set up delousing stations, and doctors studied up on the treatment of severe malnutrition. The hospital saw more cases of trench foot and frostbite suffered by men on forced marches. As the Allies pushed farther into German-occupied zones, more former captives were sent to the hospital, and the Ninety-Eighth was soon packed to capacity again.

In mid-April, Sullivan received orders that as of May 1, those patients whom doctors determined could not be returned to duty within sixty days were to be sent back to the United States. It was a signal that the war was coming to a close. And indeed, within a week, Hitler's successor, Admiral Karl Doenitz, ordered General Alfred Jodl to surrender to General Dwight Eisenhower.

On VE day, Hank was on the Champs-Élysées, waving with thousands of others as General Charles de Gaulle paraded into Paris. A few days later, Hank met his father in London and they spent a week together. "My son could have gone anywhere he wanted on his leave, but he chose to come spend it with his father," he told his friends in the Ninety-Eighth. "Isn't that something?" In his May report, Gerecke wrote, "We thank God for Victory in Europe. May victory come to our men in the Pacific area soon."

After VE Day, May 8, 1945, the flow of patients at the Ninety-

Eighth slowed to a trickle, and rumors began to circulate that its staff would be going home. Other rumors had the unit packing up and moving to the Pacific to help in the final push against the Japanese. The unit spent much of its time breaking down the hospital they'd built and sending any remaining patients to other hospitals. Orders eventually came that key doctors—the chief of surgical services, the chief of X-ray services, the heads of the neuropsychiatric, anesthetic, and gastrointestinal divisions—had been reassigned, along with some officers and enlisted men, "throwing the smoke grenade of rumor and conjecture into our midst," Sullivan wrote.

The Ninety-Eighth stopped admitting patients on May 22, and Sullivan told the staff to prepare for another ocean voyage. Finally, the commander received instructions to report to Southampton, where the Ninety-Eighth boarded the MS *Dunnottar Castle*, a troop ship named for a medieval Scottish fortress, and on June 15 crossed the English Channel to Le Havre.

Sullivan was clearly proud of his unit's success. "A newly formed and trained organization had established itself in England to perform its primary mission," he wrote. "Every type of operation which could possibly confront a fixed hospital left the unit with a wealth of experience, a pride of achievement and confidence in any future task." It was that achievement that kept most of the Ninety-Eighth in Europe. Instead of being sent home, Sullivan and his team would be sent to resurrect a battered hospital in the middle of Munich— Bavaria's capital, the newly crushed heart of Nazism.

THE NINETY-EIGHTH LANDED IN France on June 18, 1945, and after ten days at Camp Pall Mall near Le Havre, Sullivan was ordered to take his unit to Eagle Main, an Allied staging area in Verdun where Dwight Eisenhower, George Patton, and Omar Bradley had planned the final stages of the war just before Christmas. On July 2, the unit arrived in Verdun, about eighty miles from Nancy, France, where Hank was stationed. Gerecke sent a message to his son that the Ninety-Eighth was just up the Meuse River, but Hank was not on post. By the time Hank got the message and rushed to Verdun, the Ninety-Eighth had departed for Munich.

By now, Gerecke knew how to minister to a large military group, and he wasn't impressed with what he'd seen in Le Havre and Verdun. He attended a conference with eighty-five other chaplains in Reims. "There should be a Post Chaplain at Eagle-Main to coordinate the Lord's work," he wrote in his monthly report. "If the Chaplain at Etretat is in charge of Pall Mall, he should arrange for organ and hymnals. I pray God the Chaplains do not let down on our 'Fathers business' since VE Day. Seems to me our fighting men and women need special attention right now."

The majority of the Ninety-Eighth personnel arrived in Munich on Sunday, July 15, after an arduous three-day train journey aggravated by a number of detours. Almost before unloading their bags, Gerecke and Father Walsh were leading Sunday services in the hospital chapels. "Both chaplains had been with the unit in England," Sullivan wrote. "Both were devoted to their duties, kindly, tolerant."

An advance party that included Sullivan arrived at the former Municipal Hospital of Munich, known as *Schwabinger Krankenhaus,* to find "enormous problems" facing the Ninety-Eighth's mission. Schwabing, named for the district of Munich where it sat, had been a two-thousand-bed building before it was pummeled by Allied bombers, suffering seventeen direct hits, including several incendiary bombs.

The hospital consisted of seven large buildings and several smaller buildings—all connected by corridors, basements, and subbasements. Each building had three floors and each floor seventy-five beds. But when Sullivan arrived, he found Schwabing barely usable, with half its windows blown out, corridors between wards crushed, roofs open to the sky, and equipment strewn throughout the building "from attics to basements." Two bombs had destroyed the operating room, physiotherapy clinic, and X-ray clinic. The dental clinic had been reduced to a single chair.

A large incinerator hadn't been used for months, and it took two hundred German POWs from the beginning of August until the end of September to clean up the papers and garbage that the hospital's former staff had simply thrown into the basements. The heating system was decrepit and didn't work in some buildings. The mess hall was large but unusable. The kitchen had excellent gas range ovens, but there was no gas to be found in Germany and even coal was difficult to come by. The water was not chlorinated. A garage for ambulances and other vehicles had been destroyed.

Despite the conditions, eight hundred patients, most suffering from typhus fever, were being cared for by German doctors and nurses. As the Ninety-Eighth took over, Schwabing was "literally bulging with Germans," Sullivan wrote, "some working on the premises and others just living there." The mayor of Munich was living in one ward. The mass influx of Americans meant members of the Ninety-Eighth had to join them, sleeping in wards for the first weeks while other quarters were decontaminated from the typhus patients. In August, the Ninety-Eighth confronted a "full blown typhoid epidemic," necessitating the vaccination of staff and the emergency treatment of those who'd contracted the fever. In the mess, Germans had been eating spoiled food, and the condition of the latrines was "deplorable."

Sullivan also found an attitude toward illness that was symptomatic of life under Hitler. "It was found that under the Nazi period any individual who was sick was told he was sabotaging the institution," he wrote. "Apparently this fact was so ingrained into the minds of the employees that they would only report sick when ready to collapse physically. For example, a cleaning woman worked in my office for two weeks wearing a coat in summer, finally reported that she was sick, and promptly died." Six patients died from typhus, but the unit eventually got the spread of the disease under control. It helped that two parts of the campus left standing were a huge laundry facility that employed seventy-five people and a well-equipped laboratory that the Americans eventually organized into bacteriology, serology, histopathology, hematology, urinalysis, chemistry, photography, and blood bank departments.

The only members of the Ninety-Eighth who were thrilled with the facilities they found at Schwabing were the chaplains. The hospital's Catholic and Protestant chapels had both survived the bombing. "Beautiful chapel designated for Protestant Services," Gerecke wrote. The chapel seated 125 people in pews and had a two-manual pipe organ in working condition and a piano. The altar and pulpit were built into the architecture of the chapel, which meant Gerecke's army-issue chaplain outfit could largely remain packed. Each chaplain even had his own office attached to the worship spaces. Having two chapels meant each chaplain could offer more services, so Gerecke began leading worship at 9:00 A.M., 10:00 A.M., and 7:30 P.M. on Sundays.

Chaplain Walsh was greeted by fellow Catholics at the hospital—a group of one hundred nuns who worked and lived in an attached cloister. Each day, seventy-five of them worked in the laundry facility, in the kitchen, or as ward attendants. The language barrier was a problem for the Americans with all the German hospital workers, including the nuns. But in time, the sisters worked with the Ninety-Eighth's nurses and soon took over the routine menial functions, becoming the most dependable civilian employees of the hospital. Nuns were also given part of the kitchen and mess to provide food for the German hospital workers from the sisters' own stores.

Despite the typhoid epidemic, the mess, and the communication difficulties, the Ninety-Eighth began accepting patients on July 22. The initial patient load of 896 grew to 1,073 by mid-September, and the surreal experience of operating a destroyed hospital continued. The Germans introduced the Americans to a woman bathing in a tub in one corner of the hospital. She wouldn't leave the tub and told the staff she'd been immersed in it since the end of the First World War, as a treatment for a venereal disease she'd contracted from an American soldier.

In addition to doctors and nurses, 350 Germans worked for the Ninety-Eighth as cooks, housemaids, and secretaries. Nearly all of them lived "in undesirable quarters at the top of several of the ward buildings," Sullivan wrote. Polish and Hungarian workers joined the Germans as hospital employees. Aside from the work of the nuns, which he considered invaluable, Sullivan was unimpressed with the work ethic of the unit's civilian employees. "The average German worker, despite all claims to the contrary, has been found to be a somewhat slow-moving individual, who usually does a good job, but takes his time about it," he wrote. "One German bricklayer, for example, has been found to lay only 1/3 of the bricks of his American prototype."

Motivation and morale problems were not limited to Germans. After July, the Ninety-Eighth slowly began coming apart. "The juggernaut of redeployment struck in August," as the army transferred 57 officers out of the unit in the next few months, and 116 new officers in. By December, most were replacements and not happy ones. The war was over, and nobody wanted to be living in a bombed-out hospital in Munich. The possibility of a transfer to the Pacific still loomed for many, and the army's point system, which determined when individuals could go home, kept changing and was thought by most to be unfair.

The staff of the hospital remained "competent if unenthusiastic," Sullivan wrote.

> *Since arrival in Germany, redeployment remains uppermost in the minds of practically all officers, nurses and enlisted personnel, especially those that have been in the theater for any length of time. The point score's constant changing, the uncertainty of when they*

> *will return, premature information often released in the 'Stars and*
> *Stripes,' false rumors such as the fact that ASTP [Army Specialized*
> *Training Program] graduates will not be sent overseas, and a general*
> *feeling that injustice has been done in having such a discrepancy in*
> *points between those eligible to go overseas and those eligible to return*
> *in the theater, has created a feeling of unrest in the command which*
> *at this stage of operation is extremely difficult for a unit Commander*
> *to combat.*

Morale among the medical staff was especially low. "I have had to use a personal brand of psychotherapy on some highly trained professional personnel ordered into the unit recently in order to obtain useful service from them," Sullivan wrote.

For doctors, nurses, and chaplains alike, the setup of Schwabing made for time-consuming rounds. The 1,684 patients who checked into the hospital in August were spread out over twenty-one wards in seven different buildings. For Gerecke, who celebrated his fifty-second birthday that month, the pressure on his knees, from visiting up to fifteen hundred beds each month, was mitigated by the hospital's high number of ambulatory patients, which kept pastoral meetings in his office at "a high pitch."

With Geist's help, the chaplain baptized two men—a technician with the 489th Automatic Weapons Battalion and a private with the Fifty-Fifth Fighter Group—at the hospital in August. With the fighting over and the opportunity for baptisms more prevalent, Gerecke made a request of his chaplain superiors. Referencing his *Moments of Comfort* broadcasts in St. Louis, he wrote them in September with an idea to reach many more troops over the American Forces Network.

"There may be opportunity for daily devotions over AFN," he wrote. "It was my hobby during civilian ministry. May this venture have your blessings?"

In early August, Hank Gerecke took a jeep from where he was

stationed in Nancy and picked up his younger brother Corky, then stationed near Frankfurt. The brothers drove down to Munich and, without telling his father, Hank made contact with one of the Ninety-Eighth's doctors he'd met in England. The doctor and some nurses sneaked the brothers into the hospital and hid them on two gurneys under sheets. A doctor called Gerecke to the emergency room on the pretense that someone was near death. When the chaplain arrived, he approached the bodies under the sheets, at which point, his sons popped up yelling, "Happy Birthday!" Without missing a beat, Gerecke yelled back, "You boys get down from there right now!" It's possible the chaplain had never been happier in his life. His sons had survived the war and had traveled to Munich to surprise him on his birthday anniversary.

"We had a righteous time that night," Hank said later. "We surely did."

Also in August, Gerecke had asked a Captain Wesley to lead Friday evening Jewish services in the chapel, and Gerecke began a Seventh-Day Adventist service on Saturday mornings from ten to noon. Gerecke and a Jewish chaplain began organizing for High Holy Day services for troops stationed in Munich, and Gerecke convinced the hospital's department heads and chiefs of services to relieve Jewish personnel from normal duties. From September 7 to 9, 153 people attended Rosh Hashanah services at Munich's Prince Regent Theater, an opera house built by Bavarian officials to stage the works of the nineteenth-century anti-Semitic composer— and Hitler favorite—Richard Wagner. When it opened in 1901, the Prince Regent's first performance had been Act III of Wagner's *The Mastersingers of Nuremberg*. More than one hundred attended Yom Kippur services at the opera house on September 16 and 17, 1945.

The Ninety-Eighth's senior officers bunked in a large, well-furnished house called the "Villa" at one end of the administrative building, while junior officers lived in apartments at another end of the same building. Nurses lived mostly (and snugly) on the second and third floors of the administrative building. Enlisted men were housed in two former hospital buildings and slept in bunk beds. Feeding thousands in one institution in postwar Munich was a challenge. Fresh meat, fresh eggs, and fresh vegetables were scarce. The hospital's kitchen had steam vats and gas ranges, but workers had to rely on field ranges because of the lack of gas. Glass was also hard to come by, so the hospital's windows that had been broken during the bombing couldn't be replaced. The absence of screens, poor sanitation, and an unofficial dump a quarter mile away from the hospital grounds meant flies were a problem in the summer and early fall. Mess halls, kitchens, latrines, operating rooms, and dressing rooms were regularly sprayed with DDT, which "remarkably reduced this nuisance," Sullivan wrote. The DDT also took care of the cockroach issue.

Sullivan's interest in morale-building distractions continued in Munich, where he screened five movies a week in the physiotherapy gym. Playing fields for baseball and football games were a five-minute walk from the hospital, and the Ninety-Eighth's football team provided "a good spectacle even though they were out-matched in most games," he wrote. The basketball team was "uniformly victorious" and well supported. There were regular Liberty Runs into popular spots in the city, and Sunday tours to Garmisch, Starnberg, and Berchtesgaden always took the maximum number allowed on leave.

Gerecke took Geist and a group of his favorite nurses into the Alps for a week in the fall. Amid the snowball fights on the slopes of the Zugspitze, Germany's tallest mountain, one nurse spotted a beautiful little church in one of the mountain villages, and the group asked Gerecke if he could lead them in a service there the next day—a Sunday. He walked into the church and found two ministers, one old and one young, inside. The younger man, sensing an American in the room, greeted Gerecke in English. Gerecke smiled, told the men who he was, and asked if his group could worship there the next morning. He promised they'd be in and out quickly without disturbing anything in the church.

The two men conferred in German, with the older minister becoming animated, telling the young minister that the bumbling Americans, despite their promises to the contrary, would surely damage the church as they had damaged Germany, and he directed the young man to tell the American to go back home and worship in his own country. The young minister turned to Gerecke and told him in English that he was welcome to come back the next day with his group and hold a service in the church.

Gerecke thanked him, smiled at the older minister, and said in German, "Thank you, Pastor, for allowing us to use your church. We promise to leave it as beautiful as when we found it." And he walked triumphantly back out into the snow. It was always one of Gerecke's favorite stories. "The look on their faces was worth printing," he'd say.

In October, the army required all officers and enlisted personnel to take two hours of training a week in such subjects as "Aims of the Nazi Party Before 1933," "The Nazi Party in Power, 1933–39," "The Guilt of the German People," "The Nazi Strike," and "Nazi Atrocities." The last was probably the easiest to illustrate because of the hospital's proximity to Dachau, about eleven miles to the northwest.

Geist had been with Gerecke the first time each of them visited Dachau. They saw the execution mounds, the barbed wire, the SS barracks. The camp had been liberated only ten weeks before the Ninety-Eighth arrived in Munich. The evidence of mass murder was fresh. Geist took a picture of Gerecke standing next to a sign in English, below a white cross. "This area is being retained as a shrine to the 238,000 individuals who were cremated here. Please do not destroy."

Gerecke returned several times to Dachau. He never said what compelled him, nor whether his description of touching its walls as blood smeared his hands was literal or metaphorical. Whatever happened in his mind as he walked through the camp remained there for good.

As he and Geist stood next to the ovens on that first visit, Gerecke said in a soft voice, "How could they do something like this?"

He said it over and over again.

CHAPTER 5

The Sun's Light Failed

If your enemies are hungry, give them bread to eat; and if they are
thirsty, give them water to drink; for you will heap coals of fire on
their heads, and the Lord will reward you.

—PROVERBS 25:21–22

In EARLY NOVEMBER 1945, Colonel Sullivan summoned Gerecke to his office at the Munich hospital to tell him that the army had requested his transfer. Major Nazi war criminals were awaiting trial at Nuremberg, and Colonel Burton Andrus, the commandant of the Nuremberg prison a hundred miles north, had asked for Gerecke as his Protestant chaplain.

Andrus needed to protect his prisoners' spiritual welfare, but he was also thinking pragmatically. The services of a good chaplain could prevent what Andrus called "prison psychosis." Such a "mental condition," he wrote, "could only be protected by steps like this. . . . It was not so much that my prisoners were likely to become psychotic, but that it might give them the chance to feign this type of illness."

He had known that he needed chaplains since mid-August. It wasn't just a matter of regulations. Religious ministry to the prisoners was important if, Andrus wrote later, "we were going to do what, as well meaning people, we should for their possible spiritual benefit."

Andrus's situation was "urgent," and he wanted Gerecke for a number of reasons. For one, Gerecke—like so many of the Nazis at Nuremberg—was a Lutheran. He also spoke German and had worked in U.S. prisons and jails before the war.

Sullivan had told Andrus that Gerecke had served long enough. He knew Gerecke had not seen Alma in two years and that he wanted to go home, but the Nuremberg commandant had pushed to get the chaplain into his prison. "I had to go through the chaplain general to get approval for Gerecke," Andrus wrote. "But I finally got it."

Andrus had entered the army as a cavalry officer in the First World War. For reasons that were never clear to him, the army put him in charge of a military prison at Fort Oglethorpe, Georgia, for three months during the war.

The stockade held the U.S. Army's worst criminals—men who had been found guilty of murder, armed robbery, and drug violations. On Andrus's first night in charge of the stockade, the prisoners rioted. The next morning, as Andrus surveyed the damage, the prisoners informed him that they had no intention of recognizing his authority, or of doing any work. For the rest of the day, he had each prisoner brought before him. He gauged by "the defiance in their eyes" which were the ringleaders, and he assigned those men to clean the prison and repair the damages from the riot. He brought in sheet-metal workers to construct three solitary confinement cells and had the work done in full view of the prisoners. Then he instituted a new rule that sentinels would no longer have to give three warning calls to escaping prisoners before they could shoot them. One warning would now be enough.

Andrus stood a rigid five feet, ten inches and considered himself in great shape. He was furious when a reporter for *Time* described him at Nuremberg as "plump." His small brown eyes were magnified by thick, round, steel-rimmed glasses, and a pencil-thin mustache drew a line between a fleshy nose and two narrow lips. Andrus's signature feature was his green shellacked helmet, always buffed so that the golden eagle on its front shined. Those who eventually worked for him, with him, and around him at Nuremberg— lawyers, soldiers, journalists, and Nazis—called Andrus "pompous," "officious," "strict," "petty," "naive," "ridiculous," "a spit-and-polish stickler," "an insecure peacock of a man," and "not the brightest." The writer John Kenneth Galbraith wrote that it was "hard to imagine the Army could have found a better man for the job." Galbraith also said Andrus was "somewhat allergic to all of his charges."

During the Second World War, Andrus had been a combat observer with the army's G-3 Combat Lessons Branch. As his unit moved through Germany at the end of the war, he observed that the Germans were hypocrites. "They have religious statues and pictures around their houses, and try to pose as Christians, yet they are still launching rabot [*sic*] bombs on the women and children in England," Andrus wrote in a letter to the San Diego Commandery of the Masonic Order of the Knights Templar. "Many of their infernal devices have slaughtered innocent maidens, helpless widows, and defenseless orphans. They are making war on the Christian religion and all it stands for."

A week after VE Day, Andrus was ordered to Mondorf-les-Bains, a spa town with tree-lined streets, grand nineteenth-century villas, and luxury hotels in southeastern Luxembourg, where he would be the commandant of a secret interrogation center for newly captured Nazi officials. The facility, previously the Palace Hotel, was now code-named Ashcan, and it was temporarily housing some of the most important Nazis who were still alive. In the twenty-seven years since Fort Oglethorpe, Andrus had not had a single assignment dealing with a prison or prisoners. His orders to Mondorf were as surprising to him as those that took him to the Georgia stockade in the previous world war. When Andrus arrived at Ashcan three days later, the Palace was being transformed into a prison fortress. "To get in here," one guard told a reporter, "you have to have a pass from God and someone has to verify the signature."

Between May and August 1945, the Allies brought fifty-two captured Nazis to Mondorf. The town was strategically chosen for its unique positioning. Ten miles south of the city of Luxembourg, Mondorf sat on a bluff near the borders of both France and Germany. The Mosel River protected the town on one side, and observers had a clear view from nearly any vantage point high in the town.

The Palace had a veranda where the Nazis not on suicide watch could walk back and forth and take in the view over the twenty-foot-high, double-stockade coils of barbed wire. Over the fence, they could see a few square yards of green grass and a dried-out fountain that also was enclosed with barbed wire. Green slopes on three sides of the Palace's gray stucco façade meant guards could easily watch the goings-on in and around the hotel.

The war may have been over, but Andrus feared residual forces might try to free the Nazi leaders from Allied control, and he wasn't satisfied with Ashcan's defenses when he arrived. He requested floodlights, an airstrip, an electric alarm system for the outer fence, camouflaged netting to protect Ashcan from the air, more machine guns, and more guards, doctors, clerks, and typewriters. GIs carried out fine carpets and elegant furniture, replacing them with folding camp-beds and straw mattresses. Others removed chandeliers and replaced sixteen hundred of the hotel's glass windowpanes with Plexiglas and iron bars.

"I was concerned about guards being bribed, snipers shooting at prisoners or gaining information, and suicide attempts," Andrus later wrote. "I even feared murder within the enclosure; for deadly enemies were already, in some cases, being confined together. Mondorf, no one had to tell me, was a powder-keg."

Andrus wrote to a friend, "I hate these Krauts and they know it and respect me for it. I guess that's why I got this job. It's too bad we could not have exterminated them and given that beautiful country to someone who was worthy."

In April, before he was assigned to Mondorf, Andrus wrote to his wife and included some stationery lifted from an abandoned Nazi headquarters. "Here is some paper we captured in one of the places we used as a Hq. after the Natzi [sic] Hq. left," Andrus wrote. "More & more they rush out without having a chance to move or destroy everything. The more one sees of them the more one comes to detest them—they're terrible people, civillians [sic] and all."

As Andrus tried to put together a secure enclosure in Mondorf, the Nazi leaders kept arriving under the cover of darkness. Ashcan's prisoners would be the central characters in whatever production of justice the Allies decided to stage, and the prisoners knew it. Many of the Nazis were despondent that their captors were not treating them as traditional victorious warrior-gentlemen would.

Wilhelm Keitel demanded a pencil and paper to write a letter of complaint to General Eisenhower. "I am treated here in Mondorf Camp as if I were in a camp for ordinary criminals, in a jail without windows," he wrote. "In addition, it is made clear to me in every respect that I am to be expressly denied the treatment generally accorded an officer POW. . . . Recently the most extreme measures have been applied. Clothing was taken away, except for a certain limited amount, and almost all toilet articles were withdrawn. Not even military decorations of this war and the past one were left in my possession. Even spectacles were taken away."

The Germans realized, as they took in the conditions of their imprisonment at Ashcan, that the days were gone when generals on both sides came together over cognac and cigars to discuss the winning and losing strategies of particular battles after the fighting was over. The last, awful months of war—as bad as they were—may have been preferable to what lay ahead.

The Nazis were depressed and ragged. Most still wore the clothes they'd been captured in. The generals had had their ribbons torn from their chests (mostly by a giddy Andrus). The politicians wore grubby suits without ties, which had been taken away to prevent suicides, as had their belts and suspenders, so that their pants drooped. They could not shave themselves, and the staffing at Mondorf was low, so they didn't receive a shave often. The four dozen men looked more like the tenants of a bowery house than the recent leaders of a mighty nation.

One American second lieutenant, after observing the men in the Palace, said, "Who'd have thought we were fighting this war against a bunch of jerks?"

In the middle of the summer, Andrus gathered all his prisoners and dimmed the lights. "You are about to see a certain motion picture showing specific instances of maltreatment of prisoners by the Germans," Andrus told them. "You know about these things, and I have no doubt many of you participated actively in them. We are showing them to you, not to inform you of what you already know, but to impress on you the fact that we know of it, too. Be informed that the considerate treatment you receive here is not because you merit it, but because anything less would be unbecoming to us."

As the prisoners watched the film taken by American GIs who liberated the Buchenwald concentration camp, they reacted in a variety of ways. The scene would be repeated in dramatic fashion months later in the Nuremberg courtroom during the trials. Hans Frank, Hitler's lawyer and the former governor general of Poland, "held a handkerchief to his mouth and gagged on it for fifteen minutes," Andrus wrote. Joachim von Ribbentrop, Hitler's foreign minister, walked out. Julius Streicher, publisher of the anti-Semitic *Der Stürmer*, rocked back and forth in his chair, clasping and unclasping his hands. Hermann Goering ignored the film altogether. Karl Doenitz grumbled, "If this is American justice, why don't they just shoot me now?"

Ashcan was partially about collecting Nazi leaders, but it also was critical for interrogating Nazis in preparation for the Nuremberg war crimes trial. Soon Andrus and his superiors began to worry that prisoners were comparing notes on their interrogations late in the summer in order to give up less information. Andrus decided to use the Nazis' own deception and mistrust of their American captors against them. If they were comparing notes, he figured, why not eavesdrop on those conversations in order to obtain valuable evidence against them?

Andrus informed some of the prisoners that they were leaving Mondorf and being handed off to the British. He then secured a house, with a high wall around it, in Dalheim, three miles north of Ashcan. British intelligence officers helped add a room to the house that could only be accessed from the outside, and a signals and electronics expert wired the house with small microphones and a recording device. The team filled the house with German furniture and staffed the house with "courteous" British guards. Andrus worked out a circuitous, fifty-mile route around the Luxembourg countryside that would give the Nazis in the back of a windowless army ambulance the feeling that they were driving into northern Germany. Finally, he "leaked" a rumor that a small group would be moved to Germany first, followed by others.

The driver on the two-hour trip took wide left turns to avoid detection and made sharp rights to give the feeling of a southeastern trip. The rough roads Andrus chose enhanced the effect of moving through a scarred German landscape. When they arrived in Dalheim, Goering yelled, "We are at a house I know!" That night, the four Nazis slept on real mattresses and were allowed pillows for the first time all summer. The next day, the prisoners were suspicious of bugs inside the house and moved outside under a willow to talk. But the electronics expert had anticipated that move and had bugged the willow, too.

The next day, a storm kept the Nazis inside the house and

quiet—a disappointment for the team. Worse yet, Andrus got word from London that Ashcan had outlived its suitability as a prison facility. Word had leaked to the press that former Nazi leaders were being collected in Mondorf. The Nuremberg prison was far from ready, but Allied officials believed it more secure than the Palace Hotel. They ordered Andrus to move his charges there within twenty-four hours. The entire Dalheim enterprise had been a bust.

The timing of the order "shocked and annoyed" Andrus. He thought he was just about to get valuable information from Goering when they pulled the plug. He told the four Nazis at the house to pack and drove them back to Ashcan in ten minutes.

The next morning, August 12, Andrus and fifteen of the Nazis boarded two GI ambulances and drove quietly through Mondorf without motorcycle escorts and without sirens. The group boarded two dull gray C-47s whose crews had been told nothing about their cargo. Goering got out of the ambulance, carrying a red hat box in one hand and holding up his pants by his belt loop with the other. The rest of the Nazis followed him on board the two planes.

Andrus informed the lieutenant in charge about his cargo. "It is realized by everyone that these men are considered terrible people," Andrus said. "But it is not our job to judge them or to take justice into our own hands."

The lieutenant grinned at Andrus. "You mean, no leaving the plane without a 'chute,' sir?"

At the Nuremberg prison, Andrus had first recruited two other chaplains—Father Sixtus O'Connor, a Catholic priest from New York, and a twenty-eight-year-old Lutheran chaplain named Carl Eggers. The two men ministered to the Nazis for several weeks, but the senior Nazis were mostly middle-aged men, and they refused to be counseled by a junior officer of Eggers's age. Andrus had to replace Eggers, and Gerecke's experience working in St. Louis's jail system was a plus. "I absolutely needed his services," Andrus wrote later. "I knew of no one else qualified for [the situation]."

But Sullivan was loyal to Gerecke, and he resisted Andrus's request for the chaplain. So before trying to go up the chain of command to protect him, Sullivan had given Gerecke the option of taking the assignment. He had laid out the alternatives: minister to Hitler's henchmen, or go home to his wife.

Gerecke was badly shaken and asked Sullivan if he could think it over. He was terrified by the prospect of being close to the men who had tried to take over the world. Would he have to shake their hands? He imagined that simply feeling their breath on his face would be sickening. How could he comfort these Nazis who had caused the world so much heartache? How could he minister to the leaders of a movement that had taken millions of lives? How could he form a spiritual bond with these men without getting in the way of whatever God had planned for them already? He had conducted hundreds of prison services, but there were obvious differences between burglars in St. Louis and the mass murderers in Nuremberg.

Gerecke had recently traveled to Paris on leave to meet Hank, who was also on a leave, to spend a week as happy tourists in the city of light. They visited the Louvre and walked the banks of the Seine. Hank was twenty-four, and after they ate dinner together each night, he would go out on the town while his father turned in. One morning, after a particularly hard night of partying, Gerecke led Hank on a grueling schedule of sightseeing. "He was torturing me," Hank said later.

Now Gerecke found himself calling Hank for advice. Hank assured his father that he would make the right decision, and that the family would support him and love him no matter what he did. Gerecke walked outside the hospital grounds, found a bench to sit on, and prayed harder than he ever had in his life.

He thought, as any pastor might, of Jesus. According to the Gospel of Luke, Jesus was not alone when he was crucified at Golgotha. On either side of him, the Romans also had crucified two criminals, or "malefactors."

One of the criminals taunted Christ. "Aren't you the Messiah?" he asked. "Save yourself and us."

The second criminal admonished the first. "We've been punished justly for the crimes we committed," he said. "But this man has done nothing to deserve the same fate as ours." The second criminal turned to Jesus and said, "Lord, remember me when you come into your kingdom."

"Today shall you be with me in paradise," Jesus told the criminal. For Christians, Jesus's forgiveness of the criminal before his death is crucial because it represents the sacrificial moment when Christians' sins were forgiven. It also represents an atonement—the reunification of God with his creation.

Christ's forgiveness loomed large in Gerecke's thoughts as he prayed for direction on the park bench. He realized that God wanted something incredible from him. The author of the Gospel of Luke writes that after Christ told the second criminal that they'd be together in Paradise, "darkness came over the whole land . . . while the sun's light failed" in the last moments of Christ's life. Gerecke was staring into that darkness, desperately searching for light. If, as never before, he could hate the sin but the love the sinner, he thought, now was the time.

He walked back into Sullivan's office. "I'll go," he said.

TWO DECADES BEFORE GERECKE arrived, Nuremberg was an ideal place for the young Nazi movement to ground its ideology. For one, the city was the headquarters of *Der Stürmer,* Julius Streicher's newspaper that recycled medieval myths about Jews drinking the blood of Christian children. The newspaper's motto was "The Jews are our misfortune."

Hitler's vision of a Third Reich, or Third Empire, hinged on a version of the medieval idea of *translatio imperii,* or translation of empire. Under this theory, there were three Reichs. The First Reich was the Holy Roman Empire, which lasted from the crowning of the first emperor, Charlemagne, by Pope Leo III on Christmas Day in AD 800 until Emperor Francis II abdicated the throne a thousand years later.

The Second Reich took place during the much shorter period after German unification in 1871 under Chancellor Otto von Bismarck and Kaiser Wilhelm I and lasted until the end of the First World War.

Translatio imperii came from the second chapter of the Old Testament book of Daniel, in which Daniel interprets the dream of King Nebuchadnezzar. The king had dreamed of a great statue with a head of gold, chest and arms of silver, thighs of bronze, legs of iron, and feet of iron and clay. In his dream he watched the statue's feet break apart. The rest of its body soon crumbled "and became like the chaff of the summer threshing-floors; and the wind carried them away, so that not a trace of them could be found."

Daniel explains to Nebuchadnezzar that he and his kingdom are represented in the dream by the head of gold. The silver had represented another "inferior" kingdom, while the bronze was a kingdom that would "rule over the whole earth," and the iron was a kingdom that would crush and smash everything, including all the other kingdoms. In the end, Daniel says to Nebuchadnezzar, "the God of heaven will set up a kingdom that shall never be destroyed. . . . It shall crush all these kingdoms and bring them to an end, and it shall stand for ever."

Biblical scholars mostly have agreed through the centuries that the head of gold represented Nebuchadnezzar's own Babylonian empire (605–539 BC), the silver represented the Persian Empire (539–331 BC), the bronze represented the Greek-Macedonian Empire (331–146 BC), and the iron represented the Roman Empire (146 BC–AD 476). Since Daniel's prediction failed and the apocalypse didn't arrive as the Roman Empire fell—ushering in, for Christians, Jesus's second coming—medieval scholars employed the idea of *translatio imperii* to extend the fourth and final iron kingdom into their own times. They adopted the Holy Roman Empire name to ensure that it would be their own era that would precede the glory of Christ's return.

The city that Hitler would come to see as a perfect place to institute his own version of *translatio imperii* has its origins—at least in legend—in the eighth century when the parents of a Danish prince named Sebald planned their son's succession to the throne. The prince, chosen by his parents for his intellect and virtue, longed to serve God instead of country, so when he reached adulthood, he fled Denmark.

He joined the three children of Britanny's King Richard—Willibald, Wunibald, and Walpurgis—who had similar yearnings for a life of Christian service. Rather than enter a monastery, the four became *peregrinatia pro Christo*—wanderers for Christ, who undertook dangerous journeys and put themselves in harm's way for the sake of Jesus. The four men moved piously across Europe on a pilgrimage that eventually brought them to Rome and then to Germany, where Wunibald established a monastery.

But Sebald set off on his own, preferring the life of a hermit. In the depths of Germany's forest, Sebald prayed, fasted, held vigils for local peasants, and—as tradition has it—performed miracles. Accounts held that he restored the vision of a blind man, fixed broken glass with prayer, and turned water into wine and icicles into firewood. He served as the peasants' teacher and Christian model.

Sebald's harsh environment and fasting eventually caught up with him, and when a group of his beloved peasants found his body one day lying in the forest, they yoked it to two oxen and followed it in a funeral procession. The procession led out of the woods, and eventually the oxen stopped at the site of a deserted former Roman encampment. The peasants buried Sebald in that spot, which is now the center of Nuremberg.

Eventually, as more Christians made pilgrimages to Sebald's

grave, a chapel was built next to it. Sebald was not officially canon-
ized by Rome until 1425, but he was venerated by the town's citizens
for three centuries before that as the patron saint of Nuremberg.

In the early thirteenth century, construction began on a more
ambitious building atop Sebald's grave, and nearly three centuries
later, a huge Romanesque and Gothic parish church with twin
towers climbing toward the sky dominated the center of a thriving
medieval metropolis. The church was known as St. Sebald's. In
1508, church officials commissioned a grand, fifteen-foot-high brass
tomb for Sebald's bones. The artist, Peter Fischer, built the tomb,
placing Christ—"the Lord of the Worlds"—at the top.

Outside St. Sebald's, on the wall of the east choir, is a small
sculpture typical of some medieval churches. It depicts a number
of Jews suckling from the teats of a pig, a creature described in the
Hebrew Bible as unclean. The *Judensau*, as the sculpture was called,
once pointed in the direction of the city's Jewish quarter, just a few
yards to the south. And it is symbolic of Nuremberg's troubled anti-
Jewish history.

Nuremberg was built on sandy soil. Not much has ever grown
there, and its economic status and critical position in Germany's history were drawn from business and politics, rather than agriculture
and trade. The word *Norenberc* appears for the first time in a document from AD 1050 as a reference to a fortress that Emperor Henry
II built on the rocks above today's city. The fortress on Norenberc
hill became a central, and favorite, stop for emperors and their
courts as they traveled from outpost to outpost within the empire. A
settlement developed around the castle and the Pegnitz River, and
by 1400, a three-mile stone wall, with four circular guard towers
at the corners, had been built around the city—a fortress around
the fortress. A hundred years later, between forty thousand and fifty
thousand people lived within Nuremberg's walls.

Nuremberg developed a powerful city council that made decisions
of state and justice, symbolized by a sculpture above the entrance to

city hall. Visitors can still see two reclining figures, Justice and Prudence, bookending a pelican piercing her own breast to feed her chicks with her blood—an allusion to the sacrifice of Christ for man.

The city housed all kinds of tradesmen, but it was known for its metalwork in knives, candleholders, and bowls. Platers made suits of armor, bladesmiths made swords, bowyers made crossbows. It was also known for the masterworks of its medieval and early Renaissance artists who specialized in painting, engraving, woodcuts, portraiture, printmaking, and glass decoration. One artist in particular, Albrecht Dürer, was considered a great master of northern Renaissance art and created religious depictions in the fifteenth to the sixteenth centuries.

Modern historians have shown that German cities with a history of Jewish massacres in the Middle Ages had much higher proportions of anti-Semitic sentiment during the Nazi era.

At the end of the thirteenth century, Nuremberg's Jews built their section of the town on undeveloped swampy land near the Pegnitz River, which divides the city's northern and southern districts. A century later, church officials in the town of Röttingen, sixty miles west of Nuremberg, accused the Jews there of defiling Holy Communion wafers with blood. It was part of a pattern of charges leveled by Christians against the Jews during the Middle Ages that included stories of Jews stealing Communion hosts, piercing them, and draining them of Christ's blood, and Jews kidnapping Christian children, murdering them, and using their blood for Jewish rituals.

In his 1543 tract, "On the Jews and Their Lies," Martin Luther—who called Nuremberg "the eyes and ears of Germany"—wrote that if he had "power over the Jews, as our princes and cities have," he "would deal severely with their lying mouths." Luther hated Jews for both theological and social reasons. Like many medieval German Christians, his belief that Jews had killed Christ found a modern-day outlet in usury.

"We are at fault in not avenging all this innocent blood of our Lord and of the Christians which they shed for three hundred years after the destruction of Jerusalem, and the blood of the children they have shed since then," Luther wrote. "We are at fault in not slaying them."

Long before Luther cursed the Jews and advocated for their deaths, pogroms had been spreading across Europe. Dozens of Jews were killed in Röttingen in 1298 in what became known as the Rintfleisch pogroms, named after a butcher who led the months-long rampage. Over the summer that year, violence spread to more than 140 surrounding communities where roving bands of Christians killed 3,500 Jews. When the gangs arrived in Nuremberg, the city's Jews sought shelter in its fortress, but they weren't allowed in and 600 were killed by the mob.

In 1348, the Black Death began sweeping through Europe. After several Jews "confessed" under torture to starting the plague by poisoning wells and food, rumors spread from town to town in Germany and soon the Germans began burning Jews. In the German towns with Jewish populations, nearly 75 percent witnessed the massacre of their Jewish populations between 1348 and 1350.

On December 5, 1348, the townspeople of Nuremberg targeted the city's Jewish population under the consent of the Holy Roman Emperor Karl IV. The emperor had signed a document allowing for the destruction of the city's Jewish quarter to build a fruit market and a church dedicated to Mary. The result was the annihilation of six hundred people—more than a third of Nuremberg's surviving Jewish population. Not only had the emperor's signature cleared space in Nuremberg, it also solved a problem for many citizens and businesses that had owed large sums of money to Jewish bankers. Much of the borrowing had occurred a year earlier as a result of a government transition that had brought in both Karl IV and a change of control in the Nuremberg City Council.

During the destruction, Nuremberg's residents burned Jewish

homes and shops to the ground. They then constructed a large square—the Hauptmarkt—currently the site of Germany's oldest and most famous Christmas market. It is also the site of the Frauenkirche—the Church of Our Lady—which went up between 1350 and 1358 right where Nuremberg's synagogue had once stood. The emperor dedicated the church with the words: "For the glory of the empire, the honor of the Mother of God and salvation of the dead."

The scapegoating of the Jews didn't end in the medieval ages, however. In the wake of the First World War, some Germans blamed the Jewish population for the nation's defeat. In 1922, Nuremberg's Jewish population of nearly ten thousand was the second largest in Bavaria.

When Hitler walked for the first time into the hall in Frankfurt's government center where the coronation banquets were held for the Holy Roman emperors, he saw the paintings of the emperors hanging on the walls. The three Reichs, wrote Nazi historian Otto Westphal, "appeared to [Hitler's] eye as one grand, sacred, necessary connection." And just as the popes and kings of the Holy Roman Empire saw themselves as the direct descendants of the Caesars of Rome, Hitler saw himself as the historical successor to Charlemagne.

Hitler was unconcerned with the Old Testament's religious symbolism that connected the Third Reich with the Babylonians. Instead, he was interested in his nation's exalted history when the Holy Roman Empire ruled much of Europe absolutely. And he was interested in Nuremberg for its own history as one of the most important cities in the empire.

Hitler believed Nuremberg was Germany's connection to its grand past as well as to the Nazi Party's anti-Semitic rhetoric. In 1927, the year of the Nazis' first Nuremberg Rally, the ministers of St. Lawrence Church on the south bank of the Pegnitz held a ceremony blessing the Nazi swastika. The following year, the Franconia region of Germany, which includes Nuremberg, sent four times more Nazi Party members to the Reichstag than the average from other regions of the country. In 1933, the year Hitler seized power as Germany's chancellor, Nazi paramilitary brownshirts stormed hundreds of Jewish homes, confiscating cash and beating up the homeowners.

In 1933, Willy Liebel, Nuremberg's mayor, presented Hitler with *Knight, Death and the Devil,* one of Dürer's most important engravings, which portrayed a knight riding through a dark Nordic gorge, pursued by a swine-snouted devil. In the drawing, the knight ignores both the devil and death and serves as an embodiment of pious integrity, guided by Christ. The present was a gift from the city's residents, a reminder of Nuremberg's importance to the Third Reich.

The following year, Leni Riefenstahl filmed the sixth Nazi Party Congress in Nuremberg. The rallies themselves were massive propaganda events—in 1934, more than half a million German citizens and soldiers descended on the city.

Riefenstahl's film, *Triumph of the Will,* released in 1935, was propaganda about propaganda. The film begins with words against a black background: "Adolf Hitler flew again to Nuremberg to review the columns of his faithful followers." Riefenstahl carefully orchestrated her presentation of Hitler as a god. The first shot is of puffy white clouds, shot from inside an airplane. With Wagner's *The Mastersingers of Nuremberg* playing in the background, Hitler glides above the city, past the soaring, swastika-bannered spires of St. Sebald and St. Lawrence, before descending down to the adoring German citizens below.

The Nazis had worked hard to crush the Christian churches but found it too difficult, so Hitler attempted instead to co-opt its power through the use of architecture, liturgy, and propaganda. From 1933 to 1939, the Nazis built more than three hundred churches in Bavaria. A popular Nazi poster featured Hitler marching with a Nazi flag and a dove, representing the Holy Spirit, hovering above his head, as rays of light from heaven stream down.

In 1935, Hitler decided Nuremberg was the right stage to announce a new law that would make official the state's anti-Semitic policies. The Nuremberg Laws, as they were known, denied German citizenship for German Jews and prohibited them from marrying or having sex with anyone "of German or related blood." Historians have called the Nuremberg Laws "the worst in the history of human beings."

Hitler had a place for the Jews in his grand vision of a new German empire. And as he stood before the Frauenkirche in the 1930s, on the other side of the Hauptmarkt, reviewing his SA storm-troopers as they marched past him during the Nazi Party rallies, he must have been awed at how well his vision was coming together.

AFTER THE MEN AND women of the Ninety-Eighth threw a farewell party for their chaplain and said their good-byes, Gerecke asked his assistant, Tommy Geist, to come to Nuremberg with him, to be his partner in the most frightening experience of his life. But Geist had learned that he, like Gerecke, was eligible to go home to his wife, and Gerecke didn't press the issue. Geist, however, did want a final road trip with his boss, so on November 11, 1945, they packed Ge-recke's gear into a jeep for the hundred-mile trip north.

What Gerecke and Geist found when they arrived in Germany's medieval crown jewel was a city-sized debris field. According to a report by the Office of Military Government, United States (OMGUS)—the U.S. military's occupation authority in Germany—the city had become "among the dead cities of the European conti-nent," and it had been reduced to rubble by Allied bombers until it was "beyond description."

On the night of January 2, 1945, under a full moon, the Brit-ish had sent more than five hundred Lancaster heavy bombers over Nuremberg. Within an hour eighteen hundred people were killed and 90 percent of the city was destroyed. The castle, the walls, the churches, the city hall, thousands of medieval houses—almost all of it was gone. Another four thousand were killed in subsequent Allied air raids in the following weeks. By the spring of 1945, nothing remained of Nuremberg's one thousand years but rubble and the stench of death.

Yet by November, six months after the Third and Forty-Fifth Infantry Divisions of the U.S. Army had taken the city on Hitler's birthday—April 20, 1945—its population had increased 60 percent. There were now 280,000 people in Nuremberg. Thousands of German soldiers were working in Russian labor camps, and so the majority of the city's residents were women and children.

Nuremberg's remaining citizens peeked out from the lean-tos they'd built from salvaged lumber and bits of sheet metal. Some huddled in air-raid shelters, or house cellars, which were now just holes dug into the earth. Bathtubs hung halfway out from the upper floors of buildings whose front walls had been shorn completely away. Candles flickered from the darkness under the piles where people slept. The sound of the old city was the quiet of a graveyard.

Single rooms, left somehow untouched when the rest of the building had been destroyed, seemed to hover in midair. At night families cooked potatoes or cabbage, foraged from nearby farms, over open fires in the streets. Protein was hard to come by, and Allied rations consisted mostly of bread and potatoes. Some younger mothers resorted to prostitution to feed their children. The journalist Rebecca West wrote, "there was no money" in Nuremberg. "There was only cigarettes." And it was with cigarettes—or soap, or nylons—that American GIs paid the young women, and the women in turn used these to barter for food.

Outside the remains of the Museum of Gothic Art a huge stone head from a statue of God lay on the pavement. "Instead of scrutinizing the faces of men," West wrote, "He stared up at the clouds, as if to ask what He himself could be about." A British fighter plane, lodged in the broken roof of a church, was too high for anyone to remove it, or the body of its pilot. The rubble of Nuremberg, West wrote, "exhaled the stench of disinfectant and that which was irredeemably infected, for it concealed thirty thousand dead." When it rained, death flowed from the wreckage and into the city's drains.

While more than 90 percent of the city was flattened, a few structures—fountains, bridges, parts of the old castle—were miraculously untouched. The Allies chose Nuremberg over Berlin as a trial site because its courthouse—the Palace of Justice—and prison were left intact after the bombing and were connected to each other. However symbolically appropriate it was that the surviving high Nazi criminals would be put on trial in the city that represented so much to Hitler, the choice of Nuremberg was purely pragmatic.

And pragmatism prevailed in the months leading up to the trial. Resurrecting a city that had been declared dead "seemed hopeless," according to OMGUS officials. For one, Nuremberg's police force had been decimated and crime was rampant. Bandit gangs uncovered caches of machine guns and small arms across the region, and over the summer attacked farmhouses outside town, raping women and stealing whatever they could find.

To get the city running again, OMGUS first began de-Nazifying it by firing twenty-two hundred city employees. The agency then installed city government managers at the end of July 1945 and hired one thousand new workers. By November, five hundred police considered "politically clear" had been trained and were walking the beat. Prison buildings were cleaned and repaired, and OMGUS devoted one wing of a prison to housing war criminals and trial witnesses.

OMGUS officials reconstituted local courts and used thirty-four bags and two chests of gold from the Reichsbank vaults to reopen Nuremberg's banks. They turned over control of the trains to a new transport agency and allowed thirty-eight insurance companies to resume business. Scores of horses that had belonged to the German military were handed over to local farmers. Soon enough, four political parties organized, the presses of a German-edited and published newspaper began running, and a tax agency opened its doors to begin collecting public revenues.

Seventy-five percent of Nuremberg's school buildings had been destroyed. Most teachers had been Nazi Party members, and so new teachers were trained, which helped the city bring back twenty-five thousand children to class by November 1945. Because of the "acute housing problem," OMGUS officials attempted to put a roof over everyone in Nuremberg. But the scarcity of materials and labor presented a major hurdle. OMGUS considered gas, wood, coal, and food "critical items" to provide to Nuremberg's residents.

Six months after its capture, the city began to hum again, and most of Nuremberg had electricity, a water supply, and a partial sewage system. Streets and tracks had generally been cleared of rubble, and three hundred streetcars carried a million passengers across the city each week. In addition to military phone lines, OMGUS installed about a thousand civilian phone lines by November. Post office and parcel post service had resumed. Hospitals were repaired and reopened and individual health clinics established. By November, an immunization program was up and running for city residents, and Nuremberg had more hospital beds available than it had since 1939. Two cinemas started showing films again, and two more would open by the end of the year. Theatrical performances were staged for German civilians in nearby Furth and Erlangen.

The one major gripe for Nurembergers was about food and drink—beer in particular. Food had been rationed at 1,365 calories a day per person in the summer. Officials set a goal of 2,000 for the winter. The city lacked meat, partly due to a daily export of meat to Berlin, but worse was the ban on beer drinking. "The prohibition of beer for civilians deprives the population of a daily beverage to which they have become accustomed over many years and will undoubtedly be difficult to enforce," an OMGUS report stated.

"It is true that there is a long way to go and much to be accomplished," OMGUS officials wrote in their November report. "But for a city termed '91% dead' it is felt that definite progress has been made and that Military Government has done a significant job in showing the German people the way."

GERECKE WAS NERVOUS WHEN he arrived at Andrus's office at the Palace of Justice. He'd only had one commanding officer since his time in the army began, and Gerecke could hear the colonel chewing out one of his underlings from outside the door. A corporal walked out, head hung low. "It's about time you got here," Andrus said to Gerecke. "I sure need a chaplain."

You sure do, Gerecke thought.

Andrus waved everyone else out of his office and waved Gerecke in, pointing to a chair. He told Gerecke he'd been born on an army post and raised as an army brat. Andrus may not have served in combat during the First World War, but he liked to say that he'd experienced hostile fire at age two months, when his own West Point–trained father was serving in the American west, battling Indians.

The commandant told Gerecke that a Sunday school teacher had once used ice cream to entice him to attend class. "But I've never forgotten the story she [told]." It was, he said, "the story of a lost sheep, and how the master went out looking for it and brought it back rejoicing. Chaplain, you're going to find lost sheep in our prison and if God is gracious to you, you might bring back a few of them."

Andrus asked Gerecke if he planned to hold services outside the prison, and they discussed an ancient, and badly damaged, church in nearby Mögeldorf that Gerecke could take over. "I'll be out there sometime to surprise you," Andrus said.

But then he issued a warning of sorts: "Chaplain, just remember, you are here to fulfill the requirements of the Geneva Convention."

CHAPTER 6

Judas Window

Beloved, never avenge yourselves, but leave room for the wrath of God.
—ROMANS 12:19

THE NAZIS BARELY RECOGNIZED Nuremberg when they arrived. Albert Speer, an architect who had designed many of Nuremberg's Nazi edifices, could only guess at where the streets had been. "As we moved farther into the center of the city, I grew increasingly confused, for I could no longer get my bearings in this gigantic rubble heap," Speer wrote later. "There, in the midst of all this destruction, as though spared by a miracle, stood the Nuremberg Palace of Justice. How often I had driven past it in Hitler's car. Trite though the idea may be, I cannot help thinking there was a deeper meaning to the fact that this building remained undamaged."

When Andrus arrived, he had his hands full just trying to make sure the new prison was safe and manned with competent staff. The prison was in bad shape from Allied bombing, and German POWs were at work making hasty repairs. The work was being done under the watchful eyes of American GIs, but there weren't enough of them.

A trickle of occupation forces were making their way to Nuremberg, but not fast enough for Andrus, who was furious that the army had allotted only one guard for every fifty German POWs working on the repairs. At one point, Andrus's force had gone from about three hundred men to fifty, and he wasn't happy with the quality of soldier the army was providing him.

There was, at least, a show of force outside the Palace of Justice, with five M24 tanks armed with 75 mm guns surrounding the courthouse. Anyone coming into the court required documentation, and even the tribunal's judges often needed to flash their papers multiple times as they moved around the grounds. Andrus was the only person in the building allowed to carry a weapon. His guards were allowed only billy clubs, which they made from mop handles and painted white.

The Palace of Justice contained 530 offices and 80 courtrooms, all mostly spared by the bombing. The U.S. Army spent $6 million—about $75 million today—renovating Courtroom 600, where the major Nazi defendants would be tried, in a building set back several hundred yards from Fürtherstrasse, the main street Speer and Hitler had once driven down.

Before the trial, GIs removed courtroom walls, creating an additional visitors' gallery, as well as room for the world's press. To accommodate filming, they removed chandeliers and substituted floodlights, blacked out windows, and cut holes in the wooden walls to get the best camera angles.

The prison that adjoined the courthouse was designed in a four-spoked, half-wagon-wheel structure. The army built a long, wooden covered walkway that led to an elevator that deposited the prisoners directly into the defendants' dock in Courtroom 600.

The prison's four wings were divided into three tiers that each held ninety-nine cells. The wings radiated out from a central rotunda where a guard, sitting in a wooden central protective nest high above the main floor of the prison, could control entry and exit in each wing. Two of the prison's wings held civilian prisoners. The other two held Andrus's charges—the defendants and the witnesses called to testify in the trial. Altogether, Andrus oversaw about 250 people housed in the prison cells at any one time, with a total of about 450 moving through during the year of the trial. The major Nazi defendants were held on the ground floor of Wing Four, the spoke closest to Courtroom 600.

When the prison opened in 1868, it was the most modern in Europe; it represented a new concept in resocialization that gave each prisoner his own cell, rather than placing prisoners together in community cells. The prison could be run by five guards, one in each of the four wings and one in the central hub. Its structure mimicked Philadelphia's Cherry Hill Prison (now known as Eastern State Penitentiary), which was based on a correctional theory known as the Pennsylvania system. The theory held that criminals were products of their environments, and that solitude would make a prisoner regretful and penitent.

Each cell measured thirteen feet by six and a half feet. Opposite the wooden door, a window of unbreakable opaque glass opened only halfway to the outside world. The ceiling was slightly concave, giving it a vaulted look, and the floor was made of flagstone. The only thing in the cell not visible from the thick wooden door's one-foot-square peephole—which Gerecke called a "Judas window"—was a seatless toilet and tin washbasin.

Opposite the guard's large peephole in the cell door was a steel cot, fastened to the wall, with a thin straw mattress and two gray army blankets, as well as a table, and a chair. The chair was removed at night and the table was ordered specifically by Andrus to be so rickety that it would collapse under any strain. The commandant didn't want any Nazi suicides under his watch. For the same reason, Andrus ordered ties, shoelaces, belts, and nail files to be taken away from the prisoners.

Yet despite Andrus's careful efforts, two men managed to commit suicide before the trials even began. Leonardo Conti, Hitler's health minister, who took part in the Nazis' eugenics euthanasia program called Aktion T4, hanged himself with a towel fastened to the bars on his cell window on October 6, 1945. Three weeks later, Robert Ley, head of the German Labor Front, hid from his cell's guard by sitting on the toilet. He then looped his jacket zipper to the water-tank lever and created a noose with his towel. With a pair of underwear stuffed into his own mouth to quiet the death rattle, Ley leaned forward until he strangled to death. In one of the notes he left, Ley wrote, "We have forsaken God and therefore we were forsaken by God."

Until the suicides, there had been one guard for every four cells, which meant a check on each cell every thirty seconds. After Ley's death, Andrus required a guard for every prisoner, meaning constant observation for each prisoner for the rest of their time at Nuremberg.

The flagstone corridor outside the Nazis' cells stretched about 25 feet between the two walls of cells. Chicken wire, strung between the two iron catwalks on the second tier, was installed to prevent a prisoner from jumping to his death. At each end of the 175-foot-long corridor, an iron spiral staircase—also laced with chicken wire—led to the upper tiers.

The inmates on these upper tiers had more freedom and less supervision. Some were German POWs who also worked in the prison, preparing meals or doing laundry. Their cells, with larger bunks and thicker mattresses, were a major contrast to the barren cells of the major Nazi inmates' downstairs. The second tier featured a dental clinic, a physiotherapy room, and a chapel with pews for seating fifty men.

But that chapel was off-limits for the twenty-one men on trial for war crimes. Hitler's top lieutenants on the ground floor would have to make do with a smaller chapel, created by knocking down a wall in between two cells. Two candlesticks and some hymnbooks rested on an improvised altar covered by a white cloth. Above the altar, a small crucifix hung on the wall. A couple of wooden benches served as pews, and a U.S. Army chaplain's kit organ sat in the corner. The little chapel was, Andrus wrote, "a sanctified place where, we are told, at least some of these men, accused of such enormous crimes against humanity, are asking forgiveness."

Outside each cell door on the ground floor, Andrus had installed a flood lamp that the cell's guard could shine in on the prisoner at any time. At night, each guard was instructed to point the bright light at his prisoner through the door's peephole. A sympathetic guard might point it at the prisoner's body. A less sympathetic guard trained it on the prisoner's face throughout his watch.

The defendants were not allowed to turn and face the cell wall when they slept. Guards were ordered to yell at any prisoner who turned in his sleep, and even used long poles, stuck through the square hole, to prod the sleeping Nazis awake.

Andrus housed the major defendants in the middle cells along the corridor, leaving the empty cells on each side for storage. One held the defendants' own property. Another was stacked with freshly laundered underwear.

Guards woke up the prisoners shortly before breakfast each day as they changed shifts outside the cells. Twice a week the prisoners could take a hot shower or bath. Otherwise, each man was brought fresh water to wash with at 7:00 A.M. Then, a German POW would hand the prisoner a spoon and breakfast in a U.S. Army "meat can" through the square portal in the cell door. Breakfast usually consisted of "sweet soup," "biscuit soup," or "oats soup"—sometimes with noodles. Occasionally, the prisoners would get bread and sausage, oatmeal, bread with jam, or cereal. Coffee came in a standard army-issue canteen cup without a handle.

Each prisoner was responsible for keeping his own cell clean, and after breakfast, he was handed a broom to tidy up. The prisoners then received cold water to drink, or—in the winter—another cup of coffee. A POW barber, accompanied by an American guard, then visited the cells to shave each prisoner. No conversation was allowed during this process, and the barber was responsible for ensuring that every piece of equipment he brought into each cell also came out with him.

Andrus used a German POW doctor and an American doctor to check the prisoners' health in the midmorning or in the afternoon each day. The prisoners also had frequent visits by the U.S. Army psychiatrist, Dr. Douglas Kelley (and later Dr. Leon Goldensohn) or the U.S. Army psychologist, Gerecke's roommate, Dr. Gustave Gilbert. After a shave, the prisoners were allowed their twenty-minute walks in a small 140-by-100-foot exercise yard, where they were supposed to remain in a single file, but usually fell into groups to talk. A guard wielding a billy club followed eight paces behind while others with machine guns stood sentinel on the walls and in the towers.

Much of the prisoners' time early on was taken up by U.S. Army interrogations, visits with their attorneys in room 57, where they prepared legal defenses, or in discussions with the chaplains. A typical dinner might have featured a simple soup followed by hash, bread or noodles, then scrambled eggs, fish, or sausage, with a dessert of chocolate or cheese and tea. Lights went out at 9:30, and the flood lamps came on.

TRYING INDIVIDUAL GERMAN LEADERS in an international court for their crimes during the war was not an obvious enterprise. In fact, the process of figuring out who to prosecute, and over what events, was arduous and took the Allies years. The creation of the Nuremberg Laws and the destruction of Jewish property and synagogues during Kristallnacht in 1938 were early examples of Germany's wrongdoing. Then, Germany's invasion of Poland in 1939 had violated provisions of the 1929 Hague and Geneva conventions.

Beyond that, there was the persecution, including mass killings, of Jews and others. Roosevelt and Churchill both publicly condemned the reports of Nazi atrocities in the concentration camps, promising "retribution," but saying nothing about how justice would be administered. In 1942, soon after their pronouncement, representatives from nine governments-in-exile—Poland, Norway, Luxembourg, the Netherlands, Belgium, Czechoslovakia, France, Yugoslavia, and Greece—met in London. This body of representatives, known as the Inter-Allied Commission on the Punishment of War Crimes, rejected the idea of vengeance. Instead, they wrote the Declaration of St. James, which stated that "the sense of justice in the civilized world" required them to "place among their principal war aims the punishment, through the channel of organized justice, of those guilty of or responsible for these crimes, whether they have ordered them, perpetrated them or participated in them."

By the end of the year, the United Kingdom, the United States, China, Australia, and India had joined the nine governments-in-exile to form the United Nations War Crimes Commission. The commission's purpose was to investigate war crimes, identify suspected perpetrators, and collect and organize evidence against those perpetrators. In a statement, Roosevelt condemned "atrocities which have violated every tenet of the Christian faith."

Despite the international commission's early promise, its importance waned after Roosevelt, Churchill, Stalin, and their staffs became more involved in the war crimes issue in 1943. Eventually, the commission's principal function became debating the legal aspects of prosecuting war crimes: How, exactly, would the Allies deal with the Nazis once the war was won?

A year before Germany's surrender, Herbert Pell, the U.S. representative on the commission and a New York friend of Roosevelt's, wrote to Sir Cecil Hurst, the British commissioner and chairman of the body and the former president of the Permanent Court of International Justice in The Hague. Pell was growing increasingly frustrated by the lack of legal precedent to support the commission's mandate. "Every nation now at war with either Japan or Germany has expressed the intention of punishing those responsible for outrages. . . . A failure to provide what the people of the world consider to be justice will bring on us obloquy and mockery." Yet, Pell, wrote, "there is no such thing as international criminal law; there is no penalty settled for the violations of the rules of war; the list of war crimes is not a sacred thing accepted since time immemorial." He continued:

> *It seems to me silly to try and haul unsuitable precedents in by the ears to debate on how many murders make a massacre, or whether or not the law passed for the peace-time government or respectable nations can be applied in totally unforeseen conditions; kidnapping, for example, is against the law of France, but it seems rather absurd to invoke the provisions of French domestic law against German officers accused of deporting French civilians, as if they were ordinary kidnappers. . . .*
>
> *Unless we are able to provide the machinery for swift, severe and general justice we will find our work done for us more roughly by the bayonets of invading troops. It is all very well to imagine that British soldiers will pat the heads of innocent yellow-headed children or give soap to German women; this will not be the case of the soldiers of the Continent; a man who has seen his own child starved will not appreciate the beauty of the rosy infants of Germany; a man whose sister has been sent to a German brothel will not fraternize. . . . If we want to avert general massacre, we must satisfy the popular demand for justice.*

Those searching for a war crimes road map had to look back to the Hague Convention of 1899, which defined "The Laws and Customs of Wars on Land" and included a prohibition on the "no quarter" custom of attacking surrendered enemy troops. While the Hague conventions sought to regulate the customs of war, they did not restrict a sovereign state from engaging in war in the first place. Those designing the Allied response to Germany's atrocities wanted to pin responsibility on the Third Reich simply for instigating an aggressive war. But the only directly relevant multinational precedent to support these charges was a 1927 agreement put together by the U.S. secretary of state, Frank B. Kellogg, and French foreign minister Aristide Briand.

The agreement, known as the Kellogg-Briand Pact and titled the "International Treaty for the Renunciation of War," was written to celebrate a decade since the end of World War I. Forty-four countries, including Germany, had signed the pact to "condemn recourse to war for the solution of international controversies, and renounce it as an instrument of national policy in their relations with one another." The parties had also agreed to the settlement of all future disputes and conflicts only "by pacific means."

The men charged with building a trial at the end of World War II debated whether the signatories of Kellogg-Briand had engaged in a crime by breaching the pact and going to war. Kellogg-Briand had not been intended to define self-defensive war as a crime. Legally, war had always been seen as neutral ground in which both sides had the same rights. Waging aggressive war had never been defined as a crime in international law.

Only when German forces began to retreat from France and Belgium in the late summer of 1944 did the Roosevelt administration begin to think seriously about postwar Germany. Nuremberg prosecutor Telford Taylor credited "a group of New York lawyers," working in late 1944 and early 1945, for "the ideas which led to the expanded principles of the Nuremberg trials." The group included Franklin Roosevelt's war secretary, Henry Stimson; Assistant Secretary of War John McCloy; and Lieutenant Colonel Murray Bernays of the Army General Staff.

At the Yalta Conference in February 1945, Winston Churchill proposed to Roosevelt and Joseph Stalin the easiest solution: summary executions. Churchill recommended that once each wanted man was caught and identified by a senior Allied military officer, he should be shot after six hours. Churchill's proposition gained traction with Roosevelt and some in his administration who believed, as Churchill did, that putting Hitler on trial would give the dictator another global stage. In 1944, according to McCloy's papers, American lawyers mounted a mock Hitler trial and discovered that he would have had "endless opportunity for making legal mischief, and, at worst, might [have argued] himself out of a conviction," wrote historian Richard Overy. Stimson opposed the idea of summary executions and argued for a trial that would reflect democratic notions of justice, in contrast to the tyranny and mayhem the world had just witnessed.

In the early days of war crimes planning, while Roosevelt was leaning toward summary executions, Stimson was imagining a different course. He wrote to the president in September 1944 to state that he was "disposed to believe that at least as to the chief Nazi officials, [the U.S.] should participate in an international tribunal constituted to try them." That same month, McCloy summoned Murray Bernays to his office for an update on where the Office of the Judge Advocate General's staff stood on punishment of German war criminals. Bernays was a successful New York attorney before the war, and he would later become a chief intellectual architect of the Nuremberg idea.

McCloy started the meeting by telling Bernays and Colonel Archibald King, chief of the JAG's War Plans division, that there was "considerable pressure, particularly from British sources, by persons of such importance that their advice cannot be brushed aside, to the effect that trials of war criminals, particularly prominent ones, should be extremely brief and amount to little more than indentification [*sic*] of the accused as the person charged, followed by a finding and the sentence." That procedure, McCloy said, "would be especially applicable to persons of prominence whose misdeeds are well known, such as [Heinrich] Himmler. There might not be any opportunity for the accused to summon witnesses."

McCloy said this option was met with "a revulsion" within the

War Department. The "opposite view," he said, was that "there should be a full trial of every accused by military commission." The middle option, which McCloy favored, was "a brief trial of a day or two in length rather than several weeks."

The topic turned to how to define war crimes, and the jurisdiction of the courts that would try those who were accused of committing them. McCloy mentioned the difficulty of prosecuting German nationals who, while working for the German government, interred and killed German Jews.

Bernays replied that as a Jew, he deeply sympathized with the German Jewish population, but that he didn't believe their mistreatment constituted war crimes. For other governments to concern themselves with Germany's atrocities against its Jews "would invite investigations and complaints by other nations of the treatment of Negroes in the United States, Indians by Great Britain, etc."

After someone briefly mentioned "international tribunals for the trial of the most important criminals whose offenses are international in character," the three men ended the meeting with an acknowledgment that "there is at present in existence no detailed directive as to [the] investigation and trial of war crimes or the operation of military commissions."

It was a remarkable moment that would spark one of the most famous trials in history. Yet what was also remarkable was the reticence to try the Nazis for mass murder. The two men agreed that there was no set definition for war crimes, nor was there a working plan by the U.S. government or military yet to prosecute war criminals. Even the president was wavering, telling administration officials that he disliked "making detailed plans for a country which we do not yet occupy."

A week after his meeting with McCloy, Bernays wrote an influential memo that helped shape what became the International Military Tribunal. Bernays acknowledged that there were "many thousands of war criminals all over Europe," and he suggested that the Allies lean on the legal idea of criminal conspiracy to better include those thousands of war criminals under the culpability of various Nazi organizations, such as the SS, SA, SD, and Gestapo. Once the organization was found guilty of conspiracy to commit war crimes, Bernays reasoned, anyone who could be proven to be a member of that organization was also guilty.

McCloy liked Bernays's proposal and invited Bernays to present it to Stimson, who also reacted favorably and showed the plan to Roosevelt. The president "gave his very frank approval," Stimson wrote, when he recognized that "representatives of all classes of actors brought in from top to bottom, would be the best way to try it and would give us a record and also a trial which would certainly persuade any onlooker of the evil of the Nazi system."

In January 1945, Roosevelt wrote a memo to his secretary of state, requesting a report on the status of the work being done by the U.N. War Crimes Commission, "particularly . . . on offenses to be brought against Hitler and the chief Nazi war criminals." Roosevelt wrote that "the charges should include an indictment for waging aggressive war, in violation of the Kellogg Pact. Perhaps these and other charges might be joined in a conspiracy indictment."

Less than three weeks later, Roosevelt received a position paper, approved by his secretaries of state and war and his attorney general, that foresaw an international court that would try both "the highest ranking German leaders" and the Nazi organizations they led. After this major trial, smaller trials would prosecute individual members of those organizations that had already been proven to be criminal. Once prosecutors established the membership of these lesser Nazis in the criminal organizations, their individual punishment would be gauged by the facts in each case. But Roosevelt still would not make up his mind and give the plan final approval.

After Roosevelt's death in April 1945, President Harry Truman assigned Justice Robert Jackson to lead the American prosecution team, and Allied troops began rounding up German war criminals from captured territory. Truman made it clear that he opposed summary executions for the Nazi elite and supported the establishment of a military tribunal. The Americans began cornering and capturing Nazi leaders in farmhouses and basements throughout the Reich. As various SS and Gestapo members were captured, they were interrogated, and the intelligence the Allies obtained led to virtual arrest warrants—most-wanted descriptions used by Allied Nazi hunters—for more Nazis, many of whom were hiding in the vicinity of Aachen:

- *MARKOW, Ernst*
  Locksmith. Party and SA member since 1933. In 1934, became a member of the SS and NSKK [National Socialist Motor Corps]. Actively and brutally engaged in the Jewish pogrom in Nov. 38. Figure: Stocky. Hair: Blond.

- *KLOTTEN, Gerhard*
  Influential member of the SA since 1935. Became famous during the war for his brutal treatment of PW. According to available information he intended to engage himself in agricultural work in the Bergheim area in case of an Allied victory. Figure: Thick set. Hair: Blond.

- *DREESEN, Hans*
  SS officer. In July 1943 he . . . stoned an American pilot and beat him with a rubber truncheon. Residence: Jacobstrasse. Figure: Slender. Eyes: Blue.

As the war came to a close, *New York Times* London bureau editor E. Clifton Daniel Jr. wrote a letter to the U.N. commission, offering an outline for a piece on war crimes that Daniel hoped someone on the commission would write for the *Times* magazine. "Assuming that there is to be no formal reprisal against the German people as a whole, the public would undoubtedly like to know exactly who will be punished, for what reasons, and by what methods," he wrote.

Around the same time, Gordon Dean, who would become Robert Jackson's press aide at Nuremberg, wrote a memo to the Overseas section of the Office of War Information, outlining for the section's Policy Directive the reasons why the U.S. opposed summary execution for the major war criminals. "We believe that whatever their guilt, it should be established in a fair and public trial," Dean wrote, "and that not only should the major criminals be tried, but that they should be tried for their major crimes—crimes which are far more terrible, more far-reaching and more subtle than individual or even mass executions." The reasons for the U.S. position, Dean said, included:

a. *Summary execution, without a documented account of their real guilt, would only result in the world's forgetting their major sins, and these sins must never be forgotten. For current consumption the world must be able to see clearly what they did and how they did it.*

b. *For benefit of future generations, their real crimes must be spread on the history books lest the same patterns be repeated when memories are dimmed.*

c. *Such trials are perhaps the most promising medium for the development of precedents—now lacking because of our failure after the last war to develop an international criminal code—precedents which will be plain to all potential aggressors who might be tempted to repeat that pattern which these trials will expose and condemn. An effective international criminal law can and should result from these trials.*

d. *The concept that guilt should be fairly ascertained is so embedded in the charters of the countries of the civilized that we cannot afford to abandon it here simply because the guilt is great. We fought a war because of what other powers stooped to. Now that victory is here we must not allow ourselves to stoop to their leve.* [sic] *In short, we want a just judgment.*

e. *To try these war criminals only for individual cases of murder or theft of art treasures would be to miss completely—and the world might either never comprehend, or comprehending, forget—the bigger plan or conspiracy which was the real Nazi crime with its network of ramifications, conceived and directed by those in the higher echelons of the Nazi party.*

As Dean and others made clear, there was no legal precedent for framing charges against the captured Nazis. Thus, Allied leaders were still hashing out the best way to punish people whose criminal activities were so horrendous that laws barring those activities didn't technically exist.

Richard Overy wrote that the difficulty for Bernays, Stimson, Jackson, and the other architects of the Nuremberg framework came from defining the crimes in such a way that the laws could be applied to Hitler's henchmen when these men's direct participation in the atrocities at hand would be difficult to prove beyond a reasonable doubt:

> *The radical solution proposed by Jackson and the American prosecution team was to include all the actions deemed to be criminal under the single heading of a conspiracy to wage aggressive and criminal war . . . [which] could rightfully include everything the regime had done since coming to power on 30 January 1933. It could include the deliberate repression of the German people, the plans for rearmament, the persecution of religious and racial minorities, as well as the numerous crimes committed as a consequence of the launching of aggressive war in 1939. . . . Conspiracy caught everyone in the net, regardless of their actual responsibility for specific acts.*

The Americans drew up a list of one hundred candidates for a major trial, but the British wanted around a dozen defendants. At one point, the British even suggested that in the absence of Hitler—

who had killed himself in April—Goering should stand trial as Nazism's lone representative.

A compromise between the two allies put the final number of major war criminals to be tried at twenty-two, which was reduced after Robert Ley committed suicide. Some of the candidates would represent entire factions of the Nazi machinery, making for a dubious legal proposition since one man would stand for whole forces under the Hitler system. Hans Fritzsche, for instance, would represent the Third Reich's propaganda ministry in the absence of its chief, Joseph Goebbels, who had killed his wife, his six children, and himself in Hitler's Berlin bunker the day after the führer's suicide. Walter Funk and Hjalmar Schacht would represent Hitler's economic apparatus. Wilhelm Keitel and Alfred Jodl would represent the German army, the Wehrmacht.

The United States, Britain, France, and the Soviet Union would each seat one judge and one alternate on a tribunal. Each state would also staff a prosecution team to argue the cases against the defendants and Nazi organizations.

The tribunal arguably was considering "retrospective justice—creating crimes in order to punish them." Some legal minds in the West regarded the concept suspiciously, and the defendants and their counsel accused the tribunal of imparting victor's justice. In fact, the Soviet Union had already committed three of the four crimes listed in the formal indictment against Germany that came months later.

In July 1945, Robert Jackson wrote to Lord Wright of Durley, the new chair of the U.N. War Crimes Commission, outlining the plan for a major trial. The defendants, he wrote:

- *Entered into a common criminal plan or enterprise aimed at establishment of German domination of Europe and eventually the world. A plan that went back "many years before the commencement of the war" and that would result in "atrocities and other crimes."*

- *Invaded other countries, in breach of treaties between nations, and planned and launched wars of aggression.*

- *Violated the laws, rules and customs of war, part of a criminal enterprise that was calculated to result in mass murders and ill-treatment of prisoners of war and civilians.*

- *Persecuted political, racial and religious populations as part of their criminal enterprise both inside and outside Germany.*

"Those offenses were committed by members of the SS, the Gestapo, Nazi party leaders, Third Reich government officials and groups within the military establishment," Jackson wrote. "Accordingly, the defendants should be individuals who led those organizations, such as Goering, Hess, Ribbentrop and others."

Jackson went on, "The objective would be to try all the leading defendants in a single main case before an International Military Tribunal, where we shall prove the broad criminal plan and such specific acts as may be desired. Defense of sovereign unity and superior orders would not be entertained."

The four powers settled on the basic structure of the trial in August in a document known as the London Agreement and Charter, which created the International Military Tribunal. After the Allies' conference, Jackson publicly stated that for the first time, "four of the most powerful nations have agreed not only on principles of liability for war crimes and crimes of persecution, but also upon the principle of individual responsibility for the crime of attacking the international peace. . . . If we can cultivate in the world the idea that aggressive war-making is the way to the prisoner's dock rather than the way to honors, we will have accomplished something towards making the peace more secure."

The trial would be awkward, Jackson said, because the Allies would be knitting together Anglo-American criminal procedure with European continental criminal procedure. It would be slow, he said, because every word spoken in the tribunal would have to be translated into English, German, French, and Russian. "But I do not think the world would be poorer," he said, "even if it takes a month or so, more or less, to try these men . . ."

Ultimately, the Allies would have to summon all that they had "of dispassionate judgment to the task of patiently and fairly presenting the record of these evil deeds in these trials," Jackson said. "We must make clear to the Germans that the wrong for which their fallen leaders are on trial is not that they lost the war, but that they started it."

Jackson's ability to summon dispassionate judgment took conviction, but organizing the prosecution's case for the trial of the century within a few months took a lot of sweat and worry. As a start date approached, Jackson's staff of attorneys and his assistant grew increasingly anxious about their readiness. On September 6, Telford Taylor wrote Jackson a memo that opened with the words: "We are all worried about." Among his worries were: "The fact that the list of defendants is in many respects not representative of the accepted purpose of our mission," "the fact there are more defendants within the scope of our mission than can be readily dealt with in one proceeding," "the fact that the evidence in hand to date does not 'mesh well' with the published list of defendants," "drafting an indictment against these defendants with only a little of the evidence at hand," and, finally, "lots of other things."

On October 19, 1945, prosecutors filed an indictment that was broken into the four charges that Jackson had previously outlined for Lord Wright. One of those was that Germany had persecuted various populations of Europe based on politics, race, and religion.

Religion was something the Allies were also going to have to contend with, specifically, whether to supply the architects of the Holocaust with a Christian minister to comfort their spirits as they explained to the world the murder of six million Jews. The decision for adding this provision had come late and was possibly more controversial even than putting the Nazis on trial.

But those organizing the tribunal knew that if they were going to try some of the world's most notorious criminals for war crimes, they also had to follow the Geneva Convention. Article 16 of the convention's regulations regards the "Treatment of Prisoners of War" and states that prisoners of war are permitted "complete freedom in the performance of their religious duties, including attendance at the services of their faith. . . . Ministers of religion, who are prisoners of war, whatever may be their denomination, shall be allowed freely to minister to their co-religionists."

The Allies had been capturing war criminals for years. As victory, and with it the certainty of holding many more prisoners, loomed in February 1945, General Omar Bradley, leader of the Twelfth Army Group, wrote a letter to the commanding generals of several U.S. Army units. Bradley stated that all war criminals would be "granted the protection and privileges afforded by the Geneva Convention."

Several months later, the army's European Theater of Operations headquarters under General Dwight Eisenhower issued "Standing Operating Procedure No. 49: Employment of Prisoners of War," which outlined regulations for the religious rights of POWs, allowing for the freedom to attend religious services, for clergymen who were POWs to minister to prisoners, for visiting ministers to privately administer to the spiritual welfare of prisoners, and for officers at POW camps to bring in ministers from other camps.

Visiting clergy were to "discuss only matters which pertain to their religious duties" and were not to—among other things—"deliver to, or receive directly from, prisoners any letters, papers, documents or articles."

BEFORE THE NUREMBERG TRIALS, there are no records of American military chaplains being assigned to provide religious support to the enemies of their country. Throughout history, captured clerics typically ministered only to their own flocks in prisoner-of-war camps where they, too, were prisoners.

But the strict security at Nuremberg made it impossible to assign German army chaplains to look after the spiritual needs of Hitler's inner circle. Instead, with the world's attention turned to postwar Germany, the Allies decided that despite the charges of war crimes and crimes against humanity leveled against the defendants, these men deserved spiritual succor. So the U.S. Army gave the men two of its own. This would be something new for the army chaplaincy. An experiment.

The trial had not yet begun when Gerecke arrived in Nuremberg on November 15, 1945, to join the 6850th Internal Security Detachment—Andrus's Nuremberg prison unit.

"You're going to find another chaplain downstairs," Andrus told Gerecke as the commandant led him out of his office after that first meeting. "He'll be your assistant."

In the small chaplain's office, Gerecke met chaplains Sixtus O'Connor and Carl Eggers. The men filled in Gerecke on the particulars of each of the twenty-one prisoners, the witnesses, and other Nuremberg prisoners whose souls they would be responsible for.

Along with Gustave Gilbert, Gerecke and O'Connor were the only members of the prison staff who spoke German. Gerecke was impressed with O'Connor's accent. "How does a man with a name like O'Connor speak German so well?" Gerecke asked him. O'Connor explained that his mother spoke German as he was growing up, and he'd studied the language since high school. He said he'd come to Germany to study theology in Munich before the war.

As a child, Richard O'Connor, the son of a schoolteacher and construction worker who'd come to upstate New York from Ireland, had enjoyed a classical education studying the works of Virgil, Cicero, and Horace in Latin (and getting mostly Cs). He spent the latter half of his college years at St. Bonaventure in New York in philosophy classes: logic, cosmology, criteriology, ethics, metaphysics.

His grades were average—mostly Bs and Cs. In theodicy—the study of why a good and loving God allows evil—he got a B.

As O'Connor had grown as an intellectual, he became interested in how modern philosophy and science were attacking "the great Doctors of the Church."

"Materialism and positivism have attempted to replace scholastic thought as the guiding light to truth," he wrote in St. Bonaventure's literary magazine, *The Laurel*, in 1926. In Italy's universities, "science had absorbed philosophy and religion proclaiming itself the infallible guide to man in his unceasing search for truth."

O'Connor was writing about one of his heroes, Agostino Gemelli, an Italian scientist and a Franciscan. If science was infallible, Gemelli thought, the Catholic Church was only "the symbol of all that is ignorance and superstition," according to O'Connor.

Gemelli became a successful doctor and scientist, but toward the end of the nineteenth century, O'Connor wrote, "Europe began to throw off the fetters of positivism and fanatic idealism and to return to the only true guide to nature's problems. Men saw that these false systems were limited and when success and truth seemed at hand the doors were bolted, and the candle, their only guiding light wavered and went out, leaving them again in the darkness of oblivion from whence they had started."

Gemelli eventually founded the Catholic University of the Sacred Heart in Milan. In his essay, O'Connor told the story of a morning in 1903, when Gemelli was still studying for the priesthood. He had left his home in Pavia for the Franciscan novitiate in Pezzato, "high in the Alps of Brescia."

As Gemelli gazed out from his cell window and saw the landscape, filled with sunshine and the brilliant color of the meadow, his glance strayed far off where the meadow and hills converged to one point on the far horizon. "All that is real, all that is true," he mused, "converges in one absolute truth, God."

In 1929, O'Connor dropped out of St. Bonaventure College

and followed Gemelli's example into the Order of the Friars Minor. He moved to Paterson, New Jersey, and entered the novitiate—the period of training prior to taking vows when a candidate for the priesthood discerns whether the life is right for him. On August 19, 1929, O'Connor received the name "Sixtus," after Pope Sixtus IV, the fifteenth-century Franciscan pontiff who is credited with transforming Rome from a medieval city to a Renaissance hub that housed papal art collections, Vatican libraries, and the eponymously named Sistine Chapel.

O'Connor professed his temporary vows after a year in the novitiate and then made his perpetual vows years later after completing the intense spiritual reflection and academic study necessary for ordination as a priest.

After his ordination at Catholic University in Washington in 1934, O'Connor celebrated his first Mass at St. Joseph's parish, the church across from his boyhood home in Oxford, New York. His father was dying and too sick to attend, so the pastor of St. Joseph's rigged a sound system that piped the Mass into the O'Connor house.

That fall, O'Connor left for the Franciscan Monastery in Fulda, Germany, to complete his final year of theology and learn German. His plan was to become fluent enough that he could do graduate work at the great universities in Germany, and in September 1935 he began at the University of Munich.

At that time, Munich was home to the Nazi Party, which had recently assumed power in Germany. A year after O'Connor arrived, one of his professors, who was Jewish, was harassed by party thugs and fled the city. O'Connor followed, enrolling at the University of Bonn to study philosophy and the classics. Three years later, after Hitler invaded Poland in September 1939, O'Connor returned to New York and taught philosophy and classical languages at Siena College, a Franciscan school in Loudonville. It was the beginning of his love affair with teaching.

Despite his happiness at Siena, as the United States became

more involved in the war, O'Connor felt called to be a part of it. The thirty-four-year-old was anxious to become an army chaplain and the Franciscans granted his request. In his application for the chaplaincy, O'Connor listed his height as five seven and a half and his weight as 150 pounds. He listed his philosophy-teaching credentials under "experience," and under "additional experience," wrote, "Amateur theatricals, college professor four years. Track and golf." Under "languages," he said he knew Latin, German, and French. The closest person in the priest's life was his fifty-eight-year-old mother, and he listed "Mrs. E. A. O'Connor" as his contact on any official army documents that asked for one.

When he arrived in Nuremberg, O'Connor was thirty-six. He'd had a hard war, and Gerecke guessed the priest to be in his forties. After their introductions, Eggers led Gerecke to the cells on the ground floor of the prison. They stopped first at the cell of Rudolf Hess, Hitler's deputy who had flown a secret solo mission to Scotland during the war to try to broker a peace agreement between Germany and the United Kingdom. Most of the attorneys and judges at Nuremberg were sure that Hess was mentally unstable, but the tribunal had decided to go through with his trial.

Gerecke was frightened as they approached Hess's cell door. "How could I say the right thing, and say it in German?" he thought. When they entered, Hess, who was six three, stood up from his bunk, towering over Gerecke.

"This is Chaplain Gerecke, who will be on duty here from now on," Eggers told Hess. "He will conduct services and be available for counsel if you wish to have him."

Gerecke offered the Nazi his hand, and Hess took it.

The act of an army chaplain physically touching a Nazi so repelled Americans that Gerecke was later severely criticized for even shaking hands with the defendants. It wasn't an easy gesture for the chaplain to make, and it didn't mean that he was unconcerned with their crimes. Yet he wrote later that he had offered his hand "in order that the Gospel be not hindered by any wrong approach I may make. . . . I knew I could never win any of them to my way of thinking unless they liked me first."

"Furthermore," he continued, "I was there as the representative of an all-loving Father. I recalled too, that God loves sinners like me. These men must be told about the Saviour bleeding, suffering and dying on the Cross for them."

After the men shook hands, Eggers excused himself, leaving Gerecke and Hess alone. In meeting these men, Gerecke strived to remember that before their alliance with Hitler, before the choices they made that led to mayhem and murder, they had all been boys once and that they were still God's children.

Rudolf Hess was born in Alexandria, Egypt, in 1894, the son of a wealthy German import-exporter. Rudolf was being groomed to take over his father's business when the First World War broke out and he was drafted into the German army. He fought in the same regiment as Adolf Hitler, though the two didn't know each other during the war.

Rudolf later rose to the rank of first lieutenant in the army air force but was discharged after suffering a chest wound in 1917. After the war, he attended the University of Munich, where he studied with a geography professor named Karl Haushofer, founder of the theory of *geopolitik*, which bridged traditional German imperialism and the rising ideas of national socialism. Haushofer took the concept of *lebensraum*—which means habitat, or living space—and applied it to post–First World War Germany. He promoted the idea of German expansion to the east, beyond its own borders, as a means of ensuring future national growth and prosperity.

Hess entered the Nazi Party in 1920 after hearing Hitler speak. He was jailed with Hitler in 1924 for his part in Hitler's failed revolutionary attempt in Munich known as the Beer Hall Putsch, which had occurred a year earlier. In jail, Hess helped his cellmate write his autobiography, *Mein Kampf*. Hess had taken stenography before the war, and Hitler dictated much of the book to him. But some of *Mein Kampf*'s basic ideas—including those on *lebensraum*, Britain's role in history, and the organization of the Nazi Party—came from Hess.

As Hitler amassed power, he kept Hess at his side. The two had become close in prison, and while it was obvious that Hess didn't have any particularly useful skills, Hitler promoted him to deputy leader in 1933 and then, in 1939, to be third in line to lead the Reich. Hess was one of the few men whom Hitler addressed in the familiar form of "you," *du*.

Hess was introverted, shy, and insecure. He had sought out father figures such as Haushofer and Hitler and had clung to them. He had repaid Hitler's loyalty by near-comic, childlike allegiance and fetishistic devotion. "There is one man who is always above criticism," Hess said in one speech. "That is the Führer. This is because everyone knows and feels he is always right and always will be right. . . . We believe that the Führer has a higher calling to the shaping of Germany's fate." All that was needed was "faith without criticisms, surrender to the Führer, not to ask why but the silent carrying out of his orders."

Hess's take on "the Jewish problem" was aligned with Hitler's. He wanted more than just *lebensraum;* he wanted Germany and all its future holdings to be rid of Jews.

After the failed attempt at peacemaking with Britain that involved Hess flying from Germany under cover of night and parachuting into Scotland, Hess was deemed insane by Hitler. He spent years in prison, some in the Tower of London. Even so, his loyalty to Hitler remained.

Hitler may have been right about Hess's sanity. Hitler's sycophant was on trial for his part in planning Germany's invasions of Poland, Norway, and Yugoslavia, yet his mind in Nuremberg seemed to wander back to his days in prison in Britain.

In Hess's cell, Gerecke tried out his German. "Would you care to attend chapel service Sunday evening?" he asked.

"No," Hess replied in English.

Gerecke needn't have worried about his own German. Hess's English was excellent, and so Gerecke switched to English. "Do you feel you can get along as well without attending as if you did?"

"I expect to be extremely busy preparing my defense," Hess said. "If I have any praying to do, I'll do it here."

Gerecke tried to leave Hess with a copy of St. John's Gospel and a folder of other Christian materials, but Hess refused to take it, saying it would appear as if he was accepting the material only because he was facing trial, and he did not want to look weak.

Gerecke backed out of the cell, wondering if he should have done as Sullivan had suggested in Munich and played the old-age card to get a ticket home. "My first attempt and a good failure," the chaplain thought.

He paced up and down the corridor outside Hess's cell a few times, waiting for Eggers to return. The guards stared. Gerecke realized Eggers wasn't coming back, and that he could either retreat or forge ahead.

As Gerecke approached the next cell he realized it belonged to Hermann Goering, the Nazi he dreaded meeting more than any of the others.

"You want in now, Chappie?" Goering's guard asked.

"Yes, but don't push!" Gerecke said. He watched Goering through the Judas window for a minute before going in. Hitler's number two was reading a book and smoking his meerschaum pipe. Gerecke entered the cell, and Goering shot up, clicking his heels to attention. When Gerecke greeted Goering in German, Goering bowed. They shook hands.

"I heard you were coming, and I'm glad to see you," Goering said. He offered Gerecke his only chair. "Will you come in and spend some time with me?" he asked.

Like Gerecke, Goering had not seen his family in some time, and he welcomed any visitors into his cell who he believed would offer substantial conversation.

Ten weeks after Hermann Goering had been born, his mother, Franny, sailed to Haiti, where Hermann's father, Heinrich, held a ministerial post, leaving newborn Hermann with family friends. Hermann wouldn't see his mother again, nor meet the rest of his family, until he was three years old. Goering biographer Willi Frischauer wrote that later in life, Goering "was always trying to recapture the mother love which he had missed in his infancy."

When he was ten, Hermann was shipped off to boarding school in Ansbach, Germany, which he despised. He wrote about his god-father and namesake, Hermann von Epenstein, in an essay for an assignment about "the man I admire most in the world," and he was hauled into the principal's office the next day to answer why he so admired a Jew. He answered that Epenstein was Catholic, but he was forced nevertheless to write "I shall not write essays in praise of Jews" a hundred times. He was then forced to march around campus with a sign around his neck that read, *"Mein pate ist ein jude,"* which meant "my godfather is a Jew."

The next day, Hermann cut the strings of all the instruments in the school band, smashed his own violin, and hopped a train back to his parents' house. The Goerings then sent Hermann to military academies—where he thrived—for the rest of his academic career; he eventually graduated at age nineteen with a commission in an infantry unit known as the Prinz Wilhelm Regiment No. 112 and was posted to its headquarters at Mülhausen.

In his hagiography of the reichsmarshal, Charles Bewley wrote that Goering's "highest aspiration even in his most youthful days was to become an officer and play a role in his country's history. It was the typical romantic dream of a German youth, and only a greater determination to realize his dream at all costs distinguished him from thousands of contemporaries of his class."

Goering graduated from military school directly into combat in the First World War. He went on to become a war hero, flying in the Imperial German Army Air Service under Manfred von Richtofen, the famed Red Baron.

The prestige he won during the war and his aristocratic background made Goering an ideal recruit to Hitler's young political movement. In 1922, Hitler made Goering leader of the SA Brownshirts, the early paramilitary wing of the Nazi Party.

In 1923, Goering was wounded in the Munich Beer Hall Putsch, and he spent the next four years in exile in Austria, Italy, and Sweden, where he developed an addiction to morphine. In 1927, Goering and his Swedish wife, Carin, returned to Germany, where he rejoined the Nazi Party and the following year became one of its first officials elected to the Reichstag, Germany's parliament.

For the next five years, Goering's contact in the business and military worlds helped Hitler amass power. Carin died of tuberculosis in 1931, and a heartbroken Goering threw himself into politics. In 1932, he became president of the Reichstag, and the following year, Hitler became Germany's chancellor. As the Nazis claimed control of Germany, one of Goering's rewards from Hitler was authority over the party's security apparatus, and he immediately created the first concentration camps for Hitler's political opponents. In 1935, Hitler appointed Goering commander of Germany's air force, the Luftwaffe, and the following year also put him in charge of Germany's economic vision for the future, called the Four Year Plan. That position allowed Goering to accumulate a massive fortune through the state-run Hermann Goering Works, a network of industrial businesses that eventually employed seven hundred thousand people.

Goering was married a second time, in 1935, to an actress named Emmy Sonnemann, and their only child, Edda, was born in 1937. He built a huge country hunting estate in the forest northeast of Berlin and named it Carinhall, after his first wife. Goering called himself "the last Renaissance man," and he had a taste for the theatrical. He used Carinhall as an official meeting place for the Third Reich and entertained heads of state and diplomats, as well as Nazi leaders, with huge feasts during which he would descend from a staircase dressed in a sixteenth-century German hunting costume and carrying a boar spear.

Carinhall was a hunting estate, built by a man who loved animals. Tame lions padded around inside the house. Goering was Germany's chief forester and made sure laws were passed that banned the inhumane treatment of animals. Unusual or cruel traps were forbidden, as was hunting with horse and hounds. Hunters had to employ dogs that would retrieve game that had been wounded by shot.

When Goering left Carinhall, he did so in style on his own train—ten cars led by one called "the bomb clearer." The ceiling woodwork and furniture in Goering's car were made of cherry. The car included two bedrooms, a library with plush carpeting, and shelves filled with detective stories. Only Goering was allowed to use the bathroom, and when he wanted to take a bath, the train stopped for as long as that took, delaying all other trains on that section of track until he was out and dried off. The following car included a movie theater and showed films including *Gone with the Wind* and *Ninotchka*, starring Greta Garbo. On either end of the train, which staffed 171 crew and guards, 20 soldiers manned air defense batteries. The dining car served strawberries or lobster flown in from Italy by courier planes accompanying the train, or cakes baked in the train's own ovens.

In 1939, Hitler named Goering his designated successor, and the following year he promoted him to reichsmarshal—a title held previously by only one other, the eighteenth-century Habsburg military commander Prince Eugene of Savoy.

While Goering's personal anti-Semitism was restrained, compared to the obsessions of other Nazi leaders, because of his position at the top of the Nazi hierarchy, it was Goering who gave some of the most genocidal orders of the Second World War. On July 31, 1941, he sent an order to Reinhard Heydrich, head of the Reich Security Main Office, or RSHA. "I hereby charge you with making all necessary preparations with regard to organizational and financial matters for bringing about a complete solution of the Jewish question in the German sphere of influence in Europe," Goering wrote. It was the order that put in motion the Holocaust. Six months later, Nazi leaders met in Wannsee, outside of Berlin, to work out the logistics of the mass slaughter of Europe's Jews.

The timing of Goering's most famous order coincided with the end of his favor with Hitler. In 1940, Goering led Operation Eagle, the air attack on Great Britain. Tactical errors doomed the mission, and consequently Operation Sea Lion, the planned Nazi invasion of England. In 1941, the Luftwaffe failed to produce victories on the Russian front, and later it couldn't defend Germany's own soil from enemy bombers. Hitler blamed the change in momentum in the war on Goering and began isolating him, handing responsibilities and influence to his rivals—Heinrich Himmler, Joseph Goebbels, and Albert Speer.

In February 1945, as the war began to look lost for Germany, Goering was at Carinhall packing up as many rugs, tapestries, and artworks as he could before Russian tanks arrived. He supervised the packing of his drinking glasses, shot four of his favorite bison that roamed on the estate, and drove away toward Berlin.

Emmy and Edda had been sent off to relative safety in Bavaria a month earlier with four truckloads of art. More art kept coming in the weeks after their arrival. A few hours after Goering fled Carinhall, engineers from the Luftwaffe's paratroop division, following Goering's orders, mined the mansion with dynamite and turned it to rubble.

Goering reported to Berlin, and on April 20, Hitler came out of his bunker underneath the Reich Chancellery for the final time to celebrate his birthday. It was not a happy one. The Russians were already circling the city, preparing to seize it. After a final good-bye with the führer, Goering fled to Obersalzberg, a Nazi mountain retreat south of Munich, where he rejoined Emmy and Edda; there he received word from General Alfred Jodl that Hitler intended to shoot himself before being taken by Soviet troops. Goering reviewed a 1941 decree—locked away in a steel box—in which Hitler had designated him his successor: "If I should be restricted in my freedom of action, or if I should be otherwise incapacitated," it read, "Reich Marshal Goering is to be my deputy or successor in all offices of State, Party and Wehrmacht."

Goering believed that Hitler had been cut off in his Berlin bunker, and on April 23, he sent word to Hitler that he would take control of Germany unless he heard back by 10:00 P.M. that evening with different orders. In the bunker, Hitler had become hysterical and morose, and he spent his time concentrating on the logistics of suicide. He reacted to Goering's telegram with apathy, giving no hint that he believed Goering's actions to be disloyal.

Indeed, the day before, he had suggested that Goering could handle final negotiations with the Allies better without him. But Hitler's secretary, Martin Bormann, who despised Goering and had been hounding Hitler for months to dismiss him, was intent on portraying the reichsmarshal as engineering a coup d'état.

Bormann was soon handed another telegram from Goering to be passed along to the Nazi foreign minister, Joachim von Ribbentrop. The message requested that Ribbentrop join Goering in Bavaria by midnight unless he'd had alternative instructions from the führer. The message was enough ammunition for Bormann to convince Hitler that Goering was attempting to cut off his power. Hitler flew into a rage, and Bormann drew up a document that rescinded the 1941 transfer-of-power decree and ordered Goering to give himself up to avoid execution. Then Bormann sent another telegram to the SS, ordering Goering's arrest for treason.

Goering had no intention of taking control of Germany without Hitler's permission, but the SS had surrounded his house below

Obersalzberg, in Berchtesgaden, where he'd holed up with his staff, wife, and daughter. The next morning, Allied bombs destroyed Hitler's residence and most of Goering's. As Goering and the SS surveyed the destruction, Goering turned to one of the SS leaders and asked that a message be sent to Hitler. "Tell him that if he believes I have betrayed him, I am prepared to be shot."

Goering convinced the SS that they should all get out of Obersalzberg and take refuge at Mauterndorf Castle, one of Goering's homes, about 150 miles away in Austria. It took the convoy thirty-six hours to reach Mauterndorf, and when they arrived, they learned that Hitler had stripped Goering of his titles and party membership and had replaced him as successor with Grand Admiral Karl Doenitz. Goering and his family heard about Hitler's suicide on April 30 as they sat around a radio. A week later, Germany surrendered, ending the war in Europe.

The Americans had been looking for Goering since he had been in Berchtesgaden. After Goering arrived in Mauterndorf, he sent a note to Seventh Army Headquarters in Kitzbuhel, Austria, detailing the terms of his surrender. But when the Americans reached the predetermined destination—Fiéschorn Castle, near Zell am See, Austria, about fifty miles south of Berchtesgaden—Goering was not there. He'd become impatient waiting for the Americans and had gone to find them.

On May 7, Brigadier General Robert Stack, assistant division commander of the Thirty-Sixth Infantry Division, decided to search for Goering with two men. When they found him, the reichsmarshal and his entourage of eighty were having lunch on the side of the road. By 11:30 P.M., in a convoy of twenty-five vehicles led by Stack, Goering and his family entered Fischorn. Goering was now more leery of the SS than the Americans, so Stack allowed him to keep a hunting knife, a .38-caliber Smith & Wesson, and two machine-pistols, along with his reichsmarshal's baton—topped with a diamond-encrusted swastika and encased in green felt—the symbol of his rank.

The Goerings believed they had chosen a better fate by giving themselves up to the Americans, instead of surrendering to the Russians. Goering's wife, Emmy, later wrote:

> *Very fortunately for us, General Stack was a man of great tact. He had brought an interpreter with him and although my husband spoke English perfectly he had every word translated, since every detail was so important. I heard everything. Stack had telephoned to General Eisenhower to tell him of Hermann's letter.*
>
> *The American commander-in-chief had said that he was ready to see Hermann and was waiting for him to come the next day with General Stack. We were all now under Eisenhower's personal protection and were able to move into the castle of Fischorn at Bruck, near Zell-am-See until we knew whether Burg Veldenstein, Hermann's house, was still standing. We would then go and live in it. Eisenhower had given his word that my husband would be able to see him and leave again in freedom.*

But no such accommodations had been made. The American officers in charge of Goering in Augsburg had kept up the ruse of friendliness to see what information he might give up. They let him drink and he did so each night, often until 2:00 or 3:00 A.M. After two weeks, the Americans transferred Goering to the division command post at Kitzbuhel's Grand Hotel, a resort in Austria. Goering shared a drink with Stack and two other American generals, and the four men ate chicken, peas, and mashed potatoes together.

Then Goering was stuffed into a Stinson L-5 Sentinel, a two-seater plane that barely held his 264 pounds, and flown to Seventh Army Headquarters and Interrogation Center in Augsburg, Germany.

In Augsburg, the army stripped Goering of his military decorations, which included his Grand Cross of the Knight's Cross with Swords and Diamonds and his Pour le Mérite, his reichsmarshal dagger (described as the Mona Lisa of daggers), his gold epaulets, the huge diamond ring on his fourth finger, and his prized solid gold baton. Goering was questioned for two weeks.

Goering asked to speak with Eisenhower, and on May 20, he stepped off the plane, expecting to be whisked off to meet the general. Instead, he arrived in Andrus's office at Mondorf. Goering was wearing his sky blue Luftwaffe uniform, and he had brought with him sixteen matching, monogrammed suitcases, a red hat box, and his valet, Robert Kropp. Goering was sweating profusely. For some reason, his fingernails and toenails were painted bright red.

Since his capture Goering's valet had dragged around Goering's gold Luftwaffe badge with diamonds, a Movado travel clock, a gold cigarette case inlaid with amethyst and monogrammed by Prince Paul of Yugoslavia, a gold-and-velvet cigar box, a Cartier watch set with diamonds, a gold pencil, an emerald ring, a diamond ring, a ruby ring, a diamond brooch, and a gold stickpin with a swastika made of diamond chips.

Andrus found a huge stash of pills among Goering's things, and Ashcan's doctors soon learned that Goering was addicted to Paracodin, the German equivalent of Vicodin, and that he swallowed forty pills a day. He told Andrus he needed the pills "for his heart." Goering's morphine addiction had over the years turned into a reliance on pills.

The reichsmarshal's medical checkup at Ashcan wasn't good: "A very obese man about 53 years of age, perspiring profusely, short of breath but not acutely ill. . . . His skin is moist, pale and sallow, except his face, which is flushed. There is also a marked irregular tremor of both hands and he appears to be extremely nervous and excited."

Guards also found a brass shell containing a vial of cyanide—enough to kill a dozen men—inside a tin of Nescafé. They found another sewn inside one of Goering's uniforms.

In a letter addressed to Eisenhower, Goering complained about the conditions at Mondorf: it was damp, there were no electric lights, he didn't have a comb, his pipe had been taken away.

Over the next few months in Mondorf, army doctors slowly weaned Goering from his addiction, and by the middle of August he was clean and twenty pounds lighter.

From the time he arrived at Mondorf until the night of the executions at Nuremberg eighteen months later, Goering held a position of influence and authority among his Nazi colleagues. He had been the most popular of the Nazi leaders with the German people, nicknamed "Der Dicke," the Fat One, to his delight, by the people. He was the highest-ranking Nazi official still alive, and soon enough he would be the star of the Nuremberg trials.

As Gerecke sat in Goering's cell, the former reichsmarshal unloaded a considerable amount of charm on him. He spoke quickly and politely, asking about Gerecke's family and promising to come to chapel services.

Gerecke was a natural listener, but he also knew Goering was doing everything in his power to impress him. From that moment until Goering's death, Goering only called Gerecke "Pastor," never "Chaplain."

"What did Mr. Hess say about coming to chapel?" Goering asked.

Gerecke told him that Hess had declined his invitation.

"That's too bad," Goering said. "I'll tell you, Pastor, I'm going to do this for you. I'm going to try to persuade Mr. Hess to come to chapel." Later in the day, during one of the prisoners' exercise walks, Gerecke listened from a window above the courtyard as Goering did as promised and tried to convince Hess to come to chapel.

"Why did you turn down the Pastor's invitation?" Goering asked.

Hess told him.

"Listen, Herr Hess. Since the Führer is dead, it might do us both good if we were both seen in chapel services," Goering said. "Pastor Gerecke might say something nice about us."

"I have no intention of going to chapel!" Hess said.

The next time Goering saw Gerecke, he apologized for his failure to persuade Hess to come to chapel. Goering, on the other hand, never missed a service.

"Another day with the men upon whom all the world has set its eyes, and mostly for condemnation," Gerecke wrote to Alma on November 19, four days after he'd arrived in Nuremberg. "Well, maybe so but there's something going on inside their hearts since I have been seeing them that can only be measured in spiritual values."

He told Alma that the previous day he'd preached to another congregation of German prisoners, the high-ranking Nazis living on a different level of the prison, who were to be witnesses in the trial of the major war criminals. It was, Gerecke wrote, his "first German sermon in 15 years, and it wasn't too easy." The Nazi witnesses encouraged Gerecke though. "They said they were truly moved from the way I presented the Gospel to them."

The chapel had been packed. Hess's former secretary was there. She told Gerecke it was the first service she'd been to since the Nazis had taken over Germany. General Field Marshal Albert Kesselring, who had directed the bomb attacks on air bases in southeast England during the Battle of Britain and was later commander of German forces in Italy, was "moved to tears" during Gerecke's sermon. "He is one gentleman who stands out above the lot, I think," Gerecke wrote.

In his monthly report for November, Gerecke wrote that although Nuremberg was "a city of ruins, nothing has been left undone to make my stay as pleasant as possible."

CHAPTER 7

His Soul Touches the Stars

He who covers up his faults will not succeed; He who confesses and gives them up will find mercy.

—PROVERBS 28:13

At 10:00 A.M. ON November 20, 1945, Lord Geoffrey Lawrence, president of the International Military Tribunal (IMT), began the proceedings of what the world's press called "the trial of the century."

A succession of six prosecutors consumed the entire first day by reading the indictment aloud. During the course of the reading, French assistant prosecutor Pierre Mounier used the word *genocide* to describe the Nazi crimes in France. Polish lawyer Raphael Lemkin had coined the word and had urged prosecutors to include it in the indictment, and now it was being used in public for the first time.

For most of the Nuremberg prosecutors, the trial's opening was their first opportunity to see the defendants all together. To American prosecutor Telford Taylor, the defendants seemed nondescript as a unit. "Until they began to react individually to the trial itself, it would have been difficult to deduce, from visual scrutiny alone, what manner of men they were," Taylor wrote.

Historian Eugene Davidson said that the Allies chose these defendants because they were "the foremost representatives of the men and groups who had brought Hitler to power and kept him there against the aroused wrath and armed forces of almost the entire world." The Nuremberg trial would create a record for history, and while it may not have documented every moment of the war's infamy, Davidson wrote, "It would reveal one vast concentration of evil that could be exorcised."

The next day, Lawrence asked the defendants to plead guilty or not guilty. Goering stood and took a microphone handed to him by a guard. Holding a sheet of paper, he said, "Before I answer the question of the Tribunal whether or not I am guilty—"

Lawrence shut him down. "Defendants are not entitled to make a statement," he said.

Goering stared at Lawrence for a moment, then said, "In the sense of the indictment, not guilty," and sat down. Many German defendants who pleaded not guilty in subsequent trials, including Adolf Eichmann during his 1961 trial in Israel, used Goering's phrasing.

When Goering sat down, Rudolf Hess took the microphone and simply shouted "*Nein!*" to which Lawrence responded, through laughter in the courtroom, "That will be entered as a plea of not guilty."

Most of the remaining defendants pleaded simply "not guilty," though Fritz Sauckel, the Reich's labor minister, and Alfred Jodl, a general and Hitler's closest military adviser, both invoked God. "I declare myself in the sense of the Indictment, before God and the world and particularly before my people, not guilty," Sauckel said.

"Not guilty," Jodl said. "For what I have done or had to do, I have a pure conscience before God, before history and my people."

Lawrence then called upon American chief prosecutor Justice

Robert Jackson, whose opening statement is one of the most famous pieces of legal oratory in history. Taylor said that nothing else in the trial "matched its force, perception and eloquence," and that nothing else in "modern juristic literature . . . equally projects the controlled passion and moral intensity" of its language. Jackson had spent more than a month writing and rewriting it. On the podium in front of him were sixty-one typed pages. He said "the privilege" of opening the trial imposed "a grave responsibility."

"The wrongs which we seek to condemn and punish have been so calculated, so malignant, and so devastating that civilization cannot tolerate their being ignored," Jackson said, "because it cannot survive their being repeated."

Jackson then turned his attention to the defendants in the dock, whom he described as "broken." "The common sense of mankind demands that law shall not stop with the punishment of petty crimes by little people," he said. "It must also reach men who possess themselves of great power and make deliberate and concerted use of it to set in motion evils which leave no home in the world untouched."

What made the Nuremberg trial significant was not the individual fates of the twenty-one defendants, but rather the trial's challenge to the "sinister influences that [would] lurk in the world long after [the prisoners'] bodies . . . returned to dust." Jackson went on:

> *They have so identified themselves with the philosophies they conceived and with the forces they directed that any tenderness to them is a victory and an encouragement to all the evils which are attached to their names. Civilization can afford no compromise with the social forces which would gain renewed strength if we deal ambiguously or indecisively with the men in whom those forces now precariously survive.*

Jackson's statement previewed the prosecution's case and included hints at the evidence it would bring before the court: first,

Jackson mentioned how 33,771 Jews had been killed by SS Einsatz-gruppen death squads over a two-day period in a ravine called Babi Yar near Kiev "in retaliation for some fires that were set off there," and then he mentioned the destruction of the Warsaw ghetto that killed 56,065 Jews. Jackson then read letters from some of the defen-dants to others about the annihilation of millions of Soviet prisoners of war. He cited evidence of a "medical experiment" at Dachau in which prisoners were frozen in cold water and then "rewarmed with animal heat." "The victim, all but frozen to death, was surrounded by bodies of living women until he revived and responded to his en-vironment by having sexual intercourse," Jackson said. "Here Nazi degeneracy reached its nadir." Jackson spoke for four hours, stretch-ing his opening statement through most of the afternoon of the trial's second day.

The next day was Thanksgiving. The Allies did not take the day off from the trial to celebrate, but they observed the American holi-day by giving thanks in the courtroom.

Jackson asked hundreds of military and civilian Allied personnel to gather in the courtroom at 5:15 P.M. He spoke briefly, explaining the meaning of Thanksgiving to the British, French, and Russians, and invited Father Edmund Walsh, vice president of Georgetown Univer-sity and Jackson's consultant at Nuremberg, to give an opening prayer.

He also asked Gerecke, who had been in Nuremberg for just ten days, to give a benediction. As Gerecke spoke, Jackson and hundreds of others bowed their heads. When he was done, the trial resumed with the court ruling that Julius Streicher, the editor of the anti-Semitic *Der Stürmer* newspaper, was sane and fit to stand trial.

Lawyers for the U.S. counsel began making the case for Germa-ny's conspiracy to wage aggressive war. American prosecutor Major Frank Wallis spoke for much of the day and into the next session on Friday. That night, Wallis wrote in his diary that while he was standing in the courtroom in front of the prisoners' dock, the eight justices, 350 members of the press, and "cameras and more cam-

eras," he was actually speaking to the world and to future generations.

"This was history being made and recorded," he wrote. "History that would be in school books, history that would be a source of
study for years to come by International lawyers and students."

Wallis looked at the defendants as he laid out the case against
them "with a feeling of scorn and contempt—mixed with a bit of
awe when I remembered how close they came to success in their
mad undertaking." His job that day, he wrote, was "to drive a few
nails into the coffins of the bastards with words," and he did so for
four hours. "I don't think that I will ever forget Thanksgiving 1945,
and I doubt if I'll ever spend another Thanksgiving in a strange
country, in an International Court Room prosecuting such low-level
scoundrels. I certainly hope not."

Gerecke felt a grave sense of urgency as he became aware that
some, if not most, of the major criminals he'd be ministering to in
Nuremberg would be executed. A trial like this had never been attempted before, so no one really knew how long it was going to last.
Some felt it might be just a few weeks. Others believed it could go
through Christmas and possibly into the spring. Few of the partic-
ipants in the Nuremberg experiment contemplated being in Germany a year after the trial began.

As the prisoners began to accept Gerecke during the trial's initial weeks, many slowly agreed—some eagerly, others with cool
courtesy—to attend his services on Sundays. Gerecke and O'Connor used the larger chapel in the middle of the prison for services for
the witnesses confined to the prison. For the defendants, they used
the small two-cell chapel. A former lieutenant colonel of the SS, and
former Christian, was the organist. By the end of the trial, Gerecke
had brought the man back to the faith and served him Communion.
"The simple Gospel of the Cross had changed his heart," Gerecke
wrote later.

Gerecke's services were composed of three hymns, a scripture reading, a sermon, prayers, and then a benediction. Eventually, thirteen of the defendants attended the services. Each of these defendants remembered the Bible verse that was dedicated to him when he was confirmed in the Lutheran Church as a child. Four of the other defendants attended O'Connor's Catholic Masses, and five others refused all spiritual counsel.

DURING THE FIRST WEEKS, as life in the courtroom ground nearly to a halt over the slow pace of the trial, Gerecke and O'Connor were never busier. In addition to their counseling, the chaplains were also serving as translators and providing religious education lessons for the defendants. They soon developed a grim joke. "At least we Catholics are responsible for only six of these criminals," O'Connor would say. "You Lutherans have fifteen chalked up against you." Gerecke found the priest "jolly" and "delightful."

They were constantly visiting the cells of witnesses, including high-ranking Nazi officials who didn't make the Allies' defendants list. While court was in session, Gerecke bounced back and forth between watching the session in the courtroom and ministering to the Nazis.

The chaplains were also communicating with the families of those inside the prison. At one point, Gerecke, at the behest of the family of a witness—an SS chief—went to check in on the man's wife, who was staying in Nuremberg to be near him. When the chaplain arrived at the address, an American officer casually answered the door. Gerecke apologized and said he must have the wrong address, that he was looking for the wife of a Nazi officer.

"You've got the right address, Chappie," the officer said. "And she's doing just fine." Gerecke went back to the prison and told the man his wife was, indeed, doing fine.

Before his Sunday service with the defendants, Gerecke also ministered to GIs at the little church in Mögeldorf, the neighborhood where he was quartered. OMGUS vacated many of the homes around Nuremberg to house the small army of American, British, French, and Russian lawyers, judges, military officers, translators, interpreters, and secretaries employed by the tribunal. The Nuremberg war crimes community was "an island which suddenly emerged from a sea of Germanism and Germans," wrote Taylor. "Nuremberg and its people created the atmosphere in which, outside the Palace of Justice and a few social enclaves such as the Grand Hotel, we all lived."

Often a home's new temporary residents hired—somewhat awkwardly—the home's owner as a housekeeper. The journalists covering the trial all lived together in a huge mansion with beautiful gardens and greenhouses. Most of the attorneys bunked together in several houses, while each of the justices had his own residence, where he lived together with his aides.

The Germans had a complicated view of their occupiers. Some ingratiated themselves with the war's victors by smiling sweetly and offering to carry bags. Others were less friendly—for instance, one Nurembergian just stared blankly at an American lawyer who was struggling to ask directions in German. He waited for a few minutes to respond and then answered in perfect English.

For the most part, the war crimes community was always on edge. Rumors of snipers in the rubble were frequent. Many of the less adventurous stuck close to the well-guarded buildings used by the International Military Tribunal and traveled only on streets cleared of rubble and approved by the U.S. Army.

Those working on the trial worked hard and sometimes in dangerous circumstances, but they also played hard, and much of that play took place at the Grand Hotel. The Grand, a fifty-year-old luxury accommodation located directly across from the train station, was just outside the walls of the destroyed old city. During the Reich's heyday, it had housed VIPs who had come to view the Nazi Party rallies, but now it was one of the only buildings left partially standing.

Though the city was blacked out at night, the Grand Hotel was a light in Nuremberg's wreckage, attracting those looking for some relief from the often-tedious court proceedings during the day. In the immediate aftermath of the war, the Grand wasn't exactly Claridge's. Tarpaulins flapped over holes in the stone walls in one wing. Guests staying in some rooms on the upper floors had to cross a frightening, wall-less traverse along a catwalk to their rooms. Bags of water, treated with chemicals for drinking, stood in each of the hotel's corridors for guests. Yet despite the destruction to the hotel's façade, its lobbies, dining rooms, and main ballroom were intact.

As the trial progressed, the Grand Hotel became the center of social life, mostly for the American officers and civilians in the war crimes community, and also for anyone with a court pass. It was also home to the various celebrities and VIPs who came to town to visit the Palace of Justice for a day or two to "see the show," as the journalist Rebecca West put it. The food was cheap and decent, the wine cellars were well stocked, and the entertainment was frequent. One observer said the reception hall, where most conversation took place, looked like "a Hollywood set for an international spy drama. There was a great deal of red plush, and artificial marble and tarnished ormolu."

Men in uniform and others in suits were waved through the front door by two armed MPs, and then down a hall to the Marble Room, where they danced the jitterbug with the young American girls who were employed by the court as secretaries, clerks, stenographers, and interpreters. Most nights, a German band played jazz, but there were also cabarets composed of a company of singers, dancers, jugglers, acrobats, and a midget who balanced half a dozen cups and saucers on his head, then threw in lumps of sugar. The young ladies made the rounds at the dinner parties about town, and they often ended up at the Marble Room.

General Eisenhower had implemented a rule to prevent the Americans from draining the small amount of resources from the

German population by preventing married occupation forces from bringing their wives or children to Nuremberg. The result was that the American girls were hugely popular—and not just with the American men, but with the British, French, and Russians as well. A related rule said all Allied personnel in Nuremberg had to be there for official purposes. That meant judges with Czech girlfriends had to find them jobs doing translation or other menial tasks around the Palace of Justice.

"Most of the senior personnel, including the lawyers, were married men, while most of the women were single and young and not a few very attractive," wrote Taylor. "This gave the society a relaxed, tolerant and philanderous ambience which many of us found agreeable."

"There was hardly a man in the town who had not a wife in the United States, who was not on the vigorous side of middle age and who was not spiritually sick from a surfeit of war and exile," West wrote. "To the desire to embrace was also added the desire to be comforted and to comfort."

Some of the occupiers felt a visceral discomfort, however, as starving Germans pressed their faces to the glass at the Grand Hotel. "Inside, we, the conquerors who had brought their leaders to trial, were disporting ourselves in a manner certainly vulgar and virtually callous," said one member of the war crimes community.

Enlisted men frequented another building that had survived the bombing—the Opera House—which played movies downstairs and provided a dance hall and club upstairs. Allied rules against fraternization with German women were largely ignored. Those connections, along with the contact Allied personnel had with waiters and other service industry people, were the only real relations the war crimes community had with Nurembergians.

Despite the fun many of the occupiers were having with Nuremberg's locals, the war's victors eventually became bored with one another. For the most part, the Americans and British were friendly, the French less so, and the Russians largely kept to themselves. The French and British were mostly housed in a district west of the city called Zirndorf, where the French had set up their own club for drinking and dancing that was less busy and garish than the Grand Hotel.

During certain celebratory occasions, and at dinner parties thrown by the higher-ranking war crimes court officials, members of the four victorious nations mixed together. At a St. Andrew's Night party, British prosecutor David Maxwell-Fyfe had haggis flown in, entrancing the Russians. The dinner parties "were quite unrefreshing," West wrote. "For the guests at these parties had either to be co-workers grown deadly familiar with the passing months or VIPs . . . who, as most were allowed to stay only two days, had nothing to bring to the occasion except the first superficial impressions, so apt to be the same in every case. The symbol of Nuremberg was a yawn."

After several months, life on the war crimes island did become tedious for most. The day began at 8:30 and ended at 5:30. If there was no dinner party invitation, many simply ate at home and worked again until going to sleep. Because of the need to translate every word of the trial into four languages, the court proceedings themselves were slow. Despite the fact that the world was watching, in the fishbowl of Nuremberg, everyone saw the same people each day and each night. Gossip was rife. Nuremberg was "water-torture, boredom falling drop by drop on the same spot on the soul," West wrote. To live in the city "was, even for the victors, in itself physical captivity."

There was a lot of drinking, and weekends were highly anticipated events. "Those working on the trial were still mopping up the War, subject to a military atmosphere and far from home," wrote Nuremberg historians Ann and John Tusa. "If they were to be denied the satisfactions of repatriation, family, and peacetime careers, they would wring what pleasure they could from the situation they were in."

Weekends provided a chance to get out of Nuremberg, and most of the war crimes community took advantage of the countryside as frequently as possible, including a lot of skiing over the winter—in Czechoslovakia, Berchtesgaden, or Garmisch.

With 170 total staff, the British contingent was the second largest of the war crimes community. The French and Soviet staffs were much smaller, while the American staff—including the military and all the Palace of Justice (court and prison) employees—was more than a thousand.

That was the atmosphere and structure of Nuremberg. The meaning of Nuremberg, West wrote, "was that the people responsible for the concentration camps and the deportations and the attendant evocation of evil must be tried for their offenses."

GERECKE WANTED ALL THE Nazis in his care to receive Holy Communion before they were executed. But these believers in particular were likely to take more time than most to understand the significance of Communion to Gerecke's satisfaction, and with the looming prospect of the gallows for so many in his care, the chaplain knew he didn't have much time.

"I must feel convinced that each candidate not only understands its significance, but that, in penitence and faith, he is ready," he wrote later.

After several months at Nuremberg, the chaplains often arrived in their offices to find that guards had placed notes from certain prisoners expressing a desire to see the chaplains on their next visit through the cell blocks. Because the court operated from 10:00 A.M. to 1:00 P.M., and 2:00 P.M. to 5:00 P.M., the chaplains made calls before the defendants left for court in the morning or after trial in the evening. Weekends were busy for the chaplains—they often made cell calls on Saturdays and on Sundays between services.

During the proceedings, Gerecke felt it was important to visit the sessions nearly every day. It was crucial to his ministry, he thought, to "watch both sides of the story and try to keep [his] balance in speaking with the defendants by hearing a part of the evidence brought out at trial."

Yet, despite Gerecke's efforts to fully understand the situation around him, some of the defendants were skeptical. When Karl Doenitz first met Gerecke, the admiral insisted that Gerecke wouldn't be able to preach the Gospel without bringing Hitler and the war into the conversation.

"I know little about your politics," Gerecke responded. "And since you wouldn't be interested in mine, we'll simply deal with the World of God in relation to the hearts of men."

Doenitz challenged Gerecke to show him what he was talking about regarding the Gospel. "If you have the courage to come [to our cells], I'll attend your services. I think you'll probably help me," Doenitz said.

Doenitz had joined the German Imperial Navy in 1910 and had become an officer at the age of twenty-three. He was an admiral in 1942 when he engineered the rescue of about two thousand enemy survivors of the *Laconia,* a British passenger ship that a German U-boat had torpedoed in the shark-infested mid–South Atlantic between West Africa and Brazil. Doenitz had ordered the rescue against a standing rule from Hitler that waging war takes precedence over rescue missions. In ordering the rescue, Doenitz risked Allied attacks on the German submarines and U-boats taking part in the rescue, angering Hitler.

To appease the führer, Doenitz instituted a new rule known as the Laconia Order, which forbade commanders from rescuing lifeboats.

The Nazis believed that American production could replace ships, but it was much more difficult for the enemy to replace and train the men who worked those ships, so killing them would create a bottleneck and slow the U.S. Navy.

U-boat commanders later testified that Doenitz had given them verbal orders that both ships and their crews should be the target of future attacks, and so the main charge against Doenitz at Nuremberg was that he had ordered his men to fire on survivors of crippled Allied ships.

While Doenitz was on trial in Nuremberg, U-boat commander Lieutenant Heinz Eck was on trial in a British military war crimes court in Hamburg for doing just what Doenitz had ordered. Eck was the commander of U-852, which sank an Allied merchant vessel, the *Peleus,* in March 1944. The Greek steamship was torpedoed and sank within three minutes. Most of its thirty-five-member crew were able to get to two liferafts or debris floating in the water.

When Eck's U-boat surfaced, the German sailors brought aboard two men to be interrogated. Then they put the men back in the water. The sub moved about half a mile away to prepare her guns, then returned, flashed her signal light, and her crew began firing machine guns and throwing hand grenades at the *Peleus*'s crew for five hours. Three men—the Greek first officer, a Greek seaman, and a British seaman—survived the attack and were picked up twenty-five days later by a Portuguese steamship. In Nuremberg, prosecutors pointed to the *Peleus* case as a clear example of how men following the supreme commander's orders had committed a war crime.

Many prisoners were not as open to receiving help as Doenitz. Alfred Rosenberg, the Nazi's chief philosopher, told Gerecke he had no use for his childhood faith. "Don't bother with me," he told Gerecke with a smile.

Gerecke offered him a devotional book.

"No thank you," Rosenberg said. He told Gerecke politely that he felt no need for his help, but said Gerecke would be welcome to visit his cell. Rosenberg said he was a *Gottgläubig*—a believer in God but not in Christ.

In about 1936, a movement to leave the Catholic and Protestant churches began to resonate with Nazi Party members who were replacing traditional faith with a newfound faith in the Reich. Those revoking their church memberships were designated *Gottgläubige*, or "believers in God." The phrase became a way for party members to publicly differentiate themselves from both Christians and non-believers.

Rosenberg suggested Gerecke's time might be better spent with the other prisoners. "If my colleagues are naive enough to accept this, you go ahead and work with them, but don't bother with me."

Many of the prisoners were difficult to convert at first. Erich Raeder, the grand admiral and commander in chief of the German navy before Doenitz, had initially told Gerecke that he could not accept certain Christian tenets, and so the chaplain placed him as an intellectual skeptic. But after learning something of Raeder's history, it was clear to Gerecke that Raeder was actually more suspicious of the American army than he was of Christianity.

Raeder was born near Hamburg in 1876, the son of a schoolteacher, and was brought up in a religious home. He joined the navy when he was eighteen and was an officer by the time he was twenty-one. He served in the First World War, taking part in mining operations on the British coast. In 1928, Raeder was promoted to admiral and chief of the naval command, and in 1935, Hitler promoted him to commander in chief of the navy. In a fit of jealousy, Goering once told Hitler that while it was true that Raeder had built a great navy, he also went to church, and so Hitler could draw his own conclusions about whether Raeder's loyalties really stood with the Nazi Party.

In a speech in 1939, Raeder voiced enthusiasm for the "clear and relentless fight against Bolshevism and international Jewry whose nation-destroying deeds we have fully experienced." But he also used his influence to help Jews whom he knew; took up the case of Reverend Martin Niemoeller, a former submarine officer and anti-Nazi pastor who became an enemy of the state; and opposed the Nazi attack on the Lutheran and Catholic churches, including its threat to military chaplains.

In 1939, Hitler made Raeder grand admiral and placed him in charge of unrestricted U-boat warfare, but differences with Hitler later in the war forced Raeder's retirement in 1943, and his title of grand admiral went to Doenitz.

At Nuremberg, Raeder was an ardent Bible reader and one day joined Baldur von Schirach, the former Nazi Youth leader, on his way to chapel. He eventually acknowledged to Gerecke that he was interested in learning more from him. Raeder began reading the scripture for the coming Sunday's sermon. He also prepared questions for Gerecke when the chaplain visited his cell and began marking scriptural passages in the English tracts he couldn't quite understand and sending them to Schirach, who spoke English, for translation. Soon enough, Gerecke allowed him to take Holy Communion.

Joachim von Ribbentrop also proved unrepentant in the beginning. When Gerecke first visited Ribbentrop's cell, Hitler's foreign minister said, "This business of religion probably isn't so serious as you consider it." He told Gerecke that his wife had led him away from the church. Their two little boys, five and seven, had also been removed from the church and were never baptized. After receiving a few letters from Mrs. Ribbentrop saying that she would offset Gerecke's influence on her husband in any way possible, the chaplain didn't doubt it. Gerecke later called Ribbentrop's wife "the nastiest, the most disagreeable person I ever met in my life."

Born in Wesel, in northwest Germany near the Dutch border, Ribbentrop volunteered for service in the First World War at the age of twenty-one. After the war, he set up shop in Berlin exporting wines and spirits to England and France. Ribbentrop was fluent in French and he'd spent time in both England and Canada. He married into a wealthy family of German sparkling wine manufacturers, which gave him entrée with the country's elite. Those contacts were important for Hitler, and soon after Ribbentrop joined the Nazi Party in 1932, he was made an SS colonel and Hitler's adviser on foreign affairs. In 1936, Hitler named him ambassador to London, and in 1938, he became the Third Reich's foreign minister.

Hitler was, for the most part, his own foreign minister, and Ribbentrop—who was almost universally disliked by higher Nazi leadership—was his gofer. The trappings of wealth and power, which Ribbentrop both craved and aggrandized, fit him badly. He was contemptuous, incompetent, vain, and combative. Goering once called him that "dirty little champagne peddler."

As Gerecke sat in his cell, Ribbentrop began asking more questions and pointing out contradictions from the Bible. "Can a man be patriotic and Christian at the same time?" he asked.

Gerecke responded, "Of course you can be patriotic and Christian at the same time provided you do so according to Romans 13 until you come into conflict with Acts 5:29. The former will tell you what you owe your government and how to be loyal to it as a Christian. The latter will emphasize its application to Christian patriotism and tell you that you must obey God rather than man."

After several months, Ribbentrop began reading the Bible and the catechism. Gerecke said Ribbentrop "became more and more penitent, eager to turn from the past." Yet, it wasn't until the Nuremberg judges were in closed session at the end of the trial that Ribbentrop expressed any interest in taking Communion, which he eventually did.

Many of the Nazis were unresponsive at first to Gerecke's overtures to join his services in the chapel. Constantin von Neurath, the former German foreign minister and Reich protector of Bohemia, said his entire family had been Catholic, and that he'd never been a churchgoer. Eventually, Gerecke wrote, Neurath showed "genuine interest," and he agreed to try it out. Neurath's family was thankful, and they sent Gerecke letters that thanked him for helping Neurath "get right with God."

As with Rosenberg and Ribbentrop, Gerecke found that Hjalmar Schacht, the former president of the Reichsbank, responded to his requests "a little on the sharp side."

"I'll be there," Schacht said about attending chapel, "but don't ever ask me to come to Communion." That was fine with Gerecke. His only intention at first was to get each of the defendants to Sunday service. But he asked Schacht why he was so averse to Communion.

Schacht's bitterness at being accused of war crimes alongside men like Goering and Ernst Kaltenbrunner, who had overseen the concentration camp system, made him spiritually unprepared for Communion, he told the chaplain. "But if there's any degree of fairness in this trial, then I'm going to be a free man when it's over with. . . . And then I should like to go to church with my wife and take of the Lord's Supper."

Fritz Sauckel, Hitler's labor chief, became the first of the thirteen to work seriously with Gerecke. Sauckel was a short, stocky man with a bald head shaped like a bulldog's and a cramped mustache fashioned after Hitler's. He wasn't smart, but he'd been efficient enough at his job to became the most notorious slaver in history.

At Nuremberg, the fifty-one-year-old's groveling friendliness—always smiling nervously, hands constantly fluttering as he spoke—made most cringe. Sauckel had a habit of pausing between each word as he gave his testimony during the trial, which irked the judges, and the learned Germans in the room loathed his "vile" blue-collar accent. Goebbels had famously called Sauckel "one of the dullest of the dull," though one Berlin journalist said he was "one of the toughest of the Old Guard Nazis."

When Sauckel spoke to someone directly, his words seemed automatic, as if he'd prepared phrases and sentences for precise situations, shining and buffing them until a particular question demanded that exact, practiced reply. After Gerecke greeted him in his cell that first afternoon, Sauckel put his hands on Gerecke's arms and said, with great feeling, "As a clergyman, you are one person to whom I can open my heart."

Gerecke wrote later that Sauckel told him that he'd done his job as a Nazi without "any idea of committing wrong against God or man." He said he'd simply been working toward an ideal social community that he'd dreamed of since his days as a seaman and laborer.

As he'd done with the others, Gerecke tried to remember that Sauckel was once a child. Fritz had been brought up poor and considered himself a working-class success story who retained his workingman's point of view. His father had come from a long line of farmers and had been a postman, and his mother had come from a seafaring family.

At age fifteen, Fritz left home to become a merchant marine and sailed around the world, including to North America. In 1912, he was shipwrecked off the Scottish coast.

In 1914, just as the First World War was beginning, Fritz's ship, en route to Australia, was sunk by a French battleship. He spent the rest of the war in a French POW camp. When Sauckel returned to Germany in 1919, he found his savings worthless because of inflation. He took a job as a lathe operator in a ball-bearing plant in Schweinfurt and began studying engineering.

In 1923, Sauckel married a girl he'd known for ten years. Though Elisabeth was Catholic, Sauckel's parents were eventually won over by her charm. It was a happy marriage that produced ten children—eight boys and two girls—over the next fifteen years. Two of the boys were eventually killed during the Second World War.

After two years, Sauckel became a labor leader at his factory, and as early as 1921, he was making speeches and organizing for the Nazi Party. In 1923, Sauckel heard Hitler speak and was enthralled by his message of national unity. He came to feel Hitler was "the man chosen by fate to unite Germany," and eventually he began to write letters to Hitler that had a worshipful tone. Like Rudolf Hess, Sauckel "had for Hitler the loyal fidelity of a dog to its master," said one Nuremberg psychologist.

In 1933, Sauckel was elected into the Reichstag to represent

Thuringia, the region north of Bavaria, and he served as an energetic leader of the Nazi Party in the region. Eventually Hitler brought him closer into his inner circle.

Hitler saw in Sauckel what historian Eugene Davidson called a man of "tireless efficiency" who was "a good choice for the greatest slave roundup in history."

Hitler's blitzkrieg of the western front began in May 1940, and his invasion of Russia began in June 1941. From the Russian invasion until the last year of the war, Germany lost sixty thousand men each month to the eastern front alone.

To counter some of the problems created by the demand for troops, the German army lowered the minimum age of conscription and raised the maximum age in 1942. It began taking men from the arms industry who had previously been exempt from recruitment.

Germany also needed help on the home front. After Hitler assigned Sauckel the job of plenipotentiary-general for labor mobilization in 1942, Sauckel conducted slave raids into Germany's occupied territories in an attempt to slake the Reich's quenchless thirst for free labor. And they were effective. In one day, a "Sauckel action, " as they came to be called, rounded up fifty thousand men in Rotterdam. By the end of 1942, Germany was using more than 4.5 million foreign workers.

In a letter to Rosenberg in October 1942, Sauckel demanded "the ruthless application of all measures" to acquire two million Russian workers. A report three weeks later from Rosenberg's office on the roundup said that "recruiting methods were used which probably have their precedent only in the blackest periods of the slave trade. A regular manhunt was inaugurated."

There wasn't enough room in Nazi Germany for all those people brought to work there, and consequently the workers' living and work conditions were subhuman. After the SS caught civilian workers in the occupied territories, they sometimes manacled them and jammed fifty to eighty of them in freight cars headed to their destinations, often without food or water for days.

The average workday was thirteen hours, and fines, taxes, and other deductions made any promised wages theoretical. Laborers beginning work at 4:00 A.M. might have gotten a few cups of tea, followed fourteen hours later by a quart of nondescript soup and some bread—the daily ration for hard labor. Some resorted to cooking mice over fires after skinning them with bits of glass and metal. Food for workers from the east was worse than for others. If these workers were fed meat, it was from cats or horses that had been slaughtered because they had contracted tuberculosis.

Sauckel maintained that all he wanted was a workforce, and he repeatedly said that mistreating that workforce was antithetical to the Reich's goals. In March 1943, Sauckel wrote to Hitler to say that "all the workers of foreign nations are being unexceptionally treated correctly and decently, well taken care of and well clothed. . . . Never before in the history of the world have foreign workers been so well treated."

Sauckel evoked a warped sense of caring for Germany's slaves that stemmed from the utilitarianism required by his job. "Beaten, half-starved and dead Russians do not supply us with coal and are entirely useless for iron and steel production," he said.

By the fall of 1944, there were eight million foreign workers in the Reich. Foreign nationals comprised 46 percent of those working in agriculture and a third of those working in mining, construction, and the metal and chemical industries. In the last year of the war, more than a quarter of the workforce in Germany consisted of citizens of other countries. Nearly five hundred thousand of them died there during the war. A quarter, or 1.2 million, of the Reich's POWs in forced labor across Europe had died by mid-1945. At Nuremberg, Sauckel told prosecutors he was responsible only for finding Germany's labor, not for how they were treated after he delivered them to the work camps.

Within seconds of meeting Gerecke, Sauckel told the chaplain he would come to chapel services. But first, he wanted to know what arrangements were being made for serving Communion to prisoners who wanted it. "I want to ask you how I can prepare myself for the Lord's Supper," he said.

Gerecke told Sauckel to take it easy and that he would be happy to instruct him. They would go over Christian teaching with a catechism and the Bible. "This time, Mr. Sauckel, you don't want to go through the motions," Gerecke said. "You want to let the motions of God's Holy Spirit go through you."

The men discussed their children. Sauckel mentioned, proudly, how devout his wife was. When Gerecke motioned to leave, Sauckel asked the chaplain to pray with him. They knelt together on the stone floor of the cell, next to the steel cot.

Each time the chaplain visited, the two men ended their time together in prayer, kneeling on the floor by the cot. Many times, Sauckel asked for God's mercy and wiped away tears as he called himself a sinner. Sauckel would take his Bible study seriously during the months of the trial, often bringing the catechism to court with him to read during sessions.

Eventually, after one Sunday church service, Sauckel asked Gerecke if he could take Communion. "All right, Mr. Sauckel," Gerecke told him. "I'll be down to see you." When Gerecke arrived, Sauckel was on his knees, praying on the cement floor of his cell.

Gerecke entered the cell and prepared the Communion kit against the wall. Sauckel got off his knees, threw his hands in the air, and cried out so loudly that every guard on the floor came rushing to Sauckel's cell. "*Gott sei mir gnädig, ein Sünder!*" Sauckel yelled. "God, be merciful to me, a sinner!"

"I believe he meant every word of it," Gerecke said later. "He virtually crawled to the communion kit and partook of the Lord's Supper. The first one to come back!"

After Sauckel, Gerecke's success leading prisoners back to Christ continued with the three "big men," as he put it. Through Gerecke, the three prisoners learned about Sauckel's work, relearning the faith with the chaplain. They asked him for their own catechisms, and Gerecke began guiding them through the scriptures.

The first of these men was Albert Speer, the Third Reich's architect and eventually the Reich's minister for armaments and war production. In Gerecke's postwar writing, he portrayed Speer as a lively and willing congregant. "Of course I'm coming to Chapel!" Speer told Gerecke when they first met in Speer's cell. Gerecke wrote that over time he found Speer "a delightful conversationalist" who admitted to him the guilt of the Nazi regime, telling the chaplain "that the neglect of genuine Christianity caused its downfall."

As an architect, Speer had been continuing the family business. His grandfather was an architect, and his father was one of the busiest architects in Mannheim, in west-central Germany, where Speer was born. In 1930, Speer—a twenty-five-year-old student of architecture at the time—heard Hitler speak at Berlin University, and he was mesmerized. He joined the Nazi Party the following year. In 1932, he received his first commission from the party, and thereafter became the chief designer of the Nazi movement's parades and rallies. More than anyone else, Speer was responsible for the look of Nazism. Hitler called him an "architect of genius."

In 1942, Speer became minister of armaments and war production and proved useful to Hitler again as he successfully managed the massive machinery of the Reich's industrial output, largely by improving efficiencies in the bureaucracy and exploiting slave labor.

At the end of the war, Hitler gave orders to destroy much of Germany's infrastructure and factories to keep them from the Allies, but Speer refused, ordering instead for factories to be "paralyzed" by removing and hiding key parts. His view was that no one had the right to destroy Germany's postwar future.

When it became obvious that Hitler's despondency would lead to a kind of murder-suicide with the German people, Speer planned to kill him by throwing poison gas grenades in the ventilation system of Hitler's bunker. But when he found out Hitler had built a huge brick wall around the vents to prevent such an attack, he backed off the plan.

In an evangelical tract, *The Cross and the Swastika,* British writer F. T. Grossmith "tried to continue Gerecke's ministry" by corresponding with the Nuremberg defendants who were still alive in the late 1970s. For instance, he sent Karl Doenitz "some Christian literature," which he hoped "he read and applied to his life." He also wrote that he visited Speer's home in Heidelberg many years after the trials to ask about Gerecke. Speer told Grossmith that Gerecke was "a man with a warm heart . . . he cared," and that without him, he "could never have got through those days at Nuremberg."

The foreword of *The Cross and the Swastika* is attributed to Speer: "Henry Gerecke made a lasting impression on me. . . . He was sincere and forthright. His outspokenness was not upsetting to us because everyone knew that he meant well. He was liked and appreciated by all the defendants." Yet Speer never mentioned Gerecke in the famous books he wrote in Spandau, where he was imprisoned in the years following the trial.

The other two "big men" that Gerecke brought back to a belief in Christ were Hans Fritzsche, head of radio broadcasting in the Reich Ministry of Propaganda, and Baldur von Schirach, the Reich's Hitler Youth leader and governor of Vienna. Fritzsche, one historian has said, "fitted least snugly into the category of major war criminal."

For a radio propagandist, Fritzsche was a soft-spoken man. When Gerecke entered his cell, Fritzsche gave him a genuine welcome, saying he was "deeply ashamed of having turned against the church" and that he "hoped to come all the way back to Christ."

Gerecke asked Fritzsche if he would come to chapel services and he replied, "Of course I'm coming to chapel." He wanted to discuss with the chaplain "some of those important doctrines of the Scriptures," he said.

At one point during the trial, Fritzsche was walking in a public area of the Palace of Justice when a woman he recognized from court approached him. She began speaking to him in English, and before he could grasp what she was saying, the woman took Fritzsche's hand and bowed dramatically to him. He removed his hand and walked hastily away. That night, Fritzsche told Gerecke about the incident, and the chaplain promised to investigate.

The woman, Gerecke found, was an American of Russian descent who had carefully watched the entire trial. Fritzsche later recounted how the woman told Gerecke that she had been shocked by the evidence presented in court but was also ashamed that the Allies were holding all twenty-one Nazis responsible "for the misdeeds of a number of individuals." The woman "had felt the urge to demonstrate this on behalf of all the Americans who shared her opinion to at least one of the accused Germans."

Fritzsche was most likely not a man used to receiving the bows of strangers. He had come from a long line of blacksmiths and armorers in the Leipzig area in eastern Germany. His mother's family had been tulip growers from Münster, and his mother had doted on him because he was the youngest. She wore simple clothing but spoke French and played the piano and had what he called "a shining personality." Hans was close to his mother and, even as an adult, would rest his head in her lap when he needed comfort. She died of heart disease when Hans was thirty-eight.

Hans was educated in public schools, and from the ages of twelve to fourteen he was diagnosed with a "weak heart," which kept him out of school for a year and unable to play sports until he was nearly twenty. When he finally could engage in outdoor activities, he favored mountain climbing and skiing. In a nod to the maternal side of his family, Hans grew cacti and orchid collections when he was fourteen.

"My mother could be very sad about little things, but in a time of any great difficulty or crises she was always brave," Fritzsche told one of the American psychiatrists at Nuremberg. His mother had a religious phrase she would use in difficult times: "The soul is saved," she would say.

Soon after leaving university for financial reasons, Fritzsche began writing for a living. He was an editor at the *Telegraphen Union*, a wire service, and then, in the late 1920s, editor in chief of the Wireless News Service, part of the Hugenberg media empire whose press had a nationalistic tone similar to that of the Nazis.

Fritzsche's writing attracted Joseph Goebbels, Hitler's propaganda chief, who hired him in 1933 to head the News Service in the ministry's Press Section, which relayed instructions on what to print to the country's daily newspaper editors. Fritzsche's delivery was calm, learned, rational, and clear—the opposite of so many Nazis. Fritzsche could deliver precisely what Goebbels needed in order to reach a particular part of the German populace that was turned off by the rantings of other Nazi leaders.

But Fritzsche's calm demeanor belied the underlying message in his writings and his radio commentaries. For instance, he regularly attacked Franklin Roosevelt and Winston Churchill and justified Hitler's incursions into other sovereign lands. Fritzsche rose up the Nazi ranks, eventually heading the Ministry of Propaganda's Radio Division.

His views lined up well with the party's anti-Semitism. After quoting Roosevelt's line, "There never was a race and never will be a race which can serve the rest of mankind as master," Fritzsche said in a 1941 broadcast, "Here, too, we can only applaud Mr. Roosevelt. Precisely because there is no race which can be the master of the rest of mankind, we Germans have taken the liberty of breaking the domination of Jewry and of its capital in Germany, or Jewry which believed itself to have inherited the crown of secret world domination."

Later that same year, Fritzsche told his listeners, "The fate of

Jewry in Europe had turned out to be as unpleasant as the Führer predicted it would be in the event of a European war. After the extension of the war instigated by the Jews this unpleasant fact may also spread to the New World, for you can hardly assume that the nations of the New World will pardon the Jews for the misery of which the nations of the Old World did not absolve them." Jews, Fritzsche said, were prepared to murder anyone in the way of their goal.

Fritzsche's outward calm also disguised his ruthlessness. At the height of his popularity, a man named Johannes Wild wrote him anonymous letters, protesting his broadcasts. Enclosed in the letter were drawings of Hitler's great-grandfather as an orangutan wearing a helmet, and calling the führer a "bloodthirsty crook." Fritzsche turned the papers over to the Gestapo, which tracked Wild down, arrested him, and executed him.

Even when the war was lost, Fritzsche trumpeted the Nazi cause, telling Germans to "hold out to the last." After Nuremberg, Germany's own court tried Fritzsche and concluded that his propaganda helped prolong the war because it led to the drafting of German children to fight in order to sustain it.

Despite Fritzsche's early enthusiasm over discussing the scriptures, he was wary of buying into the Christian doctrines. "Don't expect me to drink it all down," he said. "I'm not going to accept it as I find it. But I want to talk to you about it." For Gerecke, that was an opening, and he took it.

Gerecke also took the openings that Baldur von Schirach gave him. When Gerecke arrived at Schirach's cell for the first time, Schirach greeted him with a boyish smile and perfect English, urging Gerecke to visit often. The energy he'd expended on Nazi youth activities "should have been used to develop loyalty to really Christian principles," Schirach told Gerecke.

Schirach had American roots. His paternal grandfather was German, but lived in the United States and fought in the Civil War.

He married an American girl in Philadelphia in 1869, then moved back to Germany. The couple's son, Schirach's father, also married an American girl on a visit to the United States.

Baldur was born in Berlin to the by-now aristocratic Schirach family and joined several youth organizations as a teenager after the First World War. In 1925, at age eighteen, he read *Mein Kampf,* and he met Hitler the following year. Hitler sent Schirach to Munich, where the party was strongest, and where Schirach attended university, becoming a student leader. For the next decade, Hitler groomed Schirach, giving him more responsibility over the Nazi Party's youth programs. By 1936, Schirach—at age twenty-nine—was one of the Reich's leaders, reporting directly to Hitler.

Schirach was responsible for the six million Hitler Youth members, whom he recruited by using a combination of militarism, nationalism, and a devotion to pagan romanticism. He was creating, in essence, the future of the SS—young people trained to believe in the supremacy of Teutonic culture. Schirach repaid Hitler's trust in him with blind devotion. And poetry:

> *That is the greatest thing about him,*
> *That he is not only our leader and a great hero,*
> *But himself, upright, firm and simple,*
> *. . . in him rest the roots of our world.*
> *And his soul touches the stars*
> *And yet he remains a man like you and me.*

The young people under Schirach's authority said prayers before their evening meal:

> *Fuehrer, my Fuehrer given me by God,*
> *Protect and preserve my life for long.*
> *You secured Germany from its deepest need.*
> *I thank you for my daily bread.*

Stay for a long time with me, leave me not.
Fuehrer, my Fuehrer, my faith, my light
Heil my Fuehrer.

In 1940, Schirach enlisted in the German army and fought in France. When he returned, Hitler made him the governor of Vienna, a city Hitler had always considered "Jew-ridden." In a speech in 1942, Schirach said the "removal" of Jews to the east would "contribute to European culture," and he deported 185,000 Viennese Jews to Poland during his tenure. Schirach admitted at Nuremberg that he had been an anti-Semite ever since reading the English author Houston Stewart Chamberlain—whose writings helped form the foundation of Nazi policy—and Henry Ford. But he also told a U.S. Army psychiatrist that those influences had been wrong.

"I have rethought all the ideas which directed me during the last fifteen or twenty years of my life," Schirach said. "Having come to the conclusion that racial policy as a whole is one of the greatest menaces to mankind."

Some weeks after Gerecke had first asked the prisoners to attend chapel services, the three "big men" asked to see him alone.

Gerecke stopped to talk to Speer first, who asked him, "If I can tell you that the blood of Jesus Christ has cleansed me of all my sins and I believe that, will you commune me?" He also heard the same request in Schirach's and Fritzsche's cells. Schirach said "that he had led people to follow blindly a kind of program, that he didn't understand himself, but now knew how wrong he was."

Gerecke arranged a service in the tiny chapel. "I shall never forget the sight of those three big men kneeling before the crucifix, asking that their sins be forgiven," Gerecke wrote. The three moved up to the altar—a white sheet covering a table—and took Communion. They looked so focused on the holiness of the moment, Gerecke thought, that the guards walked out and left the chaplain to his business.

After the war, some people who heard his story asked Gerecke whether the men in his spiritual care at Nuremberg had not actually found Christianity but rather were simply frightened by the probability that they would soon meet their deaths at the end of a rope.

"My only answer is that I have been a preacher for a long time and have decided that [finding God] is the only way a good many folk find themselves," Gerecke said later. One of "many proofs" that the prisoners had not "put on an act" at Nuremberg, he said, was a news story from the mid-1950s that said all the Nazi prisoners at Spandau—except Hess—were attending chapel regularly.

CHAPTER 8

Book of Numbers

*To be able to do harm, to inflict evil, is a power excessively hateful,
it is common to cowardice, along with flies and scorpions, and the
devil himself.*

—ERASMUS

AT THE END OF the court's session on Thursday, December 20, 1945, tribunal president Lord Lawrence adjourned the court until January 2, making for a much-welcomed twelve-day Christmas break for the trial staff. Robert Jackson threw a Christmas party at his house that night, primarily for the judges and attorneys.

At one point, Elsie Douglas, Jackson's secretary, sat down at the piano and began playing "Silent Night." A Russian officer sang, "*Stille Nacht, helige Nacht. Alles shläft, einsam wacht . . .*" The next day, the trial's lawyers, judges, and secretaries dispersed for the Christmas break. Some went home to see family. Some, like Jackson, went sightseeing in Rome, Cairo, and Jerusalem. Others went skiing in the Austrian Alps.

Nuremberg's defendants and witnesses didn't go anywhere, and neither did their jailers or chaplains. The prisoners were all worried about their families' safety, and Christmas made their ignorance more profound. "Most of us had no idea whether our nearest and dearest were still alive and our thoughts of them were clouded by anxiety and fear, by incessant futile imaginings and misgivings," Hans Fritzsche wrote. "We longed for news of them."

Despite how it seemed to the prisoners, Colonel Andrus and his chaplains were working hard behind the scenes to get the defendants' families access to the prison through petitions to the trial judges and the military government. When the answer was no— which it always was—they checked every information channel for news on the whereabouts of the defendants' families.

Colonel Andrus knew his prisoners were going through what he called "a particularly harrowing time." And rumors were only making things worse—the defense attorneys for Hermann Goering, Julius Streicher, Wilhelm Keitel, Baldur von Schirach, and Hjalmar Schacht all passed on word that their wives had been captured by American forces. "Worse," wrote Andrus, "they had been told that there was no certainty that their children had been taken with them."

In some cases, the rumors were not far from truth. On Christmas Eve, while Allied prosecutors like Jackson were singing Christmas carols in the courtyard of the Church of the Nativity in Bethlehem, Henriette von Schirach, Baldur's wife, was taken by American soldiers from a house she was living in with their children near Dresden. Henriette was put in a jeep, leaving her four young children behind with a Christmas tree, some rice, and several pounds of sugar—a gift from Gerecke. She was friendly with the chaplain throughout the trial, and in its later stages she often attended his services in Mögeldorf.

An hour after the Americans picked her up, she arrived at an Allied POW camp in Bad Tölz. She was ordered to remove her clothes and told that she'd be scrubbing toilets. It was Christmas

Eve, so Henriette was given the night off, but she was told that in the morning she would be doing her cleaning with torn red, black, and white Hitler Youth rags.

Henriette was thrown into a cell made for six people but that was holding nine. The woman next to her, a pretty, dainty wife of a former Gestapo chief, had tried to kill herself and her two children while her husband shot himself in the woods. The Allies had begun to round up Nazis and their families, and the woman had slit her children's wrists. But the children had started to scream and woke the neighbors. One of the boys survived, but the other died. Her husband had also failed in his suicide attempt in the woods. He'd been brought to the same prison in Bad Tölz and had managed to hang himself earlier that night. "He had to die," the woman told Schirach. "He saw and did terrible things."

A Swiss woman who had recently been released from the camp sent back a bottle of burgundy and a damask cloth. There was just enough burgundy for each of them to have a gulp. One woman took a red candle, a few pine tree branches, and some cakes from her suitcase and placed them on the tablecloth.

They passed around the burgundy and the prison food—sausages and white rolls. Suddenly, the cell door opened, and a guard brought in a bowl of hot punch. The scent of cloves and cinnamon filled the cell. "From Captain Lutz," the guard said. "Merry Christmas." The women drank from battered tumblers and began singing Christmas carols hesitantly. Then male voices joined in from the SS cells down the corridor.

"It sounded strong and beautiful like Christmas Mass," Henriette wrote later. "Soldiers, peasant boys and workers sang the old carols in the darkness of prison until midnight. The light of the candle fell across the faces of the V.D.-infected street girls, but as they sang their faces looked bright and clear."

For the Nuremberg prisoners back in their cells, Christmas Eve was about memories. Albert Speer was twenty on Christmas Eve in

1925 when he visited his future wife at her parents' apartment over-looking the Neckar River in southwestern Germany. He'd used his student allowance to buy her a bedside lamp with a silk shade. After celebrating with her parents, Speer went up into the mountains above the Neckar Valley to his own parents' house where the Christmas tree was always set up in the big living room. A fire snapped in a fireplace of old Delft tiles, and two buckets filled with water stood near the tree, just in case.

Speer cherished his family's Christmas rituals. His father would always try to sing a carol in a disjointed, horrible voice, before fading out after a stanza. Then, the family would head to the dining room, where Speer's mother brought out boiled Westphalian ham with potato salad served on the Speer family tableware. Speer's father sat on the board of the largest local brewery, and the family always washed down Christmas dinner with Dortmund beer. Now, in 1945, Speer sat alone with only fish, bread, and tea.

Other prisoners were less sentimental that night. Gerecke had left Julius Streicher some devotional literature in the hope that the Christmas spirit would extend even to those who rejected his faith. But Streicher told Gustave Gilbert that the Christ story didn't inspire or move him. The newspaper editor and propagandist said he was his own philosopher. "I've often thought about this business about God creating the universe," Streicher told Gilbert. "I always ask myself, if God made everything, who made God? You see, you can go crazy thinking about that. And all that stuff about Christ—the Jew who was the Son of God. I don't know. It sounds like propaganda."

Most of the men were quiet. "The silence in the big prison was so profound that it hurt," Gerecke wrote. He and O'Connor had promised their congregations Christmas Eve services, but the press had delayed them. Newspapers from across the world were demanding to know what the defendants were eating, whether they were praying, if they were allowed any celebration. "As a result," wrote Fritzsche, "the officers responsible got into a state of nervous tension approaching panic for fear they might be publicly criticized for showing humane treatment to 'inhuman creatures.' And yet—and yet—there was an island of peace in this ocean of bitterness."

The chaplains had created this island out of respect for the importance of Christmas to Germans. Later that night, Gerecke led his congregation into the chapel, and to the defendants' surprise, the guards stayed outside. Unlike typical Sunday service, where Andrus demanded that each prisoner's guard be present in the chapel at all times, the rules were relaxed. Army-green blankets lined the chapel's rough walls, and a silver cross perched on top of the portable altar covered in white cloth at the front. A tiny Christmas tree sat in one corner with lighted candles. The moment belonged to Gerecke and thirteen war criminals.

"For the first time for months, we were free from continual observation and I felt the suppressed agitation which had been a normal part of my life, slip from me like a loosened chain," Fritzsche wrote. "And it seemed to me that the nervous tension among my neighbors had likewise relaxed."

The SS organist began to play carols, and one by one, the Nazis began humming. A few started singing, and by the time they got to "Silent Night," each man was singing at full volume. No one was louder than Goering, who sat in the front row, as he always did.

The chaplain began reading from the Gospel of Luke. "And she brought forth her firstborn son, and wrapped him in swaddling clothes, and laid him in a manger; because there was no room for them in the inn," Gerecke said, in what Fritzsche called "the soft unaccustomed accents of the English tongue." Gerecke went on, "And the angel said to them, Fear not: for, behold, I bring you good tidings of great joy, which shall be to all people. For to you is born this day in the city of David a Savior, which is Christ the Lord. . . . And suddenly there was with the angel a multitude of the heavenly host praising God, and saying, Glory to God in the highest, and on earth peace, good will toward men."

The men stared at the silver cross on the altar as Gerecke spoke. The chaplain's focus was on Christ who "seemed to gather all the light of the little chapel into Himself and give it forth again," Fritzsche wrote. "Here more clearly than in the most richly-decorated church He stood out as the focal point of all action, all thought."

Gerecke continued reading from Luke: "And it came to pass, as the angels were gone away from them into heaven, the shepherds said one to another, Let us now go even to Bethlehem, and see this thing which is come to pass, which the Lord has made known to us." Gerecke's voice began to rise. "And they came with haste, and found Mary, and Joseph, and the babe lying in a manger. And when they had seen it, they made known abroad the saying which was told them concerning this child."

The light of the Star of Bethlehem guided the shepherds, and it seemed to Fritzsche as if it was guiding those in this chapel on Christmas Eve. "Did not the light that flowed from Him penetrate the darkness that encompassed the immeasurable human suffering of my country and of the whole world?" he wrote. "Man must shoulder the blame and the responsibility for those sufferings, and because of them may, indeed must, strive against his fellow man. But he has yet to acknowledge his faults before God."

"And all they that heard it wondered at those things which were told them by the shepherds," Gerecke told the men. "But Mary kept all these things, and pondered them in her heart. And the shepherds returned, glorifying and praising God for all the things that they had heard and seen, as it was told to them."

Gerecke finished with a short sermon, and then Sauckel spoke: "We never took time to appreciate Christmas in its biblical meaning," he said. "Tonight we are stripped of all material gifts and away from our people. But we have the Christmas story."

Gerecke gave a benediction and the group sat in silence for five minutes. On the way out, Gerecke wished each man the peace of Christmas. Even the guards seemed a little less grim.

During Gerecke's weekly services in the winter, Fritzsche always sat in the front row between Goering and Ribbentrop. "Again and again I noticed how, in the tiny chapel, the masks dropped and the faces relaxed," he wrote. The winter was, as Fritzsche put it, "a time of reflection."

At each service, thirteen guards stood against the chapel's back wall. The guards didn't allow any talking, and if a guard thought his charge wasn't being reverent enough, he used his baton to prod the offender. For the most part, the thirteen defendants didn't attend every service together; Goering attended them all, telling Gustave Gilbert at one point, "Prayers, hell! It's just a chance to get out of this damn cell for a half hour." But when all thirteen did attend chapel, the men had "to squeeze up close to one another to find room," according to Fritzsche.

Hjalmar Schacht, the former Reichsbank president, wrote later that he "longed for a German pastor," but that request—despite Gerecke's own support for the idea—had been turned down. "It was not so much a question of services and sermon as of the opportunity to unburden the mind in spiritual matters," Schacht wrote. He noted that Gerecke was not fluent in German, so he had to read his sermons. "And it was all the more difficult for him to carry on a pastoral conversation with any of us."

Nevertheless, Schacht continued, "there was a most moving quality in Pastor Gerecke's zeal and devotion to his task. He was a dear, good, thoroughly well-intentioned man." There was something to the chapel that comforted the doomed men. Even those who would go on to survive the trial preferred Gerecke's chapel to the one at the center of the prison. Fritzsche found the larger chapel to be "a non-descript kind of place, lacking the comfort and peace that had enfolded us in the tiny chapel."

The prisoners sang hymns together, and their sounds made lighter moments in a dark place. Schacht and Raeder were the backbone of the little choir, since many of the other defendants were less skilled vocally. Goering began and ended each hymn happily and loudly, regardless of whether he had found the correct key. Ribbentrop's singing "was almost terrifying," Fritzsche wrote. Hitler's former foreign minister typically remained silent until his voice could blend into a crescendo of others. "Then," Fritzsche added, "cautiously, he would begin with a few long-drawn-out notes which increased in volume till they rose to a trumpet-call and the singer's face assumed an ecstatic expression. A visible sign of how much this rather unprofessional performance meant to a man who, as a rule, had but little opportunity to express his feelings."

After Andrus and the chaplains found some of the defendants' families, the chaplains began to visit them, often taking food or other supplies to help a Nazi wife and her children survive postwar destitution. In February 1946, Gerecke visited Emmy Goering, Luise Funk, Margarete Frick, and Henriette von Schirach. "One defendant said it touched his heart that the American Prison Chaplain should visit his people," Gerecke wrote in his monthly report. "The families were deeply grateful."

Gerecke's responsibilities didn't end with the defendants and their families. He and O'Connor were the chaplains for the Americans, too. Gerecke conducted services at the small church in Mögeldorf each Sunday at 11:00 A.M. and provided army transportation for any member of the 6850th who wanted to attend. And, as he had during the war, he encouraged Jewish members of the unit to seek out Jewish chaplains among the vast Allied occupation of the city. He also encouraged his superiors to erect an army chapel "complete in every detail" somewhere on the two-mile road between the Palace of Justice and the Grand Hotel. "Open for prayer at all times for men and women of all faiths," he wrote in his monthly report. "Just a touch of home."

O'Connor's smaller flock of four Catholic defendants also used the tiny chapel. Two of them, Hans Frank and Ernst Kaltenbrunner, were particularly murderous.

Hans Frank had been a quiet, scholarly child who preferred his books, chess, and music to the company of other children. He had married a typist when he was twenty-five and became a doting father to five children.

In 1926, nearly straight out of law school, Frank became the chief legal authority of the Nazi Party, defending its activities in several hundred cases across Germany. Frank even served as Hitler's personal attorney before enjoying a string of party posts—Bavarian minister of justice, Reich leader of the Nazi Party, Reich minister of justice. Hitler named him governor general of Poland in 1939, where he would earn nicknames like "Slayer of Poles" and the "Butcher of Krakow."

Hitler's goal in that country was to eradicate the Polish intelligentsia by closing the universities and sending intellectuals to concentration camps. By eliminating the intellectual class, the Nazis believed they'd be left with a Polish "nomadic labor" class that they could turn into slaves for the greater good of the Reich. To that end, Frank had every professor at the University of Krakow arrested and sent to concentration camps in Germany. The Jews, on the other hand, were sent to ghettos across Poland where they would starve to death.

The position of governor general came with the perks of unlimited confiscation and endless luxury. When American troops took an inventory of Frank's house in southern Germany in 1945, they found a da Vinci portrait of Cecilia Gallerani, a landscape by Rembrandt, a gilded chalice, an ivory chest, and a fourteenth-century Madonna with child. The paintings had both been stolen from the Krakow Czartoryski gallery, the chalice and chest had been taken from the Krakow Cathedral, and the Madonna had been swiped from the Krakow National Museum.

As people were starving in the Warsaw ghetto, the Franks were tireless hosts—consuming one thousand eggs each month, along with huge quantities of meat, geese, and butter at the governor's table. Frank also owned a luxurious armored Mercedes and a private railroad car with *Governor General* inscribed in bronze.

In the labor camps, the Germans gave the Jews wages of forty cents per day, which Frank considered charity rather than earnings. In 1940, he told a gathering of German soldiers that they should tell people back home that there were fewer lice and Jews in Poland these days, adding, "of course, I could not eliminate all lice and Jews in only one year's time." Krakow, he said once, was "crawling with Jews so that a decent person would not step into the street."

In July 1941, six months after Goering signed the document that would set into motion the "final solution to the Jewish problem," Frank sent a deputy as his representative to the Wannsee Conference in the Berlin suburbs, where Nazi officials discussed how to implement the Jewish genocide. A bizarre plan to send four million European Jews to Madagascar—which Frank supported as an alternative to sending them into Poland—had fallen through.

Instead, the men at the conference decided that the Jews would be sent east, organized into giant labor camps, and worked to death. Those who survived would be sent to extermination camps. The evacuations to the labor camps would begin in Poland.

"Before I continue, I want to beg you to agree with me on the following formula," Frank told his cabinet five months after Wannsee.

> We will principally have pity on the German people only, and on nobody else in the entire world. . . . This war would be only a partial success if the whole lot of Jewry survived it, while we shed our best blood to save Europe. My attitude toward the Jews will therefore be based solely on the expectation that they just disappear. They must be done away with. . . . Gentlemen, I must ask you to rid yourselves of all feeling of pity. We must annihilate the Jews wherever we find them and wherever it is possible. . . . The General Government will have to become just as free of the Jews as the Reich.

By December 1942, the Germans had transported to the extermination camps 85 percent of the Jews of the General Government, which made for roughly 1.4 million people.

Hans Frank was Chaplain O'Connor's greatest success at Nuremberg. Over the winter, O'Connor rebaptized Frank, who seemed by all accounts to have been a serious student of the faith. He gave Frank a copy of Franz Werfel's novel *The Song of Bernadette*, which Frank read in his cell. Werfel, an Austrian Jew fleeing the Nazis across France in 1940, fictionalized the story of Bernadette Soubirous, a nineteenth-century miller's daughter who had seventeen visions of the Virgin Mary in Lourdes. Werfel first heard Bernadette's story in Lourdes, where he and his wife had found refuge from the Nazis.

If Frank sent thousands to the Reich's concentration camps, it was Ernst Kaltenbrunner who received them. Ernst was born in 1903 in Ried on the Inn, Austria, a small town near Hitler's birthplace, Braunau, and where he and Adolf Eichmann were boyhood friends.

His father and grandfather were lawyers, and Kaltenbrunner too studied law. He set up a practice in Linz in 1926, married, and had three children. He joined the Nazi Party in 1932, and in 1935 became commander of the Austrian SS. The massive intelligence network Kaltenbrunner created in Austria and spread into Hungary and Yugoslavia impressed SS chief Henrich Himmler, and after the assassination of Reinhard Heydrich in 1942, Kaltenbrunner was named head of the Reich Security Main Office.

A relative unknown among Nazi leadership at the time, Kaltenbrunner suddenly found himself controlling the Gestapo, the SD—or Security Service—and the Security Police. He had authority over the Einsatzgruppen units that roamed eastern Europe killing as many Jews as they could find, and as Eichmann's superior, he was responsible for the administrative apparatus behind the entire concentration and extermination camp system. From January 1943 until the end of the war, it was Kaltenbrunner's responsibility to see that the Final Solution ran smoothly.

Kaltenbrunner was a giant man—nearly seven feet tall with massive shoulders and bulging arms. His neck was more like a block connecting his shoulders to his head. An alcoholic who smoked a hundred cigarettes a day, Kaltenbrunner's square chin jutted forward when he spoke, which he did in a clipped, precise manner, through thin lips and crooked teeth. A scar that ran from the left side of his mouth up toward his nose was rumored to have come from a duel he fought in college but was actually the result of an accident that launched him through the shattered windshield of his car. Much of the rest of his face was pockmarked, and his eyes were narrow and brown. Rebecca West wrote that Kaltenbrunner "looked like a vicious horse."

By the end of the war, even Himmler was afraid of Kaltenbrunner, who was a terrifying combination of smart, devious, deceitful, and sadistic. He loved to hear about the various methods of execution used at his camps, and he was especially intrigued by the gas chambers. Unlike so many of the Nazis who were ideologues, Kaltenbrunner was loyal to no place and no one—not Austria, not Germany, not Himmler, not Hitler.

"He was a gangster filled with hatred and resentment and plans for improving his own condition," according to historian Eugene Davidson. He "would use any weapon to advance himself and anyone might be his victim."

When Kaltenbrunner took the witness stand at Nuremberg in April 1946 to defend himself, the prosecution asked him repeatedly about his association with the Austrian concentration camp Mauthausen. Prosecutors wanted to implicate Kaltenbrunner in the crimes that took place there, and they produced a photo of Kaltenbrunner and Heinrich Himmler on either side of Mauthausen's commandant, SS-Obersturmbannführer Franz Ziereis. In the photo Ziereis stands inside the camp and points to something unknowable in the distance, possibly something beautiful.

HIGH ABOVE THE DANUBE, on a plateau overlooking blending shades of green pastureland, purple and white wildflowers bow in the breeze. To the east, small farmhouses dot distant hills, and to the south, the snowy peaks of Mount Kremsmauer on the Austrian Alps frame the end of the Danube Valley. Atop the plateau is a granite wall enclosing Camp Mauthausen, and the best views of the Alpine scenery in the distance come while standing on stones that enclose a gas chamber just below. In this spot in the middle of Europe, nearly one hundred thousand people were tortured and murdered. Less than half of those killed have been identified.

The town of Mauthausen, with its colorful ice cream shops and comfortable pubs on the bank of the Danube, is a suburb of Hitler's childhood city of Linz, situated twelve miles northwest, up the river. In May 1938, two months after Austria was swallowed into the Third Reich, the Nazis chose Mauthausen as a site to hold Austria's political prisoners. Inmates from the German camp at Dachau built the camp with granite from nearby quarries. By November, one thousand of the former Dachau prisoners lived and worked as slave laborers in Mauthausen. In February 1939, Ziereis was named the camp's commandant. Nearly three thousand inmates were imprisoned at the camp by September 1939, almost all of them from Austria and Germany.

As the camp's population grew, so did its operations and its death toll. In 1938, as construction on Mauthausen began, thirty prisoners died, according to Ziereis's camp death register, which he called "the book of numbers." After Germany invaded Poland in September 1939, the killings at Mauthausen began to increase dramatically, and the number of those killed grew to 445. As the

German war effort ramped up, Mauthausen served as the hub to an ever-increasing array of satellite camps around Austria.

Ziereis oversaw seven SS officers and heads of divisions. Under them were ninety-one block officers and labor-gang officers, who were German SS men from the Death's Head Battalion. Below them were kapos, typically violent criminals, who were given supervisory duties over their fellow prisoners and wide latitude to punish them as they wished.

As the Nazis built more subcamps, they also needed more guards, so they brought them in from Romania, Slovakia, Hungary, and Croatia. The *volksdeutsche*, as the Third Reich called them, were ethnically German and had declared their loyalty to Hitler, and many were ready to do his bidding. Regular Wehrmacht units, municipal police officers, and Ukrainian volunteers joined them later.

The SS soon moved prisoners from other camps like Buchenwald and Sachsenhausen to Mauthausen. Polish intellectuals began arriving in 1940, followed by republican Spanish Civil War fighters, Soviet POWs, and Czech Jews. That year alone, eleven thousand prisoners were living on the beautiful plateau above the river.

Mauthausen did not have its own crematorium during that time, so the SS shipped bodies to municipal crematoriums in Steyr and Linz, which competed for the lucrative Mauthausen contracts. By the time the camp built its own, the crematoriums in the nearby cities had disposed of 2,100 bodies. By the end of 1940, 2,312 prisoners had died at Mauthausen.

In 1941, Reinhard Heydrich designed a three-tiered concentration camp system to be implemented throughout the Reich based on levels of prisoner behavior. Mauthausen was classified as a Category III camp, reserved for asocial, hardened criminals, "those who have hardly any chance at rehabilitation." This classification made Mauthausen and its largest subcamp, Gusen, situated about three miles away, "camps for murder."

That year, eighteen thousand more prisoners arrived at Mauthausen, and the SS used them in the subcamps for construction projects, such as the building of roads, tunnels, and power plants. Prisoners also worked in the armaments factories that the Nazis forced them to construct.

As the war dragged on, prisoners arrived from Yugoslavia, France, Greece, Belgium, and Luxembourg. Mauthausen's prisoners soon began to represent nearly every nation in western and eastern Europe. While there was a variety of cultures in the camp, the Jews were singled out for systematic slaughter. Most didn't last more than a few weeks. For instance, in 1941, two large groups of Jews—more than a thousand people from Czechoslovakia and the Netherlands—arrived at the camp and all were soon murdered.

At times the camp leadership focused on other groups. After Czech special agents assassinated Heydrich in Prague in 1942, Ziereis ordered 263 Czechs in the camp killed in one day. The shootings began at 8:30 A.M. and ended at 5:42 P.M. Kaltenbrunner took Heydrich's place as head of the Reich Security Main Office.

Twenty-one thousand people entered Mauthausen in 1942, and by the end of the year, 4,392 had been murdered there. Ziereis had cut food rations in February. Overcrowding in the barracks led to degraded sanitary conditions. Typhoid and dysentery epidemics followed, killing even more. Until the end of 1942, Mauthausen had the highest death rate among all Nazi concentration camps.

In the middle of 1943, when the SS decided to move the Reich's armament facilities for rocket and airplane-part production underground, it used Mauthausen subcamp labor to dig the massive caverns that housed the factories. The SS sent subcamp prisoners who were singled out for punishment to Mauthausen, where guards gassed them, worked them to death in the granite quarries, or shot them.

Mauthausen's gas chamber could kill up to 80 people at once. In the last three years of the camp's existence, the SS used Zyklon B to gas 3,445 people there. Before each gassing, the SS checked prisoners' mouths and marked a cross on the chest or back of those who had gold teeth.

At the Nuremberg trials, as a part of his defense that he'd never seen the gas chamber at Mauthausen, Kaltenbrunner said he'd only visited the camp's quarry. The quarries were a source of great economic interest to Germany—they were useful because the SS sold the granite unearthed by the camp prisoners to other departments of the Reich for use in Hitler's great building projects. Yet, as the witness testimony in Kaltenbrunner's case showed, they were also an effective murder weapon.

The quarry was first leased, and then owned, by the SS company German Earth and Stone Works. When Albert Speer was the Reich's armaments minister, he gave the Earth and Stone Works an interest-free loan of several million reichsmarks and signed a ten-year contract with the SS company to supply the granite for his great visions of Nazi buildings and monuments. One pit in particular, known as the Wiener Graben quarry, sat several hundred yards west of the main camp. This quarry was one of four between the thirty-seven-acre Mauthausen camp and the Gusen subcamp nearby, and it was one of the most evocative symbols of Mauthausen's cruelty.

The prisoners who worked in the quarry woke up at 5:30 A.M. and drank a cup of coffee before marching down the quarry's stone steps into the pit. Lunch was one cup of cabbage or turnip soup. Dinner was a sixth of a loaf of bread and a half-ounce of margarine or sausage. The SS considered any prisoner weighing ninety-five pounds well nourished, though some workers weighed as little as sixty pounds. Every prisoner worked eleven-hour days, six days a week. Those who were too exhausted to work were shot, beaten to death in the quarry, or drowned in the pools of rainwater that collected on the quarry floor. Hundreds more simply froze to death in the pit during winter.

The 186 steps to the quarry floor were badly cut into the clay, and they were also slippery. Each was eight to twelve inches tall and held in place by logs. When prisoners reached the bottom of the quarry, they strapped massive granite slabs on their backs. The prisoners were often hobbled from the sharp rocks caught inside their wooden sandals, yet the guards beat them with rifle butts as they brought the boulders up this "Stairway of Death." When a man reached the top, a guard may have directed him to throw the slab from the top of the sheared quarry wall—twelve stories high—back down to the bottom of the pit, then demand he run down and bring the same boulder back up the steps. The quarry guards regularly shot or beat the quarry workers to death if the prisoners' pace on the Stairway of Death wasn't fast enough.

Throwing prisoners twelve stories to their deaths below was also a cheap, effective murder method for the SS guards. As a witness in the case against Kaltenbrunner, the former SS guard Alois Höllriegel described a scene at the top of the quarry cliff. "I saw from my watchtower that these two SS men were beating the prisoners, and I realized immediately that they intended to force them to throw themselves over the precipice or else to push them over," Höllriegel said. "I noticed how one of the prisoners was kicked while lying on the ground, and the gestures showed that he was supposed to throw himself down the precipice. This the prisoner promptly did—under the pressure of the blows—presumably in despair."

An American prosecutor asked Höllriegel if the SS had a name for the prisoners they threw into the quarry. "Yes," Höllriegel said. "In Mauthausen Camp they were called parachutists."

This was only one horrific way to kill at Mauthausen. Many prisoners, for instance, were "bathed" to death by guards who hosed them down with cold water outside in freezing temperatures. Others were murdered with axes. Aribert Heim, Mauthausen's own version of Josef Mengele and known to inmates as Dr. Death, experimented on prisoners, frequently injecting benzine or phenol directly into the hearts of those too weak to work. In 1941, camp officials sent an eighteen-year-old Jewish prisoner—a former soccer player and swimmer—to Heim with a foot inflammation. Instead of treating the foot, Heim "anesthetized him, cut him open, castrated him, took apart one kidney and removed the second," according to a Mauthausen prisoner who witnessed the murder. Then Heim removed the victim's head and boiled the flesh off it so he could keep it on display. Heim "needed the head because of its perfect teeth," the prisoner said.

Commanders set up special areas around the camp for hangings and shootings. Hundreds of prisoners died of electrocution on the barbed-wire fence surrounding the camp. Guards drove gas vans, equipped to kill anyone in the back carriage, from Mauthausen to Gusen and back. From the summer of 1941 to the end of 1944, Ziereis sent hundreds of prisoners to Hartheim, a Nazi "euthanasia institute" near Linz.

In 1944, groups of 10,000 Hungarian Jews arrived and were mostly worked and starved to death. The SS killed 7,076 that year at the camp. At its height, in March 1945, the Mauthausen system included 84,472 prisoners, and by the time U.S. troops liberated the camp in May, 15,630 more had died. Over the seven years of the Mauthausen camp's existence, the SS brought more than 200,000 people there to use as slave labor and then to kill. Mauthausen became a death center for the entire Austrian concentration camp system.

IN THE SUMMER OF 1943, Father Sixtus O'Connor reported to Camp Barkeley, Texas, and was assigned to the Eleventh Armored Division's Combat Command "B," a brigade-sized unit of three thousand to five thousand troops. Combat Command "B" was led by Colonel Wesley Yale, who had previously set up a disciplinary training troop at Fort Bliss, Texas, for garrison soldiers whose crimes didn't rise to the level of dishonorable discharge.

A year earlier the army had created the Eleventh—known as the Thunderbolt—in response to the British defeat of German field marshal Erwin Rommel at the Battle of El Alamein in Egypt, which was a crucial victory for the Allies in North Africa. The U.S. Army wanted more than the ten tank divisions it had, so the Thunderbolt was formed in Louisiana in August 1942.

In November 1943, the Eleventh moved to Camp Ibis in California, part of the army's Desert Training Center in the Mojave along the Nevada and Arizona borders.

The division's insignia was composed of three torques—yellow for cavalry, blue for infantry, and red for artillery. In the middle, a cannon symbolizing firepower was set atop a tank track symbolizing mobility and armor protection. A red bolt of lightning flashed across both symbols, indicating the division's capability for shock action.

The Eleventh's first commanders were told to have new recruits combat-ready by April 1943. The short time frame meant that the training at Camp Polk, Louisiana, was intense. Amid the dust and dirt of western Louisiana, the men spent long hours on huge howitzers and half-track-mounted medium weapons, becoming specialists in mortars, machine guns, rifles, pistols, and artillery pieces.

O'Connor joined the unit in July 1943, and most of his responsibilities involved celebrating Mass, hearing confessions, visiting hospitals, giving "sex morality" lectures and marriage instruction, sitting in on conferences with company and battalion commanders, and presiding at weddings, baptisms, and funerals. At Camp Ibis, he took part in his unit's desert maneuvers, and in January 1944 O'Connor was promoted to captain.

On September 27, 1944, just as the war began turning for the Allies in Europe, the division's ten thousand enlisted men and six hundred officers left Staten Island on the HMS *Samaria* and the USS *Hermitage,* landing in England on October 12.

The Normandy invasion had taken place several months earlier, and Germany was reeling. In early December, after six weeks of training, the Eleventh was ordered to the European continent to relieve the Ninety-Fourth Infantry Division at Chateau Briand.

But just as the unit hit France, its orders changed. German divisions were attacking along a fifty-mile front in Belgium's Ardennes Forest. The Ardennes offensive, also known as the Battle of the Bulge for the shape it made in Allied battle lines, was Hitler's final effort at keeping Germany from being overrun. On December 19, the Eleventh began sprinting from Normandy to the Ardennes, which was six hundred miles away. The division was assigned to General George Patton's Third Army. Tanks, half-tracks, armored cars, jeeps, and trucks raced through bitter cold, rain, and snow toward battle. One soldier described it as "a wild ride in a complete blackout."

On Christmas Eve, German planes strafed the division. "Christmas morning was the first time I went to church with a forty-five . . . hanging by my side," one soldier wrote home. As the division positioned itself at the center of the bulge to await the German attack, its orders changed again. The Germans were menacing the only supply route to the 101st Airborne Division, which was fighting in Bastogne, Belgium, and the Eleventh was ordered to clear the road.

During the battle, O'Connor's unit, Combat Command "B," captured the small Belgian town of Mande St. Etienne and held on, despite a fierce counterattack. In freezing temperatures that claimed many toes, and with very little sleep, the Eleventh pushed two German divisions back six miles, liberated a dozen towns, and cleared the Bastogne supply line. After five days of fighting, the division accomplished its objective, having suffered 661 casualties.

Because of O'Connor's fluency in German, he was asked to be an interpreter between U.S. commanding officers and Germans the Eleventh captured during the battle. Many of the German POWs were afraid of reprisals for a slaughter of more than eighty unarmed American GIs in Malmedy, Belgium, by a German unit on December 16, just after the Battle of the Bulge began. O'Connor calmed the German soldiers down, telling them that American troops would never murder unarmed prisoners.

O'Connor's experience at Mande St. Etienne was his first on the front lines, but it was not his last. Thousands of other chaplains saw battle during the war as well. The U.S. Army spelled out for its chaplains their role in battle, stating that

> *when the ground forces go into action, their chaplain should be with them. This may mean he will move from one platoon to another or will minister to the wounded in exposed positions but never that he will place himself in unnecessary danger. . . . His skills may save the lives of wounded men. . . . He will do his utmost to comfort the suffering and give the consolations of religion to the dying.*

As the Thunderbolt moved east, it encountered frequent artillery and sniper fire from increasingly desperate German forces. Bodies and wrecked equipment littered the snowy landscape. Between battles, the men of the Eleventh slept in foxholes the retreating German army had left behind, drinking melted snow filtered through handkerchiefs. An outbreak of dysentery exacerbated the constant threat of frostbite.

On February 6, 1945, the Eleventh reached the Siegfried Line—a four-hundred-mile-long, three-mile-deep system of bunkers, command posts, tunnels, troop shelters, and tank traps that defended German's western border—and attacked for twelve days.

Once past the massive wall, the Thunderbolt continued deeper into Germany. When the division finally crossed the Rhine on March 28 at Oppenheim, flares, tracers, and 90 mm bursts lit up the night to repel the Luftwaffe war planes attacking from above.

Throughout the rest of March and April, the division moved through small towns toward Bavaria, where Nazi holdouts resisted Allied capture and where snipers took potshots at the Americans rolling through.

During the months of fighting, O'Connor's monthly chaplain reports are perfunctory. His January report notes only that "the troops I serve were in actual combat two of the four Sundays this month." In February, he wrote forty-six letters of condolence, a task he continued for the next three months. He celebrated Mass at least once every day for as many soldiers as could make it. And thousands did between December and April.

O'Connor had seen months of combat and had done his best to comfort those needing God. In the middle of battle, O'Connor listened to more than four thousand confessions. He also earned a Bronze Star in the process. His citation read:

> Between 30 December 1944 and 1 May 1945, Chaplain O'Connor was often in front line positions ministering to the wounded and dying and furnishing spiritual guidance to many men suffering from mental disturbances incidental to combat. In this capacity, Chaplain O'Connor has been frequently subject to heavy enemy artillery, mortar and small arms fire, especially in the area of [redacted]. By his complete devotion to duty and utter disregard of personal safety, Chaplain O'Connor has contributed to the saving of many lives and the immediate rehabilitation of many men who otherwise would have been victims of battle fatigue . . .

As the division moved south, it liberated thousands of Allied prisoners from POW camps. At Bensberg, Combat Command "B" came across its first concentration camp, with thousands of Russian and Polish slave laborers. Then, near the Regen River, the division noticed emaciated bodies on the sides of the road. As the Americans marched closer to the river, they met sixteen thousand inmates from Buchenwald who had just overrun what was left of their SS guards. In the coming days, they would see even more. When the SS were fleeing the Flossenburg concentration camp, they'd brought the prisoners with them, shooting those along the way who couldn't keep up. The SS had done the same at Stamsried and Posing, releasing prisoners who spent their newfound freedom desperately wandering the countryside scavenging for food. "For over four months we had witnessed death daily, but these people were the walking dead," wrote one officer of the Eleventh. "They were starved, barely clothed and dazed."

The Thunderbolt had pushed across Germany in one of the fastest advances in military history, and on April 25, 1945, crossed the border into Austria. On May 5, the Eleventh rolled into central Linz without firing a shot. The people of the city welcomed the American tanks, throwing flowers and waving at the GIs. Women brought bottles of wine and hard cider to the men. Polish and Czech slave laborers danced in the streets. But as the division continued down the Danube later that day, that happy scene changed drastically.

A reconnaissance patrol approaching the town of Mauthausen discovered twenty thousand people living in a camp on a hill above the town in conditions the GIs couldn't have previously imagined. The fleeing SS, unable to kill all the prisoners, had simply locked them all inside their barracks without access to food, water, or facilities. As the GIs opened some locked Mauthausen buildings, they found one or two living among the hundreds of dead.

In the camp hospital, they found evidence of cannibalism. Between the barracks at Mauthausen, five hundred bodies were stacked like wood. Another twenty thousand in Gusen rushed to greet the Americans. The division hurried all medical personnel and equipment to the camp, and cavalry patrols swept the area, catching one thousand fleeing Mauthausen guards.

The men of the Eleventh engaged Mauthausen's "walking skeletons," as one GI put it, handing out cigarettes and whatever food they had. Some of the former prisoners acted as tour guides, eager to show the Americans just what kind of hell they had survived—the bunker, the quarry, the gas showers, the crematorium. The scene was overwhelming for the soldiers. "These experiences are difficult to think about without wondering why such sadistic acts would be perpetrated purposely on any group by another," one GI wrote. "Such depravity seems foreign to most men, even in war time, and we were not psychologically prepared to really fully accept the facts before us."

Another soldier described a long trench, an open grave filled with two hundred bodies lying in a long row with flies buzzing around them. "It was hard to comprehend," the man wrote. "These men had been purposely starved to death, brutally and systematically. Their eyes stared at the sky in death as they lay grotesquely on the ground, awaiting burial in their mass grave."

Many prisoners needed instant attention. The SS had destroyed electrical and water facilities before fleeing and it would take two days for nurses from the Sixty-Sixth Field Hospital unit to make it to Mauthausen. In the meantime, O'Connor's unit acted as de facto medical personnel for five thousand survivors. GIs set to work trying to help those survivors who were near death. Many GIs flinched and vomited as they approached the survivors who lay on the ground in their own waste, covered with flies. One officer gently picked up the body of a man and his uniform became spattered with urine and excrement. His men then followed his example.

Many of the survivors who were not near death found ways to avenge their treatment at the camp. When the SS were fleeing Mauthausen, they had locked the gates and left the fences electrified. They also left many of the kapos and guards inside the prison. With numbers on their side, the prisoners had overrun what authority was left inside the camp and set up a tribunal for the execution of certain guards. On May 4, the prisoners had cut the throats of four guards. Prisoners simply beat some guards to death, while other guards were forced to run up and down the Stairway of Death before prisoners killed them. One guard was tied to a barracks bunk while prisoners took turns urinating and defecating on him.

Among the first duties of the Americans when they arrived the next day was to confiscate weapons from former prisoners and stop the lynch justice set up by the prisoners.

One Eleventh Division doctor was speaking with former inmates outside the walls of the Mauthausen camp when two Germans in civilian clothes approached. The former prisoners, weak as they were, surrounded the two men and roughly backed them into a corner by the prison fence. The Americans watched as the prisoners forced the frightened Germans—now yelling, "*Nicht SS! Nicht SS!*"—to raise their arms so that their armpits could be inspected. The doctor realized that the prisoners were looking for tattoos of serial numbers that the SS inked under their arms. When the former prisoners saw that these two men were likely regular German army, they let them go.

Had the two men been SS, "we would have seen them beaten and pulled here and there, and kicked violently to death before our eyes," the doctor wrote later. "Certainly this was a grim and sobering fact—a view of life in the raw—that seemed shocking, even to combat soldiers."

One soldier walked up to one of Mauthausen's main buildings and peered through a window. Two SS guards were locked inside, bloodied and bruised from a beating they'd suffered at the hands of their former prisoners. They'd been saved from murder by American GIs and locked away for their own safety. The next day, the same soldier peered again into the same window. One of the guards had hanged himself in his cell.

At times, even the liberators had to be held back from beating the guards. An American photographer in U.S. Army uniform followed a group of former prisoners hunting for their former captors. When they found one in an alley, the men began to beat and kick the guard to death. When the photographer produced a knife, they slit the guard's throat as the photographer took a picture.

The Americans were able to track down Franz Ziereis, the camp's commandant, and bring him to justice appropriately. Acting on a tip from former prisoners, six Thunderbolt GIs found Ziereis on May 23 in Spital, Austria, a mountainous region one hundred miles from Mauthausen. When he fled into the woods, the Americans shot and wounded him. They brought him back to the camp for questioning.

According to the camp's official rolls, Mauthausen held 66,500 prisoners the day before liberation. More than 450 died each day during the following week. The Americans turned the SS sports ground, just outside the camp walls, into a cemetery for the first 700 bodies. The next 1,500 had to be transported to a potato field between Gusen and another subcamp.

The American official in charge of the liberation had twenty of the nearby town's leading citizens brought up the hill for a tour of the camp. All of them said they were shocked and that they had absolutely no idea this kind of horror had been happening for years. As more victims died, the Americans forced the identifiable Nazi Party members in town to bury them while the townspeople watched. They also brought in four hundred regular German army POWs to get the camp back in working order. Soon, the German soldiers were under attack from former prisoners, and the Americans had to threaten to open fire to calm the situation.

Externally, and officially, O'Connor dealt with his experience at Mauthausen with documentation and numbers. "Troops of this command captured two Concentration Camps, Camp Mauthausen and Camp Gusen, and were assigned the task of directing these Camps until they could be liquidated," he wrote in his May report. He went on:

> *From 8 May until 31 May I conducted burial services for 1,834 inmates of Camp Mauthausen and for 1,077 inmates of Camp Gusen. I also visited the hospitals of these two camps and administered the last rites of the Catholic Church to more than 2,000 patients. I found Catholic priests in both camps and secured Mass kits for them and with their help arranged for both daily and Sunday Mass in these Camps. My work still continues at both places.*

In the month O'Connor spent at Mauthausen, he made nearly forty trips to the camp cemeteries and buried about one hundred people with each service.

"This unit moved to a new area on 7 June 1945," he wrote. "Thus the work at the Concentration Camps, Camp Mauthausen and Camp Gusen, came to an end." That was the last he ever wrote about it. If he ever spoke about it, he didn't do so publicly.

O'Connor told a few friends after the war that Patton had heard about his soothing of the German POWs' fears during the Battle of the Bulge, and that six months later the general personally recommended O'Connor for the Nuremberg assistant chaplain position.

In early September, O'Connor was ordered to join the Twenty-Sixth Infantry Regiment of the First Infantry Division. Within days, he was back in Germany with a new assignment as the Catholic chaplain for the Nazi war criminals awaiting trial at Nuremberg.

The army's *Technical Manual* TM 16–205 states that the chaplain who "shares the peril of battle, showing kindness that never fails and a sincere concern" for the welfare of his flock "will gain a place in their confidence that will reinforce powerfully all his efforts to give moral and religious instruction and inspiration." O'Connor's flock now included the authors of the slaughter he'd seen at Mauthausen.

BY THE TIME ERNST Kaltenbrunner took the stand in his own defense, in April 1946, O'Connor had been his pastor for eight months. The man who had been a frightening monster during the war became a sickly malcontent in prison. U.S. Army psychiatrist Douglas Kelley found Kaltenbrunner to be severely depressed just before the opening of the trial. He cried nearly every time the doctor visited.

"The hardness of character which marked him as an executioner had been replaced by this soft, sobbing personality who eagerly sought reassurance as to his future," Kelley wrote. "A great, hulking, tough-looking murderer who was at heart a shivering coward . . . he was a typical bully, tough and arrogant when in power, a cheap craven in defeat, unable even to stand the pressures of prison life."

On November 17, 1945, three days before the trials began, Kaltenbrunner had a minor brain hemorrhage that led to serious headaches. He was hospitalized and missed much of the first two months of the trials.

On the stand, Kaltenbrunner's strategy was simple: lie. Kaltenbrunner said he had never heard of most of the crimes his own attorney laid out. Others he'd heard of but had not been involved with. Any signature that looked like his, he said, was forged. The charges against him were among the most spectacular and horrific of the trials. The *Times* of London said, "probably more appalling crimes have never been charged against any man."

After Kaltenbrunner had denied signing one particular letter, the U.S. prosecutor went after him: "Is it not a fact that you are simply lying about your signature on this letter in the same way that you are lying to the Tribunal about almost everything else you have given testimony about?"

Kaltenbrunner shouted that "for a whole year I have been submitted to this insult of being called a liar!"

After his testimony, the *Times* of London said Kaltenbrunner had "put forward the ugliest defense yet heard at the Nuremberg trial . . . a flood of clumsy denial that would look stupid were it not a sorry attempt to hide behind dead men."

The newspaper said even Kaltenbrunner's codefendants "began to look embarrassed" in the dock. There's no question most, if not all, of the Nazis on trial at Nuremberg couched their own testimonies in varying levels of dishonesty, subterfuge, and fabrication, but Kaltenbrunner wasn't even trying to make it sound good. Goering couldn't stomach it and took one afternoon off, claiming to have a cold.

Kaltenbrunner testified that during the last days of the war, he'd ordered Mauthausen to be surrendered intact to Patton. But the prosecution introduced evidence and witnesses that showed Kaltenbrunner had actually ordered Ziereis to blow up all the inmates in the last days of the war. Witnesses testified that he'd given similar instructions to the leadership of other camps—Dachau, Landsberg, and Mueldorf. He'd requested some be bombed by the Luftwaffe. One SS colonel testified that a few days before the war ended, Kaltenbrunner ordered Ziereis to begin killing one thousand inmates each day.

"I consider the statement that I ever saw a gas chamber, either in operation or at any other time, wrong and incorrect," Kaltenbrunner told the court.

But then a witness for the prosecution told the tribunal that Kaltenbrunner "went laughing into the gas chamber."

"Then the people were brought from the bunker to be executed, and then all three kinds of executions: hanging, shooting in the back of the neck and gassing, were demonstrated," he continued. "After the dust had disappeared, we had to take away the bodies."

"Under my oath," Kaltenbrunner said. "I wish to state solemnly that not a single word of these statements is true."

He admitted visiting Mauthausen once but said it was the only concentration camp he'd ever seen and that he'd believed it to be a labor camp where stone was quarried to build Vienna's sidewalks. He said he'd never heard of Auschwitz until 1943, when Himmler told him it was an armaments factory.

As evidence that Kaltenbrunner had never visited Auschwitz, his attorney called as a witness Rudolf Hoess, the commandant of Auschwitz. But the legal strategy backfired when Hoess testified, in matter-of-fact tones that stunned the courtroom, that in his role at that camp he had supervised the murder of two and a half million people.

Hoess had been an SS officer for many years, and when he was designing Auschwitz, he visited Treblinka to see how the SS killed people there. He later described the gas chamber at Treblinka as a cell, about eight feet by eleven feet, that was connected to motors outside. The SS jammed about two hundred people into the cell, which was made of stone and cement. The cell doors were covered with metal sheeting and when they closed, the SS directed the exhaust from the motors into the cell, killing everyone in it within an hour. The commandant at Treblinka told Hoess they were able to kill eighty thousand people in six months this way. "He used monoxide gas," Hoess said later, "and I did not think that his methods were very efficient."

At Auschwitz, Hoess converted two old farmhouses near the camp into gas chambers, ripping out the internal walls and cementing the outsides to prevent leaks. The farmhouses were about seven hundred yards apart and closed off from the outside by woods and fences. Bunker I and Bunker II, called the red house and the white house, could kill about two thousand people at one time. They began operations in March 1942.

The previous July, a group of prisoners had been disinfecting bedding with a chemical pesticide consisting mostly of sulfuric acid called Zyklon B when the gas killed a cat that was wandering by. An SS guard took the discovery to Hoess. In September 1941, camp officers tried Zyklon B on 600 Soviet prisoners of war and 250 sick prisoners. Later that month, Hoess watched while 900 more Russian soldiers were killed using the gas.

Over the next year, as the red house and the white house were in use, Hoess began building four dedicated gas chambers—disguised as shower rooms—and crematoria. Two of the facilities consisted of an underground gas chamber with a crematorium at ground level. Two more freestanding gas chambers supplied corpses to other freestanding crematoria. SS guards lowered Zyklon B cans through openings in the chamber's ceilings, into mesh columns. The heat of the victims' own bodies turned the pellets into fatal gas.

Hoess said later that the effectiveness of the Zyklon B wasn't consistent. "After all of the observations done all of those years, I feel that it depended upon the weather, the wind, the temperature; and as a matter of fact, the effectiveness of the gas itself was not always the same," he told a U.S. Army psychiatrist in Nuremberg.

Usually it took from three to fifteen minutes to extinguish all these people, that is, for no sign of life anymore. In the farmhouses we had no peek holes so that sometimes when we opened the doors after a considerable period of time had elapsed, there were still some signs of life. Later on, in the newly erected crematory and gas chambers, which I designed, we had peek holes so that we could ascertain when these people were all dead.

An electrical ventilation system kicked on when there was no longer any movement inside the chamber. According to historian Richard J. Evans,

After twenty minutes or so, the canisters were pulled up again, to remove the possibility of any more gas escaping, while the chamber was ventilated and a special detachment of Jewish prisoners dragged the corpses out into another room, pulled out gold teeth and fillings, cut the women's hair off, removed gold rings, spectacles, prosthetic limbs and other encumbrances, and put the bodies into elevators that took them up to the crematorium room on the ground floor, where they were put into the incinerating ovens and reduced to ashes. Any remaining bones were ground up and the ashes used as fertilizer or thrown away in nearby woods and streams.

Hoess sent the hair of murdered women to Nazi workshops, where it was woven into special fittings for gaskets.

Burning the bodies of 2,000 people took about twenty-four hours. "Usually we could manage to cremate only about 1,700 to 1,800," Hoess said later. "We were thus always behind in our cremating because as you can see it was always much easier to exterminate by gas than to cremate, which took so much more time and labor."

At its most populous, the camp held 144,000 people, roughly the population of Dayton, Ohio. About 7,000 SS men worked at Auschwitz during its existence, not including secretaries and administrators. At one point, when Hoess was using prisoners to dig his many burning pits, the SS forced sixty prisoners to fill their wheelbarrows full of dirt and run as fast as they could behind one another along the rim of the deep pit. Some of the older prisoners fell into the pit with their wheelbarrows and the SS men laughed, called them "saboteurs," and began using them for target practice. A kapo named Reinhold noticed that an older Jewish man was having trouble scrambling up the side of the pit, and so he sent the man's son down after him. As the son began helping his father out, Reinhold ordered him to drown his father in the pit's standing water. After killing his father, the distraught young man found his way out of the hole, and Reinhold ordered more prisoners to throw him back down, then ordered the Jews left in the pit to drown him in the same water in which the young man had just drowned his father.

Hoess was involved in every aspect of Auschwitz's evil. He said later that he was present at most, if not all, the gassings. When typhoid broke out in one of the hospital barracks, Hoess gave the order to kill all the patients and anyone who had worked in the hospital. One day, as SS men slowly worked at the drudgery of throwing corpses into the massive burning pits, Hoess arrived, grabbed the body of a small child by the leg, and threw it into the pit. His example cheered morale, and the SS men nearby each grabbed the body of a small child and threw it into the flames.

Hoess's superior, Adolf Eichmann, had told Hoess that 2.5 million people had been murdered during his reign at Auschwitz. Hoess had thought the number was an exaggeration, but in the immediate aftermath of the war and the relatively recent discovery of the horrors of the concentration camps, he admitted to 2.5 million dead at trial. Historians now believe that despite Hoess's testimony at Nuremberg, at least 1 million and possibly 1.5 million people were killed at Auschwitz. About 90 percent of those killed were Jews, making Hoess responsible for at least 15 percent of the Jews murdered during the Holocaust.

When the war was over, Hoess went into hiding, disguising himself as a sailor at the Naval Intelligence School on the Island of Sylt in northern Germany. Afterward, he found work on a farm under the name Franz Lang, but British troops eventually arrested him in March 1946. Many Nazi officers carried a vial of cyanide with them so they could kill themselves in case they were caught by the Allies, but Hoess had accidentally broken his vial days earlier. Within a month he was sent to Nuremberg to be a witness in the trials of the major war criminals.

Those who saw or talked to Hoess at Nuremberg described the then-forty-five-year-old as "short, rather heavy set, somewhat red of face, with close-cropped hair." They remarked on his "weak, high voice" and said he "looked harmless, at least at a distance."

Nuremberg's U.S. Army psychiatrist Leon Goldensohn asked Hoess if the memories of gassings, executions, burning of corpses, if any of those thoughts "come upon you at times and in any way haunt you?"

No, Hoess said, "I have no such fantasies." He said he never had nightmares. He said he was "entirely normal. Even while I was doing this extermination work, I led a normal family life." In fact, Hoess and his family lived just outside the perimeter of the camp, where his wife's garden was filled with flowers and their children kept pet turtles and lizards. Auschwitz had provided a social life for Hoess and the other SS families who lived near the camp and had enjoyed the services of a nearby pub, a medical center, and the Dresden State Theater, which held concerts and performances.

Indeed, for many Nazis working the camps, the cruelties of war had deadened their senses of humanity. Albert Badewitz, a former Auschwitz engineer, testified at the Auschwitz atrocity trials in 1947:

A big part of the Polish intelligentsia died in the lumberyard in Auschwitz, whimpering in the snow. Some moved with a last flick-

ering of survival instinct toward a rotten piece of bone and tried to put it in their mouth. Often they died in this position. Then a fellow-sufferer took the piece of bone out of their hand. I myself and several others have in this condition gulped raw horsemeat. The horse had died several days ago, and the cadaver had already been buried in the earth. I am not ashamed for that, the instinct of self-preservation made half animals in all of us.

For Hoess, however, evil, and perhaps the ordinariness he found in his life at Auschwitz, came from an unquestioning obedience. When Heinrich Himmler gave Hoess the order to design and build a massive extermination center, "the order was authoritative—the explanation sufficient," Whitney Harris, a member of the American prosecution team who took Hoess's deposition later wrote. "In [Hoess's] mind, he had no alternative but to obey. He did so to the best of his ability, and his ability was such that he became the greatest killer of history. Devoid of moral principle, he reacted to the order to slaughter human beings as he would have to an order to fell trees."

Goldensohn asked Hoess whether the destruction of millions of people was justified in his mind.

"Not justified," Hoess said. "But Himmler told me that if the Jews were not exterminated at that time, then the German people would be exterminated for all time by the Jews."

"How could the Jews exterminate the Germans?" Goldensohn asked.

"I don't know," said Hoess. "That is what Himmler said. Himmler didn't explain."

"Don't you have a mind or opinion of your own?" asked Goldensohn.

"Yes," Hoess said. "But when Himmler told us something, it was so correct and so natural we just blindly obeyed it."

Hoess told Gustave Gilbert that "it was not always a pleasure to see those mountains of corpses and smell the continual burning," but that he "never gave it much thought to whether it was wrong. It just seemed a necessity."

Hoess was certainly aware that what he was directing in Auschwitz was wrong. He later described the small children as they made their way into the gas chambers "playing or joking with one another and carrying their toys." He recalled that "one woman approached me as she walked past, and, pointing to her four children who were . . . helping the smallest ones over the rough ground, whispered, 'How can you bring yourself to kill such beautiful, darling children? Have you no heart at all?'" He said later he "had to appear cold and indifferent to events that must have wrung the heart of anyone possessed of human feelings. I had to watch coldly, while the mothers with laughing or crying children went into the gas-chambers."

In 1942, when Hoess's wife found out what was actually happening inside the gates near her garden, she confronted Hoess, who told her the truth. "She was very upset and thought it cruel and terrible," he said later. "I explained it to her the same way Himmler explained it to me. Because of this explanation she was satisfied, and we didn't talk about it anymore. However, from that time forth, she frequently remarked that it would be better if I obtained another position."

In their final session together at Nuremberg, Goldensohn asked Hoess if he was a sadist.

"No," Hoess said. "Whenever I found guards who were guilty of treating internees too harshly, I tried to exchange them for other guards." Besides, he said, "I never struck any internee in the entire time I was commandant."

Goldensohn had also spoken with Kaltenbrunner just before his testimony began in April, and Kaltenbrunner's psychology was similar to that of Hoess, his underling.

Kaltenbrunner told Goldensohn he knew he was "thought of as another Himmler."

But "I'm not," he said, smiling. "The papers make me out as a criminal. I never killed anyone."

AN ESTIMATED SIXTY MILLION men, women, and children were murdered in the twentieth century in mass killings and genocides. After the genocide of the Native Americans in the nineteenth century came the annihilation of the Hereros of southwest Africa by the Germans in 1904, the Armenian genocide perpetrated by the Turks beginning in 1915, the manufactured starvation of the Ukrainians by the Soviets in 1932, the Holocaust in the late 1930s and 1940s, the reign of the Khmer Rouge in the 1970s, and genocides in the former Yugoslavia and Rwanda in the 1990s. Rudolf Hoess was responsible for 1.5 percent of the genocidal murders of the twentieth century.

Few people believe themselves to be capable of the extraordinary human evil perpetrated by the Nazis, and the inability to comprehend how the Holocaust occurred has reassured or comforted millions since the Second World War. "It helps side us, normal men as we take ourselves to be, against the doers, the Nazi perpetrators," wrote philosopher Arne Vetlesen. "The doers, we like to think, are not like us; indeed, their being unlike us is the very quality which explains that they could do what they did. Having committed atrocities so outrageous in nature and scope as to explode our faculties of comprehension, they, authors of the unthinkable, must surely be—or have been—abnormal men."

To think in this way, however, is to turn away from what the Holocaust means, to refuse to fully acknowledge its scope and what it says about the human condition. "It is," wrote Vetlesen, "to help perpetuate the very conditions which made its occurrence a historical fact in the first place."

Genocide scholar and social psychologist James Waller has written that:

the greatest catastrophes occur when the distinctions between war and crime fade; when there is dissolution of the boundaries between military and criminal conduct, between civility and barbarity; when political, social, or religious groups embrace collective violence against a defenseless victim group as warfare or, perhaps worse yet, as "progress." Such acts are human evil writ large.

Hoess and Kaltenbrunner certainly were killers in some capacity, but were they psychopaths? Gilbert's diagnosis of Hoess at Nuremberg was that he was "intellectually normal with the schizoid apathy, insensitivity and lack of empathy that could hardly be more extreme in a frank psychotic." If not psychotic, was he sane and evil?

Evil can be defined as any source of suffering or destruction to a living thing and can be divided into two main categories—natural and moral. Natural evil occurs outside of the control of humans and includes acts of God such as earthquakes, hurricanes, floods, and tornadoes. Moral evil begins in the human heart. It is the suffering we inflict on one another.

Waller defines moral evil as "the deliberate harming of humans by other humans." He breaks down moral evil into smaller harms, such as the destruction of property or psychological harm from the threat of physical injury, and larger harms, which include extraordinary evil. Instead of focusing on the acts of serial killers or gunmen who attack public spaces, Waller is interested in "the harm we perpetrate on each other under the sanction of political, social, or religious groups—in other words, the malevolent human evil perpetrated in times of collective social unrest, war, mass killings and genocide."

Does attempting to understand human evil create a path toward justifying or excusing the behavior that creates evil? Even Rudolf Hoess might present moral philosophers with a problem. When he was a child, Hoess's closest friend was a black pony his parents gave him for his seventh birthday. He would ride it for hours in the Black Forest near his home in Baden-Baden.

At one point, Hoess was a seemingly normal human being. And if the perpetrators of genocide can be seen as fellow human beings, do they deserve empathy, or even forgiveness, from those of us who choose to lead good lives?

In Catholic social teaching, evil is the absence of the good that God gave to humans. Because evil is a lack of something, it can only exist if something else exists. "Evil can only exist in another," wrote the philosopher Father Paul Crowley. "It is parasitic on the good." The central question, theologian Robert P. Kennedy wrote, asks why "a creature [would] spurn God's goodness and deform itself."

Evil is certainly problematic for mainstream religious belief. For one, the Hebrew Bible contains stories of God creating great suffering in the world. The prophet Amos asks, "Does disaster befall a city, unless the Lord has done it?"

Yet the existence of moral evil in humans is even trickier to understand. Kennedy wrote that "the existence of moral evil is the central enigma of human life," and the corollary of free will. In a theology that holds there is only one, all-powerful God who bestowed humans with free will, must God in some way be responsible for mass annihilation? If an omniscient God knew when he was bestowing free will on humans that "free" meant anything goes, he should have recognized that his greatest creation might commit grave evil in the world.

So how can a good and just God allow the suffering of his own creation? The medieval Christian philosopher and theologian Saint Augustine said that "either God cannot abolish evil, or he will not; if he cannot, he is not all powerful. If he will not, he is not all good." In many ways, this contradiction constitutes the central problem for students of theodicy, the study of God's relationship to evil.

If the source of the world's evil is Satan, as many Christians believe, what exactly is Satan? Some believe that Satan's arrival in Christian lore was the result of a centuries-long dissatisfaction with the mysteriousness of evil's source. T. J. Wray and Gregory Mobley, scholars who have traced Satan's biblical roots, ask: "Could it be that along with the development of monotheism is a growing existential frustration that makes it difficult for God's people to accept a deity who is responsible both for good and evil? Is it possible that at some point, God's negative attributes . . . are excised—in a sort of divine personality split—and appropriated to an inferior being (Satan)?"

In a verse from Isaiah, the Lord speaks to Cyrus, founder of the Persian Empire. "I form the light, and create darkness," God says. "I make peace, and create evil: I the Lord do all these things."

If God creates evil, but also allows his creation free will, is God or man responsible for the Holocaust? Even if evil emerges in the absence of good, in the absence of God, the free will of his creature— bent on evil—is not able to subsume God's power. So if God is master of both absolute good and absolute evil, he must also claim those of us who choose darkness.

CHAPTER 9

The Brand of Cain

Justice without kindness or mercy is the height of injustice, and mercy
without justice is indifference and caprice and the end of all order.
—ULRICH ZWINGLI

THE IMPROVISED PRISON CHAPEL may have been the only peaceful refuge in the Palace of Justice. As prosecutors presented more evidence at trial and defendants and witnesses gave more testimony, the prisoners increasingly blamed one another for the crimes being leveled at the group.

Some, led by Goering, still defended Hitler, and laid the blame for the atrocities on Heinrich Himmler, Joseph Goebbels, and Martin Bormann. Others began to disparage Hitler's legacy. Between trial sessions on June 13, Goering and Hitler's former chancellor, Franz von Papen, engaged in a shouting match. Goering defended Hitler, referring to him in the present tense as "our Chief of State."

"The Nazi Chief of State!" the normally diplomatic Papen yelled back. "A chief of state who murdered six million innocent people!"

Goering didn't relent. "You can't say Hitler ordered it," he said.

"Well then, who did order those mass murders?" Papen asked. "Did you order them?"

Goering was flustered. "No. No—Himmler," he mumbled and rushed past Papen out of the courtroom.

At lunch, Speer, Fritzsche, and Schirach laughed about how Goering's blusterings had begun to grow tiresome, even with diplomats like Papen.

"No, of course Hitler didn't order the mass murders," Fritzsche said sarcastically. "Some sergeant must have done it."

The next day Papen took the stand. It was the 155th day of the trial, and Papen, a member of O'Connor's Catholic flock, told the court about his religious background: "I grew up with conservative principles which unite a man most closely to his own folk and his native soil, and as my family has always been a strong supporter of the Church, I of course grew up in this tradition as well."

In recent days, amid all the turmoil, the other defendants had heard a rumor that senior American officials, including Gerecke, were being allowed to return home. Word was going around that Alma was calling him back to St. Louis. As Papen spoke, Fritzsche sat in the dock and wrote a letter to Alma. He passed it around and all the defendants eventually signed it, even those who didn't attend chapel services. General Alfred Jodl wrote, "I am joining this plea/request even though I don't belong to the Lutheran church. I do this heartily."

Fritzsche then gave the letter to Schirach, who translated it for Alma. It began:

> *Frau Gerecke,*
> *Your husband Pastor Gerecke has been taking religious care of the undersigned defendants during the Nuremberg trial. He has been doing so for more than half a year. We now have heard, dear Mrs. Gerecke, that you wish to see him back home after his absence of several years. Because we also*

*have wives and children we understand this wish of yours
very well.*

    *Nevertheless we are asking you to put off your wish to
gather your family around you at home for a little time. Please
consider that we cannot miss your husband now. During the
past months he has shown us uncompromising friendliness
of such a kind, that he has become indispensable for us in an
otherwise prejudiced environment which is filled with cold
disdain or hatred. . . .*

In his sessions with these men, Gerecke had listened countless
times as they moaned about being away from their families. "I had
done a little mild griping of my own," he pointed out. "I probably
mentioned my wife's health, and the fact that I had not seen her for
two and one half years. At any rate, apparently they decided that
Mrs. Gerecke would be the chief influence for my return home."

The Nazis' note, "written in almost illegible German script," had
been "the most incredible letter ever sorted by St. Louis postal clerks,"
Gerecke later wrote. The letter had made its way through regular
prison censorship and landed on Gerecke's own desk four days after it
was written. He sent it on to Alma with his own note attached:

    My Dear!

    *Here's the most unusual letter signed on the original by
the most talked about men in the world. You are, without a
doubt, the only woman in the world to get such a letter containing such a request. It is noteworthy that the Catholics too
have signed it. Keep the letter for my book, Honey.*

    Love,

    Hubby.

The last part of the Nazis' letter to Alma contained a word that
history has never associated with the Third Reich: love. "Our dear

Chaplain Gerecke is necessary for us not only as a minister but also as the thoroughly good man that he is—surely we need not describe him as such to his own wife. We simply have come to love him."

In this stage of the trial, the letter continued,

> *It is impossible for any other man than him to break through the walls that have been built up around us, in a spiritual sense even stronger than in a material one. Therefore, please leave him with us. Certainly you will bring this sacrifice and we shall be deeply indebted to you. We send our best wishes for you and your family! God be with you.*

"So I stayed on at Nuremberg," Gerecke wrote later. "Mrs. Gerecke told me to—air mail, special delivery."

In fact, the rumor the Nazis had heard was just that. Alma later told the *St. Louis Post-Dispatch* that she "really hadn't written a word about demanding that my husband give up his important task." When he first arrived in Nuremberg, before anyone knew how long the trial would last, Gerecke had committed to staying through June. He never had any intention of leaving until it was over. Gerecke later told the *Post-Dispatch*, "Chaplain Sixtus O'Connor and I were perhaps closer to them than any others. When we asked them if they would prefer German clergymen in attendance, they told us we had seen them through so much they would insist on retaining us until the end."

IN THE FINAL WEEKS of the trial, tensions seemed to ease in the prison. There was an atmosphere of peaceful resignation among the prisoners. After months in tight, stark quarters, the Nazis and prison officers had come to know each other as people, and Andrus's rules and regulations were now being administered more humanely. The weekly services in the prison chapel "became more and more solemn and moving and gave us much solace," Fritzsche wrote. "It was in such a spirit that each defendant devised the last words he was to utter at the trial." No one knew what the others were going to say—they were all too shy to share their drafts with one another.

And, over the summer, life among the occupiers in Nuremberg went on. On August 10, Gerecke officiated at the wedding of Anna Likovská, a Czech citizen working in Jackson's office who was living at the Grand Hotel, and Captain Daniel Sullivan of the Twenty-Sixth Infantry Regiment at the church in Mögeldorf. Andrus was a witness.

Gerecke was also receiving inquiries from German clergy who were curious about "the spiritual welfare of the defendants," he wrote. In some cases, the pastors left Gerecke with sermons they encouraged him to read to the defendants. "Because of the possibility of some hidden message in these manuscripts, I have never used them," he wrote. Though "I am deeply grateful for all good intentions."

On August 31, 1946, the prisoners made their final statements to the tribunal.

Goering claimed prosecutors took the defendants' words and documents they signed out of context. "The Prosecution brings forward individual statements over a period of twenty-five years, which were made under completely different circumstances and without any consequences arising from them at the time, and quotes them as proof of intent and guilt, statements which can easily be made in the excitement of the moment and of the atmosphere that prevailed at the time," he said. "There is probably not one leading personage on the opposing side who did not speak or write similarly in the course of a quarter of a century."

Goering said he hadn't wanted war, and indeed had tried to prevent it, but that after war broke out he had done everything to assure Germany a victory. "I stand up for the things that I have done, but I deny most emphatically that my actions were dictated by the desire to subjugate foreign peoples by wars, to murder them, to rob them, or to enslave them, or to commit atrocities or crimes," he said. "The only motive which guided me was my ardent love for my people, [Germany's] happiness, its freedom, and its life. And for this I call on the Almighty and my German people to witness."

Hess, whose mental state was constantly in question by Nuremberg officials, had written a letter to his wife the night before. "You most certainly heard over the radio that there has been another 'miracle' and I have completely recovered my mind," he wrote. "I hope you will see the humorous side of all this." Hess cited the writings of his mentor, the geopolitician Karl Haushofer. "Karl once wrote that for the sake of a great cause one must be able to suffer the strain of seeming to one's own people, for a time, to be a traitor. To that I would add, or seem to be crazy."

In his final statement, Hess focused on a pair of "glazed and dreamy eyes." Hitler, he said, was not "normal mentally during the last years." In those years, "the Führer's eyes and facial expression had something cruel in them, and even had a tendency towards madness." Hess said that during his imprisonment in England, people with "strange eyes" had visited him.

Fritzsche wrote that Hess's statement was "a pitiable exhibition, painful for all of us." Goering and Ribbentrop tried to get him to stop, pulling on his sleeve. "Shut up!" they pleaded. Hess, gaunt and wild-looking, yelled at them. "They were glassy and like eyes in a dream," he continued.

Justice Lawrence, president of the tribunal, interrupted Hess and asked him to conclude, which he did in a bewildering encore:

> *I was permitted to work for many years of my life under the greatest son whom my people has brought forth in its thousand year history. . . . I am happy to know that I have done my duty, to my people, my duty as a German, as a National Socialist, as a loyal follower of my Führer. I do not regret anything. . . . Some day [I will] stand before*

the judgment seat of the Eternal. I shall answer to Him, and I know
He will judge me innocent.

Ribbentrop was next. He told the court that the trial "will go down in history as a model example of how, while appealing to hitherto unknown legal formulas and the spirit of fairness, one can evade the cardinal problems of twenty-five years of the gravest human history." Hitler's foreign minister said that when he looked back "upon my actions and my desires, then I can conclude only this: The only thing of which I consider myself guilty before my people—not before this Tribunal—is that my aspirations in foreign policy remained without success."

Hans Frank, who had attempted suicide after being caught by the Allies, was in utter despair, and he began his closing statement by discussing Hitler's suicide. Hitler "left no final statement to the German people and the world," Frank said. "Amid the deepest distress of his people he found no comforting word. He became silent and did not discharge his office as a leader, but went down into darkness, a suicide. Was it stubbornness, despair, or spite against God and man?"

Frank had handed over his diary to American GIs when he was captured in 1945. He "revealed his ruthlessly brutal actions," Speer wrote. "But in Nuremberg he freely confessed his crimes, abjured them, and became a devout Catholic; his capacity to believe fervently and even fanatically had not deserted him." In fact, during the trial, Frank had come closest of any of the defendants to admitting his guilt on the witness stand.

When his own attorney asked Frank, "Did you ever participate in the annihilation of Jews?" Frank's reply had been "I say 'yes.'"

He had continued,

And the reason why I say "yes" is because, having lived through the
five months of this trial, and particularly after having heard the testi-

Henry Gerecke in the 1918 yearbook of St. John's Academy and College in Winfield, Kansas, which prepared high-school- and college-aged would-be Lutheran pastors for graduate-level seminary.

Gerecke entered Concordia Seminary in St. Louis in 1918, and married Alma Bender, the daughter of a city brewer, the following year.

Part of Gerecke's ministry was a radio show called *Moments of Comfort*—a combination of scripture recitation and soothing sermonizing. Here he is in an undated photograph doing a live broadcast in the KFUO-AM studios.

Gerecke (left) training at Fort Jackson, South Carolina, where he arrived in September 1943 at the age of fifty. He'd been assigned as a chaplain to the Ninety-Eighth General Hospital, which deployed to Hermitage, England—sixty miles west of London—five months later.

Richard O'Connor, the son of a New York schoolteacher and a construction worker, was ordained a Franciscan priest in 1934 at the age of twenty-five and took the name Sixtus. Pictured here in 1943, he volunteered to be a chaplain with the Eleventh Armored Division.

Prisoners carried large stones up the "Stairway of Death" (Todesstiege) from the Wiener Graben quarry (left), part of Mauthausen Concentration Camp near Linz, Austria, in 1942. In May 1945, after O'Connor and the Eleventh Armored Division helped liberate Mauthausen, an American soldier poses (right) near the edge of the "parachute jump" at the top of the quarry. Often the SS guards simply pushed Mauthausen's inmates over the quarry wall to their deaths, calling such victims "parachutists."

Ernst Kaltenbrunner—pictured here on the right during an inspection of Mauthausen on April 27, 1941—oversaw the Nazis' concentration camp system. Kaltenbrunner was Catholic, and O'Connor was his chaplain during the trial.

As a chaplain with the Ninety-Eighth General Hospital, Gerecke ministered to wounded GIs and to hospital staff. The Ninety-Eighth was fifteen miles east of the Ramsbury and Membury airfields, and after the D-Day landings began in June 1943, the army used the Ninety-Eighth as a transit hospital for air evacuations from the Continent.

Gerecke's two eldest sons served in Europe during the war. Hank (left) and Corky (middle) both visited their father (right) when they could get leave.

During the Second World War, Colonel Burton C. Andrus (center, pictured here with Gerecke) had been a combat observer with the Army's G-3 Combat Lessons Branch. He was variously described at Nuremberg as "pompous," "officious," "strict," and "an insecure peacock of a man." Andrus fought hard to get Gerecke to the Palace of Justice. "I knew of no one else qualified for [the situation]," he wrote later.

Along with one of the army psychologists, Gerecke and O'Connor (pictured here in an undated photo) were the only members of the prison staff who spoke German. The two men became good friends, eventually developing a grim joke. "At least we Catholics are responsible for only six of these criminals," O'Connor would say. "You Lutherans have fifteen chalked up against you."

Heraldic design of 6850th Internal Security Detachment, the unit—including Gerecke and O'Connor—that staffed the prison. Andrus, who was a member of the Masonic Order of the Knights Templar, designed the emblem, writing in a memo that the azure field stood for truth, the sable border for solemnity, and the gules (or red) flames for "the pit of wrath." The key at the top of the herald stood for security, the scales for justice, and the crushed eagle within the flames symbolized "Germany, Fallen, destroyed."

On the night of January 2, 1945, the British sent more than five hundred Lancaster heavy bombers over Nuremberg. Within an hour 1,800 people were killed and 90 percent of the city was smashed. Another 4,000 were killed in subsequent Allied air raids in the following weeks. At top, a young boy stands in Nuremberg's former Adolf Hitler Platz, in front of the ruins of St. Sebald Church. On the bottom, a boater travels through the destroyed city along the Pegnitz River.

The Grand Hotel, shown here during the trials, a fifty-year-old luxury accommodation just outside the walls of the destroyed old city, was the hub of after-court activity in the American war crimes community in Nuremberg. A German band played jazz most nights in the hotel's Marble Room.

NURNBERG OPERA HOUSE
LT. LEIGH B. BARDSLEY   SGT. ART KIDDER   SGT. SAM AVOLICINO
Special Service Officer   Non-Com in Charge

Friday, 25. January 1946, 19.00 hours

Masked Ball

OPERA IN 3 ACTS (5 SCENES) BY GUISEPPE VERDI

MUSICAL DIRECTION: ROLF AGOP
STAGEDIRECTION: BRUNO P. MACKAY

CAST:

Richard, Count of Warwick and Governor of Boston
                                               Alexander Miltschinoff
René, an officer and Richard's friend . . . . . *Herbert Knippenberg*
Amelia, Renes wife . . . . *Eugenia Estowytsch-Garcia*
Ulrica, a fortuneteller . . . . *Halli Borsforotti*
Oscar, Richard's page . . . . *Maria Seerboth*
Silvano, a sailor . . . . *Karl Hermann*
Samuel, officer, (conspirator) . . . . *Eric Joldt*
Tom, officer, (conspirator) . . . . *Alfred Stein*
Judge . . . . *Eduard Dittenroether*
Servant . . . . *Helmuth Kleiner*
Deputies, officers, sailors, guards, Ladies and gentlemen, pages, soldiers, servants folks

The action takes place in Boston, at the end of the 17th century

Scenarist: Heinz Grote   Choir-direction: Edgar Schmidt-Bredow

Costumes: Elisabeth Nilhus   Choreographie: Ruth Müller-Trapp

Intermission after the 2nd act (3rd scene)

Senior courtroom staff could take in more sophisticated culture at the Nuremberg Opera House. Pictured is the program from a January 1946 production of Giuseppe Verdi's *The Masked Ball*.

When he arrived at the Palace of Justice (shown here in aerial view), Gerecke shook the defendants' hands, a gesture for which he was later severely criticized by the American public. Shaking hands with these men didn't mean that he was unconcerned with their alleged crimes, but, he wrote later, "I knew I could never win any of them to my way of thinking unless they liked me first."

Thanksgiving fell on the third day of the trial. American prosecutor Justice Robert Jackson spoke briefly, explaining the meaning of Thanksgiving to the court. He then asked Gerecke, who had been in Nuremberg for just ten days, to say a prayer as hundreds of military and civilian Allied personnel bowed their heads.

The U.S. Army spent about $75 million (in today's dollars) renovating Courtroom 600 in the Palace of Justice—removing walls and creating an additional visitor's gallery and a room for the world's press. A long wooden covered walkway led to an elevator that deposited the prisoners directly into the Courtroom 600 defendants' dock, shown here.

Each cell in the prison where the war crimes defendants were held measured thirteen feet by six and a half feet and was accessed through a thick wooden door with a one-foot-square peephole, which Gerecke called a "Judas window."

Hermann Goering, the highest-ranking Nazi leader at Nuremberg (pictured here sitting in the courtroom) was exactly the same age as Gerecke, whom he called "pastor." Goering was head of the German Air Force and Hitler's designated successor.

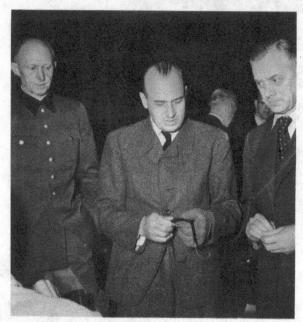

Defendants General Alfred Jodl (left), Hans Frank (center), and Alfred Rosenberg (right) in court, circa 1946. Jodl and Rosenberg largely rejected Gerecke's offer of spiritual counsel. Frank was Hitler's personal lawyer, and eventually governor general of Poland, where an estimated three million Jews were killed during the war. O'Connor baptized Frank during the trial, bringing him back into the church.

Baldur von Schirach (pictured in the Palace of Justice speaking to his attorney) led the Hitler Youth movement and was later a Nazi leader in Vienna.

Albert Speer (shown here in Courtroom 600) was Hitler's architect and designed many of the Nazi Party's grand edifices in Nuremberg. Speer and Schirach both asked Gerecke to work with them toward receiving Holy Communion while they were on trial.

Gerecke was close to General Wilhelm Keitel, seated here in the Courtroom 600 dock. The former chief of staff of the German Armed Forces High Command, he was one of Hitler's preeminent yes-men. Fritz Sauckel, shown here consulting with Keitel, was Hitler's labor chief and Gerecke's first convert back to the Lutheran faith at Nuremberg.

As the prisoners began to accept Gerecke during the trial's initial weeks, many slowly agreed to attend his services on Sundays. Gerecke and O'Connor used a small chapel fashioned by knocking down a wall between two cells. A former lieutenant colonel of the SS was the organist. In this photo, Gerecke poses for an army promotional shot.

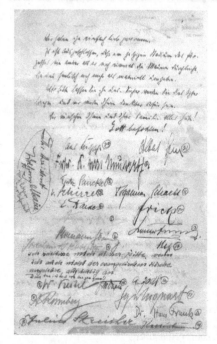

In June 1946, a rumor circulated among the defendants that Alma Gerecke had called her husband home to St. Louis. All twenty-one defendants signed a letter to Alma asking her to let Gerecke stay until the end of the trial.

Gerecke and O'Connor also ministered to the defendants' families throughout the trial. Gerecke was especially close to Goering's wife, Emmy, and daughter, Edda, whom he visited in the countryside and sent care packages to after the war. Goering signed the back of this photo of his family for Gerecke.

When the trial ended, Gerecke returned to St. Louis. He hadn't seen Alma—pictured here with Gerecke at a welcome-home party in his honor—or his youngest son, Roy, in three years. He was soon assigned to the Fifth Army's disciplinary barracks in Milwaukee, where he ministered to the U.S. Army's troubled souls.

In 1950, Gerecke, pictured here celebrating with a beer, was discharged and moved with Alma to Chester, Illinois, to be the assistant pastor of St. John Lutheran Church. But for Gerecke, Chester's real draw was the Menard penitentiary, a maximum-security facility housing 2,500 murderers and rapists, the state's worst criminals. He became the chaplain at Menard and at a hospital for the criminally insane.

After the trial, O'Connor returned to Siena College, where he taught philosophy, gardened, and played the horses at the nearby Saratoga Race Course. He never wrote about his year in Nuremberg, and rarely spoke of it, even to friends. Here he is in front of a blackboard in a Siena classroom.

In 1961, Gerecke had a heart attack in the Menard prison parking lot on his way into the prison. He drove himself home, but died later that day in Chester's hospital. He was sixty-eight years old. The cross on top of St. John Lutheran School in Chester is named in his honor.

mony of the witness, Hoess, my conscience does not allow me to throw the responsibility solely on these minor people. I myself have never installed an extermination camp for Jews, or promoted the existence of such camps; but if Adolf Hitler personally has laid that dreadful responsibility on his people, then it is mine too, for we have fought against Jewry for years; and we have indulged in the most horrible utterances—my own diary bears witness against me. Therefore, it is no more than my duty to answer your question in this connection with "yes." A thousand years will pass and still this guilt of Germany will not have been erased.

Now four months later, Frank was prepared to take back the essence of his confession. He said,

There is still one statement of mine which I must rectify. On the witness stand, I said that a thousand years would not suffice to erase the guilt brought upon our people because of Hitler's conduct in this war. Every possible guilt incurred by our nation has already been completely wiped out today, not only by the conduct of our war-time enemies towards our nation and its soldiers, which has been carefully kept out of this Trial, but also by the tremendous mass crimes of the most frightful sort which—as I have now learned—have been and still are being committed against Germans by Russians, Poles, and Czechs, especially in East Prussia, Silesia, Pomerania, and Sudetenland. Who shall ever judge these crimes against the German people?

Yet Frank did not leave the Nazis off the hook completely. Nazi leaders, he claimed,

perhaps as never before . . . still bear a tremendous spiritual responsibility. At the beginning of our way, we did not suspect that our turning away from God could have such disastrous deadly consequences

and that we would necessarily become more and more deeply involved
in guilt. . . . Hitler's road was the way without God, the way of
turning from Christ, and, in the last analysis, the way of political
foolishness, the way of disaster, and the way of death.

Arthur Seyss-Inquart, Hitler's chancellor of Austria and later
Frank's deputy in Poland, told the court that Hitler "remains the
man who made Greater Germany a fact in German history. I served
this man. And now? I cannot today cry 'Crucify him,' since yesterday I cried 'Hosanna.'"

Fritz Sauckel told the tribunal he was:

shaken to the very depths of my soul by the atrocities revealed in this
trial. In all humility and reverence, I bow before the victims and the
fallen of all nations, and before the misfortune and suffering of my own
people, with whom alone I must measure my fate. I come from a social
level completely different from that of my comrades accused with me. In
my nature and thinking, I remained a sailor and a worker.

During Keitel's pretrial interrogations by Thomas Dodd, one of
the American prosecutors at Nuremberg, the former field marshal
contemplated taking full blame for his orders to keep responsibility
from flowing down to his subordinates. Keitel's lawyer signaled to
the prosecution that his client would contemplate a deal, but prosecutors wouldn't make any promises. Rather, Dodd suggested that
Keitel do whatever his conscience told him was right.

A confession from Keitel would possibly have mitigated his eventual sentence, "but Keitel was used to acting not on suggestions but
on orders from superior officers," wrote historians Ann and John
Tusa. Keitel consulted Goering, who told him under no circumstances should he break ranks with the rest of the defendants. Keitel
wrote to his attorney that after rethinking the idea, he'd changed his
mind. He would not confess.

Keitel said during his testimony that he knew nothing of the concentration camps or conditions in the POW camps. He said he only knew about military plans at the very last minute, when Hitler gave him an order to sign. He also said he knew nothing about the handover of prisoners to the SD—the elite intelligence agency founded by Himmler to rival the Gestapo and that rooted out "enemies of the state." During cross-examination in April 1946, Keitel had implied that turning suspects in to the SD was akin to placing them in police custody.

But British prosecutor Sir David Maxwell Fyfe had asked him to be honest. "You have been at this trial too long to think that handing people over to the SD means police custody," Maxwell Fyfe had said. "It means concentration camps and a gas chamber, does it not?"

Keitel admitted under questioning by Dodd that he had knowingly transmitted criminal orders from Hitler. Justice Lawrence asked Keitel if he'd ever made any protest in writing against any of Hitler's policies. Keitel could not think of a single time when he'd done that.

Patrick Dean, a member of the British Foreign Office, said after Keitel's testimony that the field marshal was "truthful and decent according to his own standards, but his standards are those of a savage." Until the last portion of the trial the Nuremberg judges and prosecutors saw Keitel as "a weak, if not pathetic, instrument of crime." They thought he was "confused and shaken," and that during the trial he'd grown "older, greyer and more grizzled."

Now, the court was ready to hear Keitel's final words. "At the end of this Trial," Keitel said, "I want to present equally frankly the avowal and confession I have to make today." He spoke as honestly as he felt he could:

> *In the course of the trial my defense counsel submitted two fundamental questions to me, the first one . . . was: "In case of a victory,*

would you have refused to participate in any part of the success?" I
answered, "No, I should certainly have been proud of it." The second
question was: "How would you act if you were in the same position
again?" My answer: "I should rather choose death than to let myself
be drawn into the net of such pernicious methods." From these two
answers the High Tribunal may see my viewpoint. I believed, but I
erred, and I was not in a position to prevent what ought to have been
prevented. That is my guilt. It is tragic to have to realize that the best
I had to give as a soldier, obedience and loyalty, was exploited for
purposes that could not be recognized at the time, and that I did not
see that there is a limit even for a soldier's performance of his duty.
That is my fate. . . .

Keitel's honesty was rare, and it impressed many. By admitting
his weaknesses and therefore, his guilt, Keitel earned something that
approximated respect from one or two of the judges and prosecutors.
Prosecutor Telford Taylor wrote that the testimony was "the bravest
and most thoughtful statement made that day. Keitel had blamed
nobody but himself and had acknowledged his own weakness and
blindness." Taylor added, "As I sat at the American prosecution's
table and heard those balanced words, 'meine Schuld' (my guilt)
and 'mein Schicksal' (my fate), I was much moved." Airey Neave,
a member of the British prosecution team, said Keitel spoke "with
great dignity."

Even Keitel's codefendants saw something different in him after
his time in court. Speer told the prison psychologist that Keitel's statement was "more honest" than Goering's. "He not only said that he
assumed responsibility for orders he signed, but admitted that they
were crimes and that he knew that he would have to suffer the consequences." Fritzsche wrote, "We had got into the habit of disparaging Keitel's intelligence and of accusing him of spinelessness. We had
called him ugly nicknames. But in the witness stand he displayed not
only a keen, logical mentality, but more courage than most."

When the defendants had all delivered their statements, Lawrence announced that the tribunal would adjourn while the judges considered their verdicts. After all the time the chaplains had spent with the prisoners, the next ten weeks would prove to be the most intense.

The prisoners were tense and nervous during the first weeks between the end of the trial and the announcement of the verdicts. Most read or wrote in their cells. Speer, for instance, began writing his "memories of the twelve years with Hitler," which would one day become his best-selling memoir, *Inside the Third Reich.* He was able to get the first hundred pages to a friend in Coburg by smuggling them out of the Palace of Justice through one of the chaplains.

Hans Frank was also working on a memoir. O'Connor smuggled it out of the prison to Frank's attorney, Alfred Seidel, who had his secretary type the document. The attorney then returned the manuscript to O'Connor, who gave it back to Frank to make corrections, and then smuggled it out again. The epigraph of the manuscript was from Goethe: "To him entrapped in such torments and partial guilt / His God has given voice to utter what he must endure." After Frank's death, his wife, Brigitte, published the manuscript, *In the Face of the Gallows,* herself, peddling it to right-wing Catholic institutions in Germany to feed her children.

While some of the defendants wrote, others moodily took their short exercise walks in the courtyard. Gerecke held a "devotional service" every night after dinner, and the thirteen Protestants came each time. "It was gratifying to see the working of the Holy Spirit on some of these men," Gerecke wrote.

The chaplains agreed they should petition the tribunal to allow the defendants to see their families. Lawrence wrote back, "Have them come before the verdict."

Burton Andrus notified the wives that they could come to Nuremberg with their children to see their husbands. The army put the families in nearby homes and provided them with security.

After the families arrived, Gerecke helped those wives who were scrambling to maintain a normal existence for their children. He brought them whatever he thought would help—coffee, bedsheets, flour, cigarettes.

Some of the defendants, including Keitel, asked their wives not to come. "I am too emotionally unstrung, and I simply can not bear up under it," Keitel told Gerecke. Hess also refused to see his family. Hess's son Wolf said later he understood why: "He would not show the victors he accepted their dictates and wishes," Wolf said. "It would have been humiliating to him to have seen us in that way. It is very clear to me. He saw visiting as a moral concession to those who took it upon themselves to sit in judgment upon him."

Erich Raeder couldn't see his wife because the Russians had taken her prisoner. The tribunal had ordered her released for the visit, and even Lawrence had personally taken up the cause to secure her freedom. Yet, when Gerecke went to the Nuremberg airport several times to meet her, she never arrived. The Russians never explained why they didn't put her on a plane. In fact, the Russians kept Raeder's wife imprisoned until September 1949 without ever charging her with a crime, except for, as Raeder later wrote, "that of being my wife." Raeder's two children did visit the prison to see him.

For the families that did arrive, Gerecke arranged hour-long visits through his office. For any that were too difficult to set up, the chaplains resorted to desperate measures to bring the families together. In one instance, according to Schirach's wife, O'Connor smuggled Schirach's son Richard into his father's cell under his uniform coat.

Either Gerecke or O'Connor accompanied the family members to the visitation room and sat next to them while they talked. The first visits were emotional and difficult, even for the chaplains. The families sat on one side of a screen, the prisoner sat on the other side with his guard. The defendant was not allowed to touch his family members or pass anything through the screen.

Gerecke had surmised that several of the mothers were Christian, though he knew he'd have some problems with Annelies Ribbentrop, whom he considered "the most ungodly woman I ever met." In their visit, Gerecke overheard Ribbentrop plead with his wife to have the children baptized and bring them up in the church. She gave in, and Gerecke later helped her arrange for the baptism of their children at the church in Mögeldorf.

For the most part, however, Gerecke thought the wives were "unassuming." Elisabeth Sauckel, mother of ten, was "simple and kind," he thought. Julius Streicher's wife was being held at Nuremberg as a trial witness. Getting her to the visitation was easy—guards simply escorted her down from another wing of the prison.

Gerecke had traveled to Sackdilling, thirty miles northeast of Nuremberg, to tell Emmy Goering that she and her little daughter, Edda, could visit her husband.

"I almost flung my arms around his neck," she wrote later.

Gerecke considered Emmy a woman of "considerable grace and charm." He told her about the visiting restrictions such as the guards, mesh screens, and no touching.

"I was shocked by this at first," Emmy wrote, "and then I thanked Pastor Gerecke for having warned me so that I would have time to get used to the idea."

Emmy and Hermann Goering's first meeting was emotional. They hadn't seen each other since just after the war, seventeen months earlier. Emmy wanted desperately to kiss her husband, but Andrus's rules kept them apart.

At their second visit, the couple talked more freely. Emmy, determined to make Hermann laugh, told her husband funny stories about her trials over the months without him. She succeeded, but she also felt worn out, as if she had been doing "forced labor." Part of her struggle might have been due to the couple's lack of privacy.

"The only thing that embarrassed me was the presence of the American soldier who was standing beside Hermann," Emmy wrote. "I should have had one beside me too but his place had been taken by Pastor Gerecke for which I was very grateful to him."

In one of their meetings, Emmy asked Hermann, "Do you think the three of us shall ever be all free again together?"

Hermann's expression became grave. "Emmy," he said. "Don't have any hope."

Emmy later brought Edda to see her father. "Don't say anything sad in front of your papa," she instructed her daughter.

Gerecke and O'Connor grew close to the families during the trial. Most of the defendants' wives and children had been living in squalor—eating and sleeping when and where they could. Their relationship to the Third Reich was already considered contemptible among many of their German neighbors. The son or daughter of a high Nazi official was outcast in school. The chaplains learned much about the lives of the Nazi families while they were at Nuremberg, and both men did them favors—during the trial and after. Gerecke was so taken with Goering's wife and daughter that when he returned to the United States, he sent them care packages.

When the chaplains weren't escorting the families, they were babysitting. Gerecke's office soon became a temporary day-care center while the Nazis' wives visited their husbands alone. "We saw little hands and tender hearts moving about from our office to the room arranged for the visitors," Gerecke wrote. During these visits "the little ones became very dear to us."

He used the time to talk to the children about Jesus. "God forbid any boasting at this point, but I have the conviction that some of the little girls and boys who came to visit their daddies during these sessions became better acquainted with the Savior," he wrote. "Any number of them knew the same bed-time prayers that I learned as a child at mother's knee."

The chaplains especially had their hands full with Cordula and

Konstanze Schacht, who were only three and five years old. "They were Katzenjammer Kids in action," Gerecke wrote, "thinking up all sorts of deviltry to disturb the somber prison atmosphere."

Cordula's earliest memories of her father were those Nuremberg visits. "I remember the fence and the watchtower at the prison, and my mother told us not to walk on the side with the fence but instead on the other side of the street," she said later. "I saw him in the visitor's section behind a mesh screen. Next to him I remember an American soldier in a white helmet, and behind him was an open water closet. I remember it very clearly. It was the first time I saw my father knowing he was my father, and I looked at him a very long time. I remember that I then said, 'I do like you.'"

Niklas Frank was seven years old, the youngest of Hans Frank's five children, when he visited his father at Nuremberg. He entered the room with his mother and saw his father behind the screen with an American soldier with a white helmet standing next to him. His father tried to make him laugh and said it was only a few months until the family would be celebrating Christmas together at the family's lake house in Schliersee, Bavaria.

"Why is he lying?" Niklas asked himself. "He knows that he will be hanged. He knows it. Why is he lying to me?" Niklas didn't say a word. He just watched his father smile at him, and then he left. "I was very, very disappointed because my father had no real idea how to talk to his youngest child," Niklas said later. "He should have said, 'Nikky . . . you are seven years old, and we will never meet again. I will be hanged. I have earned this hanging. I have done a lot of crimes. Don't do it the same way like me.' Something like this."

In a book he later wrote, Niklas fantasized that as his father retracted his statement of guilt on the witness stand, the arm of God reached down from heaven and plunged into his father's throat and into his stomach so that Niklas, "like an eternal zombie," could feast on his father's heart:

There God's fingers grab hold, and then He, Supergod, begins to pull
His arm back, slowly, very slowly, and He turns you inside out, skin
side in, with a squishy sucking sound, so that I, amazed by this spec-
tacle of flesh, come down to you from the judges' bench and watch your
organs wriggling on your outside; your face has disappeared inside
your head. Your eyes are gone. I come closer and see your heart an-
chored to its tough arteries and veins; it's beating like crazy. . . . I will
be trying to leap away from you for the rest of my life.

Niklas never forgave his father. "Too many people [were] killed for nothing," he later said.

The other defendants had less contentious—though no less painful—interactions with their families. Fritzsche said it was "heart-rending" for the defendants to have to speak to their families "through glass and wire netting and to be unable to help them in their struggle to maintain a bare existence." The families, he wrote, "were looked after by the two American clergymen who saw to it that the grim atmosphere of the jail was not too obtrusive."

Fritzsche found it difficult to even describe "the emotional impact of these meetings" on the prisoners. "Some were hard put to maintain their composure and it was on a visiting day that, for the first time, I saw Goering's usual imperturbability forsake him," he wrote.

Edda Goering was eight years old when she visited her father for the last time at Nuremberg. Later in life, she recalled standing on a chair to get a better view of him through the screen, and the strangeness of seeing him surrounded by white-helmeted guards. She remembered seeing Niklas Frank and his older brother Norman running around the jail.

Goering and his daughter were close. He had written her a birthday letter from Nuremberg in June that she kept into old age:

My darling, sweet child! My golden treasure!
Now's the second time that your birthday has come

*around, and I can't be there. And yet, my darling, today I'm
especially close to you, and send you my warmest and most
heartfelt greetings. I pray to Almighty God from the bottom
of my heart to look after you and help you. I can't send you
any gift, but my boundless love and longing is all around you
and always shall be! . . . I hope the weather's fine so you can
spend your birthday outside in the wonderful forest. My little
sweetheart, once more all my warmest wishes for today and
always; fondest hugs and kisses from your Papa.*

Emmy had urged Edda to talk to Gerecke, and when she did, the chaplain asked her if she said her prayers.

"I pray every night," she told him.

"And how do you pray?" Gerecke asked.

"I kneel by my bed and look up to heaven and ask God to open my daddy's heart and let Jesus in."

Gerecke tried in a similar vein with Rosenberg's pretty fifteen-year-old daughter Irene, but she interrupted him. "Don't bother me with any of that prayer stuff," she said.

All right, Gerecke said, "is there anything at all I can do for you?"

"Yes," said Irene. "Got a cigarette?"

When the prisoners were not visiting with their families, they were spending time with each other. Andrus had relaxed another rule—one of association. Each man was allowed to invite three others to a maximum of two "parties," and each could accept as many invitations as he received. The parties were just meetings around a table in a special cell set up with cards and chess that the men never used. For the most part, the defendants just talked as guards stood behind them against the cell wall. Even the prisoners considered outsiders by the others—Streicher, Kaltenbrunner, Frick—received invitations. When the hour-long party was over, a guard shouted, "Finished!," and the next group would be ushered into the cell.

About a week before their scheduled deadline, the tribunal decided it needed more time to work out differences with the judgments, so they announced that the adjournment would be extended for another week, until September 30. This gave the families more time for hour-long visits every day.

The final visitation day was Saturday, September 28. On Sunday, the chaplains provided services and more counsel in an atmosphere of general gloom. Most of the prisoners had said good-bye to their wives and children, believing they'd never see them again.

On Monday, the judges arrived at the Palace of Justice in black, bulletproof cars escorted by jeeps topped with sirens and machine guns. Many of the prosecutors who had left Nuremberg after oral arguments returned for the verdicts. Andrus activated every guard in the 6850th for the occasion.

One thousand extra guards surrounded the Palace of Justice. Snipers positioned themselves at strategic points. Telford Taylor wrote that in Courtroom 600 Andrus "was at his most absurd, ordering ladies not to cross their ankles and telling his guards to wake up elderly gentlemen dozing in the heat and boredom." The prisoners filed into the dock to hear the tribunal's judgment. During the proceedings, reporters noticed that the defendants huddled close together and talked in undertones. Some thought they looked shrunken and faded.

The judges read through their opinion all day, and they spoke of the prisoners in sweeping condemnations. "Many of these men have made a mockery of the soldier's oath of obedience to military orders," the tribunal judges read. "When it suits their defense they say they had to obey; when confronted with Hitler's brutal crimes, which are shown to have been within their general knowledge, they say they disobeyed. The truth is that they actively participated in all these crimes, or sat silent and acquiescent, witnessing the commission of crimes on a scale larger and more shocking than the world has ever had the misfortune to know."

That evening, the defendants returned to their cells in a bleak mood. They would receive their individual sentences in the morning.

Days earlier, the American prosecutor Justice Robert Jackson had written to Thomas Dodd, remarking that "if there is ever to be a demonstration by the defendants, it could occur at the time of sentencing. . . . The world's eye will be focused on the courtroom on that day, and if these defendants should burst out in angry demonstrations, that will be the thing that will get the newspaper play."

When the morning came, Andrus gathered the defendants in a semicircle outside their cells. "It is your duty to yourselves and to posterity and to the German people to face this issue with dignity and manliness," he told them. "I expect you to go into that courtroom, stand at attention, listen to your sentence and then retire. You may be assured that there are people to assist you and to take care of you after you have moved out of sight of the general public."

Andrus placed a doctor and nurse in the courtroom and another doctor at the door to the elevator that carried the defendants up to the courtroom. Two soldiers stayed with the second doctor and manned a stretcher and a straitjacket "in case a prisoner went berserk," Andrus wrote.

The defendants walked into the dock together for the last time and found the courtroom strangely changed. Lawrence had banned photography while the Nazis learned the verdicts, and the bright lights that had for nearly a year shined in their faces—and that often forced the defendants to wear sunglasses in court—were dimmed.

The International Military Tribunal did not waste time. Just after 9:30 A.M., it began with its verdict on Goering, the Allies' most important prisoner. The justices said the prosecution's evidence proved that after the führer, Goering was "the most prominent man in the Nazi regime" who had "tremendous influence with Hitler." They continued:

Goering persecuted the Jews, particularly after the November 1938
riots, and not only in Germany, where he raised the billion-mark
fine as stated elsewhere, but in the conquered territories as well. His
own utterances then and his testimony now shows this interest was
primarily economic—how to get their property and how to force
them out of the economic life of Europe. As these countries fell before
the German Army, he extended the Reich anti-Jewish laws to them.
. . . Although their extermination was in Himmler's hands, Goe-
ring was far from disinterested or inactive, despite his protestations
in the witness box.

The tribunal found Goering guilty on all four counts of the indictment.

For the rest of the morning, the four voting judges alternated reading the tribunal's verdicts for each of the twenty-one defendants and for Martin Bormann in absentia.

A *Newsweek* reporter in the gallery wrote that Ribbentrop was in the "worst shape of any man on the dock . . . looks as if noose already around neck . . . sweating." When most of the defendants heard their own verdict, they took off their headphones.

The tribunal acquitted Fritzsche, Papen, and Schacht. Fritzsche's translator was just a yard away from him, behind glass, and he spoke softly: "The Tribunal finds that Fritzsche is not guilty under this Indictment, and directs that he shall be discharged by the Marshal when the Tribunal presently adjourns."

Though Fritzsche could only hear the translator through the headphones, he said that his voice "may well have seemed to me to sound like those trumpets which made the walls of Jericho crumble."

The rest were guilty on one or more counts of the indictment. The court recessed for lunch at 1:45 P.M., and because Lawrence did not want the defendants paraded through any public part of the building, Andrus served them lunch in a basement cloakroom.

The acquitted men were separated from the rest. Schacht shook hands with no one. Papen only shook hands with Keitel, Jodl, Raeder, and Doenitz—the former military leaders. Fritzsche wished an emotional good luck to each of those convicted. After receiving some congratulations in return, the acquitted men were then taken to a bizarre press conference where reporters offered them chocolate, cigars, and drinks. They were also told that an angry mob was forming to meet them outside the Palace of Justice. Schacht asked Andrus if they could stay inside the prison for a few days until security could be arranged, and the commandant agreed.

An hour after breaking for lunch, the afternoon session began, and the judges announced the sentences. Gerecke was in court that day. He had heard the evidence presented by the prosecution teams in the previous months as the defendants took the stand in their own defense.

"The request came to me to be the Spiritual Councilor to the high Nazi leaders on trial," he wrote later. "I am not a jurist. I take it the prosecution teams did their job according to the rules of their professions and the judges did what they thought was best according to the evidence brought before the tribunal." The men he had spent nearly a year ministering to "took the verdicts like soldiers and as far as I could see, not one flinched when he heard his sentence."

One by one, the defendants rode the elevator up to the dock to hear their sentences. They were handed a pair of headphones to hear the German translation of Lawrence's words. Goering was first. His face was pale, as if it were powdered.

"In accordance with Article 27 of the Charter, the International Military Tribunal will now pronounce the sentences on the defendants convicted on this Indictment," Lawrence said. "Defendant Hermann Wilhelm Goering, on the Counts of the Indictment on which you have been convicted, the International Military Tribunal sentences you to death by hanging."

Goering dropped his headset, turned, and walked back into the elevator. As he exited on the lower floor, Goering, handcuffed to a guard, saw Fritzsche standing nearby and walked toward him. He offered his hand, and Fritzsche took it. "Very glad you've been acquitted," Goering said, in a nonchalant, friendly tone.

Fritzsche couldn't muster the nerve to ask Goering what had just happened upstairs. The once powerful reichsmarshal turned to the rest of the defendants, bowed, and walked back to his cell.

Hess appeared in court next, refusing the translation headphones. "Defendant Rudolf Hess, on the Counts of the Indictment on which you have been convicted, the Tribunal sentences you to imprisonment for life."

Ribbentrop, whom Gerecke had usually found to be unemotional, stepped up to the dock afterward. He slumped as if punched in the gut when he heard his fate: "death by hanging."

Keitel nodded curtly as he heard his sentence. His fate would be the same as Ribbentrop's. Many after him were sentenced to die as well—Kaltenbrunner, Frank, Sauckel, Rosenberg, Frick, Streicher, Jodl, and Seyss-Inquart would all hang.

When Speer heard his sentence—twenty years in prison—it sounded abstract to him and almost impersonal. He was aware that many were looking at him: the judges, prosecutors, defense attorneys, and reporters. Yet he mostly just saw the dilated eyes of his own lawyer, shocked that his client had escaped the gallows. Barely conscious of what he was doing, he bowed to the judges and returned to the elevator. A guard led him back to his cell, and shortly afterward another guard ordered him to pack up his possessions and head to a new cell on the prison's second tier. Some of his codefendants had also moved tiers, while others, he saw, had remained in their ground-floor cells.

"Only a few hours ago, after our last lunch together, we did not know whether after many years of shared rule, shared triumphs, and mutual animosity we were seeing one another for the last time," Speer wrote.

Gerecke's roommate, Gustave Gilbert, visited Speer's new cell. "Twenty years—well, that's fair enough," Speer said with a nervous laugh. "They couldn't have given me a lighter sentence, considering the facts, and I can't complain."

Funk was sentenced to life in prison, as was Raeder. Schirach received a twenty-year sentence. Neurath was given fifteen years, and Doenitz received ten years. Forty-five minutes after the session began, the trial of the century was over.

That night, the acquitted men moved to the prison's third floor, where their cell doors were left open and only one guard was posted outside to make sure they didn't go down to the lower levels of the prison.

Few who had been part of the Nuremberg experiment over the previous ten months were in a celebratory mood. Whether translators or prosecutors or reporters, they had become familiar with the faces in the dock, some of whom had just been sentenced to die for their crimes. Many simply went home and prepared to leave Nuremberg. "It is a terrible thing to see a man condemned to death," wrote Ann and John Tusa, "even when you are certain that he has been responsible for the death of millions."

THOUGH THE DEFENDANTS GIVEN a death sentence had four days to appeal, Keitel refused to allow his attorney to do so. His role in the Third Reich had been too great for his frank admission of weakness to move the tribunal past a guilty verdict and death sentence. The deliberations about his fate had been the shortest of those for any defendant, requiring virtually no discussion. All four judges voted him guilty on all four counts.

Instead of appealing his sentence, Keitel appealed the form of execution. He felt that death by hanging did not become an officer. "The death sentence has come as no surprise to me, but I am very deeply upset about the way it is to be executed," he wrote his lawyer on the same day he learned his sentence. "Help me make a plea for my execution to be changed to a soldier's death by firing squad. I consider it pointless to ask more than that."

The same day, Keitel's wife, Lisa, also wrote to her husband's attorney. "We heard the judgment, but it was only as we expected," she wrote. "I hope that my husband's plea for a military execution will be granted him and Jodl. Otherwise, please, no plea for clemency."

On October 5, 1946, Keitel wrote to the Allied Control Council, the military government then running occupied Germany.

> *I will willingly give up my life in the expiation demanded by my sentence, if my sacrifice will speed the prosperity of the German people and serve to exonerate the German armed forces from blame. I have only one plea: to be granted a death by firing squad . . . the mode of execution that is the right of the soldier in every other army in the world upon whom sentence of death is pronounced as a soldier.*

Keitel was not the only one to request that his execution be conducted by firing squad. Goering also asked that if his sentence could not be commuted to life, he be shot rather than hanged. His lawyer pointed to Goering's bravery during the First World War as a reason. Jodl also asked that his death sentence be set aside, or that he be shot. Raeder, who had been sentenced to life in prison, asked that his sentence be commuted to death by shooting, "by way of mercy."

The Allied Control Council only seriously considered the requests from those Nazis who wanted to be shot rather than hanged. In the end, though, as one of the members later wrote, these men were being tried "for their responsibility in abominable crimes, and not for being soldiers." On October 11, the attorneys for the condemned men were notified that their petitions had been denied.

When Keitel discussed his German honor with the prison psychiatrists, he became emotional and the doctors were sure that he would have committed suicide if he'd been able to. "How often I have found myself seriously confronted with this as a possible way out, only to reject it because—as suicides have always demonstrated—nothing is changed and nothing bettered by such action," Keitel wrote in a note to his lawyer just after the trial began. "Quite the contrary, the armed forces, whose counselor and mediator I had so often been, would have labeled me a deserter and branded me a coward."

Hitler had chosen suicide, Keitel wrote, "shunning his own personal responsibility" and leaving it "to a subordinate to account for his autocratic and arbitrary actions, these two shortcomings will remain forever incomprehensible to me. They are my final disillusion."

Despite his depression, Keitel kept his uniform pressed, his hair immaculately brushed, and his cell in perfect order as much as he could. "One has only a bunk and a small table, with no desk or shelf, and even the wooden chair is taken out," Keitel wrote of his cell in his memoirs. "There is nothing to hang or lay one's clothes and underwear on: one is obliged to lay it on the stone floor, so it is impossible to keep one's clothes clean."

Two days after his sentence, Keitel wrote his son Karl-Heinz to say that he predicted that he would be executed two weeks later. "It has been a great help to me in facing up to the Tribunal as I did, that I have for a long time been aware of what my fate would be," he wrote. "I regret nothing that I said at my Trial, and I would never take back a word I said; I spoke the pure truth, the whole time, to every question and on every occasion. That is something I can still be proud of, and for all time in history."

Keitel wrote Karl-Heinz once more, three days before his death, noting that since his incarceration, only the women in the family had written him. "Enough said," he wrote. "What cowards we men are."

The tribunal's sentence against Keitel had been pronounced "in the name of humanity," Fritzsche later wrote. "Humanity, however, will not benefit by this sacrifice if it fails to realize that at no time in his career did Keitel bear the brand of Cain."

FRITZSCHE'S UNDERSTANDING OF THE biblical term "the brand of Cain" was as a mark that signified to the world that Cain was a murderer. Gerecke would have thought about the phrase differently. To the chaplain, the brand of Cain meant protection—even for murderers—from harm, through the grace of God.

The first five books of the Bible—called the Torah by Jews, and the Pentateuch by Christians—were first passed around orally before they were written down and finally stitched together by a later editor. The story of Cain and Abel comes in the fourth chapter of Genesis and was written by an author that modern biblical scholars refer to as "J," the Jahwist (or Yahwist), for his recurring use of the term *YHWH*, a transliteration of the Hebrew for "Lord," when referring to God.

As opposed to some of his fellow Genesis scribes who were concerned with the law, genealogies (commonly known as the "begats"), or the rules and regulations for Israelite priesthood, the Yahwist is the Torah's storyteller. He portrays what scholars call the "primeval history"—the first ten or so chapters of Genesis—as a gradual distancing between God and his creation. Throughout these chapters, the Yahwist takes his reader on a tour of this growing alienation, starting with Adam and Eve's banishment from Paradise. He then describes Noah's predicament as the rains fell and the world began to flood before moving on to report on the confusion at Babel's Tower when human language began to fragment into different dialects. Later, in the Torah, the Yahwist is responsible for the story of the plagues, the Exodus from Egypt, and the wandering in the wilderness.

In the Yahwist's hands, God is all-powerful and anthropomorphized, which makes God's humanity both reassuringly familiar and terrifying. The Yahwist is a fan of character flaws and he is an expert at exploiting them in the service of a narrative, especially when exploring the basic theological concerns about the divide between the human and the divine. The first story to illustrate this is the tale of

Adam and Eve's encounter with the serpent in the Garden of Eden.

The Yahwist brings murder into the primeval history pretty quickly, and things go badly for people from there onward. Cain is a farmer who is jealous of God's preference for his brother Abel because Abel can afford to offer "the fat portions" of his first-born sheep in sacrifice to God. Cain, on the other hand, can only offer the "fruits of the ground." Though God warns Cain not to give in to his anger over this slight, Cain can't help himself, and so he takes Abel into the field and kills him. In return, God banishes Cain from his own land to wander the earth, but he marks Cain to protect him from those who might avenge Abel's murder. Anyone who takes Cain's life, God says, "will suffer a sevenfold vengeance."

In Hebrew folk etymology, Cain means "acquisition" and Abel means "emptiness." Brothers are constantly pitted against one another in the Hebrew Bible and here the Yawhist uses the historical opposition of shepherds and farmers to illustrate that divide. Cain's story is most likely a reference to the Kenites, who were a tribe of metalworkers living in southern Palestine around 1200 BC, an era known as the "period of the Judges." Just as the Israelites favored the Kenites in the period of the Judges, God in the Old Testament must favor Cain after he kills his shepherd brother.

Cain stands for much more than one tribe, however. When the Yahwist wrote his primeval history, or "the beginning of things" as scholars call it, he wanted to connect the history to the lives of his audience. In the Yahwist's eyes, every human being is Cain and Abel, and committing sin is a universal human flaw. Cain was capable of overcoming sin, and yet he didn't just choose, of his own free will, to sin.

"The logic of sin proves stronger than the injunction to do good," writes theologian Miroslav Volf. "This is exactly what we should expect, for the logic of sin was originally designed for the very purpose of overcoming the obligation to do good." Committing a sin is not just making a wrong choice, but rather it is succumbing "to an evil power." Before he killed Abel, Cain had the ability to conquer sin or be conquered by it. He murdered his brother, according to Volf "because he fell prey to what he refused to master."

Volf, one of the world's preeminent thinkers on the Christian theology of reconciliation and forgiveness, has pointed out that traditional mythology often tells stories of sin from the perspective of the perpetrator so as to legitimize the sinner's actions and render sympathy toward him. The story of Cain and Abel condemns Cain, and though the Yahwist engenders sympathy for Abel, he twists tradition by making the story really about Cain, and by pointing the finger at his audience in doing so.

"The story about a murderous 'them' is a story about a murderous 'us,'" Volf writes. "Cain is 'them' and Cain is 'us.'" The story's great feat is that it combines "a clear judgment against the perpetrator with the commitment to protect him from the rage of the 'innocent' victim." In the story, God questions Cain again and again, asking him, why are you angry? Why has your countenance fallen? If you do well, will you not be accepted? Where is your brother Abel? What have you done?

God's constant questioning of Cain suggests a parental presence—God is someone who cares deeply about Cain's actions and their consequences. God and Cain's relationship makes God's decision to banish Cain from his presence all the more poignant. And this is not an unfamiliar trope in the Bible. For instance, Jesus's suffering on the cross didn't tear his heart, Volf suggests, but rather it was the abandonment of everyone around him, including his father: "'My God, my God, why have you forsaken me?'"

From God's perspective, the story of Cain and Abel could not have gone worse—God loses both brothers to death and banishment. Yet, according to Volf, God's mark of protection on Cain represents both armor to protect him from victimization as well as God's grace. "The same God who did not regard Cain's scanty offering, bestowed kindness upon the murderer whose life was in danger," Volf writes. God did not abandon Cain. He claimed Cain as his own by marking and protecting him, even as he sent Cain "away from the presence of the Lord."

Thousands of years later, the U.S. military assigned two chaplains to pastor the men responsible for mass slaughter. Whether the decision to make this offer came from the Geneva Conventions or from U.S. Army regulations based on them, at its heart, the decision came from ancient principles of compassion.

Those chaplains believed that God loves all human beings, including perpetrators, and so their decision was more about how to minister to the Nazis, not whether they should. The process of ministering to those who have committed evil involves returning the wrongdoer to goodness, a difficult challenge when faced with a leader of the Third Reich. For Gerecke and O'Connor that challenge meant using what they learned about each defendant to spiritually lead him back from the place where he'd fallen to a place of restoration.

The decisions Gerecke made in Nuremberg's prison were not God's decisions. They were a series of individual pastoral choices made by a middle-aged American preacher who was attempting to bring what he believed was God's light into a dark heart. The Nuremberg chaplains were not judging the members of their flocks, nor were they forgiving their crimes against humanity. They were trying to lead those Nazis who were willing to follow toward a deeper insight into what they had done. They were attempting to give Hitler's henchmen new standing as human beings before their impending executions.

CHAPTER 10

Wine and Blood

Good is opposed to evil in such a way that a good thing always elimi-nates evil as far as it can.

—J. L. MACKIE

FROM THE DAY OF the sentencing until the executions, Gerecke and O'Connor were with the eleven condemned men almost day and night. The prisoners' movements were considerably restricted. Daily exercise now consisted of a walk up and down the cell block, hand-cuffed to a guard. There would be no more walks in the courtyard and no more chapel services, and any activities outside a prisoner's cell were done in handcuffs. Some of the men asked Gerecke to stop in and visit with them four or five times a day.

The seven other convicted men, now housed in cells on the pris-on's second tier, were also only allowed to walk back and forth on the prison's ground floor. Yet the men consistently refused. "What an effect it would have on those condemned to death if they saw us strolling there," Speer wrote. "They are no longer taken for walks.

Now and then one of their cell doors opens, perhaps for the chaplain or the doctor."

But finally, after nearly two weeks in what amounted to solitary confinement, Speer relented and took Andrus up on his offer to walk on the ground floor. A guard shackled his wrist to Speer's and led him down the narrow winding staircase.

"In the silence," Speer wrote, "every step on the iron stairs sound[ed] like a thunderclap."

Once on the floor of the prison, where he'd spent so much of the last year, Speer saw eleven guards staring directly into the condemned men's cells. And as Speer passed each cell, he saw his colleagues lying on their backs, hands outside the blanket, heads turned toward the inside of the cell—just as Andrus demanded. "A ghostly sight," Speer wrote. "It looks as though they have already been laid on their biers . . . I cannot stand it for long. Back in my cell, I decide not to go back down again."

The men continued to turn inward toward themselves, and some toward God. According to Gerecke, Ribbentrop read his Bible most of the day. Hitler's foreign minister had, Speer thought, "abandoned his arrogance for a faith in Christ that sometimes strikes a grotesque note." Gerecke noticed that Keitel "was especially interested in certain Bible portions and certain hymns which spoke of the love of God in the redeeming Blood of Christ." Sauckel, on the other hand, was "much disturbed," Gerecke noted. He was "so unstrung that I feared he would not hold up under the pressure. He would pray aloud and always end our devotional sessions with, 'God be merciful to me, a sinner.'"

Ribbentrop, Keitel, and Sauckel all took Communion with Gerecke in their cells. "God had changed these hearts along the way and now in the face of losing all material things, even their life, they could hear the promises of God to penitent sinners through the lips of Jesus who receives sin-burdened souls," Gerecke later wrote.

When they were not praying, the men spent their remaining time seeking small pleasures. Some of the condemned men were stamp collectors, and they spent the time removing stamps from the letters they received. Seyss-Inquart asked Andrus if they could take cold showers, telling the commandant that as chief Nazi in the occupation of the Netherlands, he had allowed those condemned to death to take cold showers, and it often helped them. Jodl wrote to his wife that he felt like a monk in his cell—it was no longer a prison, but a refuge.

On October 12, the condemned men met with their wives for the final time. As Emmy Goering waited in her attorney's apartment for her scheduled time to proceed to the Palace of Justice, she prayed. "My God, give me the strength to bear this last visit. Afterwards, let whatever you want happen to me. But give me the courage this last time."

When they saw each other, Emmy said she had told Edda about Hermann's impending death. Hermann was crying.

"Is Papa really going to die?" Edda had asked her mother. "If Papa must die, will he find all the people he once loved in heaven?"

Yes, Emmy had assured her, most certainly.

Emmy told her husband what Edda had asked her.

"She says she wants to meet you in heaven," Emmy said. And if it weren't for Edda, "I would like to die with you."

A ray of sunlight seemed, to Emmy, to light up Hermann's face. "All signs of suffering vanished from it," Emmy later wrote. "Suddenly, he looked very young."

"Don't be afraid that they will hang me," Hermann said. "They'll keep a bullet for me."

"Do you really think they will shoot you?" Emmy asked.

"You may be sure of one thing," he said. "They won't hang me."

They spoke some more of their marriage, of Edda, and of happier days. And then it was time for Emmy to go.

"I bless you, you and our daughter," Hermann told his wife,

making a sign of blessing with his left hand. "I bless our dear Father-land, and I bless all those who will be good to you." And then a guard led him out of the room and back to his cell.

Emmy stayed in her seat for a few minutes, with Gerecke next to her. Only after a moment did she realize she was speaking through her tears, "I love you . . . I love you . . . I love you . . . "

Emmy completely lost her composure as Gerecke led her out of the room. "When I had seen a particularly dramatic scene in the theater or cinema in the past, I had often thought: 'it's exaggerated! Reality can't be so cruel!'" she later wrote. "Everything became hazy in front of my eyes, my body broke in a sweat and I felt that I was going to faint."

Gerecke had learned that photographers were camped out to get pictures of Emmy, and so he devised an alternate route out of the building that required them to exit the interview area on the other side of the partition. They passed the chair that Hermann had just been sitting in. Emmy stopped and put her hand on it. The chair was still warm.

After Gerecke got Emmy out of the building, he went to Goering's cell. Goering told Gerecke that it didn't matter what happened to him now. He had died when he'd left his wife upstairs.

THE U.S. ARMY HAD already been hanging men for several months. Even before the Nuremberg trials started, in June 1945 the Dachau trials had begun one hundred miles to the south, inside the former concentration camp. Unlike the Trial of the Major War Criminals at the Palace of Justice, the U.S. military conducted the Dachau trials to bring to justice concentration camp personnel, Nazi officials, and German civilians. Until December 1947, the U.S. Army prosecuted 1,676 lesser war criminals in 462 trials. One of the first of those trials was for officials of Dachau, and in December 1945, thirty-six were sentenced to death and sent to War Criminal Prison Number 1, or

Landsberg Prison, where Hitler and Hess had spent their time after the 1923 Beer Hall Putsch, writing *Mein Kampf.*

In May 1946, the U.S. Army's executioner, Master Sergeant John Woods, hanged twenty-eight men. Woods oversaw the construction of two gallows, which would make the process more efficient. The army hanged seven men each morning and afternoon on two successive days. Among them were Dachau's former commandant and a seventy-four-year-old doctor who had killed four hundred prisoners while experimenting with malaria.

Woods learned his trade as a teenager from a neighbor who was a prison hangman, eventually becoming the man's assistant. Woods was a short, stocky Texan who, while on duty, was a competent, friendly, and respectful soldier. But he was also a belligerent drunk off duty with a seething hatred for Germans. During the Battle of the Bulge, the German army had massacred several of his friends at Malmedy, Belgium, after taking them as prisoners. Those responsible had been tried at Dachau.

Lieutenant Stanley Tilles, who coordinated the Landsberg and the Nuremberg hangings, also was an expert in the field. "Hanging does not immediately kill a man," he wrote later:

> However, in a proper hanging he loses all consciousness and feeling the moment the large coils of the noose snap his neck. At that point his brain is disconnected from his body and his respiration stops. Complete cession of his heart beat, the official determination of death, occurs within eight to twelve minutes after he drops. During that time he does not gasp or choke; he may have bitten off his tongue and lost control of his bowels when his neck snapped, but he would not be aware of either.

After their work at Landsberg, army officials ordered Tilles and Woods to team up again. This time all the planning would be top secret. The army drafted papers stating that Tilles would be assigned to register army vehicles. In fact, he and Woods, along with a team of five military police officers, would spend from August until October coordinating the Nuremberg execution plan, constructing three mobile gallows at Landsberg, then secretly transporting them to the Palace of Justice 125 miles away.

On October 3, 1946, Colonel Phillip C. Clayton, provost marshal—head of the military police—for the U.S. Third Army, told Tilles the Nuremberg executions would take place in the early morning hours of October 16. Clayton said Tilles, Woods, and their team of MPs would arrive at the Palace of Justice under cover of darkness, set up the gallows, perform the executions, dismantle the gallows, and leave Nuremberg as soon as possible the same day. To keep the execution team's arrival secret, the army would issue orders for Woods and the MPs to join the 6850th and to take up quarters at the Grand Hotel. All orders would be verbal. There would be no paper trail assigning anyone to the execution.

The three gallows had three parts each—the frame, which had to be bolted together, the platform, and the steps. When assembled, the platform was eight feet high and eight feet wide, with thirteen steps leading up the front. A heavy black curtain obscured the area beneath the platform where the bodies would drop. The trapdoor was in the center of the platform, and the hangman's handle that released it was at the rear. An eyebolt used to secure the rope sat in the middle of the frame, which formed a square arch several feet over the platform. The entire gallows was fifteen feet high.

The men had timed themselves putting the gallows together and estimated it would take eleven to twelve hours to assemble them in the Palace of Justice. Woods spent hours testing them, stretching his ropes, making eleven black hoods, and tying nooses. By October 10, he had thirteen nooses, one for each of the condemned men and two extras. He packed a duffel bag full of leather bootlaces and army web belts that would be used to tie the prisoners' hands and feet together. Clayton told Tilles that they were to leave for Nuremberg the morning of October 14. Three semitrailer trucks would deliver the gallows the day before.

The prisoners began to hear the sound of hammering. Speer was irritated at first, thinking someone was carrying out repairs at night. Then it dawned on him what was happening. "Several times I thought I heard a saw; then there came a pause, finally several hammer blows," he wrote in his diary. "After about an hour, complete silence returned. Lying on my cot, I could not shake off the thought that the executions were being prepared. Sleepless."

Tilles's team did most of the gallows assembly on October 15. The executions would take place in the gym. The team blacked out the windows and hung a long black curtain from the basketball hoop to obscure eleven coffins before finishing the gallows. They were told to stay within the confines of the Palace of Justice until they received their final instructions at 11:00 P.M.

As Tilles's team worked, the chaplains went from cell to cell on the ground floor, sitting with each man for a few minutes, listening as they "unburdened their hearts," Gerecke later wrote, "because they felt they were soon to go into eternity."

That morning, Andrus had summoned Gerecke and O'Connor to his office. He told them the condemned men would be awakened at 11:45 P.M., served a last meal, and then walked to the gym. The executions would begin just after midnight. Andrus had ordered the chaplains not to tell the men, nor anyone else, of the execution plans. They shouldn't know until they were woken up that night, he had told them. The day should proceed normally.

In the afternoon, as the chaplains visited the men's cells, O'Connor asked Kaltenbrunner, Frank, and Seyss-Inquart whether they would like to confess their sins and receive Communion. Their eyes grew large as they realized why he was asking. What did he know? they demanded. Would it happen at dawn tomorrow?

O'Connor told them he hadn't heard anything.

Gerecke sat with each of the six condemned men in his charge—

Goering, Keitel, Ribbentrop, Rosenberg, Sauckel, and Frick—and delivered a copy of a devotion he'd written in German for them. He asked them each to join him in a prayer he'd also written. Only Rosenberg refused. "No, please do not," he said to Gerecke.

Goering demanded to know what was going on with the execution timetable. He was also refusing to leave his cell, and he was adamantly against exercising or showering. He took all the family photos that had decorated his flimsy table and put them in an envelope for this attorney. In the early afternoon, Goering requested a visit from Gerecke. "What time are the executions scheduled for, Pastor?" Goering asked. Gerecke didn't answer.

The reichsmarshal was a likable man, and Gerecke wished he could have been honest with him. Even Chaplain Carl Eggers, who hadn't known Goering for as long as Gerecke, called him a "good-natured charmer" with "a good sense of humor." Eggers had been surprised that Goering also knew quite a bit about the Bible. "Of all the doomed men, he impressed us the most," O'Connor said later. "You felt that with his brain, he could have accomplished a lot."

Goering had been fascinated with baseball, and he often discussed the game with O'Connor during routine visits. He wanted to know about the Dodgers and how baseball worked as a business. "Is there money in it?" Goering would ask. O'Connor told him that Branch Rickey, the Dodgers' general manager, made $90,000 a year. "Maybe I should have gone into that business," Goering had said.

The World Series was on the radio that night, and Gerecke's St. Louis Cardinals were playing. In between visiting the prisoners in their cells, Gerecke and O'Connor hurried to the guard booth to get caught up on the score. There was ten dollars at stake between the two chaplains.

At about 3:15 P.M., Otto, the prison's German librarian, had brought Goering a book and some writing paper. A kitchen worker brought Goering tea fifteen minutes later, and he began writing a letter. Around 7:30 P.M., Gerecke returned to Goering's cell, number 5, in a final attempt to get him to accept Christ. Goering had been a regular at the prison chapel, but he had resisted Gerecke's efforts to bring him more seriously into the fold of the church. Gerecke told Goering he'd written a special devotional for him. Goering told the chaplain to leave it on his table. He'd read it later. What he really wanted to discuss was the executions.

Gerecke tried again to steer the conversation toward how a man prepares his soul for death. He asked Goering to join him in prayer. No, Goering said. He would watch Gerecke pray from his cot.

Gerecke thought Goering seemed more depressed than he had earlier, which was not surprising given what was coming. Goering asked how the other men were doing. In particular, he was concerned about Sauckel, whom he could hear crying and moaning with fear. He asked Gerecke if he might be able to see Sauckel to help him get through this.

Then he started in on the method of execution again. Hanging, Goering said, was a most dishonorable way for him to die, given his former position with the German people.

Gerecke didn't respond. He'd heard this same complaint dozens of times from Goering since the sentencing. Silence fell between them.

Somewhat desperately now, Gerecke tried one last time to engage Goering on the "eternal values and how a man can be prepared to die, to meet his God."

"Surrender your heart and soul completely to your savior, Herr Reichsmarshal," he said.

Goering was in no mood to listen. For the last time, Goering told Gerecke that he was a member of the Christian church, but that he couldn't accept the teachings of the Christian faith. He began to make fun of the creation story in the Old Testament. He ridiculed the idea that the Bible was written by scribes divinely inspired by God. He refused the fundamental Christian doctrine of atonement—that

Jesus, through his suffering and resurrection, died for the forgiveness of man's sin and to reconcile God and his creation.

Gerecke pleaded with Goering. "This is what Jesus said," Gerecke told him. "This isn't what Gerecke is saying, but this is God speaking to you. Won't you accept this? Just say, 'Jesus, save me.'"

"No!" Goering barked. "I can't do that. This Jesus you always speak of—to me he's just another smart Jew."

"Herr Reichsmarshal," Gerecke said. "This Jesus is my savior who suffered, bled and died that I may go to heaven some day. He paid for my sins."

"Ach!" Goering yelled. "You don't believe that yourself. When one is dead, that's the end of everything."

In a softer tone, he continued, "Pastor, I believe in God. I believe he watches over the affairs of men, but only the big ones. He is too great to bother about little matters like what becomes of Hermann Goering."

He fell silent for a moment. Then he looked at Gerecke.

Pastor, he said finally, "how do you celebrate the Lord's Supper?"

Gerecke was astonished. "You claim membership in the church," Gerecke said. "You must be familiar with its sacraments."

THE LORD'S SUPPER—THE CHRISTIAN sacrament of Holy Communion—was particularly meaningful for Gerecke. As a Lutheran, the chaplain believed that when Christ offered bread to his apostles at the Last Supper, telling them it was his body, it actually became his body. When bread and wine were consecrated in Gerecke's Lutheran church, those in the pews had been taught to believe the body of Christ was "truly present . . . in, with, and under" the elements of bread and wine.

In Holy Communion, some Christians believe God is mitigating their suffering through the sacrifice of Christ, his son. Their sins disappear each time they receive Communion and they grow a little closer to God. These convictions stem from Christianity's central belief in atonement.

After Christ's death, his apostles continued to meet together, and early Christian believers received Communion in their homes on Sundays. The tradition of Sunday Mass—indeed the idea of "church"—grew directly out of Holy Communion, or the Eucharist, which derives from the Greek word *eucharistia,* meaning "thanksgiving." Eucharistic traditions are mentioned in an early-second-century Christian instruction manual called *The Lord's Teaching to the Heathen by the Twelve Apostles,* or simply the *Didache*—the *Teaching.* The pages of the manual lay out how Christians should organize their churches and worship services.

The *Didache* echoes the New Testament with a warning: "You must not let anyone eat or drink of your Eucharist except those baptized in the Lord's name. For in reference to this the Lord said, 'Do not give what is sacred to dogs.'" Similarly, in Paul's first letter to the Corinthians, Paul says that "whoever . . . eats the bread or drinks the cup of the Lord in an unworthy manner will be answerable for the body and blood of the Lord. Examine yourselves, and only then eat of the bread and drink of the cup. For all those who eat and drink without discerning the body, eat and drink judgment against themselves."

The church waited one thousand years to debate formally the theology of the Eucharist. Was it actually Christ's body and blood? In the thirteenth century, the fourth Lateran Council answered that question in the affirmative and the term *transubstantiation* entered the Christian lexicon. The council's conclusions followed from a long line of tradition still practiced in the Roman Catholic Church today. Christ's followers believed that those who consumed his flesh would receive grace and become united with him, and that the living bread of Christ would keep them supernaturally alive forever. "I am the bread of life," Jesus says in the Gospel of John. "I am the living bread that came down from heaven, so that one may eat of it and not die . . . the bread that I will give for the life of the world is my flesh."

In the Roman Catholic tradition, "when a priest consecrates the elements of bread and wine, the accidents of bread remain the same but the substance is miraculously changed by the power of God into the body and blood of Christ," writes historian of Christianity David Steinmetz. "The bread and wine still feel, smell, taste, and look like bread and wine, but appearances in this case are deceiving. The reality which is present is Christ himself."

The nature of the Eucharist was central to Martin Luther's idea of church reform, and in the early sixteenth century he rejected the concept of transubstantiation. He argued that the church had invented transubstantiation to give priests the power to perform a miracle by changing bread into the substance of Christ. Yet, he also disagreed with other reformers who said Christ's substance was completely absent from the Eucharist and that bread and wine only symbolically represented Christ's body and blood.

Luther's compromise was a 1527 tract called *That These Words of Christ, "This Is My Body," etc., Still Stand Firm Against the Fanatics,* in which he argued for an idea that combined his own beliefs about the sacraments with a theory about the promises between God and men. According to Luther, in the bread and wine of the Lord's Supper, God promises to be present for each of his children. "It is one thing if God is present, and another if he is present for you," Luther wrote. "He is there for you when he adds his Word and binds himself saying, 'Here you are to find me.'" Those who follow the Lutheran doctrine believe that Christ was making a promise to his apostles when he said, "This is my body." For Lutherans, this promise, or covenant, ran through Christ's apostles to all believers and bound them to a promise that they would remember him in return for his body.

In many ways, Lutherans tried to simplify the logic of the sacrament: here's what Christ said. We trust Christ. The rest is a mystery. For instance, Lutherans speak of "partaking" of Holy Communion because in doing so, Christians trust Christ's promise that their sins are forgiven. When Lutherans say it is a "means of grace" that God uses to pour out grace upon those who received the sacrament, they are alluding to Christ's exercise of grace in establishing the covenant with his followers to forgive all of man's sins.

This philosophy also informs the Lutheran understanding of the sacraments. The church reformers who crafted the Augsburg Confession, the sixteenth-century foundational document of the Lutheran Church, wrote that in "the Holy Supper the two essences, the natural bread and the true, natural body of Christ, are present together here on earth in the ordered action of the sacrament, though the union of the body and blood of Christ with the bread and wine is not a personal union, like that of the two natures of Christ, but a sacramental union."

The wording "in, with, and under," is crucial for Lutherans because the phrase means that the bread is simultaneously both bread and body, and that wine is both wine and blood.

IN GOERING'S CELL, GERECKE reminded Goering of the church doctrines, emphasizing that only the truly penitent should partake. He had administered communion to Keitel, Ribbentrop, Sauckel, Raeder, Speer, Fritzsche, and Schirach because they had requested it and had suffered through a great deal of self-examination under Gerecke's guidance.

"Herr Reichsmarshal," Gerecke said. "This is the way it is: Only those who believe that Jesus is really their savior, who believe in him who instituted the supper should be permitted to attend the Lord's Supper. The others are unfit."

"I have never been refused the Lord's Supper by a German pastor," Goering said. "Never."

Gerecke had been afraid of this moment. A committed member of his congregation was asking for the most central sacrament of the church with his final wish. Yet Goering had just disparaged the foundations of the Christian faith. Gerecke knew Goering was, like Rosenberg, *Gottgläubig*. As a rationalist Goering wanted to go through the motions, believing none of the mysteries of the Church while retaining some insurance in case Christianity really represented the truth.

"I cannot with a clear conscience commune you because you deny the very Christ who instituted the sacrament," Gerecke said. "You may be on the church roll, but you do not have faith in Christ and have not accepted him as your savior. Therefore, you are not a Christian, and as a Christian pastor I cannot commune you."

Then Gerecke revealed his last card. "Herr Goering, your little girl said she wants to meet you in heaven."

"Yes," Goering said slowly. "She believes in your savior. But I don't. I'll just take my chances, my own way."

Gerecke thought at that moment Goering would request a German pastor, but Goering said nothing more. Defeated, Gerecke left the cell and moved on.

Goering read in bed for thirty minutes before getting up and walking to the toilet in the corner of his cell, out of view of his guards. He urinated and then he sat back down on his bed to take off his boots and put on his slippers. He was agitated and restless. He picked up his book, walked to the table in his cell with it, and picked up his reading glasses and then put them down. He moved his suspenders and some writing utensils, placing them on a nearby chair.

At 9:15 P.M., Goering changed into his silk pajamas and got into bed, covering his chest with his hands. His left hand kept moving between his body and the cell wall while he massaged his forehead with his right hand. As usual, the prison lights were turned down at 9:30 P.M. The cell lights dimmed and the overhead corridor lights were turned out.

At 10:40 P.M., Goering turned his head to the wall and lay that way for a few minutes. Then he placed his hands at his sides again, and clenched his jaw hard, breaking the glass vial of potassium cyanide he'd placed in his cheek moments before. His guard, Private Harold Johnson, saw Goering stiffen and make a blowing, choking sound through his lips. Goering began grabbing at his throat and gurgling.

The Cardinals had tied the Red Sox, and the chaplains and a handful of guards were waiting impatiently in the guard office for the next call when they heard Johnson's voice.

"Goering's having some kind of spell!" Johnson yelled. He began unbolting the door as the acrid smell of bitter almonds wafted out of the cell.

Gerecke and prison officer Lieutenant Norwood Croner arrived within seconds. The chaplain pushed past Johnson and moved toward the cot. Goering, froth coming from his mouth, was "gurgling into death," Gerecke thought. His heart was still beating, but his eyes had rolled back in his head and the gurgling sound continued. His right arm dangled over the side of the cot. Gerecke picked up Goering's hand and felt for a pulse.

"Get the doctor, this man's dying!" Gerecke yelled at Croner.

Goering was turning green, and his gasping was growing fainter. His toes were beginning to curl toward the soles of his feet. Gerecke leaned down to Goering's ear. "The blood of Jesus Christ cleanseth us from all our sins," he said.

The prison doctor, a German POW named Ludwig Pfluecker arrived, and Gerecke stepped back to let him take Goering's pulse. It was fading.

"He's dying," Pfluecker said.

He realized Goering was not having a heart attack, but had swallowed poison, something he had no experience dealing with. Pfluecker yelled for someone to wake Charles Roska, the prison's American doctor.

Pfluecker pulled back the blanket covering Goering to check his heart and found two white envelopes in Goering's left hand. He handed them to Gerecke, telling the chaplain to remember later that he had done so. Gerecke looked inside and found the cartridge case where Goering had hidden the cyanide and folded pieces of paper.

When Roska arrived at 11:00 P.M., the bitter almond smell was stronger, and Goering's skin had turned from green to gray. One eye was partly open and dilated. His mouth was also slightly open, and Roska could see glass shards on Goering's tongue.

Captain Robert Starnes, the chief prison officer, had also arrived by then. Gerecke turned to Starnes.

"He's dead," Gerecke said, and handed Starnes the white envelopes, which were later classified top secret.

Within an hour, a three-man board of officers was formed to investigate the suicide. Investigators found a good deal of silk among Goering's belongings, including a silk dress shirt, a silk robe that was folded under his pillow, two pairs of silk socks, and silk underwear. Investigators also removed a pair of U.S.-made sunglasses, a shoeshine rag, a deck of playing cards, a book of cigarette papers, a quarter-full carton of Velvet tobacco, an eighth-full carton of Edgeworth tobacco, a full sack of Durham tobacco, six books, and two magazines.

Gerecke later wrote in his chaplain report that Goering had "denied every fundamental doctrine of the Bible. He hinted at Communion, but since he denied the Lord Jesus as Savior, I could not commune him," Gerecke noted. "Had he been sincere in his quest for Christ and Salvation, he would not have gone the way he did."

And yet, something nagged at Gerecke. He worried that he had failed Goering. The reichsmarshal had point-blank asked him about receiving the sacrament—a clear indication that Goering was ready to listen. Gerecke wondered if his rigid ministry with the Lord's Supper had kept him from understanding how to reach Goering.

Indeed, other Lutheran pastors later criticized Gerecke for withholding Holy Communion from Goering. Gerecke always defended his decision—he'd been Goering's pastor, and he knew better than anyone how the Nazi viewed Christianity. But he also noted to his accusers that he was only human, and that it was possible he'd been wrong.

"If I blundered in my approach to reach this man's heart and soul with the meaning of the Cross of Jesus, then I'm very sorry," he later wrote. "I hope a Christian world will forgive me."

The envelopes found on Goering's body contained four suicide notes. The first, addressed to the Allied Control Council, began, "Would that I be shot!" Hanging the German reichsmarshal cannot be permitted, he continued, "therefore I elect to die as the great Hannibal did."

Historians have since concluded that another note, addressed to Andrus, was meant to deflect blame from the person who had helped Goering secure the potassium cyanide. Most likely, that person was Tex Wheeler, an American MP.

"Since my imprisonment I have always kept the poison capsule on my person," Goering wrote, describing where and how he had hidden three capsules. No one in charge of the "frequent and very thorough" searches of his cell "was at fault because it was almost impossible to find the capsule," he wrote.

The other two notes were addressed to Gerecke. In the first, Goering wrote, "Dear Pastor Gerecke, please deliver this last letter to my wife." In that note, Goering told Emmy, whom he greeted as "My heart's only love," that his life had "closed when I last bid you farewell." He told her that after "intimate prayer to God," he had decided to take his own life:

> Since then I have been filled with a wonderful tranquility
> and I perceive death as the last redemption. I take it as a sign
> from God that through all the months of imprisonment he left
> me with the means to free me from earthly worry and that it
> was never discovered. Thus God in his kindness spared me

> *the worst. All my thoughts are of you, Edda and our loved*
> *ones. The last beats of my heart beat our great eternal love.*
>   *Your Hermann.*

Goering directed the last note to Gerecke. "Forgive me but I had to do it this way for political reasons," Goering wrote. "I have prayed for a long time to God and feel that I am acting correctly. Would that I might be shot. Please console my wife and tell her that mine was no ordinary suicide and that she should be certain that God will take me into his grace . . . God bless you, dear Pastor."

Investigators later questioned Gerecke because he was one of the first to arrive at Goering's side as he was dying. The Russians were especially suspicious of Gerecke's relationship with Goering.

But in the suicide's immediate aftermath, Gerecke had other things on his mind. Within minutes, Andrus asked him to tell the other prisoners what had happened and to warn them that they would be closely watched. Some of the men told Gerecke that Goering's suicide was a "craven" act. Many of them had heard Goering boast about how brave he would be to the end.

Andrus and those in charge of the executions began to panic over Goering's death, and they briefly considered carrying his body into the gallows on a stretcher so that Andrus could tell the press Goering had fainted and then hang the corpse.

A sense of urgency animated the prison as Andrus was determined to make sure the executions took place without more mistakes. Eight journalists—two from each of the four allied countries—had been selected from a lottery to be the pool reporters. They'd been brought into the prison at 8:00 P.M. and sequestered in a windowless room. At 11:30 P.M., Andrus told them about Goering, but he did not release them to contact their editors. If they wanted to witness the executions, they had to stay. A hundred other reporters waited in the Palace of Justice pressroom. They'd been warned not to wander or lean out the windows. Guards had been given orders to shoot.

Andrus ordered guards to handcuff themselves to each of the condemned men's left arm. This would leave the prisoners' right hands free to eat their final meals. Gerecke and O'Connor made a final round of visits to the cells, and the prisoners were told to dress in their court clothes. Streicher refused and was forced into them by guards.

At 12:25 A.M., the execution team, along with the doctors, press, and other witnesses, were led across the courtyard and into the gym. It was a cold night. A drizzling rain fell, and snow threatened. Wind whipped through clothing. MPs at the gym door checked each person's pass.

At the same time, those working the executions inside the gym were given their instructions. A member of Andrus's staff would lead the prisoner to the gym door and knock. One of the MPs with the execution team would open the door as Andrus and the prisoner walked three steps inside.

Andrus had wanted to allow each prisoner to walk from his cell to the gym without handcuffs, but Goering's suicide had prevented that. Once inside, Andrus would remove the prisoner's handcuffs and leave the chamber, symbolically relinquishing him to Lieutenant Tilles's staff, the MPs of the Third Army's provost marshal.

Two MPs would hold the prisoner by the arms, walking him toward the gallows. Two more MPs would follow, trailed by Gerecke or O'Connor and an interpreter. The prisoner would be led to members of the tribunal witnessing from a table near the gallows and asked to state his name.

Then one pair of MPs would lead him up the thirteen steps of the gallows to the platform and a chaplain would follow. The other MP pair would go behind the black curtain that would hide the dangling body. When the doctors present pronounced the man dead, the MPs would cut down the body and place it on a stretcher. They would then take it behind another black curtain where a plain pine coffin was waiting.

At 1:00 A.M., Andrus, trailed by two German officials, several guards, and the chaplains, went from cell to cell reading the sentences for each man—*Tod durch den Strang!* the interpreter called to each. Death by the rope. As the party left each cell, one of the chaplains spoke for a moment with the prisoner inside.

Goering would have been the first to hang, but now that position fell to Hitler's foreign minister. From the second tier, Speer heard Andrus's voice: "Ribbentrop!" A cell door opened. Speer heard muffled voices and the scraping of boots.

Gerecke entered the cell and prayed with Ribbentrop as Andrus waited outside. Ribbentrop said he "put all his trust in the Blood of the Lamb that taketh away the sins of the world. He asked that God have mercy on his soul."

When Ribbentrop was ready, Andrus called through the door. "Follow me," he said. Speer heard their footsteps reverberating in the corridor before they slowly faded away. Sitting upright on his cot, his hands icy, he was barely able to breathe.

Andrus led Ribbentrop out across the exercise yard thirty-five yards to the door of the gym. Gerecke and O'Connor followed. O'Connor wore his Franciscan habit, which consisted of a brown robe designed in the shape of a cross and tied at the waist by a white cord that ended in three knots, signifying the Franciscan vows.

"It was a long walk," Andrus wrote later, "for all of us."

When they arrived at the gym door, Andrus took off his burnished steel helmet and bowed. Ribbentrop returned the gesture.

Andrus's knock startled the execution team, which had been waiting in silence inside the gym. When the door opened, Ribbentrop walked in and shielded his eyes from the bright lights. It was 1:11 A.M. He blinked and looked around the dusty, grimy room.

Andrus removed Ribbentrop's handcuffs and left the gym. He had overseen these prisoners for too long to watch them die.

As the MPs took his arms, Ribbentrop saw the members of the tribunal, German officials, U.S. Army officers, and journalists sitting at the eight folding tables across from the gallows.

The MPs walked Ribbentrop over to face the tribunal members and asked him to state his name. He did so, and they led him to the gallows. He paused for a moment before walking up. Gerecke followed.

At the top of the steps, the MPs tied Ribbentrop's hands behind his back with the leather bootlaces, then tied his legs together with an army web belt.

As he stood on the trapdoor, he spoke his final words—a wish for peace in the world. Then he looked at Gerecke.

"I'll see you again," he said.

Gerecke spoke a brief prayer, and the moment he said "Amen," Woods draped a black hood over Ribbentrop's head, followed by the noose. Woods looked at the provost marshal officer and waited for the signal. It came quickly, and Woods pulled the hangman's lever. Ribbentrop dropped through the trapdoor at 1:16 A.M.

Gerecke and O'Connor walked out of the gym, back across the wet yard, and into the prison corridor where they waited for the signal to bring in the next man.

Speer again heard Andrus from the second tier. "Keitel!" Again, the cell door opened, and Gerecke walked in to pray with the man he would later call "my friend."

"Our period of prayer in his cell was drenched with his tears," Gerecke later wrote.

As they walked through the courtyard, Keitel recited Bible verses in German that Gerecke couldn't decipher. He also all but hummed the melody to Johann Friedrich Raeder's nineteenth-century hymn, "*Harre, Meine Seele*" ("Await, My Soul").

At the top of the gallows, Keitel said his final words, and then he recited a prayer that his mother taught him when he was a child. Gerecke's mother had said the same prayer with him when he was young, and now the two men prayed it together: "*Christi Blut und Gerechtigkeit, das ist mein Schmuck und Ehrenkleid; darin will ich vor Gott bestehen, wenn ich zum Himmel werd eingehen. Amen.*" "Christ's blood and judgment are my adornment and robe of honor; therein I will stand before God when I go to Heaven. Amen."

Keitel turned to Gerecke. "I thank you, and those who sent you, with all my heart," he said.

Woods pulled the black hood over Keitel's head and the noose around his neck and adjusted it. Keitel dropped at 1:20 A.M., and the chaplains returned to the prison.

Inside the gym, both Ribbentrop and Keitel were hanging, but still alive, so the proceedings came to an awkward pause while the doctors waited to pronounce each man dead. A colonel from the provost marshal's office finally spoke up and asked the tribunal to allow smoking. The four judges conferred and granted permission and nearly everyone produced a cigarette. As smoke filled the gym, the only sound was the scratching of reporters' pens, the buzz from the overhead lights, and the groaning of the two ropes. At 1:30 A.M., the doctor declared Ribbentrop dead. The MPs cut down his body, and Woods secured a new rope on the first gallows. Keitel was pronounced dead at 1:33 A.M.

Six minutes later, the chaplains walked in with Kaltenbrunner, and O'Connor escorted him up the gallows steps. "I did my duty according to the laws," Kaltenbrunner said when he reached the top, looking to one observer like "a haggard giant." "I regret that crimes were committed in which I had no part. Good luck, Germany." He dropped at 1:39 A.M.

Rosenberg, his cheeks sunken and complexion pasty, entered the gym next. He had refused all Gerecke's attempts at ministry, and before he died, he also refused to make a final statement. In his cell, when Gerecke asked for permission to say a final prayer, Rosenberg smiled and said, "No, thank you."

As Gerecke prayed next to Rosenberg on the platform, Rosenberg stared straight ahead, ignoring him. He dropped at 1:49 A.M., and again the proceedings silently came to a halt in a cloud of smoke as the officials waited for Kaltenbrunner and Rosenberg to die.

A doctor declared Kaltenbrunner dead at 1:52 A.M., and four minutes later, O'Connor escorted a smiling Hans Frank into the chamber.

Earlier in the evening, when Gerecke had been talking to Goering for the final time, O'Connor had been doing the same with Frank. The two men had prayed together from the service of Christ on Golgotha, when Jesus was dying on the cross. Later in the night, after the prisoners were woken and told the executions were to begin, O'Connor had given Frank Communion.

Before leaving Frank's cell for the gym, O'Connor traced a small cross on the prisoner's head, mouth, and chest—the way Frank's mother had when he was a child. As they walked to the execution chamber, just before 2:00 A.M., O'Connor gave him the last blessing of the church and forgiveness. Frank was quiet and asked the priest to tell his family that he died well, that he had accepted his death as punishment and penance for his past. As they entered the gym the men were praying to St. Joseph for a good death.

Gerecke, standing near the door, noticed that O'Connor was beginning to crack. As O'Connor followed Frank up the steps, the war hero who had ministered to troops in the midst of the Battle of the Bulge, and who had buried thousands of victims of the Holocaust, nearly fainted from the stress.

Frank thanked Andrus "for the kindness which [he] received in this incarceration." On the gallows, O'Connor read a short prayer. Frank looked at him. "May Jesus have mercy on me," he said, and then he dropped.

When Streicher entered the gym a few minutes later, he was twitching and anxious. He got his right arm free from the MP and raised it in a party salute, while yelling "Heil Hitler" at the tribunal judges. O'Connor prodded Streicher to state his name, but he refused. Finally, O'Connor lost his temper. In German he screamed, "For God's sake, Julius, tell them your name!"

"Heil Hitler," Streicher screamed instead.

When he reached the top of the gallows, Streicher spat at Woods and shouted that the Bolsheviks would hang him one day. "I am now by God my father!" he yelled. "Adele my dear wife. I die innocently."

Streicher dropped at 2:14 A.M. Tilles said later that Woods had adjusted Streicher's noose, placing the coils off center so the rope wouldn't immediately snap his neck, and he would strangle. "Unlike the other men who died soundlessly, Streicher's gasps and gurgles filled the chamber," Tilles wrote. "Everyone heard his gasps, and everyone denied hearing them. No one moved to Streicher's aid, no one objected, no one uttered any type of comment." The doctors declared Streicher dead at 2:23 A.M.

When Andrus called for Sauckel, Gerecke's breath caught. Sauckel had been the most troubled of all the condemned men in the last days. He was having difficulty composing himself, and he seemed disoriented as he walked into the gym. When Gerecke got him to the top of the platform, Sauckel yelled out, "I'm dying an innocent man." He began to talk about his wife and children, and Gerecke became unsteady. "I felt I could not go on," he said later. Gerecke shakily said a prayer and Sauckel fell through the trapdoor at 2:26 A.M. Moments later, General Jodl spoke his final words as if addressing his troops: "I salute you, my Germany."

O'Connor stood next to the final man, Seyss-Inquart, as he dropped at 2:45 A.M. The process had taken less than two hours.

As Jodl and Seyss-Inquart were still hanging, guards brought Goering's body into the gym on a stretcher. They removed a blanket to show the tribunal his body and then deposited it with the others behind the black curtain hiding the coffins. The judges announced the proceedings closed, and at 2:57 A.M., the witnesses left the gym.

The chaplains returned to the prison in silence and rested. An hour or so later, they were summoned back to the gym to give what

Gerecke called "committal prayers." They wanted the families, especially the children, to know that chaplains had performed final rites for their husbands and fathers.

Gerecke and O'Connor ducked behind the black curtain where each body was positioned atop its coffin. The Army Signal Corps had been tasked with photographing the bodies, both naked and clothed, and with the nooses still around their necks. No photographs of anyone involved with the executions were allowed, nor were photographs of the chamber itself allowed.

What the chaplains saw astonished them. The Nazis' faces were destroyed. Whether on purpose or not, Woods had miscalculated the amount of rope needed for each man. He'd also poorly designed the hinge on the trapdoor and tied the ropes improperly. The result was that the Nazis' faces smashed into the platform on their way down, breaking their noses and tearing their faces. Some, like Streicher, may have strangled to death rather than died from broken necks. Exactly what the chaplains saw, Gerecke wrote later "could never be told."

Both performed a final blessing over the bodies of the dead men, and O'Connor held a special Mass for mourning. Gerecke quickly realized that the army had other plans for the bodies, and he wouldn't be able to fulfill the favor Keitel asked of him—burial in a cemetery lot near a family chapel in Brunswick.

After the chaplains left the gym, the coffin lids were nailed shut, and at 4:00 A.M. MPs loaded the eleven coffins into two army six-by-six trucks that had pulled up to the gym.

The trucks left Nuremberg at 5:30 A.M., escorted by two machine-gun-mounted jeeps carrying armed MPs. Fifty more MPs stood at the gates of the Palace of Justice as the trucks departed. The convoy headed north, then doubled back in an effort to elude journalists who were following. Reporters were eventually dissuaded when the MPs swung the machine guns in their direction. The best guess among members of the press was that the bodies were being taken to an airfield in nearby Erlangen for a flight to Berlin.

Inside the gym, Woods and his team began the four-hour process of breaking down the gallows, which they then drove back to Landsberg and burned to prevent anyone from collecting souvenirs.

When the remaining prisoners woke up on the prison's second tier that morning, the guards escorted them down to the ground floor and instructed them to clean the cells of their dead colleagues. Inside the cells they found the remains of last meals—partially eaten sausage, bits of potato, crumbs of bread—scattered papers, and unfolded blankets. Seyss-Inquart had marked his wall calendar with a large X on October 16, the last day of his life.

In the afternoon, several guards escorted Schirach, Hess, and Speer to the gym and handed them mops and brooms. Speer tried to keep his composure. Hess stopped at what looked like a large bloodstain on the floor and raised his arm in the Nazi Party salute.

Gerecke returned to his apartment in Mögeldorf and tried to sleep. He reflected on "the gross hates and cruelties which climaxed in the careers of the Nazi leaders" that had begun with "petty hates, prejudices and compromises." He was convinced that the eleven who died "to pay a debt to the world" were "men of intelligence and ability" who, in different circumstances, could have been "a blessing to the world instead of a curse."

In his monthly report, Gerecke said he believed that Frick, Sauckel, Ribbentrop, and Keitel "died as penitent sinners trusting God's mercy for forgiveness. They believed in Jesus who shed his blood for their sins."

As he lay in bed that night, Gerecke thought about the Lutheran Church and all the good it did in the world. He thought about the work of Lutheran youth societies, the Lutheran Layman's League, the missionary program of the Lutheran Women's League, and of "all that we have," he said later. "Oh, it's a glorious thing."

In the days that followed, Emmy Goering told Edda that her father was dead. Then, Emmy later wrote, "something marvelous happened."

Gerecke came to visit them in their tiny house north of Nuremberg. "Frau Goering," he said. "I wanted to tell you that the act your husband committed is not a suicide in the eyes of God."

When he left, Edda looked at her mother. "Mummy, how happy I am!" she said. "Now I'm not worried. We shall see Papa again.'"

O'Connor also tended the families of his flock. Hans Frank's sixteen-year-old son Norman had written O'Connor on the day of the executions, and five days later, O'Connor wrote back, expressing his sympathy and telling Norman about his father's final moments.

"His last thoughts were with you," he wrote. "But he did not fear for you. He was convinced that you would understand, and that you had the courage and faith to master your future."

O'Connor told Norman that his task now was to look after his mother and siblings "with love and a man's courage," and "to represent the name of your father in this world, and to defend his honor."

He told Norman that his father had gone "straight to heaven" and that "he found a fair verdict in front of God's judgment chair. Now he surely found quiet and peace and love—those things that this world doesn't give."

He signed off, "Please be always true to God and to yourself. —O'Connor."

FORGIVENESS IS CENTRAL TO the story of Jesus of Nazareth, who, nailed to the cross, prayed to God, "Father, forgive them; for they do not know what they are doing." And it is, therefore, the core theological and ethical concept of Christianity. Forgiveness is simply what is expected of Christ's followers. When Christ taught his disciples to pray, he told them to ask God: "And forgive us our sins, for we ourselves forgive everyone indebted to us.'

The Nazis killed eleven million noncombatants, but more than half of those were Jews killed because they were Jewish. Judaism's theology is ancient and broad, and there is no one settled-upon concept of forgiveness. Maimonides, the twelfth-century Jewish philosopher, said one of the thirteen fundamental truths of Judaism was divine reward and retribution: God rewards those who keep his commandments and punishes the wicked. In Judaism, forgiveness requires that the original violation actually be removed. The Hebrew word for forgiveness is *mehillah*, the wiping away of a transgression. True forgiveness means the victim must be prepared to reestablish a relationship with the perpetrator. If God is forgiving, according to Jewish theology, in imitation of God, Jews must forgive.

But those who commit acts of violence against God's creation must also ask forgiveness of the creator. Perpetrators must do more than pray for God to pardon them. They must take an active role in the process of asking God's forgiveness: admitting the wrong they've committed, humbling themselves before God and promising not to sin again. As the author of Psalm 32 puts it: "Then I acknowledged my sin to You; I did not cover up my guilt; I resolved, 'I will confess my transgressions to the Lord,' and You forgave the guilt of my sin."

God, however, sees through false penitence. "Because that people has approached Me with its mouth and honored Me with its lips, but has kept its heart far from Me, and its worship of me has been a commandment of men, learned by rote," God says through the prophet Isaiah, "I shall further baffle that people with bafflement upon bafflement; and the wisdom of its wise shall fail, and the prudence of its prudent shall vanish."

Broadly, forgiveness in Judaism has two working parts, at extreme opposite ends of the good-evil spectrum: desisting from the evil act, and then doing good. That shift, according to Rabbi David Rosen, is summed up in a word that "dominates the penitential literature of the Bible"—*shuv*, which means "to turn." It is the central idea in the Jewish concept of *teshuva*, which literally means "return." *Teshuva* has come to mean repentance and is itself central to the holiest day of the Jewish calendar, Yom Kippur. On that day, the Day of Atonement, the victims of wrong are obligated to forgive the wrongdoer, but only after the wrongdoer has done *teshuva*: recognized the wrong he's done, stopped doing that wrong, confessed the wrong and asked forgiveness of the victim, and resolved not to repeat it. If the wrongdoer fails to go through the process, the victim can still forgive as an act of charity. But tradition generally insists that the wrongdoer earn his forgiveness through *teshuva*, rather than having it gifted to him for "free" by the victim.

Dietrich Bonhoeffer, the Lutheran pastor and theologian who was executed by the Nazis, disparaged the idea of free forgiveness, which he called "cheap grace," and which he described as "forgiveness of sins proclaimed as a general truth, the love of God taught as the Christian 'conception' of God. An intellectual assent to that idea is held to be of itself sufficient to secure remission of sins." In that framework "grace alone does everything," Bonhoeffer wrote, "and so everything can remain as it was before."

When *teshuva* is accomplished, the wrongdoer has returned to his former state of good, and all that is left to complete the process is for his victim to accept the wrongdoer's confession and recognize it by forgiving it. *Teshuva* implies "that man has been endowed by God with the power of 'turning,'" says Rosen. "He can turn from evil to the good, and the very act of turning will activate God's response and lead to forgiveness." If the wrongdoer has asked for forgiveness three times in the presence of others, and the injured party refuses to forgive him, the tables are turned and the original victim becomes the sinner.

Even when *teshuva* is completed, and a path is opened up for the resumption of a relationship between the former wrongdoer and the former victim, it isn't incumbent on the former victim to reestablish the relationship. Memory of an evil act can linger, and in Jewish tradition, reconciliation isn't required the way forgiveness is after the completion of *teshuva*. Conversely, forgiveness isn't a necessary prerequisite to reconciliation. The theologian Rabbi Elliott Dorff has said that the modern relationship between Jews and Germans illustrates such a circumstance.

Contemporary Germans who were not alive during the Holocaust don't have the moral standing to ask for forgiveness, despite the guilt some may feel for the evil acts of their parents' or grandparents' generation. Similarly, most contemporary Jews, despite the pain many may feel for the atrocities perpetrated on their families during the Holocaust, don't have the moral standing to forgive the evil acts done to their parents' or grandparents' generations. "While forgiveness between contemporary Germans and Jews is therefore not logically possible," Dorff says, "reconciliation is both possible and necessary."

Simon Wiesenthal, the Holocaust survivor and Nazi hunter, wrote about the moral impossibility of survivors of the Holocaust to forgive what was done to those who did not survive. In 1941, Wiesenthal—then thirty-one—was captured in Poland and sent to the Janowska work camp near Lvov. One day, Wiesenthal was included in a group that was taken out of the camp to work at a nearby hospital for the day. Wiesenthal was given the job of emptying cartons filled with rubbish from the operating rooms. At one point, he was approached by a nurse.

"Are you a Jew?" she asked.

He followed the nurse, who walked quickly into the Red Cross building, up a flight of stairs, and into a room with only a white bed and night table beside it. The nurse left the room, and a figure on the bed, wrapped in white, asked in a broken voice, "Please come nearer. I can't speak loudly."

As Wiesenthal approached the bed, he could see the man's white, bloodless hands and a head completely bandaged with openings for his mouth, nose, and ears. Wiesenthal sat down on the edge of the man's bed. "I have not much longer to live," the man whispered. "I know the end is near." Wiesenthal could tell the man was German.

"I am resigned to dying soon, but before that I want to talk about an experience which is torturing me," the man said. "Otherwise I cannot die in peace." The man explained to Wiesenthal that he'd been in the hospital for three months, and that he'd heard there were Jews working as laborers there. He'd asked a nurse to find a Jew and bring him to his bed, and the nurse had complied, acting on the last wish of a dying man.

The man said his name was Karl and that he was a member of the SS.

"I must tell you something dreadful, something inhuman," Karl said, grabbing Wiesenthal's hand. "I must tell you of this horrible deed . . . because you are a Jew."

Karl told Wiesenthal that he was twenty-one years old, and from Stuttgart where his father managed a factory. An only child, Karl was brought up Catholic—an altar boy whom their priest hoped would grow up to study theology. Instead, Karl had joined the Hitler Youth, and faith receded from his life. Out of fear, his parents stopped speaking much about their lives in front of him, so he found friendship in his Hitler Youth comrades. Like most of his friends, when war came Karl volunteered for the SS.

"I was not born a murderer," Karl said.

When Karl's SS platoon joined a unit of SA stormtroopers in Dnepropetrovsk on the Russian front, they found the town deserted. Cars had been abandoned. Homes were burning. Streets were blocked by hastily erected barricades. Karl's unit received an order to report to another part of the town. When they arrived at a large square, he saw a large group of civilians huddled together and under guard.

"And then the word ran through our group like wildfire: 'They're Jews,'" Karl told Wiesenthal. "In my young life I had never seen many Jews. . . . all I knew about the Jews was what came out of the loudspeaker or what was given us to read. We were told they were the cause of all our misfortunes. They were trying to get on top of us, they were the cause of war, poverty, hunger, unemployment."

The order was given and Karl, along with the rest of his unit, marched toward the huddled mass of families—150 people, maybe

200. The children stared at the approaching men with anxious eyes. Some were crying. Women held their infant children. A truck arrived with cans of gasoline, which were taken to the upper stories of one of the small houses on the square. Karl and his unit drove the Jews into the house with whips and kicks. Another truck arrived, and those Jews, too, were crammed into the small house before the door was locked.

Wiesenthal had heard the story before. Many times. He didn't need to hear the ending. He knew the ending. He got up to leave. "Please stay," Karl pleaded. "I must tell you the rest." Something in the tone of Karl's voice—or maybe the need to hear a confession from the mouth of a Nazi—convinced Wiesenthal to sit back down.

The order was given, and the SS unit pulled the safety pins from their grenades and tossed them into the upper windows of the house. Explosions, then screams, then flames and more screams. The men readied their rifles, prepared to shoot any of the Jews who tried to flee the fire. Karl saw a man on the second floor of the house, holding a child. His clothes were on fire. A woman stood next to him. The man covered the child's eyes with one hand and jumped. The woman followed. Burning bodies fell from other windows. The shooting began.

"My God," Karl whispered. "My God."

For Karl and his comrades "there could be no God," Wiesenthal wrote. "The Führer had taken His place. And the fact that their atrocities remained unpunished merely strengthened their belief that God was a fiction, a hateful Jewish invention." Weeks later, a shell exploded near Karl and he lost his eyesight. His face and upper body were torn to ribbons.

"Here was a dying man," thought Wiesenthal, "a murderer who did not want to be a murderer but who had been made into a murderer by a murderous ideology. He was confessing his crime to a man who perhaps tomorrow must die at the hands of these same murderers. In his confession there was true repentance, even though he did not admit it in so many words. Nor was it necessary, for the way he spoke and the fact that he spoke to me was a proof of his repentance."

Karl wanted to die in peace, and peace was only achievable through forgiveness. "In the long nights while I have been waiting for death, time and time again I have longed to talk about it to a Jew and beg forgiveness from him. . . . I know what I am asking is almost too much for you, but without your answer I cannot die in peace."

Wiesenthal stood up and looked at Karl's folded hands. And then he turned around and left the room.

When he returned to the camp, Wiesenthal told his fellow prisoners about Karl. "So you saw a murderer dying," one said. "I would like to do that ten times a day. I couldn't have enough hospital visits."

But another, a devout man named Josek, said that as he'd begun listening to the story of Karl, he'd feared that Wiesenthal was going to forgive the SS man by the story's end.

"You would have had no right to do this in the name of the people who had not authorized you to do so," Josek said. "What people have done to you, yourself, you can if you like, forgive and forget. That is your own affair. But it would have been a terrible sin to burden your conscience with other people's sufferings."

Wiesenthal argued that he was part of a community "and one must answer for the other." He was unsure that he'd done the right thing by remaining silent and leaving the man to die. But Josek told Wiesenthal he had done the right thing. Karl had not made Wiesenthal suffer, and what Karl had done to other people, Josek said, "you are in no position to forgive."

"If you had forgiven him," Josek said. "You would never have forgiven yourself all your life." Two years later, an SS guard shot Josek for being "work-shy."

Wiesenthal survived Janowska. He also survived Plaszow, Gross-Rosen, and Buchenwald. When he eventually landed in Mauthausen he was assigned to Block 6—the death block. The camp's gas chamber "was working at full pressure," he wrote later. But it "could not keep up with the enormous number of candidates. Day and night above the crematoria there hung a great cloud of smoke, evidence that the death industry was in full swing."

At Mauthausen, Wiesenthal befriended a young Polish man named Bolek, who had survived exhaustion, exposure, and starvation on a three-hundred-mile death march from Auschwitz only to end up in Block 6 at Mauthausen. Wiesenthal heard Bolek praying—something most of those in Block 6 had given up on—and eventually found out that the young man had been originally arrested outside the Catholic seminary in Warsaw. His time at Auschwitz had been especially diffi-cult, because the SS guards knew Bolek was a priest in training.

Wiesenthal told Bolek about his encounter years earlier with the dying Nazi. "Should I have forgiven him?" Wiesenthal asked. "Had I in any case the right to forgive him? What does your religion say? What would you have done in my position?"

Bolek thought that Karl had turned to Wiesenthal in the hospital that day because "he regarded Jews as a single condemned com-munity." For Karl, Wiesenthal was a member of that community, and therefore his last chance to confess. By simply listening to Karl's confession Wiesenthal had liberated the Nazi's conscience and al-lowed him to die in peace, returned to his childhood faith through confession, Bolek said. If the man had shown sincere repentance for his sins, as Wiesenthal believed, then he deserved the mercy of for-giveness. "In our religion repentance is the most important element in seeking forgiveness," Bolek said.

If Wiesenthal struggled with his moral authority to forgive a dying, repentant Nazi who had taken part in the massacre of Jews, what is the moral standing of a non-Jew, like Bolek, a Catholic sem-inarian, to offer mercy to a murderer of Jews? Christian theologians speak of a counterpart to forgiveness that's not quite forgiveness, but more like compassion for a wrongdoer. Forgiveness entails identi-fying the guilt of another, placing that person in a moral universe, assigning blame, lifting blame, and then letting the person go. Compassion and mercy are analogues to that.

When Bolek told Wiesenthal that in Christianity "repentance is the most important element in seeking forgiveness," he was not quite right. It is in this fissure that the difference exists in Christian forgiveness theology and Jewish forgiveness theology. Christian tradition has consistently said that forgiveness precedes repentance. Forgiveness can happen on its own, without repentance. Christians believe God has already accepted and forgiven them.

There are questions in the face of that Christian tenet: So all Christians just get a blank check? They can do whatever they want in their life because they've already been forgiven ahead of time? They're not accountable for their behavior because Christ's death on the cross has relieved them of that responsibility? Each Christian has already received God's grace so they can live their lives with a lack of morality? And historically the answer from theologians is that Christians are motivated to do good because they are loved by God, not because they are threatened.

But the Christian concept of forgiveness must be strained by the idea of genocide. Could Christians really believe that their God was crucified to forgive those who conceived of the gas showers at Auschwitz or the "parachutist" jump into the quarry at Mauthausen?

In the Christian tradition, since forgiveness isn't earned, the question about whether someone is worthy of forgiveness simply doesn't apply. Just by being human one is worthy of forgiveness. Those who are wronged forgive the wrongdoer, not the evil deed the wrongdoer committed. Forgiveness is a way of separating the doer from the deed. The person doing the forgiving—the victim who has been harmed by the wrongdoing—acknowledges the wrongdoer's evil deed, but doesn't count it against him. It's the person who is forgiven, not the deed. The deed can't be changed. The past can't be undone. Wrongdoers can be disassociated from the wrong. That's what forgiveness does.

But what right does anyone other than those who died in the

Holocaust have to forgive anyone for having created or participated in the Holocaust? Because the majority of the Holocaust's victims were Jewish, it would seem right to honor the Jewish sensibilities about forgiveness. Christians like Gerecke and O'Connor would argue that they had to act toward the Nazis in their flocks, and their families, in ways that honored their deepest understanding of humanity, and its relationship to God. The chaplains believed that their duties toward the Nazis and their families revolved around how to return them to the good.

Martin Luther would have supported the idea of offering spiritual consolation to those who have committed wrongs against others. He believed every human being is both sinner and justified as righteous through God's grace. He would have seen no principal difference between a criminal and an innocent. He would not have divided people into children of light and children of darkness. No one is innocent—neither a Gerecke nor a Kaltenbrunner—but everyone, Christians believe, is saved.

Even though Nazi war criminals had committed a different kind of wrong than ordinary people do, Gerecke would not have seen the monsters he pastored at Nuremberg as children of darkness. And he certainly would not have seen their wives and children that way. Without forgiving the deeds of those responsible for wiping out six million Jews, by the nature of their faith in God, Gerecke and O'Connor saw these men and their families as part of a single human community. Once they recognized the men in Nuremberg as just men, ministering to them, despite the horrors they'd executed, became a matter of attempting a transformation. The Nuremberg chaplains' one single burden was to return these children of God from darkness to the good of their own light.

THE DAY AFTER THE executions, Andrus announced to the press on behalf of the Allied Control Council that the bodies had been cremated and that the ashes had been "dispersed secretly." The decision for cremation countered German law, which stated that relatives had a right to the remains. The commandant said he couldn't elaborate on what "dispersed secretly" meant, but reporters surmised that the intention of the secret dispersal was, as the *New York Times* put it, "to destroy absolutely any possibility that the location of the Nazi leaders' remains ever could become a shrine for some future brand of Nazis."

Though Gerecke and O'Connor had wrestled with the idea of forgiveness of the men they had ministered to, the world's media showed less mercy. For years, the stories circulating about the fate of the Nazis' remains evoked a logic of revenge and poetic justice. For instance, in his book *Justice at Nuremberg*, published nearly forty years after the trials, Robert Conot wrote that the trucks carrying the bodies of the Nazis drove from Nuremberg to Dachau, where, at dawn, "the crematorium was fired up once again," and the bodies were burned in the concentration camp's ovens.

Though the truth was slightly less symbolic, it was no less powerful. After the trucks left Nuremberg on the morning after the executions, they drove to Ostfriedhof Cemetery on the outskirts of Munich, arriving at 9:00 A.M. The Germans who worked at the crematorium there were told that the army was delivering eleven American soldiers who had been killed and buried during the war and that their ashes were now being returned to their families. Each coffin was labeled with a fake name. Goering's was marked "George Munger," which was the name of the head coach of the University of Pennsylvania's football team at the time.

Guards surrounded the crematorium and the eleven pine boxes were taken into the basement where the fires were already blazing. The cremations—which included the nooses and black hoods—lasted until 11:00 P.M. The ashes were placed in eleven aluminum cylinders sixteen inches tall and six inches around. The next day they were taken to a white stucco villa nearby that had been transformed from the home of a wealthy merchant into U.S. Army Mortuary No. 1. The grand home was perched high on a hill above a large stream called the Contwentzbach.

A group of U.S. Army officers carried the urns to the grassy bank of the stream, where they smashed the aluminum cylinders with axes and stomped them with their boot heels. The waters of the Contwentzbach carried the Nazis' ashes to the Isar River, which took them to the Danube, and then to the sea.

CHAPTER 11

It Was You Who Invited
Me Here

Christ died for the ungodly.

—ROMANS 5:6

Two weeks after the executions, Gerecke received orders to return to the United States, and Chaplain Eggers took over Protestant Ministry duties at Nuremberg. In Andrus's push to have Gerecke promoted to major, he wrote to the army's chief of chaplains to commend Gerecke on his "sincere devotion to his faith and his constant effort on behalf of the prisoners in this jail" and to say that his efforts had "been a constant source of admiration." He believed that Gerecke should "receive recognition for this work."

Andrus also recommended that "after a reasonable time at home" Gerecke should return to Nuremberg "to continue his ministrations which he has already so nobly advanced."

On the way home, Gerecke stopped in Frankfurt to see his son Hank in the hospital. He had already been there several times. Over the summer, when stationed in Bremerhaven, Hank had been severely injured in an accident. Hank, an MP officer, had discovered that a deserter was spotted an hour south of his position and had jumped in a jeep to track down the man. Just as he was heading off, a drunk soldier in a stolen two-and-a-half-ton truck smashed into him. Hank flew out of the jeep, lost consciousness, and woke up a few minutes later on cobblestones.

At the hospital, he began running a temperature, and doctors eventually discovered that the crash had ruptured his colon in three places, giving him an infection, gangrene, and peritonitis. Doctors had determined that Hank's injuries were too severe to fly him back to the United States, and he'd been admitted to an army hospital in Frankfurt instead. At certain points during the trial, Gerecke had been worried his son might not survive.

As Gerecke disembarked in Frankfurt, a group of German teenagers ripped the suitcases from his hands and took off into the rail yard. Army MPs eventually found the cases close by. They were mostly empty, except for a pair of Goering's gloves. The reichsmarshal told Gerecke he'd worn them only once. "I won't need them again," he told the chaplain. But gifts from some of the other Nazis, including a leather cigar case Constantin von Neurath gave Gerecke after the chaplain had brought cigars into his cell to celebrate the seventy-three-year-old's birthday, were gone. Souvenirs Gerecke had collected for Alma during the war were also gone, as were the papers in another suitcase carrying extensive notes of his time in Nuremberg.

At the end of November, the army ordered Gerecke to report to Washington for two weeks to debrief the Office of the Chief of Chaplains on the trial. Gerecke was then given a leave to head home to St. Louis for Christmas before reporting to the Fifth Army's disciplinary barracks in Milwaukee. He hadn't seen Alma or Roy in three years.

While he was home in St. Louis, Gerecke spoke at various clubs, youth groups, churches, and high schools where he packed in audi-

ences by the hundreds. Even Concordia Seminary now invited Gerecke to speak, even though decades earlier it hadn't allowed him
to take classes on campus. Gerecke soon found himself telling his
story before a crowd of six hundred at the DeSoto Hotel downtown.
The reception was being held in Gerecke's honor, and the program
included a photo of Gerecke in uniform in front of his chaplain's jeep
as well as a copy of the letter that the Nuremberg defendants had
sent to Alma. Gerecke's speech was a tour through the Nuremberg
prison, and he introduced his listeners to each member of his Nazi
congregation along the way.

He also told the crowd that the children of Germany, who survived the Nazi regime, needed prayer and material help. "If we will
offer up some aid to the little folk of Europe, we shall do things for
the Kingdom of God," Gerecke said.

Before the event, Rev. E. L. Roschke wrote a letter to Gerecke
summing up what most Lutheran pastors felt about Gerecke's work.
"How very happy and proud I am that you were placed in such a
very important position of service over in Europe and that you were
privileged to render such a fine service not only to your friends and
fellow citizens but also to those who were our enemies," Roschke
wrote. "The Lutherans of St. Louis and your friends of the Western
District, both among the clergy and the laity, are extremely proud
of you."

Over the next decade, Gerecke gave his DeSoto speech hundreds
of times. He always ended it with the most dramatic and disturbing
part of his Nuremberg experience—walking the men he'd come to
know well to their deaths. Gerecke used his considerable preaching
skills to slow his tempo and lower his voice at places where he wanted
his audience to pay particularly close attention. He would pause for
dramatic effect so that the old women in the audience would nearly
fall off their chairs in anticipation, while ribbing veterans of the war
with knowing cracks about overbearing sergeants or army food.

There was always an element of a lesson in the speech, a self-effacing acknowledgment of his clumsy efforts at converting demons back into worshippers of Christ.

"For all my own blunderings and failures with them," Gerecke would say, "I ask forgiveness."

And he always ended the same way, with the prayer that wrapped up his radio show, *Moments of Comfort:* "Lord, lay some soul upon my heart and love that soul through me. And may I nobly do my part, to win that soul for thee."

But now he added a new line borrowed and often attributed to Corrie ten Boom, the Christian woman who hid Dutch Jews in her house in Haarlem during the Holocaust: "And when I come to the beautiful city, and the saved all around me appear, I want to hear somebody tell me: It was you who invited me here."

On February 1, 1947, Gerecke reported to the disciplinary barracks in Milwaukee where he began ministering to the U.S. Army's troubled souls. His work with most of the inmates at the barracks consisted of setting up personal visits, accompanying them to Alcoholics Anonymous meetings, lecturing to men who were being released back into active duty, and making hospital visits. Those in isolation, segregation, or solitary confinement all received as much attention from Gerecke as anyone else.

As he'd grown accustomed to doing during the war, Gerecke sought out the Jewish men in the detachment and urged them to attend synagogue in Milwaukee. He later partnered with the Jewish Welfare Committee "to look after the Spiritual welfare" of the Jewish inmates.

He led Christian services for the inmates on Sunday mornings and Wednesday and Friday evenings. By the middle of 1948, fifty-five inmates were doing what Gerecke called "homework"—a correspondence course through Lutheran Hour Ministries. His flock was made up of "mostly young men whom the world wanted to forget," he wrote later.

Before Hank had found himself in the Frankfurt hospital, he had married a nurse he met in France named Millie. In early 1947,

Millie gave birth to David. The Gereckes were proud grandparents and Gerecke soon took to being "Grandpopsie," as he called himself. After David's birth, Gerecke wrote to his daughter-in-law, "Congratulations darling little Mother. A kiss to you and to your first-born, David Henry. You are Mother, Hank is Daddy, I'm Grandpop and Browneyes is a pretty Grandmother. Corky is Unk and so is Roy. . . . From now on I shall speak of my grandson."

When Gerecke wasn't busying himself with the army's rehabilitated soldiers and with his grandson, he was officiating at weddings, baptisms, and funerals at the base. He also started a Wednesday evening "Youth for Christ" Bible study for the young adults on the post. He made sure there was a good organ on hand for hymns, and a decent organist to play it, and he began a bus service to pick up personnel on Sunday mornings from parts of the base that he believed were too far for them to walk to chapel.

Gerecke's speaking engagements outside the disciplinary barracks continued during his free time. His talks in Milwaukee and surrounding Wisconsin towns—to men's clubs, Lutheran churches, rotary clubs, and Jewish centers—now expanded to nearby cities, such as Chicago, Joliet, Valparaiso, Minneapolis, and Omaha. "I still feel that I have never in all my life heard any address that impressed me so much as your story," one teacher wrote to Gerecke after hearing him speak in Fort Wayne.

By March 1947, just a month after he was back to work, Gerecke had pieced together a report that the Office of the Chief of Chaplains had requested about his time at the trials. The report contained almost the same stories he'd been telling at public events and he'd hoped to publish it in two installments over the summer in a Lutheran church magazine called the *Walther League Messenger.*

At the end of March, Gerecke received a letter from Washington telling him the War Department's public relations division had rejected his report for publicity purposes.

"It is felt that the nature of the contents of the report is too personal to divulge and that it might possibly be construed as a betrayal of confidence by some readers," Major Matthew Imrie of the Chief of Chaplains office wrote. Imrie also wrote to the editor of the *Walther League Messenger,* explaining that the report "revealed intimate confidences which were deserving of the secrecy of the confessional. The War Department discourages anything that would possibly suggest to men that chaplains did not zealously guard intimate knowledge and confidences."

Gerecke reworked the report and resubmitted it to the War Department claiming that he had worked out the kinks. Yet, privately, Gerecke fumed at the hypocrisy of the War Department, which had asked him to exploit POW confessions for strategic information in England during the war. Their accusations that he had betrayed the confessional in Nuremberg implied he had committed the worst ethical breach a pastor could make. He knew what it was to keep confessional confidence, and in his report he had never crossed that line. In April, the War Department approved for publication the second version, titled "My Assignment with the International Military Tribunal as Spiritual Advisor to the High Nazi Leaders at Nuernberg, Germany, November 1945 to November 1946."

O'CONNOR ALMOST NEVER SPOKE of his experience at Nuremberg, even though he was pursued by magazine editors and book publishers who were eager for him to tell his story. Instead, he went about teaching at his alma mater, St. Bonaventure College, and Siena College, where he eventually chaired the philosophy department.

O'Connor served as vice president of Siena from 1956 until 1964, though he spent a great deal of his time caring for the flower gardens on campus. While he didn't talk about his wartime experiences, his students often called him a "chatterbox" on many other subjects. He also liked a cocktail at night and even gambled a bit at Saratoga Race Course thirty miles north.

O'Connor loved teaching, but he considered himself primarily a priest and missionary—especially in his work with the Nazis. A Franciscan missionary is both preacher and confessor, according to the Reverend Bede Hess, a former minister general of one of the three branches of the Franciscan order. As a preacher, the Franciscan missionary "moves his hearers to repentance," wrote Hess, but in the confessional "by the God-given power of absolution he forgives their sins, and grants peace and pardon in the name of Jesus Christ."

Hess invoked the Gospel of Luke, instructing confessors to "be merciful, as your Father also is merciful" to the young, perplexed, weak, the less disposed and indisposed, the shamelessly sinful and the obstinate. According to Hess, the confessor should "expend his zeal" toward the shamelessly sinful.

In 1983, O'Connor was at the Franciscans' headquarters in Manhattan when a newly ordained Franciscan priest came to him with an ethical dilemma. The new priest had just heard the confessions of two murderers at the Church of St. Francis of Assisi, known as "New York's confessional" because everyone from cops to Wall Street bankers to mobsters traveled to it for penance. After the priest heard the confessions, he went to O'Connor and asked if he'd been right to absolve the murderers of their sins. "Yes, you give them spiritual counsel, a worthy penance and unconditional absolution," O'Connor said. Then O'Connor gripped the younger priest's arm. "You absolve them of their sins, but you don't absolve them of their actions," he said.

That same year, O'Connor gave up attending to all the flowers on Siena's campus. At seventy-four, the strain of being on his feet had become too much, though he planned a full teaching schedule for the fall. On a Sunday morning in July 1983, the deacon at the local parish church arrived at the Siena friary to pick up O'Connor so the priest could celebrate the 10:00 A.M. Mass. He found O'Connor dead in his bed. He'd had a heart attack in his sleep in the middle of the night.

Thirty priests and fifty friars helped celebrate his funeral Mass three days later, then buried him in St. Agnes Cemetery in Menands, New York. At the funeral, Siena's president, Father Hugh Hines, said that O'Connor was a man who "gave totally of himself." And though O'Connor had been a popular professor, "He not only taught philosophy, he was a true philosopher."

IN 1949, THE GERECKES left Milwaukee. After Gerecke served a nine-month stint at Fifth Army Headquarters in Chicago, the army relieved him of active-duty service and he was "installed" as an assistant pastor of St. John Lutheran Church. The church, on a bluff above the Mississippi River in the small town of Chester, Illinois, was small with a white steeple and made of brick. Gerecke's installation took place on a Sunday evening. Eight hundred people jammed into the tiny church and others spilled out of its doors. The Reverend H. C. Whelp, president of the denomination's Southern Illinois district, performed the installation service and the congregation sang an eighteenth-century hymn, "Come, Thou Almighty King."

They then heard a passage from Isaiah 35: "Say to them that are of a fearful heart, be strong, fear not: behold, your God will come with vengeance, even God with a recompense; he will come and save you."

The congregation at St. John's accepted the Gereckes immediately, even becoming a bit possessive of the couple and their time. "We soon realized we would have to 'share' them with everyone in the community—black and white, rich and poor, members of the church and non-members," wrote Eileen Gordon, St. John's secretary.

Gerecke's gentleness with others continued through his years in Chester. "If the sun wasn't shining in your life that particular day, it surely was after his cheerful smile," Gordon wrote. "When someone writes of Pastor Gerecke, they must write of love, because this, indeed, was the essence of the man," she continued. "He was the personification of caring—caring for all the children of God."

Gerecke may have loved everyone in Chester, but he was frustrated by the reluctance of some parishioners to make financial contributions to the church. He groused about the man who would give only if he happened to have something left over from his paycheck at the end of the week. "And then, he expects God to know that He was mighty lucky to get that," Gerecke would say. At the same time, he didn't want people's money if it was coming to the church for the wrong reasons. After an extensive stewardship campaign one year to raise church money, Gerecke told his congregation, "Don't give unless it's from the heart. Because if it isn't, it won't help the church, or you." The sermon "probably motivated more people than all the letters and pamphlets and pleas our committee had sent out," Gordon wrote.

Later in the new year, Gerecke told his Nuremberg story to Merle Sinclair, the wife of veteran *Milwaukee Journal* crime reporter Frank Sinclair, best known for his coverage of the famous 1934 shootout between federal agents and John Dillinger's gang at the Little Bohemia Lodge in the northern Wisconsin woods. The result was a first-person narrative of Gerecke's year in Nuremberg that Sinclair wrote for the *Saturday Evening Post* that September.

Reaction to the story was mixed. More requests for Gerecke to speak to audiences rolled in, but so did hate mail calling Gerecke a "Nazi lover." These letters were painful, but not as much as the letters from Jewish Americans who called him an anti-Semite who had conspired with, and offered redemption to, men who had set out to destroy the Jewish people. Instead of throwing the letters away, Gerecke hid every piece of hate mail in the compartment behind the drawers of his desk as a reminder that his attempt to save Nazi souls could be interpreted in so many different ways.

On February 4, 1951, the church put on a concert to honor Gerecke's twenty-five years as a pastor. The seven musical numbers—

with new words to well-known songs—were a sort of "This Is Your Life" for Henry and Alma. One, set to the tune of "Sweet Genevieve," was a tribute to the Gereckes' three decades of marriage.

> *Sweet Alma Bender*
> *My Alma Bender*
> *You are so sweet, you are so tender*
> *My love songs I to you will render*
> *Will you be mine,*
> *Sweet Alma Bender.*

Gerecke preached at St. John's every other Sunday, but when he was not in church he spent the rest of his time doing other jobs. Some days he would minister to the bedridden at Chester Hospital, while on others he acted as a chaplain to two Chester veterans' groups—the VFW and the American Legion. The men in the groups regarded him as a sort of celebrity member. Gerecke also began doing radio work for a show he created called *Courage for Today* on KSGM 1450 AM. The Saturday program featured Gerecke remembering "the people in nursing homes and shut-ins," Gordon wrote, "people who had been removed from the main stream of community life and who were probably forgotten by most of us."

Often Gerecke would dedicate a birthday song on the program to an older person living in a home. Shortly afterward he might visit the same person's bedside as he lay dying. Often the elderly Lutherans were German farmers, and Gerecke would lean close and offer the Lord's Prayer in German to remind them of their youth and homeland.

Most of Gerecke's time was spent as chaplain at the Menard penitentiary, a maximum-security facility filled with twenty-five hundred murderers and rapists who he believed needed to hear the Gospel in the most desperate way. The inmates manufactured much of the underwear, clothing, caps, gloves, furniture, brooms, brushes, and other necessities utilized in the prison. Those who could be trusted to leave the prison walls worked a three-thousand-acre farm, planting and harvesting fruit, vegetables, grain, and tobacco. They helped care for herds of cattle.

Gerecke's work paid him little and wasn't easy. When he first arrived, prisoners were suspicious that he was an undercover snitch sent by prosecutors to gather information. At first, Gerecke only attracted sixty prisoners to his services. But Gerecke's fascination with technology helped him. In 1953, the chaplain tapped into television broadcasting and began showing inmates 16 mm film episodes of a half-hour drama called *This Is the Life*, created for network television by the Lutheran Church. The warden gave Gerecke permission to show the episodes in the prison's auditorium on a large screen.

The show was often casually referred to as *The Fisher Family* after the fictional midwestern family it portrayed. Each episode dealt with a problem such as racism, infidelity, or alcoholism, which was eventually tackled using a Christian solution.

Attendance at services soon quadrupled, and Gerecke had more requests for personal counseling sessions than he had time for. The chaplain told a church magazine, *The Lutheran Witness*, that as a result of the TV show, men who had considered Christianity irrelevant to their own lives suddenly made a connection with God. "Pastor, I never knew what it was all about but that picture made it plain as day," one prisoner told Gerecke, according to the magazine. "If only I had seen that picture a couple of years ago, I wouldn't be here now." Another prisoner who had been coming to the *This Is the Life* screenings for a few months tearfully told Gerecke, "If I had never seen these pictures, I would never know that Jesus is my savior. God bless you, Chaplain."

Gerecke not only worked in the correctional facility, but also the State Security Hospital, which was often referred to as "North 2." There was no chapel in North 2 so Gerecke held his services in the

IT WAS YOU WHO INVITED ME HERE

dining hall, where about 150 men from the hospital's 600 patients sat on benches at long tables bolted to the concrete floor.

Here, like every other place Gerecke had preached, music was a dominant feature, and a member of St. John's accompanied Gerecke to the asylum to play the piano. Gerecke always encouraged the men to sing the hymns loudly as he walked among their tables, smiling and singing just as loudly. As he walked, they reached out to him, and he grasped their hands or gave their shoulders a squeeze of encouragement.

"The inmates looked to Rev. Gerecke for compassion, for friendship, and for assurance of God's forgiveness," Gordon wrote.

The warden of the prison, Ross Randolph, was a Christian man, a former FBI agent, and a prison reformer. His motto at Menard was "prisoners are people," and he hoped, he wrote, to build an atmosphere among the inmates "to reclaim the maladjusted lives of men who have failed to conform to the demands of modern society."

Gerecke had written in a Lutheran magazine of an inmate at the Menard psychiatric hospital he called only "Otto—No. 25,281," whom he considered "troubled" by Satan. Otto had been baptized as a Lutheran, but "his mental capacity was not strong enough to carry through those spiritual imperatives his Christian faith dictated."

Gerecke was nevertheless able to slowly bring Otto back to the church. When Otto took Communion for the final time, Gerecke wrote that he "saw teardrops of repentance fall into the little cups on the tray. He cried for heavenly love and got it, assurance of forgiveness and all the blessings with it."

Otto died the following day. His family had provided no money for a funeral service, and a relative told prison officials the family didn't want the body. They asked the prison to bury Otto for them. Gerecke had what he called a "gentlemen's agreement" with his flock that if they died in prison, Gerecke would try and have them buried in St. John's Lutheran cemetery. St. John's senior pastor, Rev. Eric Cash, and the church's cemetery committee gave Gerecke the approval to bury Otto there. Ross Randolph provided the casket and clothing. The town funeral director prepared the body, as well as arranging for transportation from the prison hospital to the cemetery and the grave preparation.

Gerecke did not specify what crime Otto had committed, but by the time Otto died, he was completely alone in the world. Others may have concluded that, as a criminal, Otto got what he deserved, but Gerecke could barely make it through the service without breaking down. No one aside from Gerecke and the gravedigger was at the cemetery, and yet the chaplain had difficulty conducting the burial ritual.

"Otto got the same reading all 'asleep in Jesus' get," Gerecke wrote. "The wrens, the sparrows, blackbirds, and crows furnished the music" as Otto was lowered into his grave, not far from where Gerecke himself would soon be laid to rest. "The prodigal son, the lost sheep, returned this time to his heavenly home in the spirit of the publican who said: 'God be merciful to me, a sinner,'" Gerecke wrote—an echo of Fritz Sauckel's last words just before Gerecke watched him disappear through the trapdoor in the Nuremberg gymnasium.

"Just a number, perhaps to some," Gerecke wrote of Otto, "but a precious blood-bought penitent believing soul who, unworthy of himself and unwelcome among his own people, heard the angels of heaven rejoice when he came 'home.'"

In 1956, Menard welcomed Orville Enoch Hodge as an inmate. Hodge didn't fit the profile of the penitentiary's violent inmates. The burly, backslapping former politician had pleaded guilty to embezzling $1.5 million in state funds over four years as state auditor, the equivalent of $13 million today. Hodge had been a golden boy of the Illinois GOP and had been viewed as a future candidate for governor. The *Chicago Tribune* had even called him "the model of a successful small-town businessman and politician."

As an auditor, Hodge's main responsibility had been preventing the forging of state warrants authorizing the expenditure of public funds. However, the *Chicago Daily News* exposed the fact that Hodge had taken the money from his warrants and bought two private planes, four cars, a mansion on Lake Springfield in the state capital, and an apartment in Fort Lauderdale. The *Daily News* won a 1957 Pulitzer Prize for teasing apart Hodge's crimes.

When Hodge arrived at Menard, Randolph had Gerecke take charge of the politician. Randolph had also connected Gerecke with prisoner David Saunders, who edited the monthly *Menard Time*. With these influential inmates, Gerecke was able to spread the Christian Gospel more effectively through the prison.

Hodge and Gerecke piped Christian programming directly into the inmates' cells whether they wanted it or not. Hodge helped Gerecke run the A/V equipment to screen Lutheran TV shows in the auditorium, while Gerecke helped Hodge get his life back together. Each Tuesday at 8:00 A.M., Hodge and Gerecke met to discuss the "kites," which were requests for a counseling session with the chaplain that Hodge had collected from his fellow inmates. The two men would then go over each prisoner's permanent record and Hodge's notes to gauge the length of time Gerecke would spend with each prisoner.

In 1961, Hodge wrote that he'd experienced "many, many lonesome days and nights during the past five years of my imprisonment":

> *Most of us have faults that are secret from others. Yet, by contrast, others' faults are known and are associated with them throughout life. A person in prison is more or less blessed in that his imperfections are known and his debt to society satisfied. Pastor Gerecke contends, and I agree, that a person who has completed his penal sentence and returned to the free world should be accepted by society. . . . I pray that my heart will not falter or my faith weaken. Being Chaplain Gerecke's "helper" has brought me an association I will always cherish.*

Hodge believed Gerecke so inhabited the Christian way of life that when he saw Gerecke, he often thought of a sixteenth-century English prayer that Gerecke had taught him: "God be in my head, and in my understanding / God be in mine eyes, and in my looking." The prayer was typed into a small, three-ring journal of sermons and notes that Gerecke kept. At any given moment, he could page through the journal for a scripture reference, a verse from a favorite poem, or a full sermon outline.

A couple pages down from Hodge's favorite prayer, Gerecke had typed a summary of Leo Tolstoy's short story "What Men Live By." He'd typed the last lines of the story verbatim. Tolstoy tells of a poor cobbler named Simon and his wife who take in a frightened, naked stranger who'd been left for dead in the Russian winter streets. The couple gives him clothing and food and eventually a job assisting the cobbler.

The stranger, the reader learns, is actually an angel who was banished from heaven by God. At the end of the story, God forgives the angel, allowing him to return to heaven. But first, "clad with light so bright that the eyes could not endure to look upon him," he tells the cobbler about the lesson God has taught him. Gerecke typed in his journal:

> *I have learned that all men live not by care for themselves but by love. I remained alive when I was a man, not by care of myself but because love was present in a passer-by and because he and his wife pitied and loved me. . . . I knew before that God gives life to men and that he wants them to live; now I understand more than that. I understand that God does not wish men to live apart, and, therefore, he does not reveal to them what each one needs for himself. He wishes them to live united; thus he reveals to each of them what is necessary for all. I have now understood that though it seems to men that they live by care for themselves, in truth, it is love alone by which they live. He who has love is God, and God is in him, for God is love.*

At the very back of the little journal are notes from a series of sermons Gerecke preached during Lent in the final year of his life, 1961. They referenced the work of his Concordia classmate, the writer and pastor O. P. Kretzmann. It would be his last Easter, and as only seems fitting, his theme that year was forgiveness. His first sermon, on Good Friday, was on Luke 23:34, which describes Jesus's crucifixion on Golgotha between the two criminals.

"This was not the first mistake Roman justice had made," Gerecke said to the congregation. "Other innocent men had been crucified and had protested their innocence through lips swollen with agony. But here was something new on a Roman cross." Christ's words were "no cry of protest or of pain. Only a prayer that those who were doing this thing to Him might be forgiven."

Gerecke continued:

> *When men crucify their God they can expect to hear something different. His first word is His last prayer. It sweeps up to Heaven burdened as no other prayer in the history of men. Burdened with sin—all the loneliness and hate and terror of the centuries before or after. . . . The sum of man's years and man's shame and the greater sum of God's forgiveness and God's love. This is our faith. A religion without forgiveness is only the ghost of religion which haunts the grave of dead faith and lost hope.*

ON OCTOBER 11, 1961, Gerecke was parking at Menard when he had a heart attack. He slumped over the wheel, and a guard, sensing something was wrong, approached the car. Gerecke thanked the guard for his concern but waved him off. He turned around and drove back home.

Alma had him lie down on the living room couch and called the hospital, which was across the street. The doctors told her to bring her husband in. The Gereckes walked to the hospital and nurses put him in a bed there. Alma walked back across the street to call their sons. When she returned a few minutes later, just after 10:00 A.M., the doctors met her at the hospital's front door. Henry had died of a heart attack. He was sixty-eight years old.

Most of Chester's senior citizens remember where they were on a warm Wednesday in October 1961 when they heard about Gerecke's death. His official death announcement gave Chester's citizens the time and locations of his wake and funeral and also carried words from the Twenty-Third Psalm: "Yea, though I walk through the valley of the shadow of death, I will fear no evil: for thou art with me: thy rod and thy staff they comfort me."

Maybe it was apocryphal, but as news spread of Gerecke's death, so did the rumor of his last words: "How quickly God can change your plans."

At 9:00 A.M. on October 14, Gerecke's body lay in state inside St. John's. The Boy Scouts set up chairs on the church lawn and loudspeakers nearby so that the expected overflow crowd could participate in the service. Throughout the morning, people filed by the pastor's casket, and by 2:00 P.M., when the service began, more than a thousand had arrived.

Rev. Eric Cash told many grieving people that day, "No matter how many more years he might have had, Pastor Gerecke's work would never have been finished." Cash preached a funeral sermon based on the same verses from the Gospel of Matthew that Andrus had quoted to the chief of chaplains when recommending Gerecke for a promotion, and that F. W. Herzberger had used as a motto for the St. Louis Lutheran City Mission, and that Martin of Tours embodied when he tore his cape and gave half to a freezing beggar. The Gospel teaches what Jesus will say to his followers at the end of time: "Inherit the kingdom prepared for you from the foundation of the world."

For I was hungry and you gave me food, I was thirsty and you gave
me something to drink, I was a stranger and you welcomed me, I was

naked and you gave me clothing, I was sick and you took care of me,
I was in prison and you visited me.

The righteous respond, confused, asking Jesus when it was that they gave him food and drink, when it was that they welcomed him as a stranger or gave him clothing, when it was that they visited him in prison. "Truly I tell you, just as you did it to one of the least of these," Jesus replies, "you did it to me."

In his sermon at Gerecke's funeral service at St. John's, Cash said that the "pens of the multitudes" whom Gerecke had reached in his ministry, "the combined voices of thousands, rich and poor, important and unimportant, could never do justice to adequately describe the life and dedication of this man. Without any question or doubt we return to the Savior today the soul of a great man."

When the service was over, Alma took the hands of two of her grandchildren and walked out of the church.

"He had become a friend in every sense of the word; to many, he had become the personification of the love of God," Eileen Gordon wrote later. "He cared—for each and every person he met. I think if there's one thing he would want us to remember about his ministry, it would be a phrase that I heard him use many times: 'God loves you . . . so much more than you know.'"

As well attended as Gerecke's funeral was, there were hundreds of Chester residents who couldn't be there because they were behind bars. The day after Gerecke died, Warden Ross Randolph called Alma. He relayed a request from his prisoners, including some of the most hardened, that Gerecke's body be brought to the prison so they could pay their final respects. "They held him in high esteem," Randolph told the Associated Press. "He talked their language."

Alma and her sons agreed, and after state officials approved the request, the funeral home took Gerecke's body back to the prison the night before the funeral. The warden thought it was the first time in Illinois history, and maybe in the nation's history, that such arrangements had been made for prisoners to pay tribute to an individual.

At 8:00 P.M., Orville Hodge announced over the prison loudspeaker that all inmates could come to the chapel to pay their last respects. Alma, Hank, Corky, and Roy watched as eight hundred of the most dangerous men in the country filed past Gerecke's casket.

"There were tears," the warden said later.

Speaking of the Nuremberg defendants, Gerecke had once written that "evil is always its own destruction." At Menard, as in Nuremberg, good had bested evil.

"Inmates at Menard State Prison marched through the prison chapel yesterday," the Associated Press reported, "for a last look at the man many considered their only friend."

Epilogue

Highway z winds to the edge of St. Genevieve County, Missouri, past stands selling tomatoes and sweet corn, huge cylindrical steel grain bins, and front yard signs offering CUSTOM ROCK CRUSHING. Where Highway Z meets Highway H, it drops into Perry County and then enters Chester, Illinois. Population: 8,400.

The Chester Bridge winds from the bottomlands, over the Mississippi and up above the brown waters lazing by below, into Chester's bluffs. The bridge, which spans the river's narrowest point between St. Louis and New Orleans, opened in 1942, eight months after the Japanese attack on Pearl Harbor.

In downtown Chester, St. John Evangelical Lutheran Church sits across from a statue of Popeye the Sailor Man's nemesis, Bluto, an homage to Elzie Segar, a native of Chester and the cartoon's creator.

In the weeks following Gerecke's death in 1961, the prisoners at Menard took up a collection. At first, they hoped to help furnish a family prayer room at a planned new hospital as a memorial for Gerecke. But instead, the offerings—which ranged from thirteen cents to five dollars—finally went toward a white neon cross to be placed atop St. John Lutheran School, directly across the street from the church.

The cross went up in 1963, and for nearly fifty years, it stood atop the brick school. But eventually the light in the cross disappeared. It had been battered by storms and time. Wires had frayed.

Yet now a new assistant pastor was coming into the congregation. The church and wider community had raised $6,000 to replace the original Gerecke cross, and they thought it would be best to dedicate the new cross on the evening of the new pastor's installation. So, on a hot Sunday in 2010, the Lutherans of Chester gathered to witness the ordination and installation of St. John's newest assistant pastor.

Inside, the church's simple stained glass ushered in volumes of light. Twenty-eight wooden pews sat in lines below a relief of Jesus stepping out from a piece of green marble built into an array of brass organ pipes behind the altar. Banners bearing messages of faith hung down from the choir lofts above the church's altar. The top half of a red banner directly above the altar podium was decorated with a white cross that radiated yellow rays in every direction. Below the cross were words that also summed up Henry Gerecke's mission: "Tell the Good News."

Most of the elderly people in the congregation had German surnames. The women wore patterned summer dresses or matching shirt-pants sets. Some wore pearls. The men wore short-sleeved, button-down shirts—mostly plaid, some with stripes—and khakis. Everyone wore a watch.

As a number of pastors from across Illinois marched down the church's center aisle, the congregation sang them in.

The newly installed priest was twenty-six-year-old Michigan native Peter William Ill. Like Gerecke, he had spent time in a foreign land—in his case, India—on a mission to spread the Gospel. He married a girl he met when both were counselors at a Lutheran summer camp in Indiana, and now, also like Gerecke, he was an alumnus of Concordia Seminary in St. Louis.

As part of the church's old and formal ceremony, a small battalion of God's pastor-soldiers—old, young, bald, whisper voiced and booming voiced, tall, short, bespectacled and not—laid hands on Ill's head as verses from the New Testament floated from their mouths, speaking of "the Office of Holy Ministry."

One read from 1 Timothy: "Do not neglect the gift you have, which was given you by prophecy when the council of elders laid their hands on you."

St. John's senior pastor, Rev. Mark Willig, stood on the altar, dressed in a white alb and red stole embroidered with a gold Greek cross. He looked out into the pews and led its members in an invocation and exhortation.

"In the name of the Father and of the Son and of the Holy Spirit," Willig said.

"Amen," the congregation responded.

"If we say we have no sin, we deceive ourselves, and the truth is not in us," Willig said.

"But if we confess our sins," the congregation replied, "God, who is faithful and just, will forgive our sins and cleanse us from all unrighteousness."

In the next two hours, these midwesterners would, as a community, recognize a young man's call to teach and preach the Gospel. And together they would witness him become a man of God.

Just as Gerecke was, Ill was asked if he believed the canonical books of the Old and New Testaments were the inspired Word of God, if he would forgive the sins of those who repent, and if he promised never to divulge the sins confessed to him.

Yes, he would, with the help of God, Ill responded.

After Ill was welcomed to St. John's, the congregation moved across the street to the corner of High and German Streets to sit close together at long tables, on metal folding chairs. Here at St. John's Veterans Memorial Hall, which is also the gym for St. John Lutheran School, the congregation stood in line, chatting and waiting their turn among the potluck noodle casseroles and fried chicken.

Ill walked into the gym in his casual clothes, and the congregation gave him a round of applause. He shyly asked them to stop making a fuss. Then they all ate together in celebration of friendship and their faith.

At 8:30 P.M., as dusk fell, about one hundred people walked from the gym, up the hill to the front lawn of the school. Willig climbed three sets of stairs to the school's roof and stood next to the new cross. He addressed his congregation three stories below.

"Why have we called this the Gerecke Memorial Cross?" Willig asked. "It is not so much to honor Pastor Gerecke as to honor and celebrate the Gospel that he so much loved. It was Pastor Gerecke's great vision and passion to reach out to everyone with the message of God's love for us in Jesus Christ," Willig continued. "He followed that vision during World War II as a chaplain. Then he was called upon to serve as chaplain to the worst and the lost at the Nuremberg Trials. Upon coming to Chester he served as prison chaplain at Menard."

And then Willig prayed—"Stay with us, Lord, for it is evening."

And the congregation replied, "And the day is almost over."

"Let your light scatter the darkness," Willig said. He shouted down to his flock the words of Isaiah: "Arise, shine, for your light has come, and the glory of the Lord has risen upon you."

Then Rev. Ill, feet planted firmly on the school's lawn below, read from the Gospel of John. "In Him was life and the life was the light of men," Ill said. "The light shines in the darkness, and the darkness has not overcome it."

As the people sang "Lift High the Cross," St. John's bells began to clang. Willig threw the switch, sending the light from the Gerecke Memorial Cross into the night sky and across the valley below.

Acknowledgments

As a reader of books, I'm sure I appreciated in theory that a work of nonfiction took more than the diligence of its author. As a writer of a book, I've now realized in a profound and concrete way the magnitude of that understatement. Without even just one of the people named below, this would be a different book.

None of those names would be more prominent than Henry H. Gerecke, Henry and Alma's eldest son. On a cold day in December 2007, I walked into Millie and Hank Gerecke's house in Cape Girardeau, Missouri, to learn about Hank's father. It was the first of many times we sat around the Gereckes' kitchen table or at one of their favorite local restaurants (always, at Hank's insistence, his treat). Hank—a former army colonel and city police chief—is a natural storyteller, and I owe much of the color that comes through about his parents to those anecdotes. For the time Hank took with me and the stories and photos and documents he shared, but mostly for his friendship, I thank him. I also want to thank Millie and Hank's children, David, Stephen, and Jan, and their own families, for allowing me to tell their grandfather's story.

I have to thank so many more people for their help, too: Laura Marrs, Patrice Russo, Marvin Huggins, Andrea Schultz, Todd Zittlow at the Concordia Historical Institute in St. Louis. Steven Pledger and Andrew Blattner at the Cape Girardeau County Archive Center in Jackson, Missouri. The late Whitney Harris of St.

Louis. Ryan Reed of the Landmarks Association of St. Louis. Tom Geist of Eastmeadow, New York. Paul Brown, Richard Peuser, Robin Cookson, and Don Singer of National Archives in College Park, Maryland. Phil Budden of Munich, Germany. Brother Michael J. Harlan, OFM, Secretary of the Holy Name Province, and Father Brian Jordan, OFM, of St. Francis College, New York. The staff of the Missouri Historical Society Library and Research Center in St. Louis. The staff of the National Archives National Personnel Records Center in St. Louis. Peter Black, senior historian at the Center for Advanced Holocaust Studies at the U.S. Holocaust Memorial and Museum Library. The staff of the U.S. Army Heritage and Education Center in Carlisle, Pennsylvania. Marcia McManus and John Brinsfield of the U.S. Army Chaplain Museum, Fort Jackson, South Carolina. Chaplain Carleton Birch, Colonel Christopher Wisdom, Chaplain Charles Lynde of the U.S. Army Chief of Chaplains office in Washington, and Julia Simpkins of the U.S. Army Chaplain Center and School in Fort Jackson. Ambassador Stephen Rapp (and his wife, Dolly Maier), Anne Luehrs, Anna Cave, and Carolina Hidea of the U.S. State Department. Stuart W. Symington, former U.S. ambassador to Rwanda, and his wife, Susan. Philip Gourevitch. Stephan Lebert of *Die Zeit* and Birgit Asmus of *Stern*. Judge Hans-Peter Kaul and Sonia Robla of the International Criminal Court, The Hague, the Netherlands. Henrike Zentgraf and Eckart Dietzfelbinger of the Nazi Party Rally Grounds Documentation Centre, Nuremberg, Germany. Georg Schneider of the Palace of Justice prison. Irene Kornmeier of St. Louis. Jerry Legow of St. Louis. Mary Stallman, Collette and Paul Powley, Don Gentsch, and June Cash of Chester, Illinois. Irwin F. Gellman. Daun van Ee of the Library of Congress. Dennis Frank of St. Bonaventure University, New York. Father Julian Davies of Siena College in Loudonville, New York. John O'Connor of Oxford, New York. Father Moritz Fuchs of Fulton, New York. Father John Nakonachny of St. Vladimir Ukrainian Orthodox Cathedral in Parma, Ohio. Sally Ray and Larry Junker, St. John's College Alumni Association. Sabrina Sondhi, Columbia University Law School Library, Special Collections in New York City. Nick Young of the Thatcham Historical Society, Thatcham, England. The faculty of Concordia Seminary in St. Louis. Katharina Czachor of Mauthausen Memorial Archives and Library. Charles R. Hill, Eminent Commander, San Diego Commandery No. 25, Masonic Order of the Knights Templar. John Tusa. Gerhard Schorr, pastor, St. Sebald Church, Nuremberg. And Julia Gabbert for her transcription skills.

Thanks to Mark Silk of the Leonard E. Greenberg Center for the Study of Religion in Public Life at Trinity College and the faculty of the Religion Department at Trinity College in Hartford for reading and critiquing an early chapter of the book. And to Efraim Zuroff of the Simon Wiesenthal Center's Jerusalem office for a thoughtful conversation at a hectic time. To Miroslav Volf and his sons, Nathaniel and Aaron Volf, and to Peter Kuzmic. Thank you, Miroslav, for letting me tag along on Memory Lane, and for the insights of a truly great teacher. Speaking of good teachers, thanks to Sam Freedman at Columbia University for the early encouragement that the right good idea really can, and should, become a book, and to my mentor and champion at Columbia, Michael Janeway. To Steve Hayes and Brent Cunningham, for their friendship and guidance as we all became authors.

Special thanks to Professor Michael C. Rea and Professor Samuel Newlands of the University of Notre Dame's Center for the Philosophy of Religion. The center's generous grant toward my reporting, through its "The Problem of Evil in Modern and Contemporary Thought" initiative, supported by the John Templeton Foundation, helped fill a number of holes in my research.

For the time each took out of their lives to read various sections of the manuscript for accuracy, thank you to Rabbi Hyim Shafner, Rabbi Mark Shook, Rabbi Jeffrey Stiffman, the Reverend Travis Scholl, and John Q. Barrett.

Thanks to my former colleagues at the *St. Louis Post-Dispatch*, who gave me advice, moral support, and—most important—their friendship as I wrote this book. I discovered Henry Gerecke's name while writing a story for the *Post-Dispatch*. And it was also in the *P-D* newsroom that I discovered, over nearly a decade of journalism's darkest days, that great reporters and editors do inspiring and important work regardless of obstacles. They can't help it.

Thank you to my editor at William Morrow, Henry Ferris, for his patience and direction, and to Cole Hager, Danny Goldstein, and Laurie McGee.

My agent, Eric Simonoff, was the calm pool I dove for each time I felt overwhelmed or unsure or like I might die. Thank you, Eric, for your friendship, and for not letting me die.

Thank you to the Michauds for their love, their wine, and their beautiful daughters, Alabama and Hattie, who offered the best title suggestions. Thank you to Ingrid and George Gustin, the generous codirectors of the Yellow Cave Foundation for Nonfiction Immersion. The YCFNI was the only writers' colony that would have me, and I wouldn't have wanted to write the first draft of this book anywhere else. To my parents, Patty and Ted Townsend, who allowed their children to be anything they wanted to be, and celebrated them even when those choices were weird along the way. Thank you. I love you.

Finally, Georgina—as Toots said—it is you.

Source Notes

The examination of the Third Reich at the Nuremberg trials is among the most written-about events of the twentieth century. In writing this book, I read dozens of others about the Trial of Major War Criminals and the horrific events that made it necessary. But I relied most heavily on some of the classics of the genre. Especially: Eugene Davidson's *The Trial of the Germans*, Ann and John Tusa's *The Nuremberg Trial*, Telford Taylor's *The Anatomy of the Nuremberg Trials*, and Joseph Persico's *Nuremberg: Infamy on Trial*. Richard Overy's work on the legal mechanics of the run-up to the trials was essential. Robert Wistrich's *Who's Who in Nazi Germany* helped me keep the bad guys straight, and Hilary Gaskin's oral history of the trial, *Eyewitness at Nuremberg*, was invaluable in helping me set the Nuremberg scene outside the Palace of Justice (as were Taylor, and Rebecca West's *A Train of Powder*). Finally, *The Third Reich at War* by Richard J. Evans kept everything I was writing about in context.

CHAPTER 1
1   **"There had been men . . .":** West, "Greenhouse with Cyclamens I (1946)," p. 21.
1   **His voice was high pitched:** Persico, *Nuremberg*, p. 49.
2   **Andrus felt the weight:** Andrus and Zwar, *I Was the Nuremberg Jailer*, p. 158.
2   **they were treated:** Gerecke and Sinclair, "I Walked the Gallows."
2   **"I will go anywhere . . .":** Persico, *Nuremberg*, p. 50.
3   **their last meal:** "Night Without Dawn."
3   **asked for a brush and duster:** Tusa and Tusa, *Nuremberg Trial*, p. 484.

3   **He'd told Keitel:** Davidson, *Trial of the Germans*, p. 353.

3   **the general nodded curtly:** Persico, *Nuremberg*, p. 403.

3   **"Defendant Wilhelm Keitel, . . .":** Conot, *Justice at Nuremberg*, p. 505, and Harris, *Tyranny on Trial*, p. 479.

4   **he'd chosen Boston:** Powers, "A Friar's Recollection."

4   **Gerecke was the first:** Gerecke and Sinclair, "I Walked the Gallows."

4   **then sobbed uncontrollably:** See Andrus and Zwar, *I Was the Nuremberg Jailer*, p. 158; Conot, *Justice at Nuremberg*, p. 505; and Gerecke and Sinclair, "I Walked the Gallows."

4   **gave the general a final benediction:** Andrus and Zwar, *I Was the Nuremberg Jailer*, p. 158.

4   **Martin Luther's favorite:** Hank Gerecke interview, 13 July 2011.

4   **The Lord bless you:** Numbers 6:24–26, American King James Version.

5   **Henry Gerecke was late for dinner:** Henry F. Gerecke, Toastmasters speech.

5   **The eldest, twenty-two-year-old Hank:** Hank Gerecke interview, 30 June 2011.

5   **"I heard you," Alma said:** Henry F. Gerecke, Toastmasters speech.

6   **He urged church organizations:** "Army Issues Call for 859 Chaplains."

6   **there wasn't much she could do:** Hank Gerecke interview, various.

7   **most important year of his life:** Hank Gerecke interview, 2 February 2008.

7   **"one of the most singular . . .":** Hourihan, "U.S. Army Chaplain Ministry to German War Criminals."

7   **For the first time in history:** Overy, "The Nuremberg Trials," p. 2.

7   **"a bench mark in international law . . .":** Taylor, *Anatomy of the Nuremberg Trials*, p. 4.

8   **"made scarcely any impression on us":** Fritzsche, *Sword in the Scales*, p. 55.

8   **"Pastor Gerecke's view was . . .":** Ibid., pp. 55–56.

9   **They walked out the door:** Gerecke and Sinclair, "I Walked the Gallows."

9   **Near the city's ancient:** "Night Without Dawn."

9   **Looming ahead of them:** Tilles, *By the Neck Until Dead*, pp. 131–312.

9   **One of the walls had a single poster:** Tusa and Tusa, *Nuremberg Trial*, p. 482.

10   **Left of the main gallows:** Henry F. Gerecke, "My Assignment with the International Military Tribunal at Nuernberg, Germany." [hereafter Gerecke, "My Assignment"]

10   **Two MPs took Keitel:** Tilles, *By the Neck Until Dead*, pp. 130–131.

10   **He then turned on the heels:** See ibid. and "Night Without Dawn."

10   **The chaplain knew Keitel's mother:** Gerecke and Sinclair, "I Walked the Gallows."

10   **He found the field marshal penitent:** Gerecke, "My Assignment."

11   **"On his knees and under . . .":** Ibid.

12   **"Gerecke had made friends . . .":** Schirach, *Price of Glory*, p. 88.

12   **then "thanked the priest . . .":** "Defiant to the Last."

CHAPTER 2

13   **"God our Father . . .":** Luther, "The Freedom of a Christian," p. 283.

13   **the Benders were living:** See *Gould's Street and Avenue Directory of St. Louis, Red-Blue Book*. Bender, Jacob.

13   **Jacob Bender's own father:** Jacob Bender and Margaretha Bucher. Missouri Marriage Records, 1805–2002.

13   **in an apartment next to:** See *Gould's Directory* and 1900 U.S. Census. City of St. Louis, Missouri. Ward 11. District 162. Sheet 3.

13   **Henry moved in with his in-laws:** *Gould's Directory*, Henry F. Gerecke.

14   **did not allow its students:** Meyer, *Log Cabin*, p. 129.

14   **he had to go to work:** Hank Gerecke interview, 30 June 2011.

14   **New World Commercial Co.:** *Gould's Directory*, Henry F. Gerecke.

14   **Henry feared he would never:** Henry F. Gerecke, "Here's a Little Background."

14   **There was an ornately carved:** DeBellis, *100 Years of Reel Entertainment*, p. 6.

15   **Wehrenberg "saw how the crowds . . .":** Ibid., pp. 9–10.

15   **little sister, Nora, died:** Leonora Gerecke, Death Certificate.

15   **doctors cost too much:** Hank Gerecke interview, 23 March 2011.

15   **Henry was furious:** Ibid.

16   **"the beginning of my comeback":** Gerecke, "Here's a Little Background."

16   **died of a stomach hemorrhage:** See *Gould's Directory*, Henry F. Gerecke and Death Certificate for Jacob Bender.

16   **His trombone playing:** Hank Gerecke interview, 30 June 2011.

17   **Gerecke, at age thirty-two, was ordained:** Army and Navy Commission of the Evangelical Lutheran Synod of Missouri, Ohio and Other States. Chaplain Endorsement Application, 8 April 1943.

18   **the congregation threw him:** Hank Gerecke interview, 30 June 2011.

18   **often attending the wakes:** Ibid.

18   **He dragged them back:** Ibid.

19   **Preaching was perhaps:** Hank Gerecke interview, 2 February 2008.

19   **" . . . Don't kiss her back":** Ibid.

20   **Grandma Bender had died:** Alma Bender, Death Certificate.

20   **She spoke only about her dead son:** Hank Gerecke interview, 30 June 2011.

20   **Alma was shocked:** Ibid.

20   **Gerecke "followed a call":** Gerecke, "Here's a Little Background."

21   **the growing divide:** Lindberg, *European Reformations*, pp. 236–240.

22   **they signed the original constitution:** *History of Jackson, Missouri and Surrounding Counties.*

22   **When Wilhelm Gerecke arrived:** Gruhne, *Auswandererlisten des ehemaligen Herzogtums Braunschweig; ohne Stadt Braunschweig und Landkreis Holzminden, 1846–1871,* p. 124.

22   **bought 150 acres of land:** 1860 United States Federal Census. Hubble Township, Cape Girardeau County.

22   **Wilhelm had become an American citizen:** *Naturalization Records of Cape Girardeau County, 1813–1928, Vol. I.*

22   **He was a small-time farmer:** 1860 United States Federal Census. Schedule 4, Production of Agriculture in Hubble Township, Cape Girardeau County, p. 15.

22   **corn was king:** Goebel, *Länger Als Ein Menschenleben in Missouri,* Chapter 10, p. 2.

23   **Families grew potatoes:** Ibid., p. 3.

23   **William enlisted in the Union Army:** *Consolidated Lists of Civil War Draft Registrations, 1863–1865.*

23 **Caroline Luecke, two years his junior:** 1900 United States Federal Census. Hubble Township, Cape Girardeau County.

23 **and from Hanover, Germany:** 1880 United States Federal Census. Hubble Township, Cape Girardeau County, Schedule 1, p. 13.

23 **He was born on December 27, 1863:** Herman Gerecke, Death Certificate.

23 **William died at age twenty-nine:** Probate Court Records. Box 078, bundle 1445. Cape Girardeau County Archive Center. Jackson, Missouri.

23 **became the boys' guardian:** 1880 United States Federal Census. Schedule I. Hubble Township, Cape Girardeau County, p. 13.

23 **Caroline gave birth to her third son:** Ibid.

23 **received from their $693.14 inheritance:** Cape Girardeau County probate abstracts.

24 **Caroline Kelpe from Hanover, Germany:** Missouri Marriage Records, 1805–2002. Missouri State Archives.

24 **He was twenty-nine, she was twenty:** Missouri Division of Health, Standard Death Certificate. State File No. 25665. Filed Aug. 17, 1848, and Herman W. Gerecke, Marriage Certificate.

24 **was introduced to the Christian world:** *Baptism, Confirmation and Death Records*, Zion Lutheran Church, Gordonville, Missouri.

24 **Leonora Gerecke was born April 13, 1903:** Leonora Gerecke, Death Certificate.

24 **Gereckes adopted a second cousin:** 1910 U.S. Census. Hubble Township, Cape Girardeau County, Missouri.

24 **six years younger than Henry:** World War I Draft Registration Cards, 1917–19. Cape Girardeau County. FHL Roll No. 1683155.

24 **Henry and Fred worked as farm laborers:** Ibid., and 1900 U.S. Census record for Dovey Halderman. Byrd Township, Cape Girardeau County, Missouri. Roll T623_845. Page 11A. Enumeration District 23.

24 **He'd seen a man named Billy Sunday:** Hank Gerecke interview, 30 October 2010.

24 **a former center fielder:** McLaughlin, *Billy Sunday Was His Real Name*, p. 6.

24 **to devote himself full time to ministry:** The Papers of William and Helen Sunday, 1882 -[1888–1957] 1975, *A Guide to the Microfilm Edition*. Ed. Robert Shuster, p. 1.

25 **"the baseball evangelist":** McLaughlin, *Billy Sunday*, p. xvii.

25 **a "gymnast for Jesus":** Ibid., p. 155.

25 **or grab for the hand:** Ibid., p. 158.

25 **The towns where he set up:** The Papers of William and Helen Sunday, pp. 21–22.

25 **" . . . the banality of his message":** McLaughlin, *Billy Sunday*, p. xvii.

25 **" . . . the greatest since the days of the apostles":** Ibid.

25 **"the greatest preacher since John the Baptist":** *Face to Face with Satan*, p. 5.

26 **Lena didn't have much of a say:** Hank Gerecke interview, 2 February 2008.

26 **so he landed a succession of jobs:** Henry F. Gerecke, CV.

26 **the town had no "railroad shops— . . .":** *Bulletin: Academic Year 1917–1918*, p. 3.

26 **connected to downtown by streetcar:** Ibid., p. 4.

26 **" . . . a modern vacuum-cleaning apparatus":** Ibid., p. 5.

26 **was "considered self-evident":** Ibid., p. 7.

27 **"a truly Christian character":** Ibid., p. 6.

27 **"This includes all attentions . . .":** Ibid., p. 7.

27 **Pastors and congregations who wanted to join:** Todd Zittlow, Concordia Historical Institute.

28 **The core group that formed:** Todd Hertz, "Benke Suspended for 'Syncretism' after 9/11," *Christianity Today.*

28 **new synod members had to agree:** Zittlow, Concordia Historical Institute.

28 **On the denomination's centennial:** "History of the LCMS."

28 **were given Reformation Day off:** Stelmachowicz, *Johnnie Heritage,* p. 63.

28 **Young women could enroll:** *Bulletin: Academic Year 1917–1918,* p. 11.

28 **"best sent home by parcel post":** Ibid., p. 10.

28 **Wichita Natural Gas Co. struck oil:** Kansas Oil Museum.

29 **" . . . able to use also the German fluently . . .":** *Bulletin: Academic Year 1917–1918,* p. 11.

29 **He got mostly Bs in English:** Henry F. Gerecke, *Transcript.*

29 **though he hated it:** Hank Gerecke interview, 30 October 2010.

29 **"There is no feeling, except . . .":** *The Saint,* p. 80.

29 **The orchestra bought five pianos:** Ibid., p. 78.

30 **the ultimate purpose of Chrysostomos:** Ibid., p. 58.

30 **grew a beard and began smoking:** Hank Gerecke interview, 23 March 2011.

30 **He placed fourth of four:** Stelmachowicz, *Johnnie Heritage,* p. 63.

30 **"May she hold firm . . .":** *The Saint,* p. 58.

30 **the El Dorado field was producing:** Kansas Oil Museum.

30 **were among the most productive:** Price, *El Dorado,* p. 27.

31 **"You can't go to war":** Hank Gerecke interview, 26 June 2010.

31 **"Dad's Waterloo":** Hank Gerecke interview, 2 February 2008.

31 **the Baltimore-born son:** "Short History of the St. Louis Lutheran City Mission (40th Anniversary)."

32 **"He had a genuine sympathy . . .":** H. Holls, "Rev. F. W. Herzberger: Pioneer City Missionary of the Lutheran Church."

32 **"I was naked . . .":** Matthew 25:36, New Revised Standard Version.

32 **Herzberger died in August 1930:** Holls, "Rev. F. W. Herzberger."

32 **By 1938, he was running:** Henry F. Gerecke, City Mission Notes, 4 April 1938.

32 **When Gerecke took over:** Ibid., June 1940.

33 **"The large neon cross lights . . .":** Ibid., July 1941.

33 **The City Mission office moved:** "Short History."

33 **Gerecke designed:** Gerecke, City Mission Notes, December 1937.

33 **Gerecke managed about eighty-five:** Ibid., February 1939.

33 **"Ours is the busiest . . .":** Ibid., October 1941.

33 **"Your City Mission business . . .":** Ibid., November, 1940.

34 **he registered Lutheran Mission Industries:** "Short History."

34 **magazines, rags, old clothing:** Gerecke, City Mission Notes, March 1938.

34 **He borrowed a broken-down Chevrolet:** Hank Gerecke interview, 8 January 2008.

34   **Lutheran Mission Industries had three trucks:** Gerecke, City Mission Notes, October 1941.

34   **with two men each:** Hank Gerecke interview, 1 September 2011.

34   **south and southwest on Tuesdays:** Gerecke, City Mission Notes, December 1940.

34   **average of twenty-five stops a day:** Hank Gerecke interview, 1 September 2011.

34   **"Whatever the business brings in . . .":** "Short History."

34   **Poor families at the two mission congregations:** Ibid.

34   **several St. Louis stores donated clothes:** Hank Gerecke interview, 1 September 2011.

35   **"Since the first of November . . .":** Gerecke, City Mission Notes, March 1938.

35   **"We can't keep up with the calls . . .":** Ibid., 7 April 1937.

35   **"Without boasting . . .":** Ibid., March 1938.

36   **Gerecke was "much excited . . .":** Ibid., December 1940.

36   **"They seemed visibly touched . . .":** Ibid., June 1940.

36   **about $175,000 in today's dollars:** U.S. Dept. of Labor, Bureau of Labor Statistics, CPI Inflation Calculator.

36   **"We must have . . .":** Gerecke, City Mission Notes, January 1938.

36   **"When we see only money . . .":** Ibid., March 1938.

37   **When eight hundred people attended:** Ibid., November 1939.

37   **Ellwanger ran the mission day school:** "Short History."

37   **pastored his congregation:** Gerecke, City Mission Notes, 10 February 1939.

37   **Gerecke went to the City Workhouse:** Ibid., June 1940.

37   **the rounds at Koch Hospital:** Ibid., 6 October 1937.

37   **he visited the isolation patients:** Ibid., June 1940.

37   **"First service, fifteen miles . . .":** Ibid., July 1941.

38   **"The work of a city missionary . . .":** Ibid., August 1941.

38   **visits to the government's Marine Hospital:** "Short History."

38   **The three men together baptized:** Gerecke, City Mission Notes, February 1938.

38   **"The Gospel has been taught . . .":** "Short History."

39   **At the Municipal Workhouse:** Ibid.

39   **Gerecke had gained large audiences:** Gerecke, City Mission Notes, Easter 1941.

39   **"What can be done for the ex-prisoner?":** Ibid., June 1941.

40   **" . . . We enjoy a splendid spirit . . .":** Ibid., June 1940.

40   **" . . . we are after souls . . .":** Ibid., November 1938.

40   **"Quite often we find . . .":** Ibid., 4 November 1937.

40   **"Every new patient . . .":** Ibid., July 1941.

41   **"Tell it and print it":** Ibid., 4 April 1938.

41   **Cathleen, he wrote one month:** Ibid., February 1938.

41   **"Come and see for yourself . . .":** Ibid., November 1938.

41   **"The summer is on . . .":** Ibid., July 1941.

42   **KFUO-AM, founded by his mentor:** "KFUO: Streaming Worldwide on the Web."

42   **originally popular mostly in hospitals:** "Short History."

42   **bringing him fan mail:** Gerecke, City Mission Notes, October 1941.

42   **and even calls to his house:** Ibid., Easter 1941.

42   **brought his favorite musicians:** "Short History."

42   **the huge reach of radio:** Gerecke, City Mission Notes, March 1938.

42   **he promoted the show:** Ibid., Easter 1941.

42   **Gerecke recited . . . a "mission prayer":** Ibid., March 1938.

42   **a rival station, KMOX:** Hank Gerecke interview, 2 February 2008.

42   **he loved the challenge:** Hank Gerecke interview, 30 June 2011.

43   **Alma had a rule:** Ibid.

43   **Naturally that led to fights:** Ibid.

43   **they fought from the time:** Hank Gerecke interview, 23 March 2011.

43   **" . . . You're hurting them":** Ibid., 30 October 2010.

43   **a roof over their heads:** Ibid., 4 January 2008.

44   **She liked money:** Ibid., 2 February 2008.

44   **"This is Thanksgiving . . .":** Gerecke, City Mission Notes, November 1940.

44   **where they listened to a broadcast:** Hank Gerecke interview, 23 March 2011.

44   **"You've heard the sermon . . .":** Ibid., 2 February 2008.

44   **too exciting for a teenager:** Ibid., 23 March 2011.

44   **Hank enlisted in the army:** Henry H. Gerecke, U.S. World War II Army Enlistment Records, 1938–1946.

45   **"Save your old papers . . .":** Gerecke, City Mission Notes, January 1942.

45   **forced to shutter the Industries:** Hank Gerecke interview, 8 January 2008.

45   **Corky followed Hank into the army:** Carlton Gerecke, U.S. World War II Army Enlistment Records, 1938–1946.

45   **"Oliver Grosse assists . . .":** Gerecke, City Mission Notes, April 1943.

45   **application for ecclesiastical endorsement:** Army and Navy Commission of the Evangelical Lutheran Synod of Missouri, Ohio and Other States. Chaplain Endorsement Application, 8 April 1943.

45   **" . . . for the position of chaplain":** O. Rothe, Letter to Army and Navy Commission.

45   **" . . . you will have a real acquisition":** P. E. Kretzmann, Letter to Army and Navy Commission.

45   **"proven himself to be a psychologist . . .":** George W. Wittmer, Letter to Army and Navy Commission.

46   **"When I review in my mind . . .":** Louis W. Wickham, Letter to Army and Navy Commission.

46   **named Gerecke a chaplain:** Henry F. Gerecke, Orders, Chaplain.

46   **" . . . I ask your blessings . . .":** Gerecke, City Mission Notes, August 1943.

47   **" . . . when we are absent one from another":** Genesis 31:49, American King James Version.

47   **"The eternal God is your refuge . . .":** Deuteronomy 33:27, American King James Version.

47   **"God give us strength . . .":** Gerecke, City Mission Notes, November 1941.

CHAPTER 3

48   **"Before you join battle . . .":** Jewish Publication Society, Tanakh Translation.

48   **recommended for the Chaplain Corps:** Carl L. Wilberding, Letter to Henry F. Gerecke, 23 June 1943.

48   **" . . . There is no intention of backing down":** Henry F. Gerecke, Letter to Chief of Chaplains, 26 June 1943.

48   **and reported for duty at Harvard:** A. J. Casey, "Report of Entry on Active Duty," 18 August 1943 and David H. Keller, Memo. "Subject: Report of Physical Examination," 19 August 1943.

49   **"a priest in khaki,":** Cross and Arnold, *Soldiers of God*, p. 15.

49   **New York Cardinal Francis Spellman:** "Bishop Arnold."

49   **"Chaplains of all faiths . . .":** Cross and Arnold, *Soldiers of God*, p. 16.

50   **"Your earnest words . . .":** Arnold, "My dear Chaplain."

50   **a boy named for Mars:** Pernoud, *Martin of Tours*, p. 19.

50   **Martin, even as a child:** Ibid., p. 21.

51   **When Martin was fifteen years old:** Ibid., p. 24.

51   **the beggar laughed:** Ibid., p. 27.

51   **straight out of the Gospels:** Ibid., p. 28, and Matthew 25:40, New Revised Standard Edition.

51   **For centuries, French kings carried:** "The Origin of the word 'Chaplain.'" Plaque. U.S. Army Chaplain Museum. Fort Jackson, South Carolina.

52   **soldier-priests once carried maces:** Drazin and Currey, *For God and Country*, p. 5.

52   **The priests of Amun-Ra:** Armstrong, "Organization, Function and Contribution of the Chaplaincy," p. ii.

52   **to the fifty-five million Americans:** Brinsfield, Cash, and Malek-Jones, "U.S. Military Chaplains," p. 722.

52   **During King Philip's War in 1675:** "Colonial & New World Chaplains." Plaque. U.S. Army Chaplain Museum. Fort Jackson, South Carolina.

52   **among the minutemen:** Brinsfield et al., "U.S. Military Chaplains," p. 723.

52   **to support their flocks:** "During the Revolutionary War." Plaque. U.S. Army Chaplain Museum. Fort Jackson, South Carolina.

52   **and had no uniforms:** Brinsfield et al., "U.S. Military Chaplains," p. 723.

52   **militias held boisterous elections:** Drazin and Currey, *For God and Country*, p. 8.

52   **helping doctors where they could:** "Chaplain Authorization and Duties." Plaque. U.S. Army Chaplain Museum. Fort Jackson, South Carolina.

52   **Continental Congress recognized chaplains:** Brinsfield et al., "U.S. Military Chaplains," p. 723.

53   **enforcers of religious responsibility:** Drazin and Currey, *For God and Country*, p. 8.

53   **" . . . recommended to all Friends . . .":** Ibid., p. 11.

53   **Benjamin Franklin told the story:** Ibid., p. 8.

53   **"a more graceful appearance":** Ibid., p. 9.

54   **to facilitate the free exercise of religion:** Brinsfield et al., "U.S. Military Chaplains," p. 723.

54   **" . . . have been Since mutually released":** Drazin and Currey, *For God and Country*, p. 14.

54   **matters dealing with morals:** Ibid., p. 15.
54   **and Polk appointed them:** Army and Navy Chaplains Ordinariate, *United States Catholic Chaplains in the World War*, p. xiii.
54   **a "Board of Clergymen":** Brinsfield et al., "U.S. Military Chaplains," p. 724.
54   **the military employed nearly:** Ibid.
54   **allowing the first Jewish chaplain:** "Appointments to the Union Army." Plaque. U.S. Army Chaplain Museum. Fort Jackson, South Carolina.
55   **Lincoln's somewhat reluctant approval:** Armstrong, "Organization, Function and Contribution of the Chaplaincy," p. 12.
55   **a Cherokee battalion:** Brinsfield et al., "U.S. Military Chaplains," p. 725.
55   **prompting Congress:** "The Chaplaincy in the Civil War." Plaque. U.S. Army Chaplain Museum. Fort Jackson, South Carolina.
55   **he was eighty years old:** Armstrong, "Organization, Function and Contribution of the Chaplaincy," p. 11.
55   **"Evangelism [was] more than ever before . . .":** Honeywell quoted in Visser, "Evangelism," p. 8.
55   **After the Battle of Chancellorsville:** Norton quoted in Visser, "Evangelism," p. 9.
56   **"Holy barks, shouts, jerks . . .":** Ibid., p. 8.
56   **The revival reached its height:** Ibid.
56   **Chaplain Corps shrank:** Brinsfield et al., "U.S. Military Chaplains," p. 725.
56   **Some chaplains did missionary work:** Simon, "The Influence of the American Protestant Churches," p. 17.
56   **The Act of April 21, 1904:** Ibid., p. 14.
56   **created the position of chaplain assistant:** "Chaplain Assistant." Plaque. U.S. Army Chaplain Museum. Fort Jackson, South Carolina.
56   **74 Regular Army chaplains:** Simon, "The Influence of the American Protestant Churches," p. 30.
56   **the army had 2,217 chaplains:** "Army Chaplains in World War I." Plaque. U.S. Army Chaplain Museum. Fort Jackson, South Carolina.
56   **Twenty-five Catholic priests:** Army and Navy Chaplains Ordinariate, p. xiv.
57   **didn't meld well:** Ibid., p. xv.
57   **The age limits:** Ibid.
57   **religious books and literature:** Simon, "The Influence of the American Protestant Churches," p. 31.
57   **Chaplains also served as postal officers:** "Burials & Additional Duties." Plaque. U.S. Army Chaplain Museum. Fort Jackson, South Carolina.
57   **when the Japanese bombed:** "World War II." Plaque. U.S. Army Chaplain Museum. Fort Jackson, South Carolina.
58   **ministered to more than 16 million:** Brinsfield et al., "U.S. Military Chaplains," p. 726.
58   **The army required that applicants:** "World War II." Plaque. U.S. Army Chaplain Museum. Fort Jackson, South Carolina.
58   **received 4,000 applications:** Simon, "The Influence of the American Protestant Churches," p. 89.
58   **Yearbook of American Churches:** Ibid., p. 73.
58   **The army asked Methodist officials:** Ibid., p. 95.

58   **The Lutheran Church–Missouri Synod:** Ibid., 98.

58   **At its peak in 1943:** Ibid., 90.

59   **Wartime chaplains continued:** "Tell It to the Chaplain." Plaque. U.S. Army Chaplain Museum. Fort Jackson, South Carolina.

59   **tested the creativity and flexibility:** "Making do." Plaque. U.S. Army Chaplain Museum. Fort Jackson, South Carolina.

59   **chaplains also organized boxing matches:** "Troop Transports." Plaque. U.S. Army Chaplain Museum. Fort Jackson, South Carolina.

59   **"climbed mountains, crossed rivers . . .":** Simon, "The Influence of the American Protestant Churches," p. 114.

59   **the third-most combat deaths:** "In the Midst." Plaque. U.S. Army Chaplain Museum. Fort Jackson, South Carolina.

59   **classified as clerk-typists:** "Chaplain Assistants [WWII]." Plaque. U.S. Army Chaplain Museum. Fort Jackson, South Carolina.

60   **The army relaxed education requirements:** Simon, "The Influence of the American Protestant Churches," p. 106.

60   **scratched denominational quotas:** Ibid., p. 107.

60   **"a brief study outlining the plans . . .":** "A Chronicle of the United States Army Chaplain School," p. 2.

60   **founded in 1919:** Ibid., p. 1.

61   **accelerated by the Japanese attack:** Ibid., pp. 4–5.

61   **Classes would include:** Ibid., p. 6.

61   **" . . . a fraternal spirit among chaplains":** Ibid., p. 16.

61   **first class of 71 chaplains:** Ibid., p. 15.

61   **By the third class of students:** Ibid., pp. 17–18.

CHAPTER 4

62   **"When man thinks . . .":** Barth, *Church Dogmatics*, p. 451.

62   **"It is said an Eastern monarch . . .":** Abraham Lincoln, Address before the Wisconsin State Agricultural Society.

63   **the Ninety-Eighth arrived in Hermitage:** Henry F. Gerecke, "Monthly Report of Chaplains," May 1944.

63   **He searched for a local rabbi:** Ibid., August 1944.

63   **Gerecke made arrangements:** Ibid., August 1943.

63   **Gerecke recruited another local rabbi:** Ibid., February 1945.

63   **an abbreviation for "*Gamzu ya'avor*":** *Folktales of Israel*, p. 174.

63   **"Every time he felt . . .":** Ibid.

64   **It was inscribed with his motto:** Hank Gerecke interview, 13 July 2011.

64   **"To a unit closely knit . . .":** Sullivan, "Period Report, Medical Department Activities, 1 January–31 December 1945."

64   **500 enlisted men and 150 officers:** Ibid.

64   **a graduate of the Army Medical School:** Ibid.

65   **Gerecke was assigned to the Ninety-Eighth:** Arnold, "Memorandum For: The Adjutant General."

65   **The report worksheets:** Gerecke, "Monthly Report of Chaplains," September 1943.

65   **the unit's overnight training bivouacs:** Ibid., October 1943.

65   **obstacle course, infiltration crawl:** Ibid., February 1944.

65   **distributed Protestant New Testaments:** Ibid., October 1943.

66   **every item of furniture:** Hank Gerecke interview, 30 June 2011.

66   **yanked Gerecke:** Ibid.

66   **Geist had been drafted:** Thomas V. Geist, "My Experience as Assistant to Chaplain Henry F. Gerecke."

66   **Gerecke "was like a father to me . . .":** Geist interview.

67   **Gerecke gave two Thanksgiving services:** Gerecke, "Monthly Report of Chaplains," November 1943.

67   **he organized Christmas services:** Ibid., December 1943.

67   **performed his first wedding:** Ibid., February 1944.

67   **a fifteen-day leave:** Ibid., January 1944.

67   **Attendance at Sunday services:** Ibid., February 1944.

67   **starred Ronald Reagan:** *For God and Country.* Film.

67   **Sullivan received orders:** Sullivan, "Period Report, Medical Department Activities, 1 January–31 December 1945."

68   **Gerecke proved seaworthy:** Gerecke, "Monthly Report of Chaplains," March 1944.

68   **a crumbling station hospital:** Sullivan, "Historical Report, 4 April to 15 July 1944."

68   **The 834-bed hospital:** Ibid., 1 January–31 December 1945.

68   **a small wooden structure:** Photo, collection of Thomas V. Geist.

68   **a folding altar:** "The Chaplain Corps," WW2 Medical Research Centre.

69   **When the appropriate gear arrived:** Geist, "My Experience."

69   **chapel was surprisingly roomy:** Gerecke, "Monthly Report of Chaplains," May 1944.

69   **Gerecke hung black drapes:** Photo, collection of Thomas V. Geist.

69   **Sullivan encouraged exchange visits:** Sullivan, "Period Report, Medical Department Activities, 1 January–31 December 1945."

70   **built to house a gymnasium:** Ibid.

70   **The nurses organized weekly dances:** Ibid., 4 April to 15 July 1944.

70   **56 percent Protestants:** Gerecke, "Monthly Report of Chaplains," May 1944.

70   **Sullivan had the priest removed:** Hank Gerecke interview, 2 February 2008.

71   **"containing a spiritual lift":** Gerecke, "Monthly Report of Chaplains," May 1944 and December 1944.

71   **Gerecke discovered a soldier:** Gerecke, "Sickbed Sidelights," pp. 119–120.

71   **The body of a pilot:** Ibid., p. 118.

72   **dropped to their knees:** Ibid., p. 119.

72   **In the first two months:** Sullivan, "Period Report, Medical Department Activities, 1 January–31 December 1945."

72   **money coming in:** Hank Gerecke interview, 10 October 2011.

73   **the family's 1939 Chrysler Imperial:** Hank Gerecke interview, 2 February 2008.

73   **Henry sent a letter:** Henry F. Gerecke, V-Mail to Dorothy Williams, 10 May 1944.

73   **when one of Alma's admirers:** Hank Gerecke interview, 2 February 2008.
74   **For the first six weeks or so:** Sullivan, "Historical Report, 1 January to 8 May 1945."
74   **As more patients arrived:** Ibid., 1 January–31 December 1945.
74   **Six ambulances—:** Ibid., 16 July to 30 September 1944.
74   **taken to Newbury Race Course:** Ibid.
74   **From June to November 1944:** Ibid., 1 January–31 December 1945.
75   **and treated elsewhere:** Ibid., 16 July to 30 September 1944.
75   **Gerecke instituted "Moments of Prayer":** Gerecke, "Monthly Report of Chaplains," June 1944.
75   **He began noticing used condoms:** Hank Gerecke interview, 13 July 2011.
75   **"God bless you, son":** Gerecke, "Sickbed Sidelights," p. 120.
76   **encountered only three atheists:** Ibid., p. 122.
76   **Weekly bus trips:** Sullivan, "Historical Report, 16 July to 30 September 1944."
77   **visiting 2,000 patients:** Gerecke, "Monthly Report of Chaplains," January 1945.
77   **"birthday anniversary":** Hank Gerecke interview, 13 July 2011.
77   **and it showed at chapel:** Gerecke, "Monthly Report of Chaplains," June 1944.
77   **"Prayers for the sick ones . . .":** Gerecke, "Sickbed Sidelights," pp. 122–123.
77   **visit from his oldest son:** Hank Gerecke interview, 13 July 2011.
79   **silently behind the surgeons:** Gerecke, "Sickbed Sidelights," p. 123.
79   **For a moment, Gerecke froze:** Ibid., 121.
80   **"I am fortunate . . .":** Ibid., October 1944.
80   **Ninety-Eighth General Hospital Orchestra:** Sullivan, "Historical Report, 16 July to 30 September 1944."
80   **encourage the Jewish members:** Gerecke, "Monthly Report of Chaplains," May 1944.
80   **Yom Kippur services:** Ibid., November 1944.
80   **Gerecke held Thanksgiving services:** Gerecke, "Monthly Report of Chaplains," October 1944.
80   **" . . . will provide Christmas trees":** Ibid., November 1944.
81   **three thousand feet of sidewalks:** Sullivan, "Historical Report, 1 January to 8 May, 1945."
81   **" . . . but I must watch him":** Henry F. Gerecke, Letter to Dorothy Williams, 19 October 1944.
81   **a Western Union telegram:** Henry F. Gerecke, "Please rush German literature." Telegram, 24 October 1944.
81   **to extract information:** Hank Gerecke interview, 13 July 2011.
82   **to that of a general hospital:** Sullivan, "Historical Report, 16 July to 30 September 1944."
82   **"We feel highly gratified . . .":** Gerecke, "Monthly Report of Chaplains," December 1944.
82   **a note of commendation:** James P. Sullivan, Commendation letter for Gerecke, Gerecke, "Monthly Report of Chaplains," December 1944.
83   **soldiers from the front lines:** Sullivan, "Historical Report, 1 January–31 December 1945."

83   **fire destroyed the bar:** Ibid., 1 January to 8 May 1945.

83   **he began taking cigarettes:** Gerecke, "Monthly Report of Chaplains," March 1945.

83   **to sew and mend their clothing:** Sullivan, "Historical Report, 1 January to 8 May 1945.

84   **"Opportunities for individual . . .":** Gerecke, "Monthly Report of Chaplains," January 1945.

84   **"Our wounded men . . .":** Ibid., February 1945.

84   **"A cheerful, loyal, devout officer . . .":** Sullivan, "Efficiency Report for Henry F. Gerecke, 1 March 1945."

84   **Sullivan chartered a boat:** Sullivan, "Historical Report, 1 January to 8 May 1945."

85   **"An unforgettable experience . . .":** Gerecke, "Monthly Report of Chaplains," April 1945.

85   **The unit set up delousing stations:** Sullivan, "Period Report, Medical Department Activities, 1 January–31 December 1945."

85   **were to be sent back to the United States:** Ibid., "Historical Report, 1 January to 8 May 1945."

85   **Hank was on the Champs-Élysées:** Hank Gerecke interview, 13 July 2011.

85   **"We thank God for Victory . . .":** Gerecke, "Monthly Report of Chaplains," May 1945.

86   **breaking down the hospital:** Sullivan, "Period Report, Medical Department Activities, 1 January–31 December 1945."

86   **The Ninety-Eighth stopped:** Ibid., "Historical Report, 9 May to 23 May 1945."

86   **boarded the MS *Dunnottar Castle*:** Ibid., "Period Report, Medical Department Activities, 1 January–31 December 1945."

86   **" . . . and confidence in any future task":** Ibid.

86   **The Ninety-Eighth landed in France:** Sullivan, "Period Report, Medical Department Activities, 1 January–31 December 1945, Munich addendum.

87   **Gerecke sent a message:** Hank Gerecke interview, 13 July 2011.

87   **He attended a conference:** Gerecke, "Monthly Report of Chaplains," July 1945.

87   **" . . . need special attention right now":** Ibid., June 1945.

87   **"Both were devoted . . .":** Sullivan, "Period Report, Medical Department Activities, 1 January–31 December 1945, Munich addendum."

87   **"enormous problems":** Descriptions of the hospital the Ninety-Eighth took over in Munich, and the lives the unit led there, come from James P. Sullivan's, "Period Report, Medical Department Activities, 1 January–31 December 1945, Munich addendum."

89   **"Beautiful chapel . . .":** Gerecke, "Monthly Report of Chaplains," July 1945.

91   **Hank Gerecke took a jeep:** Hank Gerecke interview, 13 July 2011.

92   **Rosh Hashanah services:** Gerecke, "Monthly Report of Chaplains," August 1945.

92   *The Mastersingers of Nuremberg:* "Da Prinzeregentheater."

92   **Yom Kippur services:** Gerecke, "Monthly Report of Chaplains," August 1945.

93   **Amid the snowball fights:** Geist interview.

94   **The two men conferred:** Hank Gerecke interview, 13 July 2011.

94   **"This area is being retained . . .":** Photo, collection of Thomas V. Geist.

94   **Gerecke returned several times:** Gerecke and Sinclair, "I Walked the Gallows."

95   **He said it over and over again:** Geist interview.

CHAPTER 5

96   **"If your enemies . . .":** NRSV.

96   **had asked for Gerecke:** Andrus, Untitled manuscript draft "Gerecke."

97   **" . . . possible spiritual benefit":** Ibid.

97   **Andrus's situation was "urgent":** Ibid.

97   **"But I finally got it":** Ibid.

97   **entered the army as a cavalry officer:** Andrus and Zwar, *I Was the Nuremberg Jailer*, pp. 13–14.

98   **He was furious:** Ibid., p. 12.

98   **" . . . a better man for the job":** Galbraith, "The Cure."

98   **"somewhat allergic . . .":** Ibid.

98   **"They have religious statues . . .":** Andrus, Letter to the Recorder, San Diego Commandery No. 25, 15 March 1945.

99   **When Andrus arrived at Ashcan:** Andrus, Letter to Katherine Andrus, 18 May 1945.

99   **" . . . has to verify the signature":** Galbraith, "The Cure."

99   **any vantage point high in the town:** Ibid.

99   **The Palace had a veranda:** Ibid.

99   **the Palace's gray stucco façade:** Tusa and Tusa, *Nuremberg Trial*, p. 43.

99   **He requested floodlights:** Andrus and Zwar, *I Was the Nuremberg Jailer*, pp. 18–19.

99   **"I even feared murder . . .":** Ibid., p. 19.

100   **"I hate these Krauts . . .":** Persico, *Nuremberg*, p. 50.

100   **"Here is some paper . . .":** Andrus, Letter to Katherine Andrus, 5 April 1945.

100   **"I am treated here . . .":** Andrus and Zwar, *I Was the Nuremberg Jailer*, p. 33.

101   **" . . . a bunch of jerks?":** Galbraith, "The Cure."

101   **" . . . a certain motion picture . . .":** Andrus and Zwar, *I Was the Nuremberg Jailer*, p. 44.

101   **"held a handkerchief to his mouth . . .":** Ibid., p. 45.

102   **Andrus decided to use:** Ibid., pp. 46–50.

103   **" . . . without a 'chute,' sir?":** Ibid., p. 51.

103   **Andrus had first recruited:** "Minister Counseled Nazi Elite."

103   **they refused to be counseled:** Hank Gerecke interview, 23 March 2011.

103   **"I absolutely needed his services . . .":** Andrus, Untitled manuscript draft "Gerecke."

104   **Sullivan had given Gerecke the option:** Gerecke and Sinclair, "I Walked the Gallows."

104   **Gerecke was badly shaken:** Gerecke, "My Assignment," and Hank Gerecke interview, 30 June 2011.

104   **Gerecke had recently traveled to Paris:** Hank Gerecke interview, 30 June 2011.

104   **calling Hank for advice:** Ibid., and Gerecke and Sinclair, "I Walked the Gallows."

105   **Christ's forgiveness:** Hank Gerecke interview, 30 June 2011.

105   **Gerecke was staring:** Gerecke, "My Assignment."

105   **"I'll go," he said:** Gerecke and Sinclair, "I Walked the Gallows."

106   *Translatio imperii* **came from:** Remley, *Old English Biblical Verse*, p. 250.

106   **"the God of heaven . . .":** Daniel 2:31–44, NRSV.

106   **Biblical scholars mostly have agreed:** Miller, *New American Commentary*, pp. 94–97.

107   **a Danish prince named Sebald:** Descriptions of Sebald's life come from Collins, *Reforming Saints*, pp. 58–61.

107   *peregrinatia pro Christo*: Volz, *Medieval Church*, p. 35.

108   **Romanesque and Gothic parish:** Kootz, *Nürnberg*, p. 28.

108   **fifteen-foot-high brass tomb:** Schieber, *Nuremberg*, p. 34.

108   **critical position in Germany's history:** Kootz, *Nürnberg*, p. 3, and Schieber, *Nuremberg*, p. 8.

108   **The word** *Norenberc*: Schieber, *Nuremberg*, p. 8.

109   **The city housed:** Ibid., pp. 28–29.

109   **German cities with a history:** Voigtländer and Voth, "Persecution Perpetuated," p. 2.

109   **defiling Holy Communion wafers:** Hsia, *Myth of Ritual Murder*.

109   **"the eyes and ears of Germany":** Brockmann, *Nuremberg*, p. 181.

109   **"would deal severely . . .":** Luther, "On the Jews and Their Lies," pp. 33, f96.

110   **violence spread:** Voigtländer and Voth, "Persecution Perpetuated," p. 7.

110   **Jews sought shelter:** Schieber, *Nuremberg*, p. 44.

110   **Germans began burning Jews:** Voigtländer and Voth, "Persecution Perpetuated," p. 7.

110   **annihilation of six hundred people . . . synagogue had once stood:** Schieber, *Nuremberg*, pp. 44–45.

111   **"For the glory of . . .":** Kootz, *Nürnberg*, p. 52.

111   **In the wake of the First World War:** Dietzfelbinger interview.

111   **he was interested in Nuremberg:** Schieber, *Nuremberg*, p. 6.

111   **blessing the Nazi swastika:** Dietzfelbinger interview.

112   **four times more Nazi Party members:** Ibid.

112   *Knight, Death and the Devil*: Brockmann, *Nuremberg*, p. 181.

112   **built more than three hundred churches:** Dietzfelbinger interview.

113   **"the worst in the history of human beings":** Ibid.

113   **Gerecke didn't press the issue:** Geist interview.

113   **"among the dead cities . . .":** "Nuremberg: Historical Evolution," p. 7.

114   **had increased 60 percent:** Ibid.

114   **Nuremberg's remaining citizens:** Gaskin, *Eyewitnesses*, p. 113.

114   **seemed to hover in midair:** Ibid., p. 117.

114   **foraged from nearby farms:** Ibid., p. 104.

114   **mostly of bread and potatoes:** Ibid., p. 108.

114   **"there was no money":** West, "Greenhouse with Cyclamens I (1946)," p. 10.

114   **to barter for food:** Gaskin, *Eyewitnesses*, p. 104.

114   **"He stared up at the clouds . . .":** West, "Greenhouse with Cyclamens I (1946)," p. 16.

114   **lodged in the broken roof:** Gaskin, *Eyewitnesses*, p. 103.
115   **"exhaled the stench of disinfectant . . .":** West, "Greenhouse with Cyclamens I (1946)," p. 10.
115   **death flowed from the wreckage:** Gaskin, *Eyewitnesses*, p. 115.
115   **were miraculously untouched:** Ibid., p. 102.
115   **Resurrecting a city:** Description of the Allied rebuilding of Nuremberg comes from "Nuremberg: Historical Evolution," pp. 7–10.
115   **uncovered caches of machine guns:** Gaskin, *Eyewitnesses*, p. 109.
117   *You sure do,* **Gerecke thought:** Gerecke, Toastmasters.
117   **battling Indians:** Persico, *Nuremberg*, p. 49.
117   **"the story of a lost sheep . . .":** Gerecke, Toastmasters.
117   **" . . . to surprise you":** Ibid.
117   **"Chaplain, just remember . . .":** Persico, *Nuremberg*, p. 116.

CHAPTER 6

118   **"Beloved, never avenge . . .":** NRSV.
118   **" . . . I grew increasingly confused . . .":** Speer, *Spandau*, p. 52.
119   **Andrus, who was furious:** Andrus and Zwar, *I Was the Nuremberg Jailer*, p. 53.
119   **a show of force:** Tusa and Tusa, *Nuremberg Trial*, pp. 145–146.
119   **contained 530 offices:** "Memorium Nuremberg Trials."
119   **$75 million today:** CPI.
119   **GIs removed courtroom walls:** "Memorium Nuremberg Trials."
119   **The prison's four wings:** Schneider interview.
120   **Two of the prison's wings:** Tusa and Tusa, *Nuremberg Trial*, p. 126.
120   **Andrus oversaw about 250 people:** Andrus and Zwar, *I Was the Nuremberg Jailer*, p. 55.
120   **the ground floor of Wing Four:** Schneider interview.
120   **could be run by five guards:** Ibid.
120   **Philadelphia's Cherry Hill Prison:** "Eastern State Penitentiary."
120   **Each cell measured:** Fritzsche, *Sword in the Scales*, pp. 17–19.
120   **a "Judas window":** Gerecke and Sinclair, "I Walked the Gallows."
120   **a steel cot, fastened to the wall:** Description of the Nazis' cells is largely drawn from Andrus and Zwar, *I Was the Nuremberg Jailer*, pp. 68–74.
121   **created by knocking down a wall:** Gerecke and Sinclair, "I Walked the Gallows."
122   **Guards were ordered to yell:** Tusa and Tusa, *Nuremberg Trial*, p. 127.
122   **freshly laundered underwear:** Andrus and Zwar, *I Was the Nuremberg Jailer*, p. 68.
122   **could take a hot shower:** Tusa and Tusa, *Nuremberg Trial*, p. 127.
122   **hand the prisoner a spoon:** Andrus, "Prisoner Routine, Nurnberg Jail."
122   **Breakfast usually consisted of:** "Menus, Nuremberg prison, 17 June 1945 to 30 April 1946."
122   **he was handed a broom:** Andrus, "Prisoner Routine, Nurnberg Jail."
123   **a small 140-by-100-foot:** Tusa and Tusa, *Nuremberg Trial*, p. 128.
123   **followed eight paces behind:** Andrus and Zwar, *I Was the Nuremberg Jailer*, p. 67.
123   **they prepared legal defenses:** Tusa and Tusa, *Nuremberg Trial*, p. 130.

123   **A typical dinner:** "Menus."

123   **The creation of the Nuremberg Laws:** Unless otherwise noted, the description of how the Nuremberg trials came to be come primarily from Taylor, *Anatomy of the Nuremberg Trials* (pp. 4–39) and Overy, "The Nuremberg Trials."

124   **wrote to Sir Cecil Hurst:** Pell, Letter to Sir Cecil Hurst, 8 May 1944.

127   **"considerable pressure . . .":** Archibald King, Memorandum for the Judge Advocate General, 7 September 1944.

128   **The middle option:** Ibid.

128   **" . . . no detailed directive . . .":** Ibid.

130   **in the vicinity of Aachen:** Aachen's Wanted Nazis.

130   **"Assuming that there is . . .":** Daniel, Letter to Colonel Joseph Hodgson, 4 April 1945.

131   **"We believe that whatever their guilt . . .":** Dean, "The statement which appears below."

133   **outlining the plan for a major trial:** Jackson, Letter to Lord Wright of Durley, 5 July 1945.

134   **Jackson publicly stated:** Jackson, *Statement by Robert H. Jackson Representing the United States,* 12 August 1945.

135   **"We are all worried about":** Taylor, "We Are All Worried."

136   **"complete freedom . . .":** "Convention relative to the Treatment of Prisoners of War," Geneva, 27 July 1929.

136   **"granted the protection . . .":** Twelfth Army Group Headquarters.

136   **the religious rights of POWs:** European Theater of Operations Headquarters. "Standing Operating Procedure No. 49."

136   **there are no records:** Brinsfield interview.

137   **"He'll be your assistant":** Gerecke and Sinclair, "I Walked the Gallows."

137   **Gerecke met chaplains Sixtus O'Connor and Carl Eggers:** Ibid.

137   **"How does a man . . .":** Venzke, *Confidence in Battle.*

137   **the son of a schoolteacher:** John O'Connor interview.

137   **enjoyed a classical education:** O'Connor, Transcript of Record.

138   **interested in how modern philosophy:** O'Connor, "Augustin Gemelli," pp. 450–451.

138   **dropped out of St. Bonaventure College:** *St. Bonaventure's College and Seminary Annual Catalogue,* 1925–1926, p. 93.

139   **O'Connor professed:** Davies and Meilach, *Provincial Annals.*

139   **rigged a sound system:** John O'Connor interview.

139   **was harassed by party thugs:** Brian Jordan interview.

139   **his love affair with teaching:** Callahan, *Provincial Annals,* p. 134.

140   **was anxious to become:** Maguire, Letter to "Brothers in St. Francis."

140   **O'Connor listed his height:** Sixtus R. O'Connor, *Application for Service.*

140   **The closest person:** John O'Connor interview.

140   **on any official army documents:** Ibid. *Biographical Data,* 10 August 1944.

140   **guessed the priest to be:** Gerecke and Sinclair, "I Walked the Gallows."

140   **Gerecke was frightened:** Gerecke, Toastmasters.

140   **Gerecke offered the Nazi:** Gerecke and Sinclair, "I Walked the Gallows."

140   **It wasn't an easy gesture:** Ibid.

141   **"in order that the Gospel . . .":** Gerecke, Toastmasters.

141 **" . . . of an all-loving Father . . .":** Gerecke and Sinclair, "I Walked the Gallows."

141 **" . . . on the Cross for them":** Gerecke, "My Assignment."

141 **leaving Gerecke and Hess alone:** Gerecke and Sinclair, "I Walked the Gallows."

141 **they had all been boys:** Hank Gerecke interview, 23 March 2011.

141 **He fought in the same regiment:** Kelley, *22 Cells at Nuremberg*, p. 18.

141 **the rank of first lieutenant:** Davidson, *Trial of the Germans*, p. 110.

141 **a chest wound:** Kelley, *22 Cells at Nuremberg*, p. 18.

141 **studied with a geography professor:** Davidson, *Trial of the Germans*, p. 110.

141 **traditional German imperialism:** Wistrich, *Who's Who*, p. 126.

142 **Hess had taken stenography:** Kelley, *22 Cells at Nuremberg*, p. 19.

142 **including those on *lebensraum*:** Wistrich, *Who's Who*, p. 131.

142 **third in line to lead the Reich:** Ibid.

142 **Hitler addressed in the familiar:** Davidson, *Trial of the Germans*, p. 110.

142 **He had sought out father figures:** Wistrich, *Who's Who*, p. 131.

142 **"There is one man . . .":** Davidson, *Trial of the Germans*, p. 111.

142 **Hess's take on "the Jewish problem":** Kelley, *22 Cells at Nuremberg*, p. 20.

142 **to be rid of Jews:** Davidson, *Trial of the Germans*, p. 110.

142 **his part in planning:** Ibid., p. 125.

143 **"Would you care . . .":** Gerecke and Sinclair, "I Walked the Gallows."

143 **a copy of St. John's Gospel:** "Kesselring Cried at His Sermon."

143 **"My first attempt . . .":** Gerecke, Toastmasters.

143 **he dreaded meeting:** Gerecke and Sinclair, "I Walked the Gallows."

143 **"You want in now, Chappie?":** Gerecke, Toastmasters.

143 **"I heard you were coming . . .":** Gerecke and Sinclair, "I Walked the Gallows."

144 **his mother, Franny, sailed to Haiti:** Mosely, *Reich Marshal*, p. 8.

144 **"highest aspiration . . .":** Bewley, *Hermann Göring*, p. 19.

145 **Red Baron . . . Goering was married:** Wistrich, *Who's Who*, pp. 102–103.

146 **with huge feasts:** Ibid., p. 103, and Davidson, *Trial of the Germans*, p. 63.

146 **a man who loved animals:** Davidson, *Trial of the Germans*, p. 63.

146 **in style on his own train:** Ibid., p. 93.

146 **a title held previously:** Ibid., p. 96.

147 **"I hereby charge you . . .":** Ibid., p. 75.

147 **the end of his favor with Hitler:** Ibid., p. 60, and Wistrich, *Who's Who*, p. 104.

147 **packing up as many rugs:** Unless otherwise noted, the description of Goering's final days on the run comes from Mosely, *Reich Marshal*, pp. 338–348.

148 **Hitler had become hysterical:** Kershaw, *Hitler, 1936–45*, p. 807.

148 **better without him:** Ibid., p. 804.

148 **hounding Hitler for months:** Ibid., p. 807.

148 **Bormann drew up a document:** Ibid., p. 808.

149 **decided to search:** Lesjak, "Bagging a Bigwig."

150 **" . . . Eisenhower's personal protection . . .":** Mosely, *Reich Marshal*, p. 351.

150 **a Stinson L-5 Sentinel:** Alford, *Nazi Plunder*, pp. 45–47.

151 **his valet, Robert Kropp:** Descriptions of Goering's arrival at Mondorf taken from Andrus and Zwar, *I Was the Nuremberg Jailer*, pp. 25–37.

152   **considerable amount of charm:** Gerecke and Sinclair, "I Walked the Gallows."
152   **everything in his power:** Gerecke, Toastmasters.
153   **"Another day with the men . . .":** "Kesselring Cried at His Sermon."
153   **had directed the bomb attacks:** Wistrich, *Who's Who*, pp. 170–171.
153   **"He is one gentleman . . .":** "Kesselring Cried at His Sermon."
153   **"a city of ruins . . .":** Gerecke, "Monthly Report of Chaplains," November 1945.

CHAPTER 7

154   **"He who covers up his faults . . .":** Tanakh.
154   **A succession of six prosecutors:** Barrett, "Raphael Lemkin and 'Genocide' at Nuremberg, 1945–1946."
154   **"Until they began to react . . .":** Taylor, *Anatomy of the Nuremberg Trials*, p. 165.
155   **"the foremost representatives . . .":** Davidson, *Trial of the Germans*, p. 36.
155   **Goering stood and took a microphone:** Taylor, *Anatomy of the Nuremberg Trials*, p. 166.
155   **"Nein!":** Ibid., p. 176.
155   **"Not guilty . . .":** Trial of the Major War Criminals (TMWC), Vol. 2, p. 97.
156   **"modern juristic literature . . .":** Taylor, *Anatomy of the Nuremberg Trials*, p. 167.
156   **"The wrongs which we seek . . .":** TMWC, Vol. 2, p. 98.
157   **a ravine called Babi Yar:** Ibid., p. 124.
157   **destruction of the Warsaw ghetto:** Ibid., p. 126.
157   **the annihilation of millions:** Ibid., p. 136.
157   **evidence of a "medical experiment":** Ibid., p. 129.
157   **Jackson spoke for four hours:** Barrett, "Civilization Opens Its Case."
157   **As Gerecke spoke:** Barrett, "Thanksgiving in Nuremberg (1945)."
157   **prosecutor Major Frank Wallis spoke:** TMWC, Vol. 2, p. 177.
158   **"This was history being made . . .":** Barrett, "Thanksgiving in Nuremberg (1945)."
158   **to attend his services on Sundays:** Gerecke and Sinclair, "I Walked the Gallows."
158   **the small two-cell chapel:** Gerecke, "My Assignment."
159   **"You Lutherans have fifteen . . .":** Gerecke and Sinclair, "I Walked the Gallows."
159   **"jolly" and "delightful":** Gerecke, Toastmasters.
159   **"You've got the right address, Chappie . . .":** Hank Gerecke interview, 2 February 2008.
159   **the little church in Mögeldorf:** Gerecke, Toastmasters.
160   **OMGUS vacated:** Unless otherwise noted, the description of life in Nuremberg is drawn from Gaskin, *Eyewitnesses* (pp. 106–139), Taylor, *Anatomy of the Nuremberg Trials* (pp. 209–217), Tusa and Tusa, *Nuremberg Trial* (pp. 227–229), and West, "Greenhouse with Cyclamens I (1946)" (pp. 9–14).
161   **a German band played jazz:** Gaskin, *Eyewitnesses*, p. 131, and Jerry Legow interview.
162   **" . . . a relaxed, tolerant and philanderous ambience . . .":** Taylor, *Anatomy of the Nuremberg Trials*, p. 217.
162   **" . . . who was not on the vigorous side . . .":** West, "Greenhouse with Cyclamens I (1946)," p. 13.

162 **" . . . in a manner certainly vulgar . . .":** Tusa and Tusa, *Nuremberg Trial*, p. 229.

163 **Because of the need to translate:** Gaskin, *Eyewitnesses*, p. 130.

163 **the fishbowl of Nuremberg:** Ibid., p. 131

163 **"water-torture, boredom . . .":** West, "Greenhouse with Cyclamens I (1946)," p. 8.

163 **"There was a lot of drinking . . .":** Tusa and Tusa, *Nuremberg Trial*, p. 227.

164 **"I must feel convinced . . .":** Gerecke and Sinclair, "I Walked the Gallows."

164 **guards had placed notes:** Gerecke, "My Assignment."

165 **"I know little about your politics . . .":** Gerecke and Sinclair, "I Walked the Gallows."

165 **German Imperial Navy:** Davidson, *Trial of the Germans*, p. 403.

165 **would create a bottleneck:** Ibid., 407.

165 **Doenitz had given them:** Ibid., 408.

166 **Lieutenant Heinz Eck was on trial:** *Law Reports of Trials of War Criminals*, p. 2.

166 **When Eck's U-boat surfaced:** Davidson, *Trial of the Germans*, pp. 408–409.

166 **the Greek first officer:** *Law Reports of Trials of War Criminals*, p. 3.

166 **"No thank you," Rosenberg said:** Gerecke, "Monthly Report of Chaplains," December 1945.

166 **a movement to leave the Catholic:** Steigmann-Gall, *Holy Reich*, p. 219.

167 **might be better spent:** Gerecke and Sinclair, "I Walked the Gallows."

167 **"If my colleagues are . . .":** Gerecke, Toastmasters.

167 **Raeder was born near Hamburg:** Davidson, *Trial of the Germans*, p. 368.

167 **promoted to admiral and chief:** Wistrich, *Who's Who*, p. 239.

167 **In a fit of jealousy:** Davidson, *Trial of the Germans*, p. 372.

167 **"clear and relentless fight . . .":** Wistrich, *Who's Who*, p. 239.

167 **case of Reverend Martin Niemoeller:** Bird, *Erich Raeder*, p. 105.

168 **Hitler made Raeder grand admiral:** Wistrich, *Who's Who*, p. 240.

168 **Raeder began reading the scripture:** Gerecke and Sinclair, "I Walked the Gallows."

168 **prepared questions:** "Chaplain Gerecke Urges Aid."

168 **Soon enough:** Gerecke and Sinclair, "I Walked the Gallows."

168 **"This business of religion . . .":** Ibid.

168 **"the nastiest, the most disagreeable . . .":** Ibid., and Gerecke, Toastmasters.

168 **Born in Wesel:** Wistrich, *Who's Who*, pp. 246–247.

169 **Ribbentrop . . . was his gofer:** Davidson, *Trial of the Germans*, p. 147.

169 **He was contemptuous:** Wistrich, *Who's Who*, p. 246, and Davidson, *Trial of the Germans*, p. 148.

169 **"Can a man be patriotic . . .":** Gerecke and Sinclair, "I Walked the Gallows."

169 **" . . . you must obey God . . .":** Gerecke, "My Assignment."

169 **"became more and more penitent . . .":** Gerecke and Sinclair, "I Walked the Gallows."

169 **which he eventually did:** Gerecke, "My Assignment."

169 **Nazis were unresponsive at first:** Gerecke and Sinclair, "I Walked the Gallows."

169 **his entire family had been Catholic:** Gerecke, Toastmasters.

169 **"get right with God":** Gerecke and Sinclair, "I Walked the Gallows."

170   **"I'll be there . . .":** Gerecke, Toastmasters.

170   **Schacht's bitterness:** Gerecke and Sinclair, "I Walked the Gallows."

170   **"But if there's any degree . . .":** Gerecke, Toastmasters.

170   **" . . . go to church with my wife":** Gerecke and Sinclair, "I Walked the Gallows."

170   **a bald head shaped like a bulldog's:** Goldensohn, *Nuremberg Interviews*, p. 204.

170   **He wasn't smart:** Kelley, *22 Cells at Nuremberg*, p. 195.

170   **the most notorious slaver:** Davidson, *Trial of the Germans*, p. 506.

170   **hands constantly fluttering:** Goldensohn, *Nuremberg Interviews*, p. 204.

170   **made most cringe:** Kelley, *22 Cells at Nuremberg*, p. 195.

170   **a habit of pausing:** Taylor, *Anatomy of the Nuremberg Trials*, p. 428.

170   **"one of the dullest . . .":** Tusa and Tusa, *Nuremberg Trial*, p. 501.

170   **"one of the toughest . . .":** Taylor, *Anatomy of the Nuremberg Trials* p. 427.

170   **shining and buffing them:** Goldensohn, *Nuremberg Interviews*, p. 204.

170   **"As a clergyman . . .":** Gerecke and Sinclair, "I Walked the Gallows."

171   **working toward an ideal:** Ibid.

171   **a working-class success story:** Goldensohn, *Nuremberg Interviews*, p. 204.

171   **from a seafaring family:** Davidson, *Trial of the Germans*, p. 505, and Wistrich, *Who's Who*, p. 267.

171   **shipwrecked off the Scottish coast:** Goldensohn, *Nuremberg Interviews*, p. 206, and Wistrich, *Who's Who*, p. 267.

171   **in a French POW camp:** Evans, *Third Reich at War*, p. 347.

171   **a lathe operator in a ball-bearing plant:** Ibid., and Goldensohn, *Nuremberg Interviews*, p. 206.

171   **began studying engineering:** Davidson, *Trial of the Germans*, p. 505.

171   **It was a happy marriage:** Evans, *Third Reich at War*, p. 347.

171   **over the next fifteen years:** Goldensohn, *Nuremberg Interviews*, p. 206.

171   **Two of the boys:** Davidson, *Trial of the Germans*, p. 505.

171   **a labor leader at his factory:** Kelley, *22 Cells at Nuremberg*, p. 196.

171   **he was making speeches:** Davidson, *Trial of the Germans*, p. 505.

171   **Sauckel heard Hitler:** Evans, *Third Reich at War*, p. 347.

171   **"the man chosen by fate . . .":** Goldensohn, *Nuremberg Interviews*, p. 208.

171   **"the loyal fidelity of a dog . . .":** Kelley, *22 Cells at Nuremberg*, p. 196.

171   **elected into the Reichstag:** Wistrich, *Who's Who*, p. 267.

172   **energetic leader of the Nazi Party:** Davidson, *Trial of the Germans*, p. 504.

172   **lowered the minimum age:** Evans, *Third Reich at War*, p. 350.

172   **the Reich's quenchless thirst:** Davidson, *Trial of the Germans*, p. 506, and Wistrich, *Who's Who*, p. 266.

172   **rounded up fifty thousand men:** Davidson, *Trial of the Germans*, p. 512.

172   **4.5 million foreign workers:** Evans, *Third Reich at War*, p. 350.

172   **In a letter to Rosenberg:** Davidson, *Trial of the Germans*, p. 512.

173   **jammed fifty to eighty . . . Sauckel evoked:** Davidson, *Trial of the Germans*, pp. 509–517.

173   **eight million foreign workers:** Evans, *Third Reich at War*, p. 357.

173   **not how they were treated:** Davidson, *Trial of the Germans*, p. 507.

174   **he would come to chapel services:** Gerecke and Sinclair, "I Walked the Gallows."

174   **"how I can prepare myself . . .":** Gerecke, Toastmasters.
174   **Sauckel asked for God's mercy:** Ibid.
174   **and wiped away tears:** Gerecke, "My Assignment."
174   **"All right, Mr. Sauckel . . .":** Gerecke, Toastmasters.
175   **"big men . . .":** Ibid.
175   **"Of course I'm coming . . .":** Ibid.
175   **"a delightful conversationalist":** Gerecke and Sinclair, "I Walked the Gallows."
175   **His grandfather was an architect:** Wistrich, *Who's Who*, pp. 290–291.
175   **proved useful to Hitler:** Ibid., p. 291, and Davidson, *Trial of the Germans*, p. 483.
175   **At the end of the war . . . he backed off:** Davidson, *Trial of the Germans*, p. 485.
176   **"tried to continue Gerecke's ministry":** Grossmith, *Cross and the Swastika*, p. 121.
176   **" . . . made a lasting impression . . .":** Ibid., p. 5.
176   **"fitted least snugly . . .":** Smith, *Reaching Judgment*, p. 292.
176   **"deeply ashamed . . .":** Gerecke and Sinclair, "I Walked the Gallows."
177   **"those important doctrines . . .":** Gerecke, Toastmasters.
177   **walking in a public area:** Fritzsche, *Sword in the Scales*, p. 312.
177   **a long line of blacksmiths:** Goldensohn, *Nuremberg Interviews*, pp. 49–52.
177   **educated in public schools:** Kelley, *22 Cells at Nuremberg*, p. 81.
177   **kept him out . . . "the soul is saved":** Goldensohn, *Nuremberg Interviews*, pp. 47–50.
178   **He was an editor . . . sovereign lands:** Davidson, *Trial of the Germans*, pp. 531–532.
178   **Ministry of Propaganda's Radio Division:** Wistrich, *Who's Who*, p. 85.
178   **anti-Semitism . . . drafting of German children:** Davidson, *Trial of the Germans*, pp. 537–550.
179   **"Don't expect me . . .":** Gerecke, Toastmasters.
179   **a boyish smile:** Gerecke and Sinclair, "I Walked the Gallows."
180   **also married an American girl:** Davidson, *Trial of the Germans*, p. 285n.
180   **Baldur was born in Berlin:** Ibid., p. 286.
180   **six million Hitler Youth members:** Wistrich, *Who's Who*, p. 272.
180   **the future of the SS:** Ibid., and Davidson, *Trial of the Germans*, p. 290.
180   **"That is the greatest thing . . .":** Davidson, *Trial of the Germans*, p. 287.
180   **"Fuehrer, my Fuehrer . . .":** Ibid., p. 288.
181   **"Jew-ridden":** Ibid., p. 304.
181   **the "removal" of Jews:** Wistrich, *Who's Who*, p. 273.
181   **English author Houston Stewart Chamberlain:** Davidson, *Trial of the Germans*, p. 305.
181   **"I have rethought . . .":** Goldensohn, *Nuremberg Interviews*, p. 245.
181   **" . . . will you commune me?":** Gerecke, Toastmasters.
181   **"I shall never forget . . .":** Gerecke and Sinclair, "I Walked the Gallows."
181   **white sheet covering a table:** Gerecke, Toastmasters.
181   **left the chaplain to his business:** Gerecke and Sinclair, "I Walked the Gallows."
182   **"My only answer . . .":** Gerecke, Toastmasters.

CHAPTER 8

183   **"To be able to do harm . . ."**: Erasmus, *Enchiridon*, p. 72.

183   **Robert Jackson threw**: Persico, *Nuremberg*, pp. 181–182.

184   **"Most of us had no idea . . ."**: Fritzsche, *Sword in the Scales*, p. 123.

184   **to get the defendants' families**: Andrus and Zwar, *I Was the Nuremberg Jailer*, pp. 112–113.

184   **Christmas carols in the courtyard**: "Justice Jackson in Holy Land."

184   **was taken by American soldiers**: Schirach, *Price of Glory*, pp. 105–110.

185   **Speer was twenty on Christmas Eve**: Speer, *Spandau*, pp. 31–32.

186   **fish, bread, and tea**: "Menus, Nuremberg prison, 17 June 1945 to 30 April 1946."

186   **"I've often thought about . . ."**: Gilbert, *Nuremberg Diary*, p. 87.

186   **"The silence in the big prison . . ."**: Gerecke and Sinclair, "I Walked the Gallows."

186   **Newspapers from across the world**: Fritzsche, *Sword in the Scales*, p. 124.

187   **Gerecke led his congregation**: Gerecke and Sinclair, "I Walked the Gallows."

187   **A tiny Christmas tree**: Fritzsche, *Sword in the Scales*, pp. 124–125.

187   **The SS organist began**: Gerecke and Sinclair, "I Walked the Gallows."

187   **"And she brought forth . . ."**: Luke 2, American King James Version.

188   **"We never took time . . ."**: Gerecke and Sinclair, "I Walked the Gallows."

189   **"Again and again I noticed how . . ."**: Fritzsche, *Sword in the Scales*, p. 126.

189   **"Prayers, hell! . . ."**: Gilbert, *Nuremberg Diary*, p. 125.

189   **"longed for a German pastor"**: Schacht, *Confessions of "The Old Wizard,"* p. 404.

189   **"a non-descript kind of place . . ."**: Fritzsche, *Sword in the Scales*, pp. 126–127.

190   **Gerecke visited Emmy Goering**: Gerecke, "Monthly Report of Chaplains," February 1946.

190   **Gerecke conducted services**: Ibid., May 1946.

191   **who preferred his books**: Goldensohn, *Nuremberg Interviews*, p. 20.

191   **the chief legal authority**: Davidson, *Trial of the Germans*, p. 427.

191   **as Hitler's personal attorney**: Wistrich, *Who's Who*, p. 78.

191   **"nomadic labor" class . . . 85 percent of the Jews**: Davidson, *Trial of the Germans*, pp. 432–438.

193   **O'Connor rebaptized Frank**: Niklas Frank interview.

193   **Franz Werfel's novel**: Conot, *Justice at Nuremberg*, p. 502.

193   **Ernst was born in 1903**: Davidson, *Trial of the Germans*, p. 322.

193   **he and Adolf Eichmann**: Wistrich, *Who's Who*, p. 166.

193   **married, and had three children**: Davidson, *Trial of the Germans*, p. 322.

193   **commander of the Austrian SS**: Ibid., and Wistrich, *Who's Who*, p. 166.

193   **named head of the Reich Security Main Office**: Taylor, *Anatomy of the Nuremberg Trials*, p. 360.

193   **suddenly found himself controlling**: Davidson, *Trial of the Germans*, p. 316, and Tusa and Tusa, *Nuremberg Trial*, p. 316.

194   **Kaltenbrunner was a giant man**: Wistrich, *Who's Who*, pp. 116–117.

194   **more like a block**: Davidson, *Trial of the Germans*, p. 318.

194   **smoked a hundred cigarettes**: Ibid., p. 320.

194   **Kaltenbrunner's square chin**: Wistrich, *Who's Who*, p. 166.

194 **a clipped, precise manner:** Goldensohn, *Nuremberg Interviews*, p. 150.

194 **thin lips and crooked teeth:** Davidson, *Trial of the Germans*, p. 318.

194 **from a duel he fought:** Wistrich, *Who's Who*, p. 166.

194 **shattered windshield of his car:** Kelley, *22 Cells at Nuremberg*, p. 135.

194 **his face was pockmarked:** Tusa and Tusa, *Nuremberg Trial*, p. 316.

194 **his eyes were narrow and brown:** Davidson, *Trial of the Germans*, p. 318.

194 **"looked like a vicious horse":** Taylor, *Anatomy of the Nuremberg Trials*, p. 360.

194 **Himmler was afraid of Kaltenbrunner:** Davidson, *Trial of the Germans*, p. 318.

194 **intrigued by the gas chambers:** Wistrich, *Who's Who*, p. 167.

194 **"He was a gangster . . .":** Davidson, *Trial of the Germans*, p. 318.

194 **" . . . anyone might be his victim":** Ibid., p. 320.

195 **thirty prisoners died:** Eckstein, "Mauthausen," p. 946.

196 **oversaw seven SS officers:** Ibid., p. 949.

196 **The *volksdeutsche*:** Lechner and Dürr, "Mauthausen Subcamp System," p. 905.

196 **the SS shipped bodies:** "Construction of Mauthausen concentration camp." Plaque. Mauthausen Memorial. Mauthausen, Austria.

196 **Mauthausen was classified:** Waite, "Gusen (with Gusen II and Gusen III)," p. 901.

196 **"camps for murder":** Lechner and Dürr, "Mauthausen Subcamp System," p. 905.

197 **prisoners arrived from:** Eckstein, "Mauthausen," p. 946.

197 **Ziereis ordered 263 Czechs:** Waite, "Gusen (with Gusen II and Gusen III)," p. 901.

197 **Twenty-one thousand people:** Ibid., pp. 900–901.

197 **Typhoid and dysentery epidemics:** Eckstein, "Mauthausen," p. 948.

197 **the highest death rate:** Lechner and Dürr, "Mauthausen Subcamp System," p. 905.

197 **to dig the massive caverns:** Ibid.

197 **could kill up to 80 people:** Hagen Regional Court cited in Freund and Greifeneder, Mauthausen Memorial.

198 **marked a cross on the chest:** Freund and Greifeneder.

198 **he'd never seen the gas chamber:** TMWC, Vol. 11, p. 321.

198 **SS company German Earth and Stone Works:** Marsálek and Hacker, *Concentration Camp Mauthausen*, pp. 9–10.

198 **the Wiener Graben quarry:** Eckstein, "Mauthausen," p. 946.

198 **as little as sixty pounds:** Marsálek and Hacker, *Concentration Camp Mauthausen*, p. 14.

198 **Hundreds more simply froze:** Ibid., p. 15.

199 **"I saw from my watchtower . . .":** TMWC, Vol. 4, p. 388.

199 **version of Josef Mengele:** Rising, "On Trail of Most Wanted Nazi."

200 **Guards drove gas vans:** Waite, "Gusen (with Gusen II and Gusen III)," p. 901.

200 **hundreds of prisoners to Hartheim:** "The Concentration Camp System at Mauthausen." Plaque. Mauthausen Memorial. Mauthausen, Austria.

200 **10,000 Hungarian Jews arrived:** Waite, "Gusen (with Gusen II and Gusen III)," p. 901.

200   **known as the Thunderbolt:** Craig, *11th Armored Division: Thunderbolt.*

201   **Amid the dust and dirt:** Steward, *Thunderbolt.*

201   **joined the unit in July 1943:** O'Connor, "Monthly Report of Chaplains," September 1943 to August 1944.

201   **his unit's desert maneuvers:** Ibid., January 1944.

201   **left Staten Island on the HMS *Samaria*:** Unless otherwise noted, the description of the Eleventh's march through Europe is drawn from Steward and Craig.

202   **asked to be an interpreter:** Brian Jordan interview.

203   **"when the ground forces . . .":** *Technical Manual, TM 16–205: The Chaplain. U.S. Army*, July 1944, p. 64.

203   **"the troops I serve . . .":** O'Connor, "Monthly Report of Chaplains," January 1945.

203   **forty-six letters of condolence:** Ibid., February 1945.

204   **He also earned a Bronze Star:** Conley, "Award of Bronze Star Medal."

205   **evidence of cannibalism:** Eckstein, "Mauthausen," p. 951.

206   **de facto medical personnel:** Pike, *Spaniards in the Holocaust*, p. 242.

207   **even the liberators had to be held back:** Pike, *Spaniards in the Holocaust*, p. 240.

207   **they slit the guard's throat:** Ibid., p. 242.

208   **More than 450 died:** Ibid., p. 240.

208   **German soldiers were under attack:** Ibid., p. 243.

208   **" . . . I conducted burial services . . .":** O'Connor, "Monthly Report of Chaplains," May 1945.

209   **"This unit moved . . .":** Ibid., June 1945.

209   **O'Connor told a few friends:** Brian Jordan interview.

209   **"shares the peril of battle . . .":** *Technical Manual*, p. 64.

209   **He cried nearly every time:** Kelley, *22 Cells at Nuremberg*, pp. 133–134.

210   **a minor brain hemorrhage:** Ibid., and Goldensohn, *Nuremberg Interviews*, p. 139.

210   **He was hospitalized:** Davidson, *Trial of the Germans*, p. 321.

210   **Kaltenbrunner's strategy:** Ibid., p. 323, Taylor, *Anatomy of the Nuremberg Trials*, p. 360, and Tusa and Tusa, *Nuremberg Trial*, p. 318.

210   **"probably more appalling crimes . . .":** Tusa and Tusa, *Nuremberg Trial*, p. 317.

210   **" . . . I have been submitted . . .":** Taylor, *Anatomy of the Nuremberg Trials*, p. 362.

210   **" . . . the ugliest defense yet heard . . .":** Tusa and Tusa, *Nuremberg Trial*, p. 318.

210   **"began to look embarrassed":** Ibid., p. 319.

210   **ordered Mauthausen to be surrendered:** Davidson, *Trial of the Germans*, p. 321.

211   **" . . . that I ever saw a gas chamber . . .":** TMWC, Vol. 11, p. 317.

211   **brought from the bunker:** Ibid.

211   **to build Vienna's sidewalks:** Tusa and Tusa, *Nuremberg Trial*, p. 318.

211   **an armaments factory:** Ibid., and Taylor, *Anatomy of the Nuremberg Trials*, p. 361.

212   **killing everyone in it:** Goldensohn, *Nuremberg Interviews*, p. 301.

212   **"He used monoxide gas . . ."**: Harris, *Tyranny on Trial*, p. 336.

212   **The farmhouses**: Goldensohn, *Nuremberg Interviews*, p. 310.

212   **the red house and the white house**: Evans, *Third Reich at War*, p. 298.

212   **could kill about two thousand**: Goldensohn, *Nuremberg Interviews*, p. 311.

212   **They began operations**: Evans, *Third Reich at War*, p. 298.

212   **when the gas killed a cat**: Ibid., p. 297.

212   **four dedicated gas chambers**: Ibid., p. 299.

212   **supplied corpses**: Harris, *Tyranny on Trial*, p. 338.

212   **The heat of the victims' own bodies**: Ibid., and Evans, *Third Reich at War*, pp. 299–300.

212   **"After all of the observations done . . ."**: Goldensohn, *Nuremberg Interviews*, p. 303.

213   **" . . . the canisters were pulled up again . . ."**: Evans, *Third Reich at War*, p. 300.

213   **special fittings for gaskets**: Goldensohn, *Nuremberg Interviews*, p. 298.

213   **" . . . always behind in our cremating . . ."**: Ibid., p. 304.

213   **roughly the population of Dayton, Ohio**: 2008 U.S. Census.

213   **About 7,000 SS men worked**: Evans, *Third Reich at War*, p. 304.

214   **many burning pits . . . His example cheered morale**: Harris, *Murder by the Millions*, pp. 46–49.

214   **90 percent of those killed were Jews**: Evans, *Third Reich at War*, p. 304.

215   **Hoess went into hiding**: Ibid., p. 743.

215   **Franz Lang**: Harris, *Murder by the Millions*, p. 32.

215   **Within a month he was sent**: Evans, *Third Reich at War*, p. 743.

215   **"short, rather heavy set . . ."**: Harris, *Tyranny on Trial*, p. 334.

215   **"weak, high voice"**: Taylor, *Anatomy of the Nuremberg Trials*, p. 363.

215   **"I have no such fantasies"**: Goldensohn, *Nuremberg Interviews*, p. 315.

215   **" . . . I led a normal family life . . ."**: Gilbert, *Nuremberg Diary*, p. 237.

215   **his wife's garden**: Evans, *Third Reich at War*, p. 306.

215   **which held concerts and performances**: Ibid., p. 304.

215   **"A big part of the Polish intelligentsia . . ."**: Harris, *Murder by the Millions*, p. 83.

216   **"the order was authoritative . . ."**: Harris, *Tyranny on Trial*, p. 335.

216   **"Not justified . . ."**: Goldensohn, *Nuremberg Interviews*, p. 296.

216   **"it was not always a pleasure . . ."**: Gilbert, *Nuremberg Diary*, p. 238.

217   **"playing or joking with one another . . ."**: Evans, *Third Reich at War*, p. 299.

217   **"had to appear cold and indifferent . . ."**: Ibid., p. 305.

217   **"She was very upset . . ."**: Goldensohn, *Nuremberg Interviews*, p. 308.

217   **"I never struck any internee . . ."**: Ibid., p. 309.

218   **" . . . I never killed anyone"**: Ibid., p. 150.

218   **An estimated sixty million men**: Waller, *Becoming Evil*, p. 15.

218   **"It helps side us . . ."**: Vetlesen, *Evil and Human Agency*, p. 14.

219   **"the greatest catastrophes occur . . ."**: Waller, *Becoming Evil*, p. xv.

219   **"intellectually normal . . ."**: Gilbert, *Nuremberg Diary*, p. 239.

219   **suffering or destruction . . . "the harm we perpetrate . . ."**: Waller, *Becoming Evil*, pp. 12–14.

219   **Hoess's closest friend**: Harris, *Murder by the Millions*, p. 22.

220   **"Evil can only exist . . .":** Crowley, "Evil," p. 495.

220   **"spurn God's goodness . . .":** Kennedy, "Evil, moral," p. 497.

220   **"Does disaster befall a city . . .":** Amos 6:3, NRSV.

220   **"either God cannot abolish evil . . .":** McCloskey, *God and Evil*, p. 1.

221   **" . . . growing existential frustration . . .":** Wray and Mobley, *Birth of Satan*, p. 3.

221   **"I form the light, . . .":** Isaiah 45:7, King James Version.

CHAPTER 9

222   **"Justice without kindness . . .":** Zwingli, "An Exposition of the Faith."

222   **Some, led by Goering:** Gilbert, *Nuremberg Diary*, pp. 346–347.

223   **"I grew up with . . .":** TMWC, Vol. 16, pp. 235–236.

223   **who translated it for Alma:** Schirach's English translation was not quite faithful to Fritzsche's German original, and he seems to have used his knowledge of American colloquialism for Alma's benefit. Based on a transcription of Fritzsche's original handwriting by Zieghart Rein provided to me by the Concordia Historical Institute in St. Louis at my request in August 2011, and translated by Ingrid Gustin, an accurate English translation of Fritzsche's original wording follows. Rein's transcription of Fritzsche's original follows that. I chose to quote from Schirach's translation in the body of this chapter because that is the version that both Henry and Alma Gerecke read in 1946.

Gustin translation:

Mrs. Gerecke.

Dear honorable Lady!

Your husband Pastor Gerecke looked after the accused in the Nuremberg trials as pastor to the signatories. He held this office for the last six months.

It has come to our attention that you, dear lady, after the absence of your husband for many years, have expressed the wish that he return home. We understand this wish very well because we also have wives and children.

But we have a request of you: delay this wish to gather your family at home. Please consider that we at this time cannot do without your husband. In the past few months he has displayed a steady friendship. He has become indispensable for us. Especially in surroundings in which we find prejudice, cold denial and even hatred.

He is for us indispensable, not only as a pastor, but also as the good person that we probably don't have to describe to his wife.

He simply has become dear to us. It is incomprehensible, that at this juncture of the trial, someone other than him can break through these walls that more than physically surround us spiritually. Please spare him for us. Surely you can bear this sacrifice and we will be grateful.

We wish you and your family the best. God be with you.

Rein transcription:

Frau Gerecke.

Sehr verehrte gnädige Frau!

Ihr Gatte Pastor Gerecke, betreut als Seelsorger die Unterzeichner unter den lutherischen Ange-klagten im Nürnberger Prozess. Er tut dies seit über einem halben Jahr.

Wir haben nun gehört, daß Sie, gnädige Frau, nach der mehr jährigen Abwesenheit Ihres Gatten den Wunsch nach seiner Heimkehr haben. Wir verstehen diesen Wunsch sehr gut, denn auch wir haben frauen und Kinder.

Aber wir haben eine Bitte an Sie: Stellen Sie den Wunsch, ihre Familie wieder zu Haus versammeln, zurück.

Bitte bedenken Sie, daß wir auf ihren Gatten jetzt nicht verzichten können. Er hat uns in den vergangenen Monaten eine so bewegungslose Freundlichkeit gezeigt, daß er für uns unentbehrlich geworden ist, zumal in einer Umgebung in der wir sonst.

Vorurteil, kalte Ablehnung oder sogar Hass finden. Er ist uns unentbehrlich nicht nur als Seelsorger, sondern auch als der gute Mensch— als den wir ihn seiner Frau sicher nicht erst zu beschreiben brauchen.

Wir haben ihn einfach lieb gewonnen. Es ist ausgeschlossen, daß im jetzigen Stadium des Prozesses ein anderer als er noch einmal die Mauern durchbricht, die uns seelisch noch mehr als materiell umgeben. Also bitte lassen Sie ihn uns. Sicher werden Sie dies Opfer tragen—und wir werden Ihnen dankbar dafür sein.

Wir wünschen Ihnen und Ihrer Familie alles gute!

223   **"Frau Gerecke":** Fritzsche et al., Letter to Alma Gerecke, 14 June 1946.

224   **"I had done a little mild griping . . .":** Gerecke and Sinclair, "I Walked the Gallows."

224   **"the most incredible letter . . .":** Ibid.

224   **"My Dear!":** Henry F. Gerecke, Letter to Alma Gerecke, 18 June 1946.

224   **"Our dear Chaplain Gerecke . . .":** Fritzsche et al., Letter to Alma Gerecke.

225   **"So I stayed on at Nuremberg . . .":** Gerecke and Sinclair, "I Walked the Gallows."

225   **"really hadn't written a word . . .":** "Nuernberg Nazi Leaders Urged St. Louis Chaplain."

225   **Gerecke had committed:** Gerecke, "Monthly Report of Chaplains," December 1945.

225   **" . . . perhaps closer to them . . .":** "Nuernberg Nazi Leaders Urged St. Louis Chaplain."

225   **"became more and more solemn . . .":** Fritzsche, *Sword in the Scales*, pp. 316–317.

226   **officiated at the wedding:** Gerecke, "Monthly Report of Chaplains," August 1946.

226   **inquiries from German clergy:** Ibid.

226   **Goering claimed prosecutors:** TMWC, Vol. 22, p. 364.

226   **"I stand up for the things . . .":** Ibid., p. 366.

227   **"You most certainly heard . . .":** Manvell cited by Persico. *Nuremberg*, p. 374.

227   **"glazed and dreamy eyes . . .":** TMWC, Vol. 22, p. 370.

227   **"a pitiable exhibition . . .":** Fritzsche, *Sword in the Scales*, p. 317.

227   **tried to get him to stop:** Neave, *On Trial at Nuremberg*, p. 302.

227 " . . . under the greatest son . . .": TMWC, Vol. 22, p. 373.

228 "will go down in history . . .": Ibid., pp. 373–375.

228 "Amid the deepest distress . . .": Ibid., p. 383.

228 "And the reason why I say 'yes . . .' ": Ibid., Vol. 12, p. 13.

229 " . . . which I must rectify . . .": Ibid., Vol. 22, p. 385.

229 " . . . a tremendous spiritual responsibility . . .": Ibid., p. 384.

230 " . . . I cannot today cry . . .": Ibid., p. 405.

230 "shaken to the very depths . . .": Ibid., p. 396.

230 " . . . Keitel was used to acting . . .": Tusa and Tusa, Nuremberg Trial, p. 259.

231 when Hitler gave him an order: Ibid., p. 308.

231 "You have been at this trial too long . . .": Ibid., p. 311.

231 could not think of a single time: Gilbert, Nuremberg Diary, p. 228.

231 "truthful and decent . . .": Tusa and Tusa, Nuremberg Trial, p. 310.

231 "a weak, if not pathetic, instrument . . .": Smith, Reaching Judgment, p. 186.

231 " . . . two fundamental questions . . .": TMWC, Vol. 22, pp. 376–377.

232 something that approximated respect: Smith, Reaching Judgment, p. 186.

232 "the bravest and most thoughtful . . .": Taylor, Anatomy of the Nuremberg Trials, pp. 537–538.

232 "with great dignity . . .": Neave, On Trial at Nuremberg, p. 304.

232 "more honest": Gilbert, Nuremberg Diary, p. 227.

232 " . . . disparaging Keitel's intelligence . . .": Fritzsche, Sword in the Scales, p. 176.

233 smuggling them out: Speer, Spandau, p. 8.

233 O'Connor smuggled it: Niklas Frank interview.

233 The epigraph of the manuscript: Frank, In the Shadow, p. 333.

233 peddling it to right-wing: Ibid., p. 332.

233 short exercise walks: Andrus and Zwar, I Was the Nuremberg Jailer, p. 142.

233 "It was gratifying . . .": Gerecke, "My Assignment."

233 " . . . before the verdict": Gerecke and Sinclair, "I Walked the Gallows."

233 in nearby homes: Gerecke, "My Assignment."

234 wives who were scrambling: Hank Gerecke interview, 1 April 2008, and Niklas Frank interview.

234 "I am too emotionally unstrung . . .": Gerecke, "My Assignment."

234 "He would not show the victors . . .": Posner, Hitler's Children, p. 54.

234 Erich Raeder couldn't see his wife: Gerecke and Sinclair, "I Walked the Gallows."

234 Lawrence had personally: Raeder, My Life, p. 400.

234 The Russians never explained: Gerecke and Sinclair, "I Walked the Gallows."

234 without ever charging her: Davidson, Trial of the Germans, p. 391.

234 "that of being my wife . . .": Raeder, My Life, p. 400.

234 O'Connor smuggled Schirach's son: Schirach, Price of Glory, pp. 211–212.

234 accompanied the family members: Gerecke, "My Assignment."

235 "the most ungodly woman . . .": Gerecke and Sinclair, "I Walked the Gallows."

235 escorted her down: Fritzsche, Sword in the Scales, p. 320.

235 Gerecke had traveled to Sackdilling: Goering, My Life with Goering, pp. 154–155.

236 **was outcast in school:** Klaus von Schirach interview.

236 **he sent them care packages:** Hank Gerecke interview, 4 January 2008 and Niklas Frank interview.

236 **"We saw little hands . . .":** Gerecke, "My Assignment."

237 **"They were Katzenjammer Kids . . .":** Gerecke and Sinclair, "I Walked the Gallows."

237 **Cordula's earliest memories:** Posner, *Hitler's Children*, p. 103.

237 **tried to make him laugh:** Niklas Frank interview.

237 **"like an eternal zombie . . .":** Frank, *In the Shadow*, p. 371.

238 **" . . . killed for nothing":** Niklas Frank interview.

238 **"heart-rending" . . . "emotional impact . . .":** Fritzsche, *Sword in the Scales*, p. 320.

238 **standing on a chair . . . "My golden treasure! . . .":** Posner, *Hitler's Children*, p. 198

239 **Emmy had urged Edda:** Gerecke and Sinclair, "I Walked the Gallows."

239 **"Got a cigarette?":** Ibid.

239 **Andrus had relaxed another rule:** Fritzsche, *Sword in the Scales*, pp. 318–319.

240 **would be extended for another week:** Conot, *Justice at Nuremberg*, p. 492.

240 **gave the families more time:** Gerecke and Sinclair, "I Walked the Gallows."

240 **an atmosphere of general gloom:** Conot, *Justice at Nuremberg*, p. 492.

240 **One thousand extra guards:** Tusa and Tusa, *Nuremberg Trial*, p. 467.

240 **Snipers positioned themselves:** Ibid., p. 466.

240 **"was at his most absurd . . .":** Taylor, *Anatomy of the Nuremberg Trials*, p. 574.

240 **". . . have made a mockery . . .":** TMWC, Vol. 22, pp. 522–523.

241 **in a bleak mood:** Fritzsche, *Sword in the Scales*, p. 321.

241 **"if there is ever to be . . .":** Taylor, *Anatomy of the Nuremberg Trials*, p. 571.

241 **"It is your duty . . .":** Andrus and Zwar, *I Was the Nuremberg Jailer*, p. 142.

241 **Lawrence had banned photography:** Fritzsche, *Sword in the Scales*, p. 321.

242 **"Goering persecuted the Jews . . .":** TMWC, Vol. 22, pp. 524–527.

242 **"worst shape of any man . . .":** Persico, *Nuremberg*, pp. 397–398.

242 **they took off their headphones:** Fritzsche, *Sword in the Scales*, p. 322.

242 **" . . . Fritzsche is not guilty . . .":** TMWC, Vol. 22, p. 585.

242 **" . . . the walls of Jericho crumble":** Fritzsche, *Sword in the Scales*, pp. 323–324.

243 **Schacht shook hands with no one:** Speer, *Spandau*, p. 5.

243 **some congratulations in return:** Fritzsche, *Sword in the Scales*, p. 324.

243 **a bizarre press conference:** Persico, *Nuremberg*, p. 402.

243 **" . . . the Spiritual Councilor . . .":** Gerecke and Sinclair, "I Walked the Gallows."

243 **"took the verdicts like soldiers . . .":** Gerecke, "My Assignment."

243 **rode the elevator up to the dock:** Reactions of the defendants to their sentences are drawn from Persico, *Nuremberg*, p. 403, and TMWC, Vol., 22, pp. 588–589.

244 **it sounded abstract:** Speer, *Spandau*, pp. 3–4.

245 **Forty-five minutes after:** Taylor, *Anatomy of the Nuremberg Trials*, p. 598.

245 **cell doors were left open:** Fritzsche, *Sword in the Scales*, p. 325.

245 **"It is a terrible thing . . .":** Tusa and Tusa, *Nuremberg Trial*, p. 473.

245 **Keitel refused to allow:** Davidson, *Trial of the Germans*, p. 342.

245 **frank admission of weakness:** Smith, *Reaching Judgment*, p. 186.

245 **". . . no surprise to me . . .":** Keitel, *Memoirs*, p. 237.

246 **"I will willingly . . .":** Ibid., p. 238.

246 **Goering's bravery:** Taylor, *Anatomy of the Nuremberg Trials*, p. 601.

246 **or that he be shot:** Ibid., p. 602.

246 **". . . and not for being soldiers":** Ibid., p. 607.

246 **he became emotional:** Kelley, *22 Cells at Nuremberg*, p. 124.

247 **"shunning his own personal responsibility":** Keitel, *Memoirs*, p. 235.

247 **Despite his depression:** Tusa and Tusa, *Nuremberg Trial*, p. 485, and Kelley, *22 Cells at Nuremberg*, p. 126.

247 **"One has only a bunk . . .":** Keitel, *Memoirs*, p. 31.

247 **"I regret nothing . . .":** Ibid., p. 237.

247 **"in the name of humanity":** Fritzsche, *Sword in the Scales*, pp. 180–181.

248 **a gradual distancing:** Childs, *Introduction to the Old Testament*, p. 154.

249 **"will suffer a sevenfold vengeance":** Genesis 4:15, NRSV.

249 **In Hebrew folk etymology:** Rosenberg, "Genesis: Introduction," p. 10.

249 **a tribe of metalworkers:** Miller and Hayes, *History of Ancient Israel and Judah*, p. 80.

249 **he wanted to connect the history:** Westermann, *Genesis 1–11: A Commentary*, p. 318, cited in Volf, *Exclusion & Embrace*, p. 93.

249 **"The logic of sin proves stronger . . .":** Volf, *Exclusion & Embrace*, p. 96.

250 **"The story about a murderous 'them' . . .":** Ibid., p. 93.

250 **Jesus's suffering on the cross:** Ibid., p. 26.

250 **". . . why have you forsaken me?":** Mark 15:34, NRSV.

250 **armor to protect him:** Lapide, *Von Kain bis Judas: Ungewohnte Einsichten zu Sünde und Schuld*, cited in Volf, *Exclusion & Embrace*, p. 98.

250 **". . . Cain's scanty offering . . .":** Volf, *Exclusion & Embrace*, p. 98.

251 **"away from the presence of the Lord":** Genesis 4:16, NRSV.

251 **not whether they should:** Volf interview, 26 August 2010.

CHAPTER 10

252 **"Good is opposed to evil . . .":** Mackie, "Evil and Omnipotence," p. 1.

252 **almost day and night:** Gerecke, "My Assignment."

252 **a walk up and down:** Taylor, *Anatomy of the Nuremberg Trials*, p. 607.

252 **no more chapel services:** Gerecke and Sinclair, "I Walked the Gallows."

252 **four or five times a day:** Gerecke, "My Assignment."

252 **"What an effect . . .":** Speer, *Spandau*, pp. 6–10.

253 **Ribbentrop read his Bible:** Gerecke, "My Assignment."

254 **if they could take cold showers:** Conot, *Justice at Nuremberg*, pp. 502–503.

254 **"My God, give me the strength . . .":** Goering, *My Life with Goering*, pp. 156–158.

255 **He had died when:** Gerecke, "My Assignment."

255 **Until December 1947:** "U.S. Army Trials in Post-War Germany."

256 **hanged twenty-eight men:** Unless otherwise noted, the description of the execution preparations is drawn from Tilles, *By the Neck Until Dead*, pp. 40–49 and pp. 111–113.

258   **Speer was irritated at first:** Speer, *Spandau*, p. 10.

258   **The team blacked out:** Tilles, *By the Neck Until Dead*, p. 124.

258   **their final instructions:** Ibid., p. 128.

258   **the chaplains went from cell to cell:** Gerecke, "My Assignment."

258   **Andrus had summoned:** Persico, *Nuremberg*, p. 417.

258   **he hadn't heard anything:** Ibid.

259   **refusing to leave his cell:** Swearingen, *Mystery of Hermann Goering's Suicide*, p. 68.

259   **"What time are the executions . . .":** Persico, *Nuremberg*, p. 420.

259   **Eggers had been surprised:** Swearingen, *Mystery of Hermann Goering's Suicide*, p. 157.

259   **"Is there money in it?":** Ibid., p. 158.

259   **he began writing a letter:** Ibid., p. 70.

260   **Gerecke returned to Goering's cell:** In writing about these final meetings with Goering, Gerecke's own affidavit to the military's investigators of Goering's suicide is at odds with his later telling of the tale. In later writings, he conflated two separate meetings on the final two nights of Goering's life into one meeting on the final night. In describing it here, I've restored the two-night sequence under the logic that what the chaplain told investigators in the hours immediately after the events was more accurate than what he wrote down from memory years later.

260   **He would watch Gerecke pray:** Persico, *Nuremberg*, p. 420.

260   **more depressed than he had earlier:** Gerecke, "My Assignment."

260   **"Surrender your heart . . .":** *Report of the Board Proceedings in Case of Hermann Goering (Suicide), Nuremberg, Germany*, October 1946.

260   **to make fun of the creation story:** Gerecke, "My Assignment."

261   **"This is what Jesus said . . .":** Gerecke, Toastmasters.

261   **" . . . When one is dead, . . .":** Gerecke, "My Assignment."

261   **"Pastor, I believe in God . . .":** Stokes, "St. Louis Chaplain Tells of Rushing."

261   **Gerecke was astonished:** Gerecke and Sinclair, "I Walked the Gallows."

263   **"when a priest consecrates . . .":** David C. Steinmetz quoted in Lindberg, *European Reformations*, p. 186.

263   **"It is one thing . . .":** Martin Luther in Placher, *Readings in the History of Christian Theology*, p. 25.

263   **here's what Christ said:** Travis Scholl interview.

264   **"the Holy Supper the two essences . . .":** Book of Concord, VII.37.

264   **"Herr Reichsmarshal . . .":** Gerecke and Sinclair, "I Walked the Gallows," and Gerecke, "Toastmasters."

265   **Gerecke knew Goering was:** Stokes, "St. Louis Chaplain Tells of Rushing."

265   **wanted to go through the motions:** The conversation between Gerecke and Goering is drawn from Gerecke and Sinclair, "I Walked the Gallows," Gerecke, "My Assignment," and Gerecke, "Toastmasters."

265   **Goering read in bed:** Unless otherwise noted, the narrative of Goering's suicide is drawn from the *Report of the Board Proceedings in Case of Hermann Goering (Suicide), Nuremberg, Germany*, October 1946.

266   **and felt for a pulse:** Stokes, "St. Louis Chaplain Tells of Rushing."

266   **"The blood of Jesus Christ . . .":** Gerecke, Toastmasters; and Gerecke and Sinclair, "I Walked the Gallows."

267   **"He's dead . . ."**: Tusa and Tusa, *Nuremberg Trial*, p. 483.

267   **Within an hour**: Swearingen, *Mystery of Hermann Goering's Suicide*, p. 92.

267   **"denied every fundamental doctrine . . ."**: Gerecke, "Monthly Report of Chaplains," October 1946.

267   **pastors later criticized Gerecke**: Hank Gerecke interview, 2 February 2008 and 30 June 2011.

268   **"If I blundered . . ."**: Gerecke, "My Assignment."

268   **"Would that I be shot!"**: Goering, "To The Allied Control Council," 11 October 1946.

268   **"I have always kept the poison capsule . . ."**: Ibid., "To the Commandant," 11 October 1946.

268   **"My heart's only love"**: Ibid., "My heart's only love," 11 October 1946.

269   **" . . . I had to do it this way . . ."**: Ibid., "Dear Pastor Gerecke," 11 October 1946.

269   **The Russians were especially suspicious**: Hank Gerecke interview, 4 January 2008.

269   **Goering's suicide was a "craven" act**: Gerecke and Sinclair, "I Walked the Gallows."

269   **briefly considered carrying Goering's body**: Swearingen, *Mystery of Hermann Goering's Suicide*, p. 79.

269   **At 11:30 P.M.**: Tilles, *By the Neck Until Dead*, p. 129.

269   **If they wanted to witness**: "Army Takes Bodies."

270   **Guards had been given orders**: Tusa and Tusa, *Nuremberg Trial*, p. 482.

270   **Andrus ordered a guard**: Andrus and Zwar, *I Was the Nuremberg Jailer*, p. 156.

270   **It was a cold night**: Tusa and Tusa, *Nuremberg Trial*, p. 482.

270   **checked each person's pass**: Tilles, *By the Neck Until Dead*, pp. 130–131.

270   **without handcuffs**: Tusa and Tusa, *Nuremberg Trial*, p. 485.

270   **would hold the prisoner**: Tilles, *By the Neck Until Dead*, p. 131.

271   **Death by the rope**: Conot, *Justice at Nuremberg*, p. 505.

271   **"Ribbentrop!"**: Speer, *Spandau*, p. 10.

271   **Gerecke entered the cell**: Gerecke, "My Assignment."

271   **"Follow me . . ."**: Andrus and Zwar, *I Was the Nuremberg Jailer*, p. 158.

271   **reverberating in the corridor**: Speer, *Spandau*, pp. 10–11.

271   **Andrus led Ribbentrop out**: Persico, *Nuremberg*, p. 425, and Gerecke and Sinclair, "I Walked the Gallows."

271   **"It was a long walk . . ."**: Andrus and Zwar, *I Was the Nuremberg Jailer*, p. 158.

271   **Ribbentrop returned the gesture**: Persico, *Nuremberg*, p. 425.

271   **dusty, grimy room**: Tilles, *By the Neck Until Dead*, p. 132, and Tusa and Tusa, *Nuremberg Trial*, p. 482.

271   **He had overseen these prisoners**: Persico, *Nuremberg*, p. 425.

272   **sitting at the eight folding tables**: Tilles, *By the Neck Until Dead*, p. 132.

272   **"I'll see you again"**: Gerecke, "My Assignment."

272   **Woods pulled the hangman's lever**: Tilles, *By the Neck Until Dead*, p. 133.

272   **Gerecke and O'Connor walked out**: Gerecke, "My Assignment."

272   **"Keitel!"**: Speer, *Spandau*, p. 11.

272   **"my friend"**: Gerecke, Toastmasters.

272 **" . . . drenched with his tears . . ."**: Gerecke and Sinclair, "I Walked the Gallows."

272 **hummed the melody:** Gerecke, Toastmasters.

273 **Keitel dropped . . . Keitel was pronounced dead:** Tilles, *By the Neck Until Dead*, pp. 133–134.

273 **" . . . Good luck, Germany":** Taylor, *Anatomy of the Nuremberg Trials*, p. 610.

273 **complexion pasty:** Tilles, *By the Neck Until Dead*, p. 134.

273 **"No, thank you":** Gerecke, "My Assignment."

274 **a cloud of smoke:** Tilles, *By the Neck Until Dead*, p. 135.

274 **from the service of Christ:** O'Connor, Letter to Norman Frank, 21 October 1946.

274 **nearly fainted from the stress:** Hank Gerecke interview, 21 October 2009.

274 **"for the kindness . . .":** Taylor, *Anatomy of the Nuremberg Trials*, p. 610.

274 **"May Jesus have mercy . . .":** O'Connor, Letter to Norman Frank.

274 **"Heil Hitler . . .":** Tilles, *By the Neck Until Dead*, p. 135.

275 **"For God's sake, Julius . . .":** Hank Gerecke interview, 21 October 2009.

275 **Streicher screamed instead:** Taylor, *Anatomy of the Nuremberg Trials*, p. 610.

275 **Woods had adjusted Streicher's noose:** Tilles, *By the Neck Until Dead*, p. 136.

275 **"I felt I could not go on":** Gerecke, "My Assignment."

275 **Sauckel fell through the trapdoor:** Tilles, *By the Neck Until Dead*, p. 137.

275 **as if addressing his troops:** Harris, *Tyranny on Trial*, p. 487.

275 **the final man, Seyss-Inquart:** Tilles, *By the Neck Until Dead*, p. 137.

275 **guards brought Goering's body:** Ibid., p. 138.

276 **"committal prayers":** Gerecke, "My Assignment."

276 **photographing the bodies:** Conot, *Justice at Nuremberg*, p. 507.

276 **No photographs of anyone:** Tilles, *By the Neck Until Dead*, p. 138.

276 **astonished them:** Gerecke, Toastmasters.

276 **breaking their noses:** Taylor, *Anatomy of the Nuremberg Trials*, p. 611.

276 **a final blessing:** Gerecke, Toastmasters.

276 **a special Mass for mourning:** O'Connor, Letter to Norman Frank.

276 **the favor Keitel asked of him:** "Chaplain Gerecke Urges Aid to Europe."

276 **and at 4:00 A.M.:** "Army Takes Bodies."

276 **army six-by-six trucks:** Persico, *Nuremberg*, p. 429.

276 **The trucks left Nuremberg:** "Army Takes Bodies."

277 **breaking down the gallows:** Tilles, *By the Neck Until Dead*, p. 139.

277 **instructed them to clean:** Speer, *Spandau*, p. 11.

277 **"the gross hates and cruelties . . .":** Gerecke, "My Assignment."

277 **"a blessing to the world . . .":** Gerecke and Sinclair, "I Walked the Gallows."

277 **"died as penitent sinners . . .":** Gerecke, "Monthly Report of Chaplains," October 1946.

277 **Gerecke thought about:** Gerecke, Toastmasters.

277 **"something marvelous happened":** Goering, *My Life with Goering*, p. 159.

278 **O'Connor wrote back:** O'Connor, Letter to Norman Frank.

278 **"Father, forgive them . . .":** Luke 23:34, NRSV.

278 **the core theological and ethical concept:** Williams, *Forgiveness*, p. 31.

278 **"And forgive us our sins . . .":** Luke 11:4, NRSV.

278 **eleven million noncombatants:** Snyder, "Hitler vs. Stalin."

279   **forgiveness requires that:** Dorff, "Religious Perspectives," p. 20.

279   **They must take an active role:** Rosen, "The Concept of Forgiveness in Judaism."

279   **"Then I acknowledged my sin . . .":** Psalm 32:5, Tanakh.

279   **"Because that people . . .":** Isaiah 29:13–14, Tanakh.

280   **that the wrongdoer earn:** Dorff, "Religious Perspectives," p. 32.

280   **" . . . proclaimed as a general truth . . .":** Bonhoeffer, *Cost of Discipleship*, p. 43.

280   **the tables are turned:** Dorff, "Religious Perspectives," p. 23.

280   **relationship between Jews and Germans:** Ibid., p. 36.

281   **"Are you a Jew?" she asked:** Wiesenthal's account is taken from his book, *The Sunflower: On the Possibilities and Limits of Forgiveness.*

287   **children of light:** Volf interview, 26 August 2010.

288   **relatives had a right:** Tusa and Tusa, *Nuremberg Trial*, p. 486.

288   **"dispersed secretly":** Schmidt, "11 Nazis Cremated."

288   **"to destroy absolutely . . .":** Ibid.

288   **"the crematorium was fired up . . .":** Conot, *Justice at Nuremberg*, p. 507.

288   **Ostfriedhof Cemetery:** Swearingen, *Mystery of Hermann Goering's Suicide*, p. 81.

288   **Goering's was marked:** Persico, *Nuremberg*, p. 429.

288   **eleven aluminum cylinders:** Swearingen, *Mystery of Hermann Goering's Suicide*, p. 81.

289   **home of a wealthy merchant:** Persico, *Nuremberg*, p. 429.

289   **they smashed the aluminum cylinders:** Ibid.

CHAPTER 11

290   **"Christ died for . . .":** NRSV.

290   **Gerecke received orders:** Suchara, Orders, Chaplain (Captain) Henry F. Gerecke.

290   **"sincere devotion to his faith . . .":** "List No. 86, Control Approval Symbol SPXOM–6-PO."

290   **"to continue his ministrations . . .":** Andrus, Letter to Chaplain Miller.

291   **Hank had been severely injured:** Hank Gerecke interview, 13 July 2011.

291   **"I won't need them again":** "Nuernberg Nazi Leaders Urged St. Louis Chaplain."

291   **to debrief the Office of the Chief of Chaplains:** Gerecke, "Monthly Report of Chaplains," December 1946.

292   **before a crowd of six hundred:** Ibid., January 1947.

292   **held in Gerecke's honor:** "Reception. Chaplain 'Major' Henry F. Gerecke." Program.

292   **" . . . some aid to the little folk . . .":** "Nuernberg Nazi Leaders Urged St. Louis Chaplain."

292   **"How very happy . . .":** Roschke, Letter to Henry F. Gerecke, 27 December 1946.

293   **"For all my own blunderings . . .":** Gerecke and Sinclair, "I Walked the Gallows."

293   **"Lord, lay some soul . . .":** Gerecke, Toastmasters.

293   **His work with most:** Gerecke, "Monthly Report of Chaplains," July and August 1948.

293   **urged them to attend synagogue:** Ibid., March 1947.

293   **doing what Gerecke called "homework":** Ibid., June 1948.

293   **" . . . whom the world wanted to forget":** "Pastor Henry F. Gerecke, 1950–1961."

294   **"Youth for Christ" Bible study:** Gerecke, "Monthly Report of Chaplains," November 1947.

294   **he began a bus service:** Ibid., January 1948.

294   **during his free time:** Ibid., April, May, and June 1947, and February 1948.

294   **" . . . that impressed me so much . . .":** Butch, Letter to Henry F. Gerecke, 10 May 1947.

294   **had pieced together a report:** Henry F. Gerecke, Letter to Chaplain Matthew Imrie, 26 March 1947.

294   **" . . . is too personal to divulge . . .":** Imrie, Letter to Henry F. Gerecke, 10 March 1947.

295   **"revealed intimate confidences . . .":** Ibid., Letter to Alfred P. Klausler, 22 April 1947.

295   **resubmitted it to the War Department:** Ibid., Letter to Henry F. Gerecke, 17 April 1947.

295   **Gerecke fumed at the hypocrisy:** Hank Gerecke interview, 30 June 2011.

295   **the War Department approved:** Edgerton, "Report entitled 'My Assignment with the International Military Tribunal as Spiritual Advisor to the High Nazi Leaders at Nurenberg, Germany, November 1945 to November 1946.'"

295   **even though he was pursued:** Brian Jordan interview.

295   **served as vice president of Siena:** Davies and Meilach, *Provincial Annals.*

296   **both preacher and confessor:** B. Hess, "Franciscan Mission."

296   **confessions of two murderers:** Brian Jordan interview.

296   **strain of being on his feet:** Maguire, Letter to "Brothers in St. Francis."

297   **took place on a Sunday evening:** Gordon, "Heritage Sunday."

298   **John Dillinger's gang:** "Frank Sinclair Dies; Reporter."

298   **calling Gerecke a "Nazi lover":** Hank Gerecke interview, 4 January 2008.

299   **Gerecke preached at St. John's:** Gordon, "Heritage Sunday."

299   **the Menard penitentiary:** Gerecke, "Agreement of Worker."

299   **a maximum-security facility:** "A Reel of Celluloid."

300   **Gerecke's work paid him little:** Gerecke, "Agreement of Worker."

300   **the chaplain tapped into television:** "A Reel of Celluloid."

300   **showing inmates 16 mm film:** Hodge, "Aid to a Prison Chaplain."

300   **The warden gave Gerecke permission:** "A Reel of Celluloid."

301   **tables bolted to the concrete floor:** Gordon, "Heritage Sunday."

301   **" . . . assurance of God's forgiveness":** Ibid.

301   **Ross Randolph, was a Christian man:** Hodge, "Aid to a Prison Chaplain."

301   **whom he considered "troubled":** Henry F. Gerecke, "Otto—No. 25,281," *The Lutheran Witness.*

302   **pleaded guilty to embezzling:** "Orville Hodge, Auditor Who Robbed State."

302   **$13 million today:** CPI.

303   **take charge of the politician:** Hodge, "Aid to a Prison Chaplain."

303   **piped Christian programming:** Ibid.

305   **preached during Lent:** Henry F. Gerecke, "Seven Words for Lent."

305   **"This was not the first mistake . . .":** O. P. Kretzmann, *The Pilgrim,* p. 44.

305　**when he had a heart attack:** Hank Gerecke interview, 13 July 2011.

306　**remember where they were:** Gordon, "Heritage Sunday."

306　**His official death announcement:** "In Memory of Rev. Henry F. Gerecke," Death Notice.

306　**"How quickly God can change your plans":** Gordon, "Heritage Sunday."

306　**Gerecke's body lay in state:** Blumenkamp, "Chaplain Henry F. Gerecke."

306　**The Boy Scouts set up chairs:** Gordon, "Heritage Sunday."

306　**more than a thousand:** Blumenkamp, "Chaplain Henry F. Gerecke."

306　**"No matter how many . . .":** Gordon, "Heritage Sunday."

306　**"For I was hungry . . .":** Matthew 25: 34–40, NRSV.

307　**"pens of the multitudes":** Blumenkamp, "Chaplain Henry F. Gerecke."

307　**Warden Ross Randolph called Alma:** "800 Menard Convicts."

EPILOGUE

309　**the narrowest point between:** "A Bit of a Chester History Lesson."

309　**they hoped to help furnish:** "800 Menard Convicts."

Bibliography

BOOKS

Alford, Kenneth D. *Nazi Plunder: Great Treasure Stories of World War II.* Cambridge, MA: Da Capo Press, 2008.

Andrus, Burton C., and Desmond Zwar. *I Was the Nuremberg Jailer.* New York: Tower Publications, 1969.

Army and Navy Chaplains Ordinariate. *United States Catholic Chaplains in the World War.* New York: ANCO, 1924.

Atrocities at Camp Mauthausen: A Visual Documentation of the Holocaust. Atglen, PA: Schiffer Publishing, Ltd., 2003.

Barrett, John Q. "Raphael Lemkin and 'Genocide' at Nuremberg, 1945–1946." In *The Genocide Convention Sixty Years After Its Adoption*, eds. Christoph Safferling and Eckart Conze. The Hague: T.M.C. Asser Press, 2010.

Barth, Karl. *Church Dogmatics, Vol. IV.1.* London: T&T Clark, 1956.

Bewley, Charles. *Hermann Göring and the Third Reich.* New York: The Devin-Adair Company, 1962.

Bird, Keith W. *Erich Raeder: Admiral of the Third Reich.* Annapolis: Naval Institute Press, 2006.

Bonhoeffer, Dietrich. *The Cost of Discipleship.* 1937. Trans. R. H. Fuller. New York: Macmillan, 1959. New York: Touchstone, 1995.

Brockmann, Stephen. *Nuremberg: The Imaginary Capital.* Rochester, New York: Camden House, 2006.

Brueggemann, Walter. *Genesis: A Bible Commentary for Teaching and Preaching.* Atlanta: John Knox Press, 1982.

Childs, Brevard S. *Introduction to the Old Testament as Scripture.* Philadelphia: Fortress Press, 1979.

Church of St. Sebald, Nuremberg. Nuremberg: Verlag Hans Carl GmbH, 2005.

Collins, David J. *Reforming Saints: Saints' Lives and Their Authors in Germany, 1470–1530.* Oxford: Oxford University Press, 2008.

Conot, Robert E. *Justice at Nuremberg.* New York: Carroll & Graf Publishers, Inc., 1984.

Craig, Berry. *11th Armored Division: Thunderbolt.* Paducah, KY: Turner Publishing Company, 1988.

Cross, Christopher. In collaboration with William R. Arnold. *Soldiers of God: The True Story of the U.S. Army Chaplains*. New York: E.P. Dutton & Company, 1945.

Davidson, Eugene. *The Trial of the Germans*. New York: The MacMillan Company, 1966.

DeBellis, Steven J. *100 Years of Reel Entertainment: How Wehrenberg Theaters Became the Longest-Running Picture Show in America*. St. Louis: Fred Wehrenberg Circuit of Theaters, Inc., 2006.

Drazin, Israel, and Cecil B. Currey. *For God and Country: The History of a Constitutional Challenge to the Army Chaplaincy*. Hoboken, NJ: KTAV Publishing House, Inc., 1995.

Erasmus. *Enchiridon*. Trans. John P. Dolan. *The Essential Erasmus*. New York: Penguin Books USA (Meridian), 1964.

Evans, Richard J. *The Third Reich at War*. New York: The Penguin Press, 2009.

Folktales of Israel. Ed. Dov Noy. Trans. Gene Baharav. Chicago: University of Chicago Press, 1963.

Frank, Niklas. *In the Shadow of the Reich*. New York: Alfred A. Knopf, 1991.

Fritzsche, Hans. *The Sword in the Scales, as Told to Hildegard Springer*. Trans. Diana Pyke and Heinrich Fraenkel. London: Allan Wingate, 1953

Gaskin, Hilary. *Eyewitnesses at Nuremberg*. London: Arms and Armour Press, 1990.

Gerecke, Henry F. "Sickbed Sidelights." In *Marching Side by Side: Stories from Lutheran Chaplains on the Far-Flung Battlefronts*, ed. Frederick C. Proehl. St. Louis: Concordia Publishing House, 1945.

Gilbert, G. M. *Nuremberg Diary*. Toronto: Signette/New American Library, 1947.

Goebel, Gert. *Länger Als Ein Menschenleben in Missouri*. St. Louis: Missouri Historical Society, 1877. Trans. Martin W. Heinrichsmeyer, 1956.

Goering, Emmy. *My Life with Goering*. London: David Bruce & Watson, 1972.

Goldensohn, Leon. *The Nuremberg Interviews*. Ed. Robert Gellately. New York: Alfred A. Knopf, 2004.

Grossmith, F. T. *The Cross and the Swastika*. Boise, ID: Pacific Press Publishing Association, 1984.

Harris, Whitney R. *Murder by the Millions: Rudolf Hoess at Auschwitz*. Jamestown, NY: The Robert H. Jackson Center, Inc., 2005.

———. *Tyranny on Trial: The Evidence at Nuremberg*. 2nd ed. New York: Barnes & Noble Books, 1995.

Holy Bible. New Revised Standard Version. New York: HarperCollins, 1993.

Hsia, R. Po-chia. *The Myth of Ritual Murder: Jews and Magic in Reformation Germany*. New Haven: Yale University Press, 1990.

Keitel, Wilhelm. *The Memoirs of Field-Marshal Keitel*. Ed. Walter Gorlitz. Trans. David Irving. New York: Stein and Day, 1966.

Kelley, Douglas M. *22 Cells at Nuremberg: A Psychiatrist Examines the Nazi Criminals*. New York: Greenberg, 1947.

Kershaw, Ian. *Hitler, 1936–45: Nemesis*. New York: Norton & Company, 2000.

Kootz, Wolfgang. Revised and expanded by Karin Ecker. *Nürnberg*. 3rd ed. Lübeck, Germany: Schöning Verlag, 2006.

Kretzmann, O. P. *The Pilgrim*. St. Louis, MO: Concordia Publishing House, 1944.

Lapide, Pinchas. *Von Kain bis Judas: Ungewohnte Einsichten zu Sünde und Schuld*. Munich: Gütersloher Verlagshaus, 1994.

Lindberg, Carter. *The European Reformations*. Malden, MA: Blackwell Publishing, 1996.

Luther, Martin. *The Babylonian Captivity of the Church*. Trans. A. T. W. Steinhäuser. Philadelphia: Fortress Press, 1959.

———. "The Freedom of a Christian." Trans. W. A. Lambert. *Three Treatises*. Minneapolis: Fortress Press, 1957.

Marsálek, Hans, and Kurt Hacker. *Concentration Camp Mauthausen: National Socialist Concentration Camps Mauthausen, Gusen, Ebensee und Melk*. Trans. Paul Catty. Vienna: Österreichische Lagergemeinschaft Mauthausen, 1995.

McLaughlin, William G., Jr. *Billy Sunday Was His Real Name*. Chicago: University of Chicago Press, 1955.

McCloskey, H. J. *God and Evil*. The Hague: Martinus Nijhoff, 1974.

Meyer, Carl S. *Log Cabin to Luther Tower*. Madison, WI: Concordia Publishing House, 1965.

Miller, J. Maxwell, and John H. Hayes. *A History of Ancient Israel and Judah*. Philadelphia: The Westminster Press, 1986.

Miller, Stephen R. *The New American Commentary—Daniel, Vol. 18*. Nashville: B&H Publishing Group, 1994.

Mosely, Leonard. *The Reich Marshal: A Biography of Hermann Goering*. Garden City, New York: Doubleday & Co., 1974.

Neave, Airey. *On Trial at Nuremberg*. Boston: Little, Brown and Company, 1978.

Overy, Richard. "The Nuremberg Trials: International Law in the Making." In *Nuremberg to the Hague: The Future of International Criminal Justice*, ed. Philippe Sands, 1–29. Cambridge: Cambridge University Press, 2003.

Pernoud, Régine. *Martin of Tours: Soldier, Bishop, and Saint*. San Francisco: Ignatius Press, 2006.

Persico, Joseph E. *Nuremberg: Infamy on Trial*. New York: Penguin Books, 1995.

Pike, David Wingeate. *Spaniards in the Holocaust: Mauthausen, The Horror on the Danube*. London: Routledge, 2000.

Placher, William C. *Readings in the History of Christian Theology, Vol. 2: From the Reformation to the Present*. Philadelphia: The Westminster Press, 1988.

Posner, Gerald L. *Hitler's Children: Sons and Daughters of Leaders of the Third Reich Talk About Their Fathers Themselves*. New York: Random House, 1991.

Price, Jay M. *El Dorado: Legacy of an Oil Boom*. Charleston, SC: Arcadia Publishing, 2005.

Raeder, Erich. *My Life*. Trans. Henry W. Drexel. Annapolis: United States Naval Institute, 1960.

Remley, Paul G. *Old English Biblical Verse*. Cambridge: Cambridge University Press, 1996.

Schacht, Hjalmar. *Confessions of "The Old Wizard."* Trans. Diana Pyke. Boston: Houghton Mifflin Company, 1956.

Schieber, Martin. *Nuremberg: The Medieval City*. Nuremberg: Geschichte Für Alle e.V., 2009.

Schirach, Henriette von. *The Price of Glory*. Trans. Willi Frischauer. London: Frederick Muller, Ltd., 1960.

Smith, Bradley F. *Reaching Judgment at Nuremberg*. New York: Basic Books, 1977.

Speer, Albert. *Spandau: The Secret Diaries*. Trans. Richard and Clara Winston. New York: MacMillan Publishing, 1976.

Steigmann-Gall, Richard. *The Holy Reich: Nazi Conceptions of Christianity, 1914–1945*. Cambridge: Cambridge University Press, 2003.

Steinmetz, David C. *Luther in Context*. 2nd ed. Grand Rapids, MI: Baker Academic, 2002.

Stelmachowicz, M. J. *Johnnie Heritage, 1893–1976*. Winfield, KS: St. John's College, 1976.

Steward, Hal D. *Thunderbolt: The History of the 11th Armored Division*. Nashville: The Battery Press, 1948.

Strickland, Debra Higgs. *Saracens, Demons & Jews: Making Monsters in Medieval Art.* Princeton: Princeton University Press, 2003.

Swearingen, Ben E. *The Mystery of Hermann Goering's Suicide.* New York: Harcourt Brace, 1985.

Taylor, Telford. *The Anatomy of the Nuremberg Trials.* New York: Alfred A. Knopf, 1992.

"Teaching of the Twelve Apostles, Commonly Called the Didache." In *Early Christian Fathers.* Ed. Cyril C. Richardson. New York: Touchstone, 1996.

Tilles, Stanley. *By the Neck Until Dead: The Gallows of Nuremberg,* with Jeffrey Denhart. Bedford, IN: JoNa Books, 1999.

Tusa, Ann, and John Tusa. *The Nuremberg Trial.* New York: Atheneum, 1984. Ed. Notable Trials Library, 1990.

Venzke, Roger R. *Confidence in Battle, Inspiration in Peace: The United States Army Chaplaincy, 1945–1975.* Washington, DC: Office of the Chief of Chaplains, Department of the Army, 1977.

Vetlesen, Arne Johan. *Evil and Human Agency: Understanding Collective Evildoing.* New York: Cambridge University Press, 2005.

Volf, Miroslav. *The End of Memory: Remembering Rightly in a Violent World.* Grand Rapids, MI: Eerdmans Publishing Company, 2006.

———. *Exclusion & Embrace: A Theological Exploration of Identity, Otherness, and Reconciliation.* Nashville: Abingdon Press, 1996.

———. *Free of Charge: Giving and Forgiving in a Culture Stripped of Grace.* Grand Rapids, MI: Zondervan, 2005.

Volz, Carl A. *The Medieval Church: From the Dawn of the Middle Ages to the Eve of the Reformation.* Nashville: Abingdon Press, 1997.

Waller, James. *Becoming Evil: How Ordinary People Commit Genocide and Mass Killing.* 2nd ed. New York: Oxford University Press, 2007.

West, Rebecca. "Greenhouse with Cyclamens I (1946)." *A Train of Powder.* New York: The Viking Press, 1955.

Westermann, Claus. *Genesis 1–11: A Commentary.* Trans. John J. Scullion, S.J. Minneapolis: Augsburg Publishing House, 1984.

Wiesenthal, Simon. *The Sunflower: On the Possibilities and Limits of Forgiveness.* Symposium Ed. Harry James Cargas and Bonny V. Fetterman. 2nd ed. New York: Schocken Books, 1997.

Wistrich, Robert. *Who's Who in Nazi Germany.* London: Weidenfeld and Nicolson, 1982.

Wray, T. J., and Gregory Mobley. *The Birth of Satan: Tracing the Devil's Biblical Roots.* New York: Palgrave Macmillan, 2005.

ARTICLES, COLLECTIONS, DISSERTATIONS, DOCUMENTS, AND LETTERS

Aachen's Wanted Nazis. n.d. Record of the Office of the United States Commissioner, U.N. War Crimes Commission. NM–66. Entry 52K. File 153: United Nations War Crimes Commission, Research Officer. General Correspondence (Red Files). National Archives Collection of World War II War Crimes Records (RG238). National Archives II, College Park, Maryland.

"A Bit of a Chester History Lesson." City of Chester. www.chesterill.com/index.php?id=23.

"Alphabetical List of Graduates, 1898–1955." St. John's College & Academy, Winfield, Kansas.

Andrus, B.C. Letter to Chaplain Miller. Chaplains Reports and "201" Files. Entry 484. File: Gerecke, Henry F. Records of the Office of the Chief of Chaplains (RG247). National Archives II, College Park, Maryland.

Andrus, Burton C. Letter to the Recorder, San Diego Commandery No. 25. 15 March 1945. Burton C. Andrus Collection. Box 3. Folder 29. U.S. Army Military History Institute. United States Army War College. Carlisle, Pennsylvania.

———. Letter to Katherine Andrus. 18 May 1945. Burton C. Andrus Collection. Box 7. Folder 9. U.S. Army Military History Institute. United States Army War College. Carlisle, Pennsylvania.

———. Letter to Katherine Andrus. 5 April 1945. Burton C. Andrus Collection. Box 7. Folder 9. U.S. Army Military History Institute. United States Army War College. Carlisle, Pennsylvania.

———. "Prisoner Routine, Nurnberg Jail." Memo. Burton C. Andrus Collection. Box 33. Folder 74. U.S. Army Military History Institute. United States Army War College. Carlisle, Pennsylvania.

Andrus, Burton C. Untitled manuscript draft "Gerecke." n.d. Burton C. Andrus Collection. Box 52. Folder 34. U.S. Army Military History Institute. United States Army War College. Carlisle, Pennsylvania.

Armstrong, Warren Bruce. "The Organization, Function and Contribution of the Chaplaincy in the United States Army, 1861–1865." Ph.D. diss. University of Michigan, 1964.

Army and Navy Commission of the Evangelical Lutheran Synod of Missouri, Ohio and Other States. Chaplain Endorsement Application, 8 April 1943. Gerecke Collection. Concordia Historical Institute.

"Army Issues Call for 859 Chaplains." *New York Times.* 9 September 1943.

"Army Takes Bodies of Nazis from Jail." *New York Times.* 16 October 1946.

Arnold, William R. "Memorandum For: The Adjutant General." 24 August 1943. Chaplains Reports and "201" Files. Entry 484. File: Gerecke, Henry F. Records of the Office of the Chief of Chaplains (RG247). National Archives II, College Park, Maryland.

———. "My dear Chaplain." Letter. 19 August 1943. Chaplains Reports and "201" Files. Entry 484. File: Gerecke, Henry F. Records of the Office of the Chief of Chaplains (RG247). National Archives II, College Park, Maryland.

"Baptism, Confirmation and Death Records." Zion Lutheran Church, Gordonville, Missouri. Cape Girardeau County Archive Center.

Barrett, John Q. "Civilization Opens Its Case at Nuremberg." The Jackson List: http://www.stjohns.edu/academics/graduate/law/faculty/profiles/Barrett/Jackson List.sju. November 21, 2010.

———. "Thanksgiving in Nuremberg (1945)." The Jackson List: http://www.stjohns.edu/academics/graduate/law/faculty/profiles/Barrett/JacksonList.sju. November 25, 2008.

Bender, Alma. Death Certificate. 7 January 1921. File No. 355742. Missouri State Board of Health.

Bender, Jacob. Death Certificate. DOD 5 February 1922. File No. 6296. Missouri State Board of Health.

Bender, Jacob, and Margaretha Bucher. Missouri Marriage Records, 1805–2002. 27 August 1870. St. Louis, Missouri, 139.

"Bishop Arnold, 83, Aide to Spellman." *New York Times.* 8 January 1965.

Blumenkamp, Edwin. "Chaplain Henry F. Gerecke." *Der Lutheraner.* 7 November 1961.

Brauer, Oscar P. Letter to Army and Navy Commission. 1 June 1943. Henry F. Gerecke Collection. Concordia Historical Institute. St. Louis, Missouri.

Brinsfield, John W., Jr., Tierian Cash, and Thomas Malek-Jones. "U.S. Military Chaplains." In *A Companion to American Military History,* Vol. II, ed. James C. Bradford, 722–732. Malden, MA: Blackwell Publishing, 2010.

Bulletin: Academic Year 1917–1918. Winfield, KS: St. John's Lutheran College, 1917.

Butch. Letter to Henry F. Gerecke. 10 May 1947. Private collection of Henry H. Gerecke.

Callahan, Adalbert, O.F.M., ed. *The Provincial Annals,* Vol. IV, No. 3. New York: Province of the Most Holy Name, July 1943.

Cape Girardeau County probate abstracts, 1808–1919. Box 78, No. 1445. Cape Girardeau County Archive Center, Jackson, Missouri.

Casey, A. J. "Report of Entry on Active Duty." 18 August 1943. Chaplains Reports and "201" Files. Entry 484. File: Gerecke, Henry F. Records of the Office of the Chief of Chaplains (RG247). National Archives II, College Park, Maryland.

———. "Report of Entry on Active Duty." 13 June 1943. Chaplains Reports and "201" Files. Entry 484. File: O'Connor, Sixtus Richard. Records of the Office of the Chief of Chaplains (RG247). National Archives II, College Park, Maryland.

"The Chaplain as Counselor." Pamphlet No. 16–60. Department of the Army, 1958.

"Chaplain Gerecke Urges Aid to Europe." *St. Louis Post-Dispatch.* 9 January 1947.

"A Chronicle of the United States Army Chaplain School During the Second World War, the First Two Years." n.p., n.d. [Chaplain School Library, Fort Jackson, South Carolina.]

Conley, Edgar T., Jr. "Award of Bronze Star Medal." 19 May 1945. Chaplains Reports and "201" Files. Entry 484. File: O'Connor, Sixtus Richard. Records of the Office of the Chief of Chaplains (RG247). National Archives II, College Park, Maryland.

Consolidated Lists of Civil War Draft Registrations, 1863–1865. NM–65, entry 172, 620 Volumes. Records of the Provost Marshal General's Bureau (Civil War), Record Group 110. National Archives, Washington, D.C.

"Convention relative to the Treatment of Prisoners of War." Geneva July 27, 1929. www .icrc.org/ihl.nsf/full/305?opendocument.

Crowley, Paul. "Evil." In *HarperCollins Encyclopedia of Catholicism,* ed. Richard P. McBrien. New York: HarperCollins, 1995.

Daniel, E. Clifton, Jr. Letter to Col. Joseph Hodgson. 4 April 1945. Record of the Office of the United States Commissioner, U.N. War Crimes Commission. NM–66. Entry 52K. File 150: Miscellaneous. General Correspondence (Red Files). National Archives Collection of World War II War Crimes Records (RG238). National Archives II, College Park, Maryland.

"Da Prinzeregentheater." prinzregententheater.de/de/geschichte/zusammenfassung.html.

Davies, Julian A., O.F.M., and Michael D. Meilach, O.F.M., eds. *The Provincial Annals,* Vol. XXXIII. New York: Province of the Most Holy Name of Jesus, 1984.

Dean, Gordon. "The statement which appears below was furnished to the Overseas Branch of OWI as a basis for their Directive on Policy which was distributed 22 May 1945." Memo. n.d. TTP-CLS: Series 4; Sub-series 1–2. Box No. 1, Folder 9. Telford Taylor Papers, Arthur W. Diamond Law Library, Columbia University Law School, New York, New York.

"Death Marches." United States Holocaust Memorial and Museum. ushmm.org/wlc/en/article.php?ModuleId=10005162.

"Defiant to the Last." United Press via the *New York Times*. 16 October 1946.

Dorff, Elliot N. "Religious Perspectives on Forgiveness." With Mark S. Rye, Kenneth I. Pargament, M. Amir Ali, Guy L. Beck, Charles Hallisey, Vasudha Narayanan, and James G. Williams. In *Forgiveness: Theory, Research and Practice*, ed. Michael E. McCullough, Pargament and Carl E. Thoresen. New York: The Guildford Press, 2000.

Eastern State Penitentiary. http://www.easternstate.org/learn/timeline.

Eckstein, Benyamin. "Mauthausen." In *Encyclopedia of the Holocaust*, Vol. 3, ed. Israel Gutman. New York: MacMillan Publishing Company, 1990.

Edgerton, Joseph S. "Report entitled 'My Assignment with the International Military Tribunal as Spiritual Advisor to the High Nazi Leaders at Nurenberg, Germany, November 1945 to November 1946' by Chaplain (Major) Henry F. Gerecke, for use by the Army and Navy Commission of the Missouri Synod and publication in the WALTHER LEAGUE MESSENGER." Memo. 16 April 1947

"800 Menard Convicts File Past Bier of Prison Chaplain." Associated Press. 14 October 1961.

European Theater of Operations Headquarters. "Standing Operating Procedure No. 49: Employment of Prisoners of War." Memo. 9 May 1945. General Administrative Records. 1942–1957. Judge Advocate Division, War Crimes Branch. File: "Old File Copies SOP's." HM1989. Box 10, "WC Directives (Maj. Haefele) thru Nuremberg Trials." Records of United States Army Europe (USAEUR). Record Group 549. National Archives II, College Park, Maryland.

Face to Face with Satan. Billy Sunday Collection. Grace College and Seminary. Winona Lake, Indiana.

For God and Country. Short film. Perf. Ronald Reagan. U.S. War Department, 1943.

"Frank Sinclair Dies; Reporter." *Milwaukee Sentinel*. 19 February 1973.

Freund, Florian, and Harald Greifeneder. Mauthausen Memorial. en.mauthausen memorial.at/.

Fritzsche, et al. Letter to Alma Gerecke. 14 June 1946. Henry F. Gerecke Collection. Concordia Historical Institute. St. Louis, Missouri.

Gaeth, Arthur. "Witness Tells of Nazis' Last Hours in Cells." *St. Louis Post-Dispatch*. 16 October 1946.

Galbraith, John Kenneth. "The Cure at Mondorf Spa." *Life*. 22 October 1945.

Geist, Thomas V. "My Experience as Assistant to Chaplain Henry F. Gerecke." Unpublished manuscript, n.d.

Geneva Convention Relative to the Protection of Civilian Persons in Time of War (Geneva IV).

Geneva Convention Relative to the Treatment of Prisoners of War (Geneva III).

Gerecke, Carlton. U.S. World War II Army Enlistment Records, 1938–1946. National Archives and Records Administration.

Gerecke, Caroline. Death Certificate. Filed 17 August 1948. File No. 25665. Missouri State Board of Health.

Gerecke, Henry F. "Agreement of Worker to Participate in the Pension Fund." Henry F. Gerecke Collection. Concordia Historical Institute. Concordia Seminary. St. Louis, Missouri.

————. "Assignment with the International Military Tribunal as Spiritual Advisor." *Army and Navy Chaplain.* July–August 1947.

————. City Mission Notes, 1937–43. Henry F. Gerecke Collection. Concordia Historical Institute. Concordia Seminary. St. Louis, Missouri.

————. CV. Henry F. Gerecke Collection. Concordia Historical Institute. Concordia Seminary. St. Louis, Missouri. 1958.

————. "Here's a Little Background . . ." n.d. Henry F. Gerecke Collection. Concordia Historical Institute. Concordia Seminary. St. Louis, Missouri.

————. "I Thirst." Private collection of Henry H. Gerecke.

————. Letter to Chief of Chaplains. 26 June 1943. Chaplains Reports and "201" Files. Entry 484. Records of the Office of the Chief of Chaplains (RG247). National Archives II, College Park, Maryland.

————. Letter to Chaplain Matthew Imrie. 26 March 1947. Chaplains Reports and "201" Files. Entry 484. Records of the Office of the Chief of Chaplains (RG247). National Archives II, College Park, Maryland.

————. Letter to Dorothy Williams. 19 October 1944. Henry F. Gerecke Collection. Concordia Historical Institute. Concordia Seminary. St. Louis, Missouri.

————. Letter to Mildred Gerecke. 13 March 1947. Private collection of Henry H. Gerecke.

————. "My Assignment with the International Military Tribunal at Nuernberg, Germany." (Early draft of the *Army and Navy Chaplain* article, circa 1946.)

————. Letter to Alma Gerecke. 18 June 1946. Gerecke Collection. Concordia Historical Institute. Concordia Seminary. St. Louis, Missouri.

————. "Monthly Report of Chaplains." [Specific month indicated in citation.] Chaplains Reports and "201" Files, 1946-48. Geiger, Leo, thru Gibbons, Robert G. Entry 484, Box 120. File 202: "Gerecke, Henry." Records of the Office of the Chief of Chaplains (RG247). National Archives II, College Park, Maryland.

————. Orders, Chaplain. "S.O.196, Par. 20, W.D." Chaplains Reports and "201" Files. Entry 484. Records of the Office of the Chief of Chaplains (RG247). National Archives II, College Park, Maryland.

————. "Otto—No. 25,281." *The Lutheran Witness.* n.d.

————. "Please rush German literature . . ." 24 October 1944. Henry F. Gerecke Collection. Concordia Historical Institute. Concordia Seminary. St. Louis, Missouri.

————. "Seven Words for Lent." Private collection of Henry H. Gerecke

————. "The Prisoner." Sermon notes. Private collection of Henry H. Gerecke.

————. Telegram to Paul Kretzmann. 24 October 1944. Collection of Concordia Seminary, St. Louis, Missouri.

————. Toastmasters speech. n.d. (1950s) Evansville, Indiana. St. John Lutheran Church. Chester, Illinois.

————. Transcript, 1914–1918. St. John's College. Winfield, Kansas.

————. V-Mail to Dorothy Williams. 10 May 1944. Henry F. Gerecke Collection. Concordia Historical Institute. Concordia Seminary. St. Louis, Missouri.

Gerecke, Henry F., and Merle Sinclair. "I Walked the Gallows with the Nazi Chiefs." *Saturday Evening Post.* 1 September 1951.

Gerecke, Henry H. U.S. World War II Army Enlistment Records, 1938–1946. National Archives and Records Administration.

Gerecke, Herman W. Death Certificate. Filed 11 November 1942. File No. 33403. Missouri State Board of Health.

———. Marriage Certificate. To Caroline Kelpe. Filed 7 November 1892. Randol Township, Cape Girardeau, Missouri. Henry R. English, recorder.

Gerecke, Leonora. Death Certificate. 7 January 1921. File No. 355742. Missouri State Board of Health.

Goering, Hermann. "Dear Pastor Gerecke." 11 October 1946. Telford Taylor Papers, Series 20; Subseries 1; Box No. 2, Folder 19. Arthur W. Diamond Law Library, Columbia University Law School, New York, New York.

———. "To the Allied Control Council." 11 October 1946. Telford Taylor Papers, Series 20; Subseries 1; Box No. 2, Folder 19. Arthur W. Diamond Law Library, Columbia University Law School, New York, New York.

———. "My heart's only love." 11 October 1946. Telford Taylor Papers, Series 20; Subseries 1; Box No. 2, Folder 19. Arthur W. Diamond Law Library, Columbia University Law School, New York, New York.

———. "To the Commandant." 11 October 1946. Telford Taylor Papers, Series 20; Subseries 1; Box No. 2, Folder 19. Arthur W. Diamond Law Library, Columbia University Law School, New York, New York.

Gordon, Eileen. "Heritage Sunday." 1985. Henry F. Gerecke Collection. Concordia Historical Institute, St. Louis, Missouri.

Gould's Street and Avenue Directory of St. Louis, Red-Blue Book. St. Louis: Polk Gould Directory Co.

Gruhne, Fritz. Auswandererlisten des ehemaligen Herzogtums Braunschweig; ohne Stadt Braunschweig und Landkreis Holzminden, 1846–1871, Brunswick, Germany: Braunchschweigeischen Geschichtsverein, 1971.

Hess, Bede. "The Franciscan Mission." *Report of the Ninth Annual Meeting.* The Franciscan Educational Conference. Athol Springs, New York. September 1927.

History of Jackson, Missouri and Surrounding Counties. Paducah, KY: Turner Publishing Co., 2002. Cape Girardeau County Archive Center, Jackson, Missouri.

"History of the LCMS." Lutheran Church–Missouri Synod, www.lcms.org/page.aspx ?pid=463.

Hodenfield, G. K. "St. Louis Chaplain Offers a Theory." *St. Louis Post-Dispatch.* 16 October 1946.

Hodge, Orville. "Aid to a Prison Chaplain." *This Day,* October 1961.

Holls, H. "Rev. F. W. Herzberger: Pioneer City Missionary of the Lutheran Church." n.d. Henry F. Gerecke Collection. Concordia Historical Institute, St. Louis, Missouri.

Hourihan, William J. "U.S. Army Chaplain Ministry to German War Criminals at Nuremberg, 1945–1946." *The Army Chaplaincy,* Winter–Spring 2000.

Imrie, Matthew H. Letter to Henry F. Gerecke. 10 March 1947. Chaplains Reports and "201" Files. Entry 484. Records of the Office of the Chief of Chaplains (RG247). National Archives II, College Park, Maryland.

———. Letter to Henry F. Gerecke. 31 March 1947. Chaplains Reports and "201" Files. Entry 484. Records of the Office of the Chief of Chaplains (RG247). National Archives II, College Park, Maryland.

———. Letter to Henry F. Gerecke. 17 April 1947. Chaplains Reports and "201" Files. Entry 484. Records of the Office of the Chief of Chaplains (RG247). National Archives II, College Park, Maryland.

———. Letter to Alfred P. Klausler. 22 April 1947. Chaplains Reports and "201" Files. Entry 484. Records of the Office of the Chief of Chaplains (RG247). National Archives II, College Park, Maryland.

"Imprisoned Nazi Leaders Still Cherish Memory of U.S. Chaplain They Met During Nuremberg Trial." National Catholic Welfare Conference News Service. 16 September 1954.

"In Memory of Rev. Henry F. Gerecke." Death Notice. Collection of Irene Kornmeier.

"Installation of the Rev. Henry F. Gerecke" Program. 9 July 1950. Collection of Irene Kornmeier.

Jackson, Robert H. Letter to Lord Wright of Durley. 5 July 1945. Record of the Office of the United States Commissioner, U.N. War Crimes Commission. NM-66. Entry 52L. File 15. United Nations War Crimes Commission, Research Officer. Correspondence with Military Officials (Black Files). National Archives Collection of World War II War Crimes Records (RG238).

————. Statement by Robert H. Jackson Representing the United States. 12 August 1945. Record of the Office of the United States Commissioner, U.N. War Crimes Commission. NM-66. Entry 52L. File 15. United Nations War Crimes Commission, Research Officer. Correspondence with Military Officials (Black Files). National Archives Collection of World War II War Crimes Records (RG238).

Kansas Oil Museum. www.kansasoilmuseum.org.

Keller, David H. "Subject: Report of Physical Examination." Memo. 19 August 1943. Chaplains Reports and "201" Files. Entry 484. File: Gerecke, Henry F. Records of the Office of the Chief of Chaplains (RG247). National Archives II, College Park, Maryland.

Kennedy, Richard P. "Evil, moral." In *HarperCollins Encyclopedia of Catholicism*, ed. Richard P. McBrien. New York: HarperCollins, 1995.

"Kesselring Cried at His Sermon, Says St. Louis Chaplain for Nazis." *St. Louis Post-Dispatch*. 6 December 1945.

King, Archibald. Memorandum for the Judge Advocate General. 7 September 1944. Record of the Office of the United States Commissioner, U.N. War Crimes Commission. NM–66. Entry 52L. File 15. United Nations War Crimes Commission, Research Officer. Correspondence with Military Officials (Black Files). National Archives Collection of World War II War Crimes Records (RG238).

Kretzmann, P. E. Letter to Army and Navy Commission. 31 May 1943. Henry F. Gerecke Collection. Concordia Historical Institute. St. Louis, Missouri.

Law Reports of Trials of War Criminals. United Nations War Crimes Commission, Vols. I-V. Buffalo, NY: William S. Hein & Co., 1997.

Lechner, Ralf, and Christian Dürr. "Mauthausen Subcamp System." *The United States Holocaust Memorial Museum Encyclopedia of Camps and Ghettos, 1933–1945. Vol. I: Early Camps, Youth Camps and Concentration Camps and Subcamps Under the SS-Business Administration Main Office (WVHA)*. Vol. ed. Geoffrey P. Megargee. Part B. Bloomington: Indiana University Press, 2009.

Lesjak, David. "Bagging a Bigwig: Interview with Lester Leggett." World War II. January–February 2006.

Lincoln, Abraham. Address before the Wisconsin State Agricultural Society. Milwaukee, Wisconsin. 30 September 1859.

"List No. 86, Control Approval Symbol SPXOM–6-PO." Memo. 29 October 1946. Chaplains Reports and "201" Files. Entry 484. Records of the Office of the Chief of Chaplains (RG247). National Archives II, College Park, Maryland.

Luther, Martin. "On the Jews and Their Lies." In *Luther's Works,* trans. Franklin Sherman. Philadelphia: Fortress Press, 1971.

Mackie, J. L. "Evil and Omnipotence," *Mind,* Vol. 64, No. 254. (April, 1955), pp. 200–212.

Maguire, Alban A. Letter to "Brothers in St. Francis." 25 July 1983. Sixtus O'Connor Papers. Franciscan Friars Holy Name Province. New York, New York.

"Memorium Nuremberg Trials." Ed. Matthias Henkel and Hans-Christian Täubrich. Nuremberg: Museen Der Stadt Nürnberg, 2011.

Menus. Nuremberg prison, 17 June 1945 to 30 April 1946. National Archives Collection of World War II War Crimes Records (RG238). National Archives II, College Park, Maryland.

"Minister Counseled Nazi Elite." Associated Press via *The Spokesman Review.* 22 May 1982.

"Night Without Dawn." *Time Magazine.* October 28, 1946.

"Nuernberg Nazi Leaders Urged St. Louis Chaplain Stay with Them." *St. Louis Post-Dispatch.* 29 December 1946.

"Nuremberg: Historical Evolution." Memo. Office of Military Government, Nuremberg. November, 1945. TTP-CLS: Series 4; Subseries 1–2. Box No. 1, Folder 8. Telford Taylor Papers, Arthur W. Diamond Law Library, Columbia University Law School, New York, New York.

O'Connor, Richard J. "Augustin Gemelli, O.F.M." *The Laurel.* St. Bonaventure, New York. October, 1928.

———. "Genius." *The Laurel.* St. Bonaventure, New York. October 1928.

———. Transcript of Record. St. Bonaventure College. 8 October 1947.

O'Connor, Sixtus R. Application for Service. n.d. Office of Chief of Chaplains, War Department, 23–27182. Chaplains Reports and "201" Files. Entry 484. Records of the Office of the Chief of Chaplains (RG247). National Archives II, College Park, Maryland.

———. Army Services Forces memo. Office of Chief of Chaplains, War Department, 23–27182. Chaplains Reports and "201" Files. Entry 484. Records of the Office of the Chief of Chaplains (RG247). National Archives II, College Park, Maryland.

———. Biographical Data. 10 August 1944. Office of Chief of Chaplains, War Department, 23–27182. Chaplains Reports and "201" Files. Entry 484. Records of the Office of the Chief of Chaplains (RG247). National Archives II, College Park, Maryland.

———. Letter to Norman Frank. 21 October 1946.

———. "Monthly Report of Chaplains." [Specific month indicated in citation.] Chaplains Reports and "201" Files, 1946–48. O'Connor, Martin Joseph, through O'Connor, Stephen J. Entry 484. Box 261. File 201—"O'Connor, Sixtus R." Records of the Office of the Chief of Chaplains (RG247). National Archives II, College Park, Maryland.

"Orville Hodge, Auditor Who Robbed State." *Chicago Tribune.* 1 January 1987.

"Pastor Henry F. Gerecke, 1950–1961." n.d. Henry F. Gerecke Collection. Concordia Historical Institute. St. Louis, Missouri.

Pell, Herbert. Letter to Sir Cecil Hurst. 8 May 1944. Record of the Office of the United States Commissioner, U.N. War Crimes Commission. NM–66. Entry 52K. File 150: Miscellaneous. General Correspondence (Red Files). National Archives Collection of World War II War Crimes Records (RG238). National Archives II, College Park, Maryland.

Powers, Jimmy. "A Friar's Recollection of the Nürnberg Trials." *New York News*. 1947.

Randolph, Ross V. "Our Goal in a Prison." *This Day*. October 1961.

"Reception. Chaplain 'Major' Henry F. Gerecke." Program. Henry F. Gerecke Collection. Concordia Historical Institute. St. Louis, Missouri.

"Reel of Celluloid and a Spool of Tape," *The Lutheran Witness*. 9 September 1958.

Report of the Board Proceedings in Case of Hermann Goering (Suicide). Nuremberg, Germany. October 1946.

"Rev. H.F. Gerecke Dies, Prison Adviser." *St. Louis Post-Dispatch*. 11 October 1961.

"Rev. Henry F. Gerecke Funeral to Be Saturday." *St. Louis Post-Dispatch*. 12 October 1961.

Rising, David. "On Trail of Most Wanted Nazi." Associated Press. 30 April 2008.

Roschke, E. L. Letter to Henry F. Gerecke. 27 December 1946. Private collection of Henry H. Gerecke.

Rosen, David. "The Concept of Forgiveness in Judaism." January 2003.

Rosenberg, Joel W. "Genesis: Introduction." In *The HarperCollins Study Bible: New Revised Standard Version*. Ed. Wayne A. Meeks. New York: HarperCollins, 1993.

Rothe, O. Letter to Army and Navy Commission. 27 May 1943. Henry F. Gerecke Collection. Concordia Historical Institute. St. Louis, Missouri.

Schmidt, Dana Adams. "11 Nazis Cremated, Ashes 'Dispersed.'" *New York Times*. 18 October 1946.

"Short History of the St. Louis Lutheran City Mission (40th Anniversary)." n.d. Henry F. Gerecke Collection. Concordia Historical Institute. St. Louis, Missouri.

Simon, Edward A. "The Influence of the American Protestant Churches on the Development of the Structure and Duties of the Army Chaplaincy, 1914–1962." Ph.D. diss. Princeton Theological Seminary, 1963.

Snyder, Timothy. "Hitler vs. Stalin: Who Killed More?" *New York Review of Books*. 10 March 2011.

"Song Sheet." "25th anniversary of P. Gerecke's Installation as pastor." 4 February 1951. Collection of Irene Kornmeier.

St. Bonaventure's College and Seminary Annual Catalogue, 1925–1926. Allegany, New York.

Stokes, Richard L. "Goering Had Poison Vial from Day of His Arrest." *St. Louis Post-Dispatch*. 27 October 1946.

———. "Inquiry Begun on How Goering Got the Poison." *St. Louis Post-Dispatch*. 16 October 1946.

———. "St. Louis Chaplain Tells of Rushing to Goering's Cell as He Killed Self." *St. Louis Post-Dispatch*. 17 October 1946.

Suchara, T. W. Orders, Chaplain (Captain) Henry F. Gerecke. Memo. 31 October 1946. Chaplains Reports and "201" Files. Entry 484. Records of the Office of the Chief of Chaplains (RG247). National Archives II, College Park, Maryland.

Sullivan, James P. "Efficiency Report for Henry F. Gerecke, 1 March 1945." Chaplains Reports and "201" Files. Entry 484. Records of the Office of the Chief of Chaplains (RG247). National Archives II, College Park, Maryland.

———. "Historical Report, 4 April to 15 July 1944." Written 7 July 1944. WWII Operations Reports, 1941–48. Medical. MDGH 97.0.3 to MDGH 98.1.13. Entry 427. Box 17283 Records of the Adjutant General's Office, 1917–(RG407). National Archives II. College Park, Maryland.

———. "Historical Report, 16 July to 30 September 1944." Written 13 October 1944.

WWII Operations Reports, 1941–48. Medical. MDGH 97.0.3 to MDGH 98.1.13. Entry 427. Box 17283 Records of the Adjutant General's Office, 1917–(RG407). National Archives II. College Park, Maryland.

———. "Historical Report, 1 January to 8 May, 1945." Written 21 May 1945. WWII Operations Reports, 1941–48. Medical. MDGH 97.0.3 to MDGH 98.1.13. Entry 427. Box 17283 Records of the Adjutant General's Office, 1917–(RG407). National Archives II. College Park, Maryland.

———. "Historical Report, 9 May to 23 May 1945." Written 2 June 1945. WWII Operations Reports, 1941–48. Medical. MDGH 97.0.3 to MDGH 98.1.13. Entry 427. Box 17283 Records of the Adjutant General's Office, 1917–(RG407). National Archives II. College Park, Maryland.

———. "Period Report, Medical Department Activities, 1 Jan.–31 Dec. 1945." Memo. WWII Operations Reports, 1941–48. Medical. MDGH 97.0.3 to MDGH 98.1.13. Entry 427. Box 17283 Records of the Adjutant General's Office, 1917–(RG407). National Archives II. College Park, Maryland.

———. "Period Report, Medical Department Activities, 1 Jan.–31 Dec. 1945, Munich addendum." Memo. WWII Operations Reports, 1941–48. Medical. MDGH 97.0.3 to MDGH 98.1.13. Entry 427. Box 17283 Records of the Adjutant General's Office, 1917–(RG407). National Archives II. College Park, Maryland.

Sunday, Papers of William and Helen, 1882 -[1888–1957] 1975. A Guide to the Microfilm Edition. Ed. Robert Shuster. Billy Graham Center, Wheaton College. Wheaton, Illinois.

Taylor, Telford. "We Are All Worried." Memo. 6 September 1945. TTP-CLS: Series 4; Subseries 1–2. Box LC4, Folder 5: "Memoranda July–October '45." Telford Taylor Papers, Arthur W. Diamond Law Library, Columbia University Law School, New York, New York.

Technical Manual, TM 16–205: The Chaplain. U.S. Army. July, 1944. Cited in "The Military Chaplaincy of the U.S. Army, Focusing on World War II Chaplains in Combat" by Patrick G. Skelly. Ph.D. diss. Norwich University, 2007.

This Is the Life. Short film. Lutheran Hour Ministries, 1952.

Trial of Major War Criminals (TMWC): Yale Law School Avalon Project: avalon.law .yale.edu/subject_menus/imt.asp.

Twelfth Army Group Headquarters. Memo. 13 February 1945. General Administrative Records, 1942–1957. Judge Advocate Division, War Crimes Branch. File: "Organization 1945." HM1989. Box 1, "Organization 1943 thru Organization 1947." Records of United States Army Europe (USAEUR). Record Group 549. National Archives II, College Park, Maryland.

U.S. Army Regulation 190–8: Enemy Prisoners of War, Retained Personnel, Civilian Internees and Other Detainees. Washington, DC: Headquarters Departments of the Army, the Navy, the Air Force, and the Marine Corps, 1997.

Visser, Jacob Carl. "Evangelism in the Military Chaplaincy." Ph.D. diss. Nazarene Theological Seminary, Kansas City, Missouri. 1964.

Voigtländer, Nico, and Hans-Joachim Voth. "Persecution Perpetuated: The Medieval Origins of Anti-Semitic Violence in Nazi Germany." Working paper. University of California Los Angeles. April 2011.

Wade, H. H. Staffs of the German Concentration Camps: Mauthausen. Record of the Office of the United States Commissioner, U.N. War Crimes Commission.

NM–66. Entry 52K. File 153: United Nations War Crimes Commission, Research Officer. Wade file. General Correspondence (Red Files). National Archives Collection of World War II War Crimes Records (RG238). National Archives II, College Park, Maryland.

Waite, Robert G. "Gusen (with Gusen II and Gusen III)." *The United States Holocaust Memorial Museum Encyclopedia of Camps and Ghettos, 1933–1945. Vol. I: Early Camps, Youth Camps and Concentration Camps and Subcamps Under the SS-Business Administration Main Office (WVHA).* Vol. ed. Geoffrey P. Megargee. Part B. Bloomington: Indiana University Press, 2009.

———. "Mauthausen Main Camp." *The United States Holocaust Memorial Museum Encyclopedia of Camps and Ghettos, 1933–1945. Volume I: Early Camps, Youth Camps and Concentration Camps and Subcamps Under the SS-Business Administration Main Office (WVHA).* Vol. ed. Geoffrey P. Megargee. Part B. Bloomington: Indiana University Press, 2009.

Wilberding, Carl L. Letter to Henry F. Gerecke. 23 June 1943. Chaplains Reports and "201" Files. Entry 484. File: Gerecke, Henry F. Records of the Office of the Chief of Chaplains (RG247). National Archives II, College Park, Maryland.

Wittmer, George W. Letter to Army and Navy Commission. 2 June 1943. Henry F. Gerecke Collection. Concordia Historical Institute. St. Louis, Missouri.

Zittlow, Todd. Concordia Historical Institute. St. Louis, Missouri. 2009.

Zwingli, Ulrich. "An Exposition of the Faith," 1531.

INTERVIEWS

Unless noted otherwise, all interviews were conducted by the author in person.

Black, Peter. Washington, D.C. 8 March 2008

Brinfield, John. Fort Jackson, South Carolina. 18 August 2010

Cash, June. Chester, Illinois. 12 July 2011

Collins, David J. Personal telephone interview. 7 December 2011

Dietzfelbinger, Eckart. Nuremberg, Germany. 31 August 2010

Frank, Niklas. Itzehoe, Germany. 5 May 2011

Fuchs, Moritz. Fulton, New York. 19 July 2011

Geist, Tom. East Meadow, New York. 10 March 2008

Gentsch, Don. Chester, Illinois. 12 July 2011

Gerecke, Hank. Cape Girardeau, Missouri. 4 January 2008

Gerecke, Hank. Cape Girardeau, Missouri. 2 February 2008

Gerecke, Hank. Cape Girardeau, Missouri. 20 August 2008

Gerecke, Hank. Cape Girardeau, Missouri. 21 October 2009

Gerecke, Hank. Cape Girardeau, Missouri. 26 June 2010

Gerecke, Hank. Cape Girardeau, Missouri. 30 October 2010

Gerecke, Hank. Cape Girardeau, Missouri. 23 March 2011

Gerecke, Hank. Cape Girardeau, Missouri. 30 June 2011

Gerecke, Hank. Cape Girardeau, Missouri. 13 July 2011

Harris, Whitney. St. Louis, Missouri. 26 April 2008

Jordan, Brian (Rev.) New York, New York. 21 June 2013

Kaul, Hans-Peter. The Hague, Holland. 20 August 2010

Kornmeier, Irene. Arnold, Missouri. 22 March 2011

Legow, Jerry. St. Louis, Missouri. 24 March 2011

Nischwitz, Ruth and Harvey. Gordonville, Missouri. 23 March 2011
O'Connor, John. Oxford, New York. 19 July 2011
Powley, Colette and Paul. Chester, Illinois. 12 July 2011
Schirach, Klaus von. Munich, Germany. 6 May 2011
Schneider, Georg. Nuremberg, Germany. 30 August 2010
Scholl, Travis. St. Louis, Missouri. 2010
Volf, Miroslav. Osijek, Croatia. 25 August 2010
Volf, Miroslav. Novi Sad, Serbia. 26 August 2010
Willig, Mark. (Rev.) Personal e-mail interview, 29 September 2011
Zentgraf, Henrike. Nuremberg, Germany. 30 August 2010

All Bible verses quoted in this book are from the New Revised Standard Version, the Jewish Publication Society's Tanakh Translation, or the American King James Version—the Bible Henry Gerecke read and used in his ministry.

Index